THE SURRENDER OF THE
U-BOAT FLEET 1945

THE SURRENDER OF THE
U-BOAT FLEET 1945

DEREK WALLER

Seaforth
PUBLISHING

Copyright © Derek Waller 2025

First published in Great Britain in 2025 by
Seaforth Publishing,
A division of Pen & Sword Books Ltd,
George House, Beevor Street, Barnsley S71 1HN

www.seaforthpublishing.com

A catalogue record for this book is available from the British Library

ISBN 978 1 0361 3549 2 (HARDBACK)
ISBN 978 1 0361 3551 5 (EPUB)

The Publisher's authorised representative in the EU for product
safety is Authorised Rep Compliance Ltd., Ground Floor,
71 Lower Baggot Street, Dublin D02 P593, Ireland.
www.arccompliance.com

Typeset by Mac Style in Garamond 11.5/14
Printed and bound in Great Britain by CPI Group (UK) Ltd, Croydon, CR0 4YY

Contents

List of Plates

Between pages 212 and 213

'Instrument of Surrender'. (Alamy)
U-249 alongside at Weymouth. (Alamy)
U-1305 arrives in Loch Eriboll. (Alamy)
U-278 en route to Loch Eribol. (Alamy)
U-1231 in Loch Eribol. (Seaforth library)
U-541 arriving in Gibraltar. (Seaforth library)
U-532 in Liverpool. (Wikimedia Commons)
U-776 visiting London. (Alamy)
U-1009 entering Loch Foyle. (Wikipedia Commons)
U-boats in Loch Ryan. (Seaforth library)
U-boats at Lishally. (Seaforth library)
U-530 and *U-977* in Rio de Janiero. (Official US Navy Photograph)
Two scuttled U-boats in a German harbour. (Seaforth library)
U-1105 undertaking Royal Navy trials. (Royal Navy Submarine Museum)
U-1171 undertaking Royal Navy trials. (Royal Navy Submarine Museum)
U-1407 as HMS *Meteorite*. (Seaforth library)
U-2513 in service with the US Navy. (Official US Navy photograph)
U-234 destroyed by the US Navy. (Official US Navy photograph)
U-2529 in Russia. (Seaforth library)
U-995 displayed near Kiel. (Wikipedia Commons)

Preface

IN THE MINUTE SHEET of Admiralty file ADM 199/22 – 'Operation Pledge' held in the National Archives in Kew there is a suggestion by the Director of Plans dated 17 September 1945 that 'DTSD might like to consider adding *The Surrender of the U-boat Fleet* to the list of Admiralty histories to be compiled'. However, this suggestion fell on stony ground when the Admiralty's Director of Tactical and Staff Duties Division replied on 3 October 1945: 'The subject will form an interesting episode in the *General History of the War at Sea*. It is considered too limited to form a subject in itself.'

Subsequently when the official British history *The War at Sea* was written by Captain S W Roskill, RN, its Volume III, Part II published in 1961 summarised the surrender of the U-boat fleet in just two pages.

This book then is at least a partial means of complying with the Admiralty's Director of Plans' original suggestion, albeit some 80 years too late.

Introduction

Eighty years after the capitulation of Germany and the surrender of the surviving U-boats, there are four Second World War U-boats still in existence:

U-995 (Type VIIC/41) in Laboe, Kiel, Germany
U-2540 (Type XXI) in Bremerhaven, Germany
U-505 (Type IXC) in Chicago, USA
U-534 (Type IXC/40) in Birkenhead, UK

U-995 surrendered in an unserviceable state in Trondheim on 9 May 1945. It was taken over, repaired, and put into service by the Royal Norwegian Navy. It was decommissioned in 1962 and sold to the German Navy Association in 1965.

U-2540 was scuttled in the Baltic near Flensburg on 4 May 1945. It was raised in June 1957 and renovated for use by the then West German Navy before being retired in 1982 and acquired by the German Maritime Museum.

U-505 was captured by the US Navy (USN) at sea off West Africa on 4 June 1944 and hidden in Bermuda for the remainder of the war. After languishing for 10 years in the USN's Portsmouth Navy Yard in New Hampshire, it was donated to the Chicago Museum of Science and Industry in 1954.

U-534 was sunk in an Allied air attack off the east coast of Denmark on 5 May 1945. It was raised in 1993 and transported to Liverpool in 1996. Its condition precluded exhibition as a complete vessel, so it was cut into four sections and is on display at the Woodside Ferry Terminal in Birkenhead.

However, since the end of the Second World War considerably more U-boats have seen the light of day. A total of 156 surrendered at the end of the war in Europe in May 1945, of which 155 were German-built and one was an ex-Dutch submarine. Of these, forty-nine surrendered either at or directly from sea, eighty-seven surrendered in Norwegian ports, sixteen surrendered in German ports, three surrendered in a Danish port and one surrendered in a French port. Seven of the U-boats had surrendered at sea in the Western Atlantic in May: five to the USN and two to the Royal Canadian Navy (RCN). And two more belatedly surrendered from sea in Argentina in July and August 1945.

The 156 U-boats included *U-1406* and *U-1407*. These were examples of the latest Type XVIIB hydrogen peroxide-powered 'Walter' U-boats and had surrendered in Cuxhaven on 5 May 1945. On 7 May they were illegally scuttled in Cuxhaven harbour by a German naval officer who was not a member of either crew. Nevertheless, they were quickly raised and were included with all the other Kriegsmarine submarines which had surrendered when decisions were made about the fate of the surviving U-boats.

When the war in the Far East ended in August 1945, seven of the Imperial Japanese Navy's (IJN) submarines which surrendered were ex-Kriegsmarine U-boats. Two surrendered to the Royal Navy in Singapore, two surrendered to the Royal Navy in Java and three surrendered to the US Navy in Japan. Of the seven U-boats, one was already in the IJN, having been donated to Japan by Germany and being commissioned into the IJN in September 1943. The others had been handed over to the Japanese on 7 May. These six U-boats were commissioned into the IJN in July 1945, but none of them was fully serviceable nor were they used operationally before the Japanese surrender.

Two others deserve mention. As one of the two U-boats which were captured during the war, *U-505* was captured by the US Navy off West Africa in June 1944 and was then towed to Bermuda where it was held in complete secrecy until May 1945. Additionally, *U-760*, which had been interned in Spain since September 1943 after being damaged in an air attack, was handed over to the Royal Navy in July 1945 for disposal and was thus treated as though it had surrendered.

This book, which is based on research that began in the mid-1960s, brings together the contents of many articles published by the author in a variety of magazines and journals, including the American *Warship International*, the Canadian *Argonauta* and the UK's World Ship Society's *Warships*, as well as the Internet site Uboat.net between 2010 and 2023, and it provides a comprehensive record of all the U-boats which surrendered in 1945. It also includes the story of the 200 or so U-boats which were scuttled rather than surrendering in the final days of the war, as well as mentioning others which have been raised since.

It begins by describing the development of Allied policy in 1943, 1944 and early 1945 for the surrender and disposal of any surviving U-boats. It describes the surrender arrangements, as well as the discussions about U-boats at the Potsdam Conference in July 1945 and by the Tripartite Naval Commission (TNC) in Berlin between August and December 1945. The uses and fates of all the surrendered U-boats are then recorded, particularly those which were formally allocated to the UK, the USA and the USSR, before concluding with a schedule showing the final disposal details of each of the U-boats which surrendered.

Finally, the production of the book would not have been possible without the provision of wise advice and assistance from many people from across the world, and I am most grateful to all of them. There are far too many to mention them all individually, but prime amongst them have been Martin Pegg, David Hird and George Malcolmson from the UK, Axel Niestlé, Horst Bredow, Peter Monte, Jochen Hiller and General Manfred Rode from Germany, Sander Kingsepp from Estonia, Dani Akerberg from Spain, Walter Cloots from Belgium, Mark McShane from Ireland, Svein Aage Knudsen from Norway, Warren Sinclair, Michael Whitby, Owen Cooke and Jerry Mason from Canada, and Colonel Mark Gifford, Wendy Gulley, Mark Jones, Keith Allen, Aaron Hamilton and Ken Deshaies from the USA. I am also very grateful to my two specialist researchers; Roger Nixon who searched the UK TNA Kew records for me, and Mike Constandy who did the same in relation to the US NARA records in Washington and Boston.

Derek Waller
May 2025

CHAPTER 1

Allied Policy for the Surrender of the U-Boats

THE SURRENDER ARRANGEMENTS AND the question of what should happen to the surviving vessels of the German Navy at the end of the war had exercised the three Allies (UK, USA and USSR) in late 1943, throughout 1944 and in early 1945. The Russians had indicated in early 1944 that in line with the precedent set by the division of the Italian fleet in 1943 they expected to be allocated a share of the surviving German warships. In contrast, the total elimination of the German Navy and the associated destruction of any remaining U-boats was a long-held UK policy objective.

Two overlapping strands of staff work relating to the surrender of Germany took place in the second half of 1943 and early 1944. One was political and concentrated on matters far wider than the question of what was to be done about the German Navy. The other was military and related to the possible capitulation of Germany prior to the planned Normandy invasion.

The political debate was initiated via the European Advisory Commission (EAC) which had been established after the Conference of Foreign Ministers held in Moscow in October 1943, the purpose of which was to study and make recommendations to their governments on European questions connected with the termination of hostilities. The EAC then comprised British, American and Russian representatives, and one of its earliest projects was to produce a draft paper setting out the terms for an unconditional German surrender which included matters dealing with the German armed forces.

Initial British thoughts in support of the EAC's aim were set out on 15 January 1944 in EAC Paper (44) 1 under the heading 'Terms of Surrender for Germany', and included the proposals:

Hostilities to cease in all theatres of war. German forces to stay where they are pending future instructions and to surrender their arms, etc. When no United Nations [UK, USA and USSR] forces are present, the local German commander will store arms, etc, and be responsible for their eventual surrender.

German warships to be assembled in specified ports and surrendered or dealt with as directed. No transfer to other flags. No scuttling.

German armed forces to be progressively demobilised and totally disbanded.

All war material, complete or incomplete, to be surrendered, destroyed or dealt with as directed.[1]

Similar American proposals were set out on 25 January 1944 in EAC Paper (44) 4. They included:

The German High Command should be required to acknowledge the total defeat and the unconditional surrender of Germany's armed forces.

German land, sea and air forces should be completely demobilised.

All German forces should be disarmed immediately.

All arms, ammunition and implements of war should be delivered … to the occupation authorities for such disposition as they may wish to make of them.

The German authorities should be required to prevent the destruction of such materials … until ordered to deliver, destroy or otherwise dispose of them.[1]

The military debate, which was conducted under the code name Operation 'Rankin', had started when the Chief of Staff to the (then) vacant Supreme Allied Commander post (COSSAC) was directed to prepare a plan in May 1943 to cover: 'A return to the Continent in the event of German disintegration at any time from now onwards with whatever forces may be available at the time.'[2]

As a result, an outline plan (COSSAC (43) 60) covering the worst-case situation, called Operation 'Rankin Case C', was published on 30 October 1943, saying: 'The conditions under which this operation will be put into effect are those arising from the surrender of the Germans, and the cessation of all organised resistance. Such a situation is likely to be brought about in the winter of 1943/44 by either a military disaster, impending or actual, in Russia; or by a collapse of morale in Germany; or by a combination of both.'[3]

The COSSAC plan focussed on the broader military aspects of the occupation of Germany and, as part of the ongoing planning process, the

Allied Naval Commander Expeditionary Force (ANCXF) and the Royal Navy's Commander-in-Chief Nore who was part of the planning team, asked the Admiralty in late November 1943 for guidance concerning the policy to be followed in respect of the surviving vessels of the German Navy in the event of an early German surrender.

In response, the UK's naval proposals were set out by the RN's First Sea Lord on 25 February 1944 in a formal report to the British Chiefs of Staff Committee, COS(44)201(0), which said:

> The Allied Naval Commander, Expeditionary Force has asked for guidance concerning the general policy to be followed in enforcing the surrender of the German Fleet under 'Rankin Case C' conditions in order that appropriate plans and directives may be prepared.
>
> It is assumed that any instrument of surrender signed with Germany will secure for the United Nations [UK, USA and USSR] the right to give to the German Naval Forces any directions that may be required.
>
> As soon as practicable, arrangements should be made for all surviving units of the German Fleet, down to and including torpedo boats and U-Boats, to assemble, steam out and surrender in UK ports. U-Boats and any other ships at sea should similarly be given orders to surrender in appropriate Allied ports, according to their positions at the time.[4]

The proposal that the surviving units of the German Navy should steam out and surrender in UK ports was recognised as contentious, and although it was not eventually taken forward, it was justified in the COS Paper, viz:

> Apart from the fact that the Royal Navy has played the leading part against the German Navy, the surrender of German main units in UK ports is recommended because:
>
> (a) The Royal Navy, at this stage of the war, is better equipped to organise the surrender of the German Fleet than the Soviet Navy.
> (b) It will be easier for Allied Naval Forces from the UK to get into contact with German Naval Headquarters.
> (c) The enemy are more likely to surrender their ships intact in a UK than in a Soviet port.[4]

As far as the subsequent disposal of any warships of the German Navy which surrendered was concerned, the COS Paper concluded with the words:

> Surrender in UK ports would, of course, be without prejudice to the ultimate disposal of the ships, which would be a matter for settlement between Governments. It is recognised, however, that the Soviet

Navy, for prestige and other reasons, may insist that a proportion of the German Fleet surrenders at Kronstadt. Moreover, a number of the more important units, if not scuttled, may be lying in Baltic ports within the area provisionally assigned to the Soviet for the purpose of the administration of the Armistice. It is important that agreement should be reached on the ports of surrender if the issue of contradictory instructions to the German Navy is to be avoided.

The question of the future disposal of the German Fleet and the Soviet share will therefore be examined.[4]

Thus, the two originally separate military and political strands of planning were converging, and firm proposals about the eventual surrender of the German Navy, including the disposal of any surviving U-boats, were beginning to take shape in Britain and America in early 1944. The Russians were also taking a close interest in the topic and on 28 February the Soviet Naval Mission in London asked the Admiralty to be reminded of the arrangements for the surrender of the Imperial German Navy at the end of the First World War. Their questions included:

The organisation for the surrender of the German fleet.
The methods and means for controlling German naval bases after the Armistice.
The number of naval officers engaged in the process.[4]

At that stage of the war, it was unclear as to the precise procedure to be adopted to obtain Allied agreement to the UK proposals particularly from the Russians, and the UK Chiefs of Staff were therefore asked to approve discussions with the Soviet Government at an opportune date. It was suggested that: 'The procedure might be either to table the directive at the European Advisory Commission or to raise the question at the highest level.'[4]

In support of the 'Rankin Case C' proposals, the First Sea Lord's COS paper was shared with both the USN and ANCXF. However, the need to concentrate on the invasion of Normandy meant that the 'Rankin Case C' planning activity was put on hold in March 1944. There was also disagreement between the UK and US authorities about the process to be followed to obtain Allied agreement to the proposals. This was because the UK Chiefs of Staff were keen that they should be agreed unilaterally by the British and Americans before they were presented to the Russian representative on the EAC. In contrast, a US Joint Chiefs of Staff (JCS) paper dated 13 April 1944 stated:

It would be inappropriate for the United States and British representatives on the European Advisory Commission to approach the Soviet representative with previously agreed views prior to consultation with the Soviet representative.

The United States Chiefs of Staff should present their views to the State Department for transmission to the European Advisory Commission where the final matter should be negotiated on the basis of the three Powers.[5]

As a result, the UK COS re-considered their approach, and instead sought broad acceptance of the proposals from the US JCS in the form of an informal indication of their views to avoid any embarrassing US/UK disagreements during the three-way EAC discussions. After further consideration in Washington, a satisfactory compromise was reached when the JCS advised the State Department on 21 April 1944 that:

Should the United States Chiefs of Staff act to agree formally with the British, at this time, concerning these or other similar proposals, we should in effect be placing Mr Winant [the US representative on the EAC] in the undesirable position of confronting the Russians with a previously agreed US-British policy on a matter which is also properly of interest to Russia.

The United States Chiefs of Staff recommend that the British proposals be furnished [to] Mr Winant, with instructions that they are in general satisfactory as a basis for his negotiations.[5]

The specific question of what should happen to the German Navy, particularly the U-boats, at the end of the war was also exercising the USN, early evidence of which was a letter from the Chief of Naval Operations (CNO) to the Commander of US Naval Forces in Europe (ComNavEu) on 24 May 1944. The letter was titled 'German Submarines for the United States', and it spelt out just what the USN required and why, viz:

The following views of the Commander-in-Chief regarding the disposition of German submarines, upon the unconditional surrender of Germany, are furnished [to] you in connection with your position as the US Naval Advisor to the European Advisory Commission.

It is assumed that, upon the unconditional surrender of Germany, the United States will become entitled to the possession of one-third of all German submarines.

Because of their value in research and development and in order to provide for operational test employment in the Western Pacific, it is desired to obtain actual physical possession of certain submarines of the United States' share with minimum delay.[6]

This statement from the CNO to ComNavEu in the latter's role as the USN's Advisor to the EAC, which was based in London, was by no means premature. This was evident from an Admiralty letter on 1 July 1944 to ANCXF, who was by then part of Supreme Headquarters Allied Expeditionary Force (SHAEF). This was a response to ANCXF's earlier request for advice in relation to planning for the 'Rankin Case C' and said that the co-ordination of any instructions to the German Naval High Command to be issued with the Armistice terms would rest with the Admiralty, and that planning for the surrender of the U-boats would rest with the RN's Commander-in-Chief Western Approaches (C-in-C WA).

On the same day, the Admiralty advised the C-in-C WA:

> The arrangements for the surrender of German naval forces when an armistice with Germany is concluded or hostilities cease, have been engaging the attention of Their Lordships, and the policy in regard to this will shortly be considered with the American and Soviet Delegates to the European Advisory Commission.
>
> In the interim Their Lordships request that you will give consideration to the problems which will arise with the surrender of the surviving German U-Boat Fleet.[7]

The formal consideration by the EAC of the terms of an unconditional German surrender, which was the result of the lengthy debate, during which the Russian delegation played a full part in relation to German warships (surface and submarine), took place at its 7th (44) Meeting on 25 July 1944. The result was an agreement by the British, American and Russian representatives that: 'In virtue of the Terms of Reference of the European Advisory Commission, agreed upon at the Moscow Conference, the Commission has given attention to the terms of surrender to be imposed on Germany and submits herewith, for the consideration of the three Governments, a draft Instrument entitled 'Unconditional Surrender of Germany.'[8]

The EAC's draft surrender document contained two important statements in relation to the German Navy:

> Article 4. The German authorities will issue orders to all German or German-controlled naval vessels, surface and submarine … wherever such vessels may be at the time of surrender … to remain in or proceed immediately to ports and bases as specified by the Allied representatives.
>
> Article 5. The German authorities will hold intact and in good condition at the disposal of the Allied Representatives, for

> such purposes and at such times and places as they may
> prescribe:- all naval vessels of all classes, both surface and
> submarines ... whether afloat, under repair or construction,
> built or building.[8]

Having settled the overall Allied policy in relation to the surrender of
Germany, the Admiralty then took action to produce a draft of what it
called 'The Special Orders for German Naval Command upon Surrender
or Cessation of Hostilities'. Whilst the majority of the German Navy and
its facilities were expected to be found in the British Zone of Germany
after the surrender, there was no question that these Special Orders
were seen as the sole preserve of the RN. It was appreciated that they
would have to be agreed, ideally via the EAC, by the Americans and the
Russians as well as by SHAEF/ANCXF, but there were nevertheless time
constraints, and the Admiralty decided to take the initiative in respect of
these Special Orders.

The unilateral British initiative began on 7 August 1944, with an
Admiralty minute setting the scene and explaining the reasons for it:

> The European Advisory Commission has agreed the terms of the
> military Instrument of Surrender. The Instrument of Surrender
> is being supplemented by what we term a General Order, which in
> effect contains additional terms of surrender not thought suitable for
> inclusion in the purely military Instrument. The General Order is on
> broad lines, and though it contains some military points, deals largely
> with economic, political and other matters. The British view is that in
> addition to the Instrument and the General Order, it is desirable to
> have certain agreed Special Orders to the German High Command
> or German Government concerning action to be taken immediately
> following the cessation of hostilities. Obviously one subject for a
> Special Order is the action to be taken by the German Navy.[9]

The first draft of the proposed Special Orders for the German Navy was
published by the Admiralty on 12 August 1944, and during the following
three months it was refined during discussions both within the Admiralty
and with ANXCF, the USN, the Soviet Navy and the EAC. Thus, by the
end of 1944, the Special Orders had been agreed by all concerned, and
was ready to be issued by ANCXF on behalf of SHAEF as soon as any
German capitulation occurred.

As far as the surrender of the U-boats was concerned, the emphasis was
on those that were at sea at the time of the capitulation, with the Special
Orders stating: 'The German High Command will transmit by W/T

[Wireless Telegraph] on appropriate frequencies the two messages in Annexures "A" and "B" which contain instructions to submarines at sea.'[9]

Annexure A set out details of the action to be taken by the U-boats in order to surrender, and Annexure B contained the instructions to be followed in order to effect safe transit from the points of surrender to a number of specified Allied reception ports and other locations.

In parallel with the British actions relating to the EAC and to the production of the Special Orders, a third strand of work was underway in London in August 1944 to draft the plan for the naval disarmament and control of Germany in accordance with the terms of surrender which were being considered. It was recognised that any such plan would have to be agreed by both the Americans and the Russians, but the covering minute of the draft of the 'Outline Plan for the Control, Disarmament and Disbandment of the German Navy' (N.F.D.(44)1) dated 28 August 1944 nevertheless contained an unequivocal statement of British policy, viz:

> Unlike the terms of the Armistice of 1919 which permitted Germany a reduced navy and left intact the German naval system of administration and command, we this time intend that no vestige of the German Navy, either in respect of its personnel, its material, its dockyards, its manufacturing establishments, its schools, its depots, its barracks, or anything which might assist in keeping alive any form of German naval esprit de corps (such as it is), or permit of a revival of a German Navy, shall remain.[10]

There was therefore no doubt whatsoever about the British attitude towards the German Navy once the war was over, as well as the baseline for the necessary negations with the Allies. At the same time, the US Joint Chiefs of Staff sent a message to the US Secretary of State on 4 September 1944 concentrating on the eventual disposal of any surviving German surface warships and U-boats, saying:

> It is understood that the immediate disposition of units of the German fleet in connection with the imposition of surrender terms upon the defeat of Germany is presently under advisement in the European Advisory Commission, and that it has been tentatively agreed that the ultimate disposition of the units of the German fleet will be a matter for decision by the governments of the United Nations concerned.
>
> It is the view of the Joint Chiefs of Staff that, except for the retention of a limited number of ships for experimental and test purposes, the German fleet should be completely destroyed. In the event that

agreement cannot be reached with the Russians and the British on this basis, the United States should press for either:

a. A one-third share of each category of ships in the German fleet, or
b. Agreement that all capital ships, such as battleships, pocket-battleships and heavy cruisers, and submarines should be destroyed, while smaller craft and more lightly armed vessels be shared equally by the United States, Russia and Great Britain.[8]

Subsequently, American policy was refined as a result of consultations between the Joint Chiefs of Staff, the Secretary of State and the President himself, and this was formally articulated on 23 November 1944 by the submission to the EAC of a 'US Draft Directive on Disposition of German and German Controlled Naval Craft, Equipment and Facilities' (EAC/44/34), which included two significant proposals concerning the future of the German Navy:

Para 6: Except as provided in para 8 [below] you [the Commanders-in-Chief of the respective occupation zones] will immediately render unfit for combat and as quickly as possible thereafter destroy or scrap all naval craft designed primarily for combat.

Para 8: You will safeguard for ultimate disposition by the Control Council all such German ... naval craft ... mentioned in para 6 [above] as you determine to be of new or experimental design, or which you consider merit special examination, or which the accredited representatives of either of the other two Allied Commanders-in-Chief may designate for retention as experimental or new types.[11]

In essence, the American proposal to the EAC was that except for a small number of naval vessels to be retained for experimental and other purposes the entire German Navy, both surface ships and submarines, should be destroyed or scrapped. There was no mention of a one-third split between each of the UK, USA and USSR, there was no differentiation between surface ships and submarines, and there was no mention of the fall-back positions set out in the US JCS letter of 4 September.

The EAC, which by that time comprised British, American, Russian and French representatives, was not the most dynamic of organisations. Also, the EAC was only an advisory body, and there were a considerable number of Draft Directives and other more weighty matters to be considered in the latter half of 1944 and in early 1945. Progress with the American Draft Directive EAC/44/34 concerning the future of the German Navy, which was one of a series of twenty-three such US submissions to the EAC covering a wide variety of topics, was therefore slow.

Nevertheless, the American Draft Directive provoked a great deal of interest in Britain, where it was apparent that in principle the USN and the RN had similar policy objectives concerning the disposal of the German Navy. However, whilst agreeing that it would lead to the total elimination of German naval power, the UK took an equivocal view about the fate of the surface fleet in the expectation that the Russians would demand to be allocated at least a fair share of the surviving warships. In return, it was hoped that as part of the negotiations it would be possible to achieve the specific UK objective of destroying almost all the remaining U-boats.

The need for these Allied discussions was then overtaken by the end of the European war in early May 1945, by which it had already been accepted by the three Allies that the ultimate disposition of the surviving units of the German Navy would need to be a matter for decision by the governments of the UK, USA and USSR. It was clear that the Russians would be likely to demand to be allocated at least one third of the German Navy's surviving warships, an action that was initiated personally by Marshal Stalin within two weeks of the end of the war in Europe.

One of the important aspects of the consideration of the Draft EAC Directive 44/34 was that it helped to formalise British and RN views about the future of any U-boats that were likely to surrender at the end of the war, and these were highlighted in the Admiralty File on the topic which, for example, recorded comments such as:

22 Jan 45: The policy of destruction proposed by the US is, in my view, in the best interests of the Royal Navy and of the United Nations as a whole and will, I believe, commend itself to the Board.

15 Feb 45: The question of manpower required to maintain surrendered vessels ... is of vital interest to Admiral (Submarines). Every German U-Boat which we have to maintain means a direct reduction in our effort against the Japanese, for the maintenance personnel can only be skilled submarine ratings. Apart from U-Boats required for experimental purposes it is therefore very desirable for them to be scrapped at the earliest opportunity.

21 Mar 45: If the U-Boat fleet was destroyed and German war making industry obliterated, I do not think there would be any harm in letting the Russians have what remains afloat of the German surface fleet. I would therefore say that we can

enter upon a policy of supporting the American attitude
wholeheartedly.

29 Mar 45: I agree. If a policy of total scrapping [of the whole fleet]
cannot be agreed then [we should] go for a policy of
scrapping the whole U-Boat fleet.[11]

By April 1945 the British attitude, as well as that of the Americans and
the Russians, towards the future of any U-boats that might surrender at
the end of the war was therefore clear. They each accepted that the final
decisions about the ultimate disposal of any surviving U-boats would
need to be taken jointly and that detailed negotiations would be required.

In the meantime, the Allies were aware that the instructions to be given
to the German Navy concerning the detailed surrender arrangements
had been drafted and agreed in late 1944, and that there was a need for
these to be reviewed and updated in the light the impending cessation
of hostilities. The updating exercise was led by the Admiralty and the
C-in-C WA and, whilst U-boats in port were to be covered by the general
order that all warships in harbour were to remain there pending further
directions, it was recommended that the U-boats at sea should be given
more specific instructions, viz:

All submarines at sea are to surface at once, fly a black flag or pendant
and report their position in plain language immediately to the nearest
British, US or Soviet coast W/T station on 500 KCS (600 metres) and
to the call sign GZZ 10 on one of the following high frequencies –
16845, 12685 KCS or 5970 KCS and proceed on the surface to the
nearest German or Allied port or such port as the Allied Representatives
may direct, and remain there pending further directions from the Allied
Representatives. At night they are to show lights.[12]

A revised version of the Special Orders was therefore circulated to all
concerned by the Admiralty on 1 May 1945, opening with the statement:

Cominch [Commander-in-Chief of the US Navy] and NSHQ
[Canadian Naval Staff Headquarters] Ottawa have agreed. Subject
to Soviet Concurrence, following is amended version of the Special
Orders to German Navy. Begins: The following special orders are to
be complied with by the German High Command and by all German
naval authorities.[12]

Despite the recommendations of the Admiralty, it was by then too late
for SHAFE and ANCXF to include all aspects of the proposed revision.
Thus, in their final versions, albeit with some amendments, the Special

Orders still said, in respect of the U-boats, that the German High Command was to transmit the two messages containing the instructions to be followed by submarines at sea, firstly the surrender procedure and, secondly, the transit instructions from the points of surrender to a number of prescribed reception ports and other locations.

After the German capitulation at the surrender ceremony in Reims (codenamed Operation 'Eclipse'), the updated versions of the 'Special Orders by the Supreme Commander Allied Expeditionary Force to the German High Command Relating to Naval Forces' were personally handed to the Commander-in-Chief of the German Navy by ANCXF in the early hours of the morning of 7 May 1945.[9]

A short time later, the messages in the Special Orders began to be transmitted to the U-boats at sea by the German authorities in both German code and plain language. This was followed by the surrender process itself, together with discussions about the initial arrangements for the high-level Allied meeting at Potsdam in July which, amongst other more weighty topics would decide the fate of the surviving U-boats.

CHAPTER 2

UK Plans for the Surrender of the U-Boats

WITH THE OBJECTIVE OF ENSURING total German naval disarmament, the Royal Navy intended that at the cessation of hostilities any U-boats that surrendered in and around Europe and in the Eastern Atlantic would be moved to the UK prior to their destruction. Thus, in mid-1944, as a by-product of the earlier 'Rankin Case C' and EAC-related German surrender studies, the RN began its detailed planning for the post-war transfer of the surviving German U-boats to British ports, albeit that there would need to be Allied agreement about the future of the U-boat fleet.

To this end, a letter from the Admiralty to the Commander-in-Chief Western Approaches (C-in-C WA), Admiral Sir Max Horton, on 1 July 1944, stated:

> Their Lordships request that you will give consideration to the problems which will arise in connection with the surrender of the surviving German U-Boat Fleet. They accordingly issue the following instructions which are to be considered provisional only, pending agreement being reached on matters of policy with the Soviet Union and the United States of America.
>
> Their Lordships direct that you shall undertake the planning and co-ordination of the operations necessary to receive the surrender of the surviving German U-Boat Fleet.
>
> You should accordingly confine your plans to those U-Boats which will be in ports in the British zone, in Atlantic ports or at sea to the west of Lubeck at the time of the armistice and 'Stand Still' order or may be directed to proceed to ports within the British zone.
>
> You should keep their Lordships informed of your intentions, including the ports to which the German submarines will be brought.[1]

The letter did not give any indication of the number of U-boats thought likely to surrender, and thus the number that would need to be accommodated in British ports. The C-in-C WA therefore initially responded to the Admiralty on 30 July saying: 'It is fully appreciated that it is impossible to forecast with any accuracy how many U-Boats will have to be accepted in the event of surrender. Nevertheless as a basis for planning an expression of Admiralty opinion regarding the probable number would be helpful.'[1]

On 5 August, in a further response to the Admiralty, Admiral Horton estimated that up to 238 U-boats could be stored at four UK naval anchorages. These were at Lisahally in Northern Ireland (70 U-boats), Loch Ryan in south-west Scotland (100 U-boats) and 68 U-boats at two anchorages in the Gare Loch in western Scotland: Roseneath and Faslane. The figure of 238 was simply an indication of the number of U-boats that could be accommodated at the four locations rather than an assessment of the number likely to surrender. The latter figure only became available on 14 August when the Admiralty advised that:

> It is impossible to give anything more than a rough estimate of the number of U-Boats in the proposed British zone, in Atlantic Ports or at sea to the west of Lubeck, at the time of surrender, but for planning purposes, the number may be taken as 160. In the event this number will probably be smaller.[1]

In response to the C-in-C WA's letter of 5 August, the Admiralty advised on 21 September 1944 that:

> I am to state that Their Lordships' final decision on your proposals will be delayed by the consideration of the commitment in personnel which the maintenance of surrendered U-Boats in the UK entails. Questions of high policy are involved which affect also the treatment of surrendered surface ships. Their Lordships are in particular exploring the possibility of obtaining the agreement of the US and USSR to scrapping the majority of U-Boats at an early date after their surrender, in order to reduce the number of British officers and ratings required for guard and maintenance duties.
>
> I am, however, to state that the general lines upon which your planning is proceeding are considered acceptable subject to the decisions on the questions of policy above mentioned, and that the appropriate authorities are being notified of the possibility of a special requirement arising in respect of surrendered U-Boats at Loch Ryan, Faslane and Roseneath.[1]

Despite this clarification, there remained the question of the locations to be selected as laying-up ports. Admiral Horton had advised the Admiralty that his preference was to use Lisahally, Roseneath and Faslane where the U-boats could be berthed alongside jetties, as opposed to Loch Ryan where the U-boats would need to be moored in open water. There was then considerable debate about which locations should be used, which only ended when, on 3 November, the Admiral advised the Admiralty:

> It is now intended to use Lisahally and Loch Ryan only for berthing surrendered U-Boats.
>
> Arrangements can be made to berth 81 at Lisahally and 100 at Loch Ryan. The total of 181 allows a margin on the Admiralty estimate of 160 given in the Admiralty letter of 14 August.
>
> In view of the above, and the figures given in my letter of 15 August, delete all references to Roseneath and Faslane.[1]

Thus, by the end of 1944, the RN's plans for the storage of the U-boats that were likely to surrender in the British zone of interest became focussed on the port at Lisahally where the U-boats would be berthed alongside the jetties and the anchorage in Loch Ryan where the U-boats would be moored in the shallow open water.

By mid-March 1945, the approach of the end of the war was becoming increasingly obvious and there was an urgent need for more detailed planning. The Admiralty therefore arranged for a meeting to be held in London on 20 March (later postponed until 27 March) to discuss the outstanding matters. Prior to the meeting, the C-in-C WA sent a message to the Admiralty on 19 March setting out almost a dozen points on which he sought clarification. Whilst it had already been agreed that the U-boats would be held at Loch Ryan and Lisahally, the outstanding queries included:

> Procedure for issuing orders and instructions to German U-Boats at sea on the cease fire.
> Disposal of German U-Boats that surrender off a British port.
> Any change in Admiralty estimate of 160 German U-Boats that may surrender in British zone.[1]

The meeting was attended by a wide cross-section of UK naval authorities, as well as representatives from the US Navy (USN) and the Royal Canadian Navy (RCN). Whilst the minutes of the meeting show that all of the C-in-C WA's points were considered, there was disagreement about the arrangements to be made for handling the U-boats that surrendered from sea. The C-in-C WA had assumed that all such U-boats should be directed initially to German ports, but the Chairman of the meeting,

Rear Admiral McCarthy, the Admiralty's Assistant Chief of Naval Staff, made it clear that:

> Although C-in-C WA's proposals had been generally agreed in principle, he had thought that the preparation in Germany of U-Boats for laying-up was intended only in the case of vessels found in German ports. U-Boats at sea would have to be dealt with first, and it seemed that the administrative difficulties ... would have to be accepted. Vessels at sea in the British zone would have to be brought direct to a British port.[1]

The decisions made at the meeting related to three main strands of action. First, the updated surrender orders to be issued to U-boats at sea at the time of the expected German capitulation. Second, the reception arrangements for U-boats surrendering from sea. Third, arrangements for the reception of U-boats that had surrendered in German and German-controlled (mostly Norwegian) ports and which were then to be transferred to the UK.

For planning purposes, it was still estimated that no more than 160 U-boats were likely to surrender in the British zone of interest, which included Germany, Denmark and Norway. Whilst, in the event, this estimate of 160 turned out to be remarkably accurate, it was more by good luck than judgement. This was because, if so many U-boats had not been scuttled by their crews in the northern German ports and in the western Baltic during the first week in May in Operation 'Regenbogen', the number that surrendered would have been in the region of 380.

'Regenbogen' was the Kriegsmarine's plan to scuttle rather than surrender all the U-boats remaining in German ports when the war ended. The intention had been to initiate their scuttling on receipt of the codeword from German Naval HQ, but the speed of the Allied advance through northern Germany and the swift capture of the Baltic ports caused many U-boat COs to anticipate the expected order. The scuttling process began on 1 May and continued for the next seven days even though the 'Regenbogen' order was withdrawn in the early hours of 5 May. However, by then the die had been cast and the COs of many of the remaining U-boats in the German ports and at sea in the Baltic continued their scuttling actions until Germany's capitulation on 8 May, by which time some 220 had been scuttled in and around the harbours and bays of northern Germany. This was the reason why the British estimate, first made in August 1944, that only some 160 U-boats would surrender at the end of the war, turned out to be almost exactly correct.

It was also confirmed at the Admiralty meeting that the U-boats which surrendered in ports in mainland Europe would be transferred to the UK, where they would be held at Lisahally and in Loch Ryan. However, only minimal maintenance was intended, because Britain was planning to seek Allied agreement for the wholesale scrapping or sinking most of the remaining U-boats as early as possible. This latter point did not go down well with the USN in Washington, with a post-meeting memorandum to the Commander of US Naval Forces in Europe (ComNavEu) dated 28 March recording that:

> There is a difference of opinion between the US and British view relative to holding enemy equipment, which includes all naval craft (captured or surrendered) in good condition for the eventual disposal by the Allied representatives.
>
> The British view interprets this trusteeship as merely 'guarding and prevention of theft or sabotage'. The US Naval Division has interpreted this to mean 'sufficient maintenance to keep vessels in an operating condition ready for sea'.[2]

Following the meeting, detailed arrangements were made for the reception of U-boats surrendering from sea and for the transfers from Germany, Denmark and Norway. Loch Eriboll near Cape Wrath in the far north-west corner of Scotland was designated as a 'Port for Preliminary Examination', Loch Alsh in north-west Scotland near the Isle of Skye was designated as a 'Port for Final Examination', and Lisahally and Loch Ryan were designated as 'Ports for Laying-Up'. Loch Eriboll was chosen for the preliminary examinations because it was a remote anchorage where minimum damage could be done by any rogue U-boat and Loch Alsh was selected because it was sheltered, could accommodate thirty-three U-boats on buoys at any one time, and possessed both a resident Naval Organisation and a railhead. These arrangements were then specified in the Operation Order, code-named Operation 'Pledge', issued by the C-in-C WA on 19 April 1945.[3]

At the same time as these detailed surrender plans were being worked out, during the previous nine months the RN had also been considering the possibility of conducting trials on a small number of U-boats that it wished to retain for the same technical assessment and experimental purposes as had been set out in the American Draft EAC Directive 44/34 in November 1944.

The idea of such trials had first been suggested in mid-1944, culminating in a letter from the Royal Navy's Admiral (Submarines) to the Admiralty on 15 October 1944 titled 'Types of German U-Boats Required for Post War Experiments and Tests'. This showed that the RN already possessed a great deal of intelligence about the various U-boat types operated by and being developed for the Kriegsmarine, some of which had been gained from the early Type VIIC U-boat, *U-570* (HMS *Graph*), which had been captured by the RN in 1941, and which had been used operationally in 1942 and 1943. The Admiral's letter included the statements:

> A close study of the characteristics of all German U-Boats construction will be of great value, and to this end it is proposed that a certain number of each type shall be taken over by the Navy for this purpose.
>
> From both an operational and experimental point of view the Type XXI U-Boat is of the greatest importance, followed by the Type XXIII.
>
> Types and numbers required are as follows, in order of priority:

Type	Number	Purpose
XXI	2 minimum	2 in commission
XXIII	2	1 in commission, 1 to cannibalise
XIV	1	strip and examine
IXD2	1	strip and examine
XB	2	1 in commission, 1 to cannibalise

> Of the above, submarines in 'commission' would be kept available for seagoing trials. Submarines 'cannibalised' would primarily be required to provide spare parts for submarines in commission, but would also be available for stripping and detailed examination.[4]

These proposals, which were made well before the war had ended, and which included reference to three types of U-boat which were never built, before any U-boats had surrendered, and before it had been decided exactly how many U-boats would be retained by each of the three Allies, were modified by Admiral (Submarines) on 7 March 1945, when he added the HTP-powered 'Walter' U-boats to his list, saying:

> Since that letter [dated 15 October 1944] was written, fresh information has been received of newer types of U-Boat than the Type XXI and XXIII … (Types XVII and XXVI). Admiral (Submarines) considers that numbers of these and any other new types will be required to at least the same scale as for the Type XXIII, ie. two, one to commission and one to cannibalise.[4]

After the meeting in London on 27 March and in parallel with the production of the 'Pledge' Operation Order, the Admiralty considered how to encourage the surrender of individual U-boats at sea prior to the end of hostilities. To this end, the First Sea Lord submitted a memorandum to the UK Chiefs of Staff Committee (COS (45) 74) on 17 April saying:

> It is proposed to make known to U-Boat officers and crews, through clandestine propaganda channels, a detailed procedure for surrender at sea in the presence of Allied air and naval units.
>
> If U-Boat crews believe in the existence of a definite procedure for surrender, it will encourage them to give practical expression to any spirit of defeatism that may exist within the individual U-Boat.
>
> The propaganda channels which would be employed … are unofficial and are recognised as not committing HM Government to any official line of policy. The instructions would appear to come from an ostensibly German source, and would be described as the best procedure for a U-Boat to adopt in order to avoid unnecessary casualties.[5]

The proposal was approved at the 105th COS Meeting on 20 April subject to the approval of the US Joint Chiefs of Staff in Washington. However, whilst US, Canadian and UK naval and air forces, including the C-in-C WA and the Commander-in-Chief of RAF Coastal Command (C-in-C CC) were forewarned of the procedure to be adopted in the event of any such premature surrender, not a single U-boat CO took the bait. Their loyalty to the Kriegsmarine in general and to Admiral Dönitz in particular precluded any such defeatist action. It was even the cause of some admiration, as recorded in the Admiralty's 'U-Boat Trend' report dated 9 May 1945: 'It is very remarkable proof of the tenacity and discipline of the U-Boat fleet that no one had previously surrendered during the long phase of cumulating military defeats.'[6]

The surrender of German forces, including U-boats, in north-west Germany and Denmark to Field Marshal Montgomery's 21st Army Group on 5 May prompted the C-in-C WA to reinforce his earlier action by sending a precautionary signal message on 5 May detailing the actions to be taken should any U-boat unexpectedly surrender before the general German capitulation. Any U-boat that surrendered in the Irish Sea or in the South-West Approaches was to be escorted to Beaumaris Bay in Anglesey, North Wales, and any U-boat that surrendered elsewhere in his command area was to be escorted to Loch Alsh.[7] However, as no U-boats surrendered prematurely, there was no requirement for these orders to be implemented.

Also, it was realised that whilst the emphasis had been concentrated on defining the surrender arrangements for the U-boats still at sea as well as for their subsequent handling after arrival at the ports designated for preliminary examination, no arrangements were in place to notify the British anti-U-boat forces, warships and aircraft, how to handle the situation once Germany had capitulated. As a result, the C-in-C WA wrote to the Admiralty on 19 April 1945 saying:

> When the scheme for the surrender of the German U-Boat fleet at sea is brought into operation it will be necessary for all Allied warships, merchant vessels and aircraft to be warned accordingly.
>
> It is requested that arrangements be made for a warning on the following lines to be issued by the Admiralty to all concerned:
>
> > All German U-Boats at sea have been ordered to report their positions and remain surfaced. Orders have been issued that they are to fly a large black or blue flag by day and burn navigation lights at night.
> >
> > U-Boats have been ordered to proceed direct to the nearest standard route and thence to Loch Eriboll.
> >
> > Any U-Boat sighted approaching or on one of these [standard] routes and on the surface and flying the appropriate distinguishing signal or burning navigation lights by night, is to be immune from attack, unless he commits a hostile act.[1]

This was followed up by the Admiralty which then set out a clear procedure detailing what was to happen between the initial surrender of the U-boats at sea and their reception at Loch Eriboll (or elsewhere). The Vice Chief of Naval Staff sent a message to all RN home and foreign stations on 2 May, saying:

> As soon as hostilities with Germany cease, U-Boats will be given the following surrender orders:
>
> > Surface, remain surfaced and report position
> > Fly black or dark blue flag by day and burn navigation lights at night
> > Jettison ammunition, render torpedoes safe by removing pistols, andrender mines safe
> > Proceed by fixed routes to prescribed ports for preliminary examination
>
> Any U-Boat sighted and obeying orders in para 1 is not to be attacked unless it commits a hostile act. Position, course and speed of U-Boats is to be reported.
>
> Further details including fixed routes and prescribed ports will be signalled to HM ships when the operation is brought into force.

British and Allied merchant ships in areas concerned will be given all necessary instructions.

Codeword for this operation follows.[7]

A short time later the Admiralty advised that the codeword to be used would be 'Adieu', and this was followed by a message to RAF Coastal Command, saying: 'Request you will arrange Air Co-operation in connection with Operation "Adieu" as Commanders-in-Chief and Cominch [the Commander-in-Chief of the USN] may require'.[7]

As a result, a similar message was sent out by the C-in-C CC, and the necessary orders were therefore in place with all RN and RAF anti-U-boat forces (warships and aircraft) to ensure the safe surrender of any U-boats at sea, together with directions to the agreed ports. It was then simply a case of awaiting the expected capitulation of Germany and the receipt of the codeword 'Adieu'.

CHAPTER 3

US Plans for the Surrender of the U-Boats

IT WAS CLEAR TO the US Navy that most of the surviving German U-boats were likely to surrender within the British sphere of influence. Thus, the USN's prime early concern was to put in place arrangements that would ensure its post-war access to the latest German submarine technology. To this end, the CNO's letter titled 'German Submarines for the United States' to the Commander of US Naval Forces in Europe (ComNavEu) on 24 May 1944 included the statement:

> Because of their value in research and development and in order to provide for operational test employment in the Western Pacific, it is desired to obtain actual physical possession of certain submarines of the United States' share with minimum delay. It is important that these submarines be of the latest type and that they should be in the best obtainable operating condition, fully armed and equipped, and with maximum spare parts and munitions, particularly torpedoes. By types, the numbers desired for the purposes outlined in this paragraph are:

> | | |
> |---|---|
> | 250 ton type | 1 |
> | 517 ton type | 6 |
> | 740 ton type | 6 |
> | 1200 ton type | 2 |
> | 1600 ton type | 1 (mine-laying) |
> | 1600 ton type | 1 (supply) |

> At the proper time you should make request for appropriate personnel for selecting and manning the submarines to be taken over to the extent [that] such personnel are not available within the limits of your command.[1]

So, by the time the European war ended, the idea that the USN should obtain and conduct trials on a small number of U-boats was not new. It had been an item on the USN's agenda for well over a year and was based on intelligence information possessed by the USN concerning the various types of U-boat operated by and being developed for the Kriegsmarine. The USN was particularly interested in obtaining examples of the latest high-tech German U-boats, not only for general assessment and experimental purposes, but also perchance they might be of assistance in the ongoing war against Japan.

In support of this intention to obtain the maximum possible advantage from the latest German submarine technology, the USN's CNO, who was dual-hatted as Commander-in-Chief United States Fleet (Cominch), announced on 26 December 1944 that:

On 4 December 1944 the Secretary of the Navy approved the establishing of a US Naval Technical Mission in Europe (NavTecMisEu), with the following mission and task:

Mission   To exploit German science and technology for the benefit of the Navy Department technical Bureaux and the Co-ordinator of Research and Development.

Task   To co-ordinate all the United States Naval activities engaged on the continent of Europe in exploiting German scientific and technological intelligence.[1]

NavTecMisEu, located in Paris, was activated on 20 January 1945 to be followed, as far as the search for specific German U-boats was concerned, in the spring of 1945 by another parallel, smaller and secretive organisation called the US Submarine Mission in Europe (SubMisEu).

The purpose of SubMisEu was to implement the CNO's U-boat acquisition policy which he had set out in his letter of 24 May 1944, and thus to locate and take back to the United States for study some of the high-technology German U-boats that had been identified by the USN. To this end, a small team was formed at the USN submarine base at New London in March 1945. It was not formally part of NavTecMisEu, but nevertheless liaised with it very closely.

The USN had similar aspirations to the RN concerning the urgent acquisition of the Kriegsmarine's high-tech U-boats, and in April 1945 it updated the list of the types and numbers in which it was especially interested. This opportunity arose on 18 April, when the Admiralty wrote to ComNavEu, saying:

I am commanded by My Lords Commissioners of the Admiralty to acquaint you that they have had under consideration the types of German U-Boats which should be retained for experimental purposes

in the event of their surrender on the cessation of hostilities, and I am
to invite you to state the requirements of the United States Navy in this
matter so that the responsible British Naval Authorities may be given a
complete list of U-Boats to be specially preserved.[2]

On 25 April ComNavEu referred the question to Washington, asking
if the list of U-boats originally set out in the CNO's letter of 24 May
1944 was still the USN's up-to-date requirement. The CNO's reply on
30 April was less imprecise than previously and ComNavEu was able to
advise the Admiralty on 4 May that:

> The Commander-in-Chief, United States Fleet and Chief of Naval
> Operations has indicated the requirements of the United States Navy
> for German U-Boats, which should be retained for experimental
> purposes, as follows:
>
> Two of each type: VIIC/42, IXC, IXD, IXD2, XB, XIV, XVII, XXI,
> XXIII, XXVI.
>
> In addition, two each of any further types which show promise for
> experiments and tests are required.[2]

This update of the USN's earlier statement of requirements was, like
that of the RN, made before the war had ended, before any U-boats
had surrendered and before it had been agreed just how many U-boats
would be retained by each of the Allies. As it happened, only five U-boats
surrendered at sea to US naval forces in May 1945, and the USN's
eventual requirement was therefore modified in terms of U-boat types
and numbers both by events and Allied policy.

The result of this pre-planning meant that the British and American
ground forces which were advancing into north-west Germany in 1945
included a special unit (T-Force) which, amongst its many tasks, was
charged by the joint US/UK Naval Intelligence staffs with capturing
and preserving all equipment and facilities connected with the very
latest U-boat technology. There was very close liaison between T-Force,
NavTecMisEu and SubMisEu, all of which had similar, albeit overlapping,
interests in certain of the surviving German U-boats, particularly the
Types XXI and XVII that were specifically required by the USN, thus
ensuring their early availability for assessment and experiments.

Whilst the overall arrangements for the surrender of U-boats at sea
to British, American and Canadian forces in the North Atlantic were
orchestrated by SHAEF, the Allied Naval Commander Expeditionary
Force (ANCXF), the Admiralty in London and the RN's C-in-C WA,

the detailed arrangements for the surrender of U-boats off the eastern seaboard of the USA were the responsibility of the USN.

In anticipation of the end of the war in Europe, the USN's Commander of the Eastern Sea Frontier (CESF) issued a preliminary instruction to all his subordinate formations in a message on 30 April 1945 titled 'Information on German Submarines', saying:

> Due consideration must be given to possibility German submarines may surrender prior cessation hostilities in Germany. Desire to surrender may be indicated by surfacing with engines stopped, showing white flag, raising periscopes or exhibiting rubber dinghies with crew on deck.
>
> If such happens air or surface vessels must be on guard against treachery such as attacks on themselves or nearby merchant vessels or scuttling. Such treachery will be dealt with ruthlessly by attack and destruction. Keep them clear of any nearby shipping.
>
> Aircraft will keep sub covered and immediately inform CESF who will send surface vessel. Surface vessels will start escorting to points previously indicated by Cominch.
>
> Submarines will be directed to jettison ammunition and remove torpedo pistols and burn running lights.
>
> At night keep submarine illuminated by searchlight.[3]

However, no U-boats surrendered prematurely in the western North Atlantic, so there was no requirement for these instructions to be implemented.

After receiving an Admiralty message on 2 May outlining the orders that were to be issued to all U-boats in the event of the German surrender, as well as a copy of the Admiralty's Operation 'Adieu' message, the USN Commander-in-Chief Atlantic Fleet (CincLant) advised all the naval units and vessels under his command in a general message on 3 May that:

> If U-Boats offer to surrender to Atlantic Fleet ships at points other than [the designated] points of surrender [that were specified in the SHAEF Special Orders], procedure is as follows:
>
> (A) Place armed guard aboard. At earliest moment force all officers and crew below decks and keep them there. Impress on them that if U-Boat is scuttled they sink with her and take steps to ensure this. Be ruthless if necessary.
> (B) Carry out inspections required. At discretion remove excess U-Boat personnel not required for surface operations.
> (C) Report immediately by operational priority despatch to CincLant and Cominch, info CESF when steps (A) and (B)

have been accomplished. Include identification [of] U-Boat and other pertinent information. CincLant will then issue necessary instructions for delivery of U-Boat and crew into port.

(D) Escort the U-Boat toward the nearest point of surrender until further instructions. At surrender points or at other points directed by later despatch the submarine will be turned over to Naval District authorities acting as representatives of East Sea Frontier.[3]

In the event, no U-boats arrived directly and unannounced at any of the designated points of surrender, and the surrender arrangements in the area off the eastern seaboard of the USA were therefore conducted in accordance with more comprehensive formal USN orders, the prime one of which was Operation Order No 2-45[3] issued by the Commander of the Northern Group of the ESF, who was also Commandant of the 1st Naval District, from his headquarters in Boston on 5 May.

Any U-boat which indicated its intention to surrender within the waters controlled by the Northern Group of the ESF was to be directed to proceed on the surface to a preliminary 'Point of Surrender' near Casco Bay, Maine. The USN was then to accept the surrender and take formal custody of the U-boat, before conducting it to an 'Examination Anchorage' in Lower Portsmouth Harbour. If any U-boat intending to surrender appeared in coastal waters to the south of Casco Bay, its surrender was to be accepted at sea, and it was then to be escorted directly to the examination anchorage. After the examination process had been completed and the majority of the German crew had been removed the U-boat was to be towed to Portsmouth Navy Yard (PNY) for inspection and retention.

A similar procedure was adopted by the Commander of the Delaware Group of the ESF, from his Headquarters in Cape May, New Jersey. In his instruction (A4-3/JOO), any U-boat which sought to surrender off the coast of New Jersey was to be directed to a point of surrender at sea 15 miles due east of the Delaware South Channel for the preliminary surrender arrangements. It was then to be towed to a designated examination anchorage in Delaware Bay 'under the guns of Fort Miles'. However, this Operation Order did not include details of the planned final location of any U-boat that might be examined in Delaware Bay, saying instead that disposition directions would be issued as required.[3]

Having put these arrangements in place, it was then just a matter of the USN awaiting notification of the German capitulation (Operation

'Eclipse'), together with confirmation that the 'Special Orders by the Supreme Commander Allied Expeditionary Force to the German High Command Relating to Naval Forces' had been issued to the Commander-in-Chief of the German Navy and that they had been implemented by the German Naval High Command.

Whilst all the actions following the German capitulation were carried out as planned, and whilst the units of the US Atlantic Fleet were at readiness to implement the surrender arrangements when they came into effect at 0001 on 9 May, the limited number of U-boats operating in the western North Atlantic meant that the actual surrender process itself got off to a slow start. So much so that on 10 May CincLant sent a message to all his operating units advising extreme caution and saying:

> Although the German High Command has unconditionally surrendered all forces, the U-Boat situation in the Atlantic remains obscure. Some may not have received the surrender order, others may not intend to abide by it. Until the situation clarifies proceed as follows:
>
>> Do not take offensive action such as air or surface searches
>> Maintain alert escort of convoys and take all measures to protect shipping
>> Regard any sub not in our physical possession as potentially dangerous
>> Be ruthless in suppressing any offensive action by subs. Any sub submerged in vicinity our convoys or forces shall be regarded as operating offensively
>> Previous instructions as to method of accepting surrender apply. While accepting surrender exercise extreme caution against treacherous acts and employ 2 or more vessels where practical.[3]

As it happened, the five U-boats that surrendered to the USN gave no cause for concern during the surrender process, but it was clearly wise for the naval authorities to remain alert to any unexpected reactions from the U-boat COs.

CHAPTER 4

The Surrender of the U-Boats

On 4 May 1945, on behalf of Admiral Dönitz, the German Navy's Captain (U/B) West, in a message which was repeated several times in the following days, ordered all U-boats at sea to cease operations and to return to Norwegian ports:

> The following order has been promulgated by the Gross Admiral: 'All U-Boats including the East Asia boats are to cease offensive action forthwith and begin return passage unseen. Ensure absolute secrecy. Manifestation of this step must not reach the outer world for the time being'. When on return passage, avoid all possibilities of being attacked by hunting groups. Norwegian ports of arrival will be given later.[1]

Early in the afternoon of 5 May, there was a further message from the German Naval War Staff, repeated by BdU (Ops) (Befehlshaber der Unterseeboote – HQ of Commander Submarines – Operations Division), to all U-boats, reinforcing the order for them to: 'Cease action forthwith against the British and Americans.'[1]

Thereafter, the formal surrender of the Kriegsmarine took place in two entirely separate phases, but not before Admiral Dönitz had sent a personal message to all the U-boat COs and their crews on 5 May:

> My U-Boat men: Six years of U/B warfare lie behind us. You have fought like lions. An overwhelming superiority in material has forced us into a very narrow space. From this small basis a continuation of our battle is no longer possible – U/B men, unbroken and unashamed you are laying down your arms after a heroic struggle without an equal. We think respectfully of our fallen comrades, who have sealed with death their loyalty to the Führer and the Fatherland. Comrades, keep your U/B spirit, with which you have fought bravely, toughly and undeviatingly through the long years, also in the future for the best of our Fatherland. Long live Germany. Your Grand Admiral.[1]

This was followed, first, by the surrender of the German armed forces in Holland, Denmark and north-west Germany including the Frisian Islands, Heligoland and all the islands in Schleswig-Holstein to Field Marshal Montgomery's 21st Army Group. The Montgomery-related 'Instrument of Surrender' was signed on the evening of 4 May and came into effect at 0800 on 5 May. It required all German forces in these areas to lay down their arms and to surrender unconditionally and, in the Field Marshal's hand-written addition it specifically included all naval ships in the area.

As part of the SHAEF Mission to Denmark, Rear Admiral Reginald Holt arrived in Copenhagen on the afternoon of 5 May where he lost no time in making it clear to the resident German naval staff that, despite the lack of any other Allied presence, he expected the terms of the surrender to be observed without question. He emphasised what he called 'the standstill order' verbally on 6 May and in writing on 7 May although it seemed that the Royal Navy was more interested in the fate of the Kriegsmarine's surface ships in Denmark such as cruisers, destroyers, minesweepers and other smaller warships rather than in any U-boats which might surrender there.

In support of this first phase of the surrender process, the German Naval War Staff at Flensburg sent a message to all subordinate naval organisations on the morning of 6 May reinforcing the earlier instructions, and spelling out the details of the surrender document, which included the statements that:

> All hostilities at sea by German forces to cease at 0800 hours (British Double Summer Time) on 5 May.
> The German command is to carry out at once, and without argument or comment, all further orders that will be issued by the Allied Powers on any subject.[2]

Admiral Dönitz, by then Head of State, had made clear to the German Armed Forces High Command on 4 May that it was essential that the terms of the surrender were followed to the letter, including the requirement that there should be no demolitions or sinking of warships, including U-boats. Thus, the terms of the surrender were known to the naval authorities in north-west Germany, especially those in the Cuxhaven area, who were clear that operations were to cease, that all warships were to surrender and that proposals to scuttle any U-boats were forbidden.

Despite this, the orders in relation to scuttling were ignored by many of the U-boat COs. This was perhaps not surprising as there was considerable confusion in relation to these orders, the result of which was that by the end of 5 May only nineteen U-boats had surrendered in port as instructed: sixteen in the German ports of Heligoland, Cuxhaven and Flensburg, and three in Baring Bay, near Fredericia in Denmark. Subsequently, just two more U-boats arrived from sea at ports which had already surrendered: one, *U-806*, in Aarhus (Denmark) on 6 May and the other, *U-1198*, in Cuxhaven on 8 May:

Heligoland (5 May)
U-143, U-145, U-149, U-150, U-368, U-720 and *U-1230*

Cuxhaven (5 May)
U-291, U-779, U-883, U-1103, U-1406, U-1407, U-2341 and *U-2356*

Flensburg (5 May)
U-2351

Baring Bay (5 May)
U-155, U-680 and *U-1233*

From sea in Aarhus (6 May)
U-806

From sea in Cuxhaven (8 May)
U-1198

Of the sixteen U-boats which surrendered in German ports, two were the Type XVIIB 'Walter' U-boats, *U-1406* and *U-1407*. They had arrived in Cuxhaven on 3 May, and after their COs' requests to be allowed to scuttle their U-boats had been refused they had surrendered on 5 May. However, once the crews had been taken off and whilst the two U-boats were moored in Cuxhaven harbour they were scuttled on 7 May by a German naval officer who had not been a member of either crew.

The twenty-one surrenders that occurred following the agreement with 21st Army Group all took place before the ports in question had been occupied by Allied forces, and the Allies' orders were implemented by the local German naval authorities who accepted the need to co-operate fully. However, this was not the case in the other north-west German locations where most of the remaining U-boats were based, and many of them were scuttled by their COs rather than surrendering. Despite this, such action did not raise many Allied concerns particularly as by their sinking some 200 commissioned U-boats had conveniently been put beyond future warlike use which was one of the long-term British objectives.

The Montgomery-related surrender action was followed by the general German capitulation, codenamed Operation 'Eclipse', which was signed on 7 May, and which came into effect at 0001 on 9 May. This dealt with all naval ships (including U-boats) in port and, in considerable detail, with those which were still at sea. The U-boats in port were covered by the 'Act of Military Surrender', and the U-boats at sea were covered separately by the related 'Special Orders by the Supreme Commander Allied Expeditionary Force (SCAEF) to the German High Command relating to Naval Forces'.

As a result of the capitulation, SHAEF released a message at 0410 on 7 May, saying: 'A representative of the German High Command signed the unconditional surrender of all German land, sea and air forces in Europe at 0141 hours under which all forces will cease active operations at 0001 hours on 9 May.'[3] This was followed at 1629 on 7 May by a similar message from the UK's First Sea Lord in London to all RN Flag Officers ashore and afloat, as well as to HQ RAF Coastal Command, adding: 'Instructions to cease offensive operations will be promulgated generally to the Fleet by Admiralty at earliest moment this can be done.'[4] A short time later, at 1725 on 7 May, the Assistant Chief of Naval Staff advised the Commander-in-Chief of RAF Coastal Command (C-in-C CC) to: 'Cease attacks on all shipping, [but] attacks on U-Boats should continue as heretofore.'[3]

Thus, the U-boat war continued despite Dönitz' orders on 4 and 5 May to cease operations against the British and American forces, despite the limited surrender to 21st Army Group and despite the signing of the German capitulation document on 7 May, and it was not formally ended until 0037 on 9 May when the UK's Vice Chief of Naval Staff issued the instruction: 'Carry out Operation "Adieu".'[3]

In accordance with 'Adieu' and the SHAEF Special Orders, the U-boats at sea began to surrender and to be directed and/or escorted by warships and aircraft to the defined initial examination locations. As set out in the Special Orders, the main UK surrender port for the U-boats at sea in the North Sea, the English Channel and the Eastern Atlantic was Loch Eriboll, with Portland in the south of England as a second UK surrender port. Kiel and Gibraltar were also defined as surrender ports. In the Western Atlantic there were four nominated surrender points. Two in Canada, one east of Newfoundland and one south of Nova Scotia, and two in the USA, one east of Casco Bay in Maine and one east of the Delaware River in New Jersey.

The surrender of the U-boats in port after the German capitulation on 9 May, eighty-seven in Norway and one in France (*U-510* in St Nazaire), was a relatively straightforward affair, albeit that in Norway there were very few Allied forces present on 9 May. Instead, as in Denmark and the north-west German ports, the Allies used the German military infrastructure to facilitate the surrender process. The U-boats which surrendered in Norway were:

Horton (9 May) – 10
U-170, U-874, U-975, U-1108, U-2502, U-2513, U-2518, U-3017, U-3041 and *U-3515*

Kristiansand (S) (9 May) – 17
U-281, U-299, U-369, U-712, U-1163, U-2321, U-2325, U-2334, U-2335, U-2337, U-2350, U-2353, U-2354, U-2361, U-2363, U-2529 and *U-4706*

Narvik (9 May) – 12
U-294, U-295, U-312, U-313, U-363, U-427, U-481, U-668, U-716, U-968, U-997 and *U-1165*

Bergen (9 May) – 28
U-298, U-324, U-328, U-539, U-778, U-868, U-875, U-907, U-926, U-928, U-930, U-991, U-1002, U-1004, U-1022, U-1052, U-1057, U-1061, U-1104, U-1202, U-1271, U-1301, U-1307, U-2328, U-2506, U-2511, U-3514 and *UD-5*

Trondheim (9 May) – 13
U-310, U-315, U-483, U-773, U-775, U-861, U-953, U-978, U-994, U-995, U-1019, U-1064 and *U-1203*

Stavanger (9 May) – 7
U-637, U-1171, U-2322, U-2329, U-2345, U-2348 and *U-3035*

The terms of surrender had been notified to the German C-in-C in Norway by Field Marshal Keitel on 7 May, and this was followed by a message from the German Naval War Staff in Flensburg on the morning of 8 May. The latter made it clear to the Head of the Kriegsmarine in Norway that he was responsible for the notification of the conditions of surrender to all relevant naval headquarters as well as to the Admiral commanding the U-boats. To avoid the confusion that had overtaken events in Denmark and north Germany on 5 May in relation to surrender versus scuttling, the Kriegsmarine's Captain (U/B) West issued a clear order to all U-boat bases in Norway on 8 May saying:

Do not allow any U-Boats to sail, nor permit transfers of any kind between the bases.

The Admiral of the Fleet has ordered: U-Boats in Norway are neither to be scuttled nor destroyed, because only in that way can hundreds of thousands of German lives in the east be saved.[1]

Also, on 8 May, Admiral Dönitz sent his final personal message to the U-boat COs:

U-Boat men. After a heroic fight without parallel you have laid down your arms. You have unprecedented achievements to your credit. You must now make the hardest sacrifice of all for your Fatherland by obeying the [surrender] instructions unconditionally. This casts no slur on your honour but will prevent serious consequences for your native land. The order to proceed on return passage to Norway is cancelled. Your Grand Admiral.[5]

The surrender process in Norway began in Oslo on 8 May with a meeting between Commodore Per Askim of the Royal Norwegian Navy, representing the RN's Flag Officer Norway, Rear Admiral James Ritchie, and the Kriegsmarine's Admiral Krancke, who was clear about the need to cooperate fully with Allied naval representatives. The local German naval authorities in Norway therefore followed the Allies' surrender and disarmament orders, passed via the Kriegsmarine HQ in Oslo, in order to ensure the prompt surrender of all the U-boats in Norwegian ports on 9 May.

The surrender of the U-boats at sea did not go quite as smoothly as the surrender of those in port. The results were affected by the position of each U-boat at midnight on 8 May, difficulties with the receipt of the surrender messages, the date on which the U-boat surfaced and sent its initial PCS message, the surrender port chosen by the CO and the attitudes of the individual U-boat COs to the prospect of captivity for themselves and their crews.

Most COs received the surrender messages on either 8, 9 or 10 May, and most accepted the inevitability of the German defeat and thus the need to surrender forthwith. However, some of them were unhappy about the situation and a few chose to disobey the Allied surrender orders. On the other hand, there were real signals-reception difficulties, a fact well recognised by the Allies, and some of the U-boats at sea either never received the formal surrender orders, did not receive them on time or received them in such an unconventional manner as to suggest that they might be invalid.

The pattern of the surrenders from sea was therefore varied. Several of the U-boats in the vicinity of Norway and Germany headed directly for ports in those countries without first broadcasting any surrender messages. But the majority of those at sea surfaced and transmitted their surrender messages on 9, 10 and 11 May and then as instructed headed for the appropriate surrender port either solo or with an aircraft and/or surface warship escort. Fifteen U-boats surrendered whilst still at sea on 9 May, ten on 10 May and seven on 11 May. Others took a little longer to surface and either send their first PCS message and/or to fly a black flag or to arrive at an Allied port without prior notice.

Most of the U-boats which surrendered at sea in the Eastern Atlantic headed for Loch Eriboll in the UK. The first U-boat to enter the Loch after surrendering on 9 May (*U-1009*) arrived on the morning of 10 May. Between then and 18 May a further seventeen U-boats arrived in Loch Eriboll. These included *U-2326* which had surrendered to an aircraft in the North Sea on 11 May and, after first heading for Kiel, had arrived in Dundee on 14 May.

The most extreme example of delay after its surrender at sea occurred in the case of *U-3008*. This U-boat had surrendered to an aircraft whilst at sea off the north-east tip of Denmark on 11 May and had been ordered to sail to Kiel. However the CO was loath to travel south without either an escort or a copy of the charts showing the local minefields. He therefore anchored in Frederickshaven Roads in north-east Denmark from 12 to 19 May before obeying his orders and heading for Kiel, where *U-3008* eventually arrived on 21 May.

By mid-May there were still thought to be thirty-eight U-boats at sea which were unaccounted for, albeit that most of them had been sunk in the last few weeks of the war. Thus, on 18 May on Allied instructions BdU (Ops) signalled the thirty-eight 'missing' U-boats, including *U-530*, *U-963*, *U-977*, *U-979* and *U-1277*, saying:

> Your conduct is wrong in not acting in accordance with the unconditional surrender signal. This entails a breach of the obligations undertaken by the Grand Admiral and the laws of war. Serious consequences for yourselves and Germany may ensue. Surface at once and report position. Remain on the surface and wait for further instructions.[1]

By 21 May it was estimated that between ten and twelve U-boats were probably still at sea and therefore potentially dangerous, with the Admiralty's 'U-Boat Situation Report' for the week ending 21 May recording:

What the remaining U-Boats are doing or intend to do is a fruitful and intriguing subject for speculation [and] it is still possible though increasingly improbable that some of them have failed to intercept or have hitherto refused to believe any of the surrender messages which are so constantly transmitted.[6]

As a result, the order transmitted on 18 May was reinforced on 24 May in another message, this time to all U-boat COs, from the German Admiral West Norwegian Coast, again on behalf of the Allies, stating:

> You are acting wrongly by not surrendering. Your refusal represents a violation of our signature and the rules of war. Serious consequences can arise for you and for Germany. Surface forthwith and report your position in plain language. Remain surfaced and await further orders.[1]

Despite this message being repeated regularly until 1 June, by the end of May there were still three U-boats at sea. Of these, two (*U-530* and *U-977*) were on their way to Argentina where they eventually surrendered, one in July and one in August, and one (*U-1277*) was on its way to Portugal where it was scuttled in early June.

Between 9 May and 17 August, a total of forty-seven U-boats surrendered either at sea to British, US and Canadian naval forces or arrived directly at harbours on either side of the Atlantic without prior notice:

UK	21	Canada	2
Norway	9	Argentina	2
Germany	6	Gibraltar	2
USA	5		

UK

U-249	Surrendered whilst at sea on 9 May, arrived at Portland on 10 May
U-802	Surrendered whilst at sea on 9 May, arrived at Loch Eriboll on 11 May
U-826	Surrendered whilst at sea on 9 May, arrived at Loch Eriboll on 11 May
U-1009	Surrendered whilst at sea on 9 May, arrived at Loch Eriboll on 10 May
U-1058	Surrendered whilst at sea on 9 May, arrived at Loch Eriboll on 10 May
U-1105	Surrendered whilst at sea on 9 May, arrived at Loch Eriboll on 10 May
U-293	Surrendered whilst at sea on 10 May, arrived at Loch Eriboll on 11 May

U-516	Surrendered whilst at sea on 10 May, arrived at Loch Eriboll on 14 May
U-532	Surrendered whilst at sea on 10 May, arrived at Loch Eriboll on 13 May
U-825	Surrendered whilst at sea on 10 May, arrived at Loch Eriboll on 13 May
U-1023	Surrendered whilst at sea on 10 May, arrived at Portland on 10 May
U-1109	Surrendered whilst at sea on 10 May, arrived at Loch Eriboll on 11 May
U-1305	Surrendered whilst at sea on 10 May, arrived at Loch Eriboll on 10 May
U-956	Surrendered whilst at sea on 11 May, arrived at Loch Eriboll on 13 May
U-1010	Surrendered whilst at sea on 11 May, arrived at Loch Eriboll on 14 May
U-1231	Surrendered whilst at sea on 11 May, arrived at Loch Eriboll on 13 May
U-2326	Surrendered whilst at sea on 11 May, arrived at Dundee on 14 May
U-244	Surrendered whilst at sea on 12 May, arrived at Loch Eriboll on 14 May
U-764	Surrendered whilst at sea on 13 May, arrived at Loch Eriboll on 14 May
U-255	Surrendered whilst at sea on 14 May, arrived at Loch Eriboll on 17 May
U-776	Surrendered whilst at sea on 14 May, arrived at Portland on 16 May

Norway

U-245	Surrendered in Bergen after direct arrival from sea on 9 May
U-278	Surrendered in Narvik after direct arrival from sea on 9 May
U-318	Surrendered in Narvik after direct arrival from sea on 9 May
U-992	Surrendered in Narvik after direct arrival from sea on 9 May
U-2324	Surrendered in Stavanger after direct arrival from sea on 9 May
U-1272	Surrendered in Bergen after direct arrival from sea on 10 May
U-218	Surrendered in Bergen after direct arrival from sea on 12 May
U-1005	Surrendered in Bergen after direct arrival from sea on 14 May
U-901	Surrendered whilst at sea on 13 May, arrived at Stavanger on 15 May

Germany

U-1194   Surrendered in Cuxhaven after direct arrival from sea on 9 May

U-3008   Surrendered whilst at sea on 11 May, arrived at Kiel on 21 May

U-739   Surrendered whilst at sea on 14 May, arrived at Emden on 14 May

U-1102   Surrendered in Hohwacht Bay after direct arrival from sea on 13 May

U-1110   Surrendered whilst at sea on 14 May, arrived at List, Sylt on 14 May

U-2336   Surrendered in Kiel after direct arrival from sea on 15 May

USA

U-805   Surrendered whilst at sea on 9 May, arrived at Portsmouth, NJ on 15 May

U-858   Surrendered whilst at sea on 9 May, arrived at Lewes, Delaware on 14 May

U-1228   Surrendered whilst at sea on 9 May, arrived at Portsmouth, NJ on 17 May

U-873   Surrendered whilst at sea on 11 May, arrived at Portsmouth, NJ on 16 May

U-234   Surrendered whilst at sea on 12 May, arrived at Portsmouth, NJ on 19 May

Canada

U-889   Surrendered whilst at sea on 10 May, arrived at Shelbourne on 13 May

U-190   Surrendered whilst at sea on 11 May, arrived at Bay Bulls on 19 May

Argentina

U-530   Surrendered in Mar del Plata after direct arrival from sea on 10 July

U-977   Surrendered in Mar del Plata after direct arrival from sea on 17 August

Gibraltar

U-541   Surrendered whilst at sea on 10 May, arrived at Gibraltar on 12 May

U-485   Surrendered whilst at sea on 12 May, arrived at Gibraltar on 12 May

Since the war there has been much uncertainty concerning the dates on which the forty-seven U-boats that were at sea on 9 May actually surrendered. On the one hand the Admiralty was clear that such surrenders took place where and when the U-boats surfaced and either sent their first PCS messages or were located flying their black flags or when they arrived unannounced at the various ports. On the other hand many historians have maintained that the surrenders only took place when the U-boats arrived in port despite having already surrendered at sea. Despite the latter view, the initial surrender dates which are recorded in the Admiralty War Diary,[3] as well as being illustrated on an excellent Admiralty summary chart held in the UK National Archive at Kew (*MFQ 1/589/16*), are considered to be the most accurate.

Following the signing of the two formal surrender documents, 156 U-boats surrendered to the Allies on both sides of the Atlantic, of which only nine put into ports in the Western Atlantic: five in the USA, two in Canada and two in Argentina. Not a single U-boat surrendered in any Soviet-controlled port nor did any of the six U-boats in the Far East surrender to the Allies in May 1945. Instead the latter were handed over to the Imperial Japanese Navy (IJN) just before the German capitulation came into effect.

As well as the nine U-boats which surrendered from sea in the Western Atlantic, there was one other U-boat in the area in May 1945 and that was *U-505* which had been captured by the USN off the west coast of Africa on 4 June 1944 by a USN carrier task group. It was then towed to the USN base at Port Royal Bay in Bermuda for technical examination. Because of the security imperative to create the illusion that it had been sunk rather than captured, *U-505* was temporarily renamed as USS *Nemo* and kept secretly in Bermuda for the remainder of the war.

After its arrival in Bermuda on 19 June 1944, *U-505* was dry docked for the repair of the damage that had occurred during its capture. Fortunately, this was not significant, and the USN was able return *U-505* to the water with an American crew for trials under the control of the USN's Office of Naval Intelligence (ONI).

Of the U-boats at sea on 8 May, there were four whose COs chose to scuttle their vessels rather than obey the surrender orders. Two were on their way back to Germany, and two were heading for Portugal on the supposition that internment in a neutral country was preferable to captivity in the UK. These were:

U-287 – Scuttled in the Elbe Estuary on 16 May

U-963 – Scuttled off Nazare, Portugal on 20 May

U-979 – Scuttled off Amrum, N Frisian Islands on 24 May

U-1277 – Scuttled north west of Oporto, Portugal on 3 June

U-287 was patrolling to the east of the Orkneys in early May and it remained at sea after the formal surrender on 8 May, the CO (Meyer) preferring to disregard the Allies' orders and to return to Germany rather than head for Loch Eriboll. *U-287* entered the Elbe Estuary on 16 May where it was scuttled on the riverbank off the village of Altenbruch some 10km east of Cuxhaven. The crew went ashore hoping to escape detection and when they were inevitably discovered they said that *U-287* had sunk after hitting a mine.

After *U-963* received Dönitz' cease-fire/recall order but before receiving the formal surrender order it was damaged during an aircraft attack on 6 May whilst west of the Hebrides. As a result *U-963* was said to be unable to send or receive any radio messages. The CO (Wentz) decided to head south towards the Iberian Peninsula instead of returning to Norway. On the evening of 19 May when *U-963* was off Nazare (north of Lisbon) on the north-west coast of Portugal the main pumps failed and the U-boat began to settle. Wentz therefore ordered *U-963* to be scuttled in the early hours of 20 May.

U-979 was operating to the east of Iceland when it torpedoed a British tanker in early May. It was immediately counter-attacked with depth charges but managed to escape with only minor damage. The CO (Meermeier) decided to return to Bergen for repairs but after receiving the surrender order he decided to return to Germany instead. There was damage to one of the U-boat's propeller shafts, so the journey towards the western German ports at periscope depth was slow. *U-979* eventually reached the North Frisian Islands (south-west of Denmark) and the CO's intention was to anchor off Amrum Harbour prior to going ashore to investigate the situation and then hopefully to escape capture. However when manoeuvring just after midnight on 23/24 May near the southern tip of Amrum Island the U-boat ran aground at high tide on sandbanks close to the shore and could not be re-floated.

In early May *U-1277* had orders to patrol in the Western Approaches. However whilst he had received and acted on the German cease-fire instruction on 4 May telling him to return to Norway the CO (Stever) decided that the subsequent surrender order and the other plain-language signals were not authentic. Instead the U-boat remained at sea in and around the Iceland-Faeroes gap whilst the CO decided what he should do. By mid-May he learned of the Allied occupation of Norway and the capitulation in Germany but he was still loath to surrender. In Stever's view Norway was no longer an option and a return to Germany was precluded by the lack of charts showing the minefields in the North Sea and Baltic. Stever therefore decided that his best option was to head for a neutral country. Thus *U-1277* set course for Spain and Portugal and after a mostly-submerged journey arrived in the vicinity of Cape Finisterre off the north-west corner of the Iberian Peninsula at the beginning of June. Stever's original intention had been to scuttle his U-boat off Vigo in Spain but instead he headed to Oporto in Portugal and at about midnight on 2/3 June *U-1277* surfaced close to the shore north-west of Oporto where Stever scuttled his U-boat.

Whilst there was a view in some British naval circles that the scuttling of these four U-boats was to be welcomed, there was also a view that as their COs had deliberately contravened the surrender orders they deserved to be punished. In the case of the CO of *U-1227* (Stever) who was the last to scuttle his U-boat (almost four weeks after the end of the war) he was charged and found guilty of deliberately failing to surrender as instructed and, specifically, of scuttling his U-boat; actions for which he was sentenced in 1946 to imprisonment as a war criminal. The Admiralty and the British military authorities in Germany were initially also inclined to prosecute the other three COs (Meyer of *U-287*, Wentz of *U-963* and Meermeier of *U-979*). However, whilst preliminary work on the legal cases was initiated no court actions transpired. As time passed it had been decided that it was no longer necessary to make an example of another U-boat commander.

In relation to the surrender of the, by then, ex-U-boats in Japanese waters, the Admiralty's Vice Chief of Naval Staff had advised the RN's Commander-in-Chief East Indies on 5 May that:

> It is not intended to include special orders for U-Boats in Japanese controlled waters.
>
> If German naval authorities are co-operative, ANCXF [Allied Naval Commander Expeditionary Force] should instruct them to issue special orders to U-Boats in the Far East.
>
> If German naval authorities will not co-operate, C-in-C East Indies should himself issue [suitable] special orders.[3]

After the German capitulation on 8 May and the initiation of the process for the surrender of the U-boats still at sea, the Allies were keen to ensure that any U-boats still in the Far East followed a similar surrender procedure to those in the Atlantic. Although it was not known that by then it was far too late, ANCXF advised the Admiralty on 12 May that the following instruction had been passed to the German naval authorities:

> The German Naval High Command is to order all German U-Boats in or based on Japanese controlled harbours to leave such harbours. They are to proceed in the manner which the Commanding Officer sees fit until they are over 300 miles from such harbours, when they are to surface, fly a black flag or pennant, report their position in plain language to the nearest British, US or Soviet coast W/T station and proceed to the nearest Allied port, or such port as Allied representatives may direct, and remain there pending further directions from Allied representatives. At night they are to show lights.[3]

This instruction was followed up by a message from BdU(Ops) on 16 May to the COs of *U-181*, *U-195*, *U-219* and *U-862* but it produced no positive results as not only had the U-boats still in the Far East already been taken over by the IJN but also because they were all unfit to proceed to sea. This was confirmed in a message from the RN's Flag Officer Kiel to ANCXF on 17 May, saying: 'German Naval HQ Kiel today informed me [that] High Command have complied with your 121100 and reported that only one of the German U-Boats in Japanese waters is fit for sea. This latter [*U-183*] has acknowledged the order.'[7]

By that stage the fog of war had well and truly taken over, as this single U-boat which was reported to be fit for sea had already been sunk in the Java Sea by a US submarine on 23 April. Yet despite this it was reported that *U-183*'s acknowledgement of the order to surrender had been made in mid-May when it was said to have been south of the Philippines and in transit to Fremantle in Western Australia. The net result was that none of the U-boats in the Far East surrendered to the Allies in May.

At the same time as the 21st Army Group's 'Instrument of Surrender' which specifically included all naval vessels was being signed on 4 May, there was a parallel US/UK policy in effect which stated that any warships and merchant ships captured in north-west German and Danish ports prior to any total German capitulation were to be treated as 'prizes'.

This complicated matters as it implied that the twenty-one U-boats that had surrendered in Denmark and north-west Germany between 5 and 8 May would be at the disposal of whoever had captured them. Although this policy was primarily concerned with the future of German merchant shipping it also referred to warships and in this respect it was contrary to the agreement that the disposal of any German naval vessels which surrendered would be subject to joint decisions by the Allies. The policy had been first set out in a directive (FACS 113) from the Combined US/UK Chiefs of Staff (CCS) to General Eisenhower at SHAEF on 4 December 1944, and it included in its paragraph 3 the statement: 'Captured enemy warships should be at the disposal of SCAEF who should refer to the Combined Chiefs of Staff for direction concerning their assignment.'[8]

As the end of the war in Europe approached, this policy was re-visited, primarily in relation to merchant ships, and on 20 April 1945 the UK Chiefs of Staff (COS) sent a message to the UK Joint Staff Mission in Washington, saying:

> Following is proposed directive to SCAEF:
> Unless otherwise directed FACS 113, paragraph 3 is to be applied to all German shipping captured by forces under your command in German ports before the surrender or declaration of defeat of Germany.
> Shipping not required within your theatre is to be sailed as soon as possible to the United Kingdom.
> Captured shipping is to be seized in prize.
> Seizure in prize should be effected by the Naval Authorities in control of ports where ships are captured.
> You will receive further instructions regarding the treatment of shipping falling into your hands upon surrender or declaration of defeat.
> Warships should be disarmed, their flag lowered, and reference made to CCS in accordance with paragraph 3 of FACS 113.[8]

This was followed by a message from the Admiralty to ANCXF on 3 May saying:

> Proposal to seize in prize German ships captured before cessation of hostilities was telegraphed to CCS on 20 April. Reply not yet received.
> If policy of taking captured ships in prize is approved, intention is that this should be effected by Naval authorities controlling the ports concerned. Action must however await CCS directive.
> Should urgent need arise of establishing claim to captured ships against Russians, e.g. in Lubeck, White Ensign should be hoisted under procedure in [the] Naval Prize Manual.[9]

It was therefore not surprising that in early May there was thorough confusion in northern Germany about which policy should be followed, viz:

9 May: 21st Army Group: German seagoing ships captured at Lubeck are being claimed as prizes. Request instructions whether similar action should be taken at Kiel and Flensburg observing [that] this appears to be a partial surrender on the field of battle.

9 May: Commodore Hamburg: Unless orders to the contrary, propose to sail destroyer and German U-Boat to UK as soon as mine clearance has been completed. Request instructions with regard to remainder of ships.

10 May: ANCXF: No German warships, U-Boats or merchant ships are to be sailed to UK ports until further instructions are issued.[9]

On the same day as the instruction that no ships were to be sailed to UK ports was issued, ANCXF sent a message to SHAEF and the Admiralty setting out the proposals for the disposal of German warships and merchant ships, viz:

All German Warships, Naval Auxiliaries and Merchant Ships which were in German ports, westward from Lubeck (inclusive), and in all Dutch and Danish ports at the time of surrender to 21st Army Group, or who entered these ports subsequently but previous to the general capitulation, should be dealt with as captured enemy ships in accordance with FACS 113, paragraph 3.[9]

In view of the need for clarity but in effect achieving just the opposite, and after some urgent hastening action from London to Washington in view of the situation in Lubeck, the policy was re-iterated in a message (FACS 221) from the CCS to General Eisenhower on 14 May, saying:

Unless otherwise directed paragraph 3 of FACS is to be applied to all German shipping captured by forces under your command in German ports before the surrender or declaration of defeat of Germany.

Accordingly all shipping not required within your theatre is to be sailed as soon as possible to the United Kingdom.

Warships should be disarmed, their flag lowered, and reference made to the CCS in accordance with paragraph 3 of FACS 113.[8]

As requested, whilst the CCS agreed to the move of the U-boats from Norway to the UK, they failed to react to the Admiralty's somewhat late Machiavellian suggestion aimed at thwarting Russian ambitions in respect of the U-boats which had surrendered to 21st Army Group in Germany and Denmark. The British suggestion was quietly dropped and it was assumed that the U-boats which surrendered before 9 May fell into the same category as those which surrendered on or after 9 May, Thus, they would all to be available for disposal as agreed by the Allies. This was subsequently belatedly confirmed in a US Joint Chiefs of Staff (JCS) paper dated 5 July 1945, which included the statement: 'No distinction should be made between war vessels captured before or surrendering after the capitulation.'[11]

CHAPTER 5

The Kriegsmarine's Operation 'Regenbogen'

AFTER THE RED ARMY captured Danzig on 30 March 1945 and began to advance westwards along the southern Baltic coast, the Kriegsmarine was progressively forced to abandon the ports and harbours in the eastern Baltic, and to move the remaining U-boats towards Kiel and the ports and anchorages in the western Baltic. At the same time British and Canadian forces were advancing from the west towards Schleswig-Holstein, thus putting pressure on the U-boat bases to the south-west of the Danish peninsula, such as Wilhelmshaven, Wesermunde and Hamburg.

In late April 1945 the Kriegsmarine therefore needed to consider how best to continue the war and what should be done with the remaining surface warships and U-boats if, as seemed inevitable, Germany was forced to capitulate. Thus, whilst he was still C-in-C of the Kriegsmarine Admiral Karl Dönitz' thoughts turned to consideration of the fate of the remaining warships and, as he later wrote:

> The officers of Supreme Headquarters were of the opinion that to hand over weapons, and particularly warships, the most strikingly outward and visible manifestation of armed strength, would be a violation of the tenets of military honour.
>
> I fully realised that if I handed over our warships I would be acting contrary to the traditions of our Navy and of the navies of every other nation. It was in an effort to conform to this code of honour which is accepted by all nations that the German Navy sank the fleet in Scapa Flow at the end of the First World War.[1]

Almost all the publications which describe the end of the U-boat war refer at least briefly to the Kriegsmarine's Operation 'Regenbogen', and their authors almost invariably assert that the scuttling of so many U-boats in early May 1945 was contrary to the conditions of the 'Instrument of Surrender' agreed with Field Marshal Montgomery's 21st Army Group in

North Germany. The latter was signed at 1830 on the evening of 4 May
and became effective from 0800 on 5 May.

Whilst confusion and the fog-of-war had settled over northern
Germany in the first week of May, especially on the night of 4/5 May
and before the total German capitulation came into effect at 0001 on
8/9 May, there was a standing German Navy instruction that the COs of
all warships were expected to scuttle their vessels rather than surrender
or allow them to be captured. Thus, it was not surprising when, as the
end of the war in Europe approached, the Kriegsmarine's Naval War Staff
(Seekriegsleitung [Skl]) reinforced this expectation by sending a message
on 30 April to all German naval headquarters, including the Office of
the Commander-in-Chief U-boats (BdU), concerning what it called the
'self-destruction' (scuttling) of any remaining German naval ships and
submarines, saying:

1. In case of a non-predictable development of the situation it is
   intended to sink the nucleus of the fleet upon dissemination of
   codeword Regenbogen [Rainbow], and to retire units from the
   service still useful for civilian purposes.
2. Codeword Regenbogen signifies:
   a. The following war ships are to be sunk immediately respectively
      to destroy themselves: battleships, cruisers, destroyers, torpedo
      boats, S-boats, U-boats.
   b. All ships still with the potential for later civilian use such as
      fishing or transportation are to be retired. Their armament has to
      be destroyed.
   c. Ships still usable for any kind of minesweeping operations are to
      be retired. Their armament is to be destroyed.[2]

During the final week of the war, the BdU directed that all the remaining
operational and potentially operational U-boats, especially those in the
Baltic, were to transfer to Norway from where the U-boat war would
continue. This left large numbers of U-boats in the Baltic and the north-
west German ports and anchorages, particularly many new Type XXI and
Type XXIII U-boats which were undergoing their working-up exercises
prior to becoming operational.

At the same time the Allied armies in the vicinity of Hamburg and Kiel
were closing in on the German forces in northern Germany and by 2 May
British forces had reached the Baltic coast near Lubeck. Almost all the
U-boat ports and anchorages to the west and east of the Danish peninsula
but south of the Danish border were therefore under immediate threat

of capture. Thus, with effect from 1 May the planned scuttling of the U-boats in lieu of surrender began. At the time such action was contrary to neither Allied nor Kriegsmarine policy: rather, it was exactly what the Kriegsmarine expected.

It was therefore no surprise when Admiral (U/B), who by then was Admiral Hans-Georg von Friedeburg, sent a message on 1 May to the U-boat bases at Wesermunde and Wilhelmshaven with copies to the CO of the 31st U-Boat Flotilla, as well as to Captain (U/B) Baltic, saying: 'For U-boats the orders issued will continue to apply, namely the destruction of U-boats by order of Admiral (U/B), unless the local O.I/C Base is compelled by the situation to act independently.'[3] In response the reaction from the CO of the 31st U-Boat Flotilla in Wesermunde confirmed on 2 May that: 'In agreement with Admiral, Navy Office Hamburg, the following boats ... will be towed at once to Markwaerderhafen, ready for blowing up.'[3] On the same day the CO of the 25th U-Boat Flotilla in Travemünde advised Admiral U/B: 'Arrival of enemy tanks in Travemünde reported at 1515. Am giving order to scuttle.'[4] Similarly on 3 May BdU (Ops) instructed the CO of the 5th U-Boat Flotilla in Kiel: 'Boats ready for Norway are to leave Geltinger Bay for Norway immediately. If at all possible make provision for Regenbogen in Geltinger Bay.'[5]

Operation 'Regenbogen' was therefore well underway from the very start of May and all those in charge of the U-boats remaining in North Germany, from Dönitz and the admirals in the various headquarters down to the individual U-boat COs, were aware of the Kriegsmarine's scuttling policy and were implementing it as circumstances demanded. Thus, three U-boats were scuttled in Warnemunde on the Baltic coast on 1 May, thirty-two were scuttled off the Baltic coast on 2 May, mostly in Travemünde, and a further forty-six were scuttled in a variety of north-west German and Baltic locations on 3 May.

The specific 'Regenbogen' warning order of 30 April was reinforced late on 3 May, or early on 4 May, when the Naval War Staff advised the whole fleet including Admiral (U/B) that: '[The] basic order remains in force that old battleships, cruisers, destroyers, new torpedo boats, S-boats, U-boats and small battle units may not fall into enemy hands, but in the existing situation are to be sunk or destroyed.'[4]

Shortly thereafter early on 4 May BdU (Ops) sent a further message to Admiral U-Boats and all U-boat COs and U-boat bases on the north German coast advising them:

1. The U-boat war goes on.
2. Boats coming from Kiel are to go not to Flensburg, but to Geltinger Bay. Cdr. Liebe of BdU (Ops) will settle which boats can be made ready for front line operations and be despatched to Norway.
3. On keyword 'Regenbogen', which may also be given for single areas, U-boats are to be scuttled or destroyed outside the fairways.
4. Over and above this, the order is: No boat is to fall into enemy hands. Every man must scuttle on his own responsibility in case of danger.[5]

This order was reinforced yet again on 4 May when the Naval War Staff emphasised: 'Local C's-in-C are authorised, taking account of [the] situation, to issue code word "Regenbogen" on their own responsibility.'[4]

The U-boat COs had thus been very clearly reminded of their duty and they could be in no doubt about it. If they were not able to sail their U-boats to Norway, they were expected to scuttle them rather than surrender them to either the Russians or the Western Allies. The plethora of messages despatched by the OKM (the Kriegsmarine HQ), the Skl and the BdU in the first few days of May 1945 made it quite clear that this was a Kriegsmarine policy requirement and as a result a further five U-boats were scuttled on 4 May.

Whilst these initial scuttling actions were underway many of them overlapped with the negotiations which led to the surrender to Field Marshal Montgomery's 21st Army Group of all German armed forces in Holland, Denmark and north-west Germany. The negotiations took place on 3 and 4 May the formal surrender agreement was signed at 1830 on 4 May and it came into effect at 0800 on 5 May. It required all German armed forces in those areas to lay down their arms and surrender unconditionally and a last-minute addition to the typed 'Instrument of Surrender' document, written by the Field Marshal himself included the condition that the surrender also applied to all naval ships (including U-boats).

There is nevertheless confusion relating to the date and time when Admiral Dönitz, who was now Head of State, became aware of Montgomery's late condition concerning the surrender of all warships. Dönitz in his 1959 *Memoirs* wrote:

At our morning conference on May 4 I therefore directed Supreme Headquarters to issue orders that no arms were to be destroyed. At the same time I instructed the Chief of Naval Staff to ensure that the signal

'Regenbogen' – the code word for the sinking of warships – should not be issued and explained to him the reason for my instructions.[1]

There is no doubt that the main topic of the meeting on 4 May, which was attended by Field Marshal Keitel and Admiral von Friedeburg as well as by Dönitz' Minister for Foreign Affairs, Johann Ludwig Count Schwerin von Krosigk, and Dönitz' adjutant, Commander Walter Ludde-Neurath, was the implication of the proposed local surrender. But it is not clear if there were any specific discussions about 'Regenbogen'. This is especially so as it appears that no specific 'Regenbogen'-related orders or instructions were originated as a result. Perhaps by 1959 Dönitz' memory had let him down.

There is no evidence to confirm that the standing 'Regenbogen' warning order of 30 April was ever formally rescinded during 4 May either by Dönitz himself, the Supreme Command Staff (OKW), the Skl staff at the OKM or by Admiral (U/B) at the BdU. No such instructions are recorded in either the OKW or the OKM War Diaries and no copy of the May 1945 BdU War Diary survived the war.

On the other hand, on 4 and 5 May Dönitz had initiated two specific actions relating to the impending end of the war. First, on the afternoon of 4 May he ordered all U-boats at sea to cease operations and return to Norwegian ports. As a result in a message to Field Marshal Montgomery on 5 May the Head of the German Armed Forces, Field Marshal Keitel, advised that: 'The Grossadmiral [Dönitz] has issued orders already on 4 May at 1614 to all U-boats to cease combat operations and to sail homeward.'[6] Second, on Dönitz' behalf BdU (Ops) advised all U-boat COs on 5 May that the OKM had ordered that they were to: 'Cease hostilities against the English and Americans forthwith.'[5]

It is therefore possible that neither Dönitz nor the OKW staff may have realised the specific need to order the cancellation of the standing 'Regenbogen' instruction until late on 4 May probably after the surrender document had been signed. Specifically, after Admiral von Friedeburg, Dönitz' senior representative at the Luneburg Heath negotiations, had reported back to him in Flensberg at 1940 on the evening of 4 May that the 'Instrument of Surrender' now included Montgomery's late hand-written statement indicating that all warships were required to surrender.

As recorded by Dönitz' Adjutant, Commander Ludde-Neurath, in the 1999 version of his book *Regierung Dönitz: Die Letzten Tage des Dritten Reiches* (first drafted in 1948):

On the same evening at 19:40 hrs we received a radio message concerning the signing of the instrument of surrender in the HQ of Montgomery which had taken place in the meantime. In the Northern Area, weapons were to be silent from the 5th of May at 08:00 hrs. As desired by the Grossadmiral, the OKW issued orders forbidding the destruction of weapons and – with a short explanation of the reasons – the order to pass all weapons to the enemy.[7]

As a result, at some time after 1940 on 4 May and most probably in the very early hours of 5 May Field Marshal Keitel caused the OKW to send a short but unfortunately untimed message notifying all the German armed forces, including the Kriegsmarine, of the 21st Army Group's surrender conditions, including the requirement, to use his own words, that there should be 'no scuttling', viz:

As of 05 May 1945 0800 hrs of German summertime ceasefire with respect to the troops of Field Marshal Montgomery. It comprises all formations of the Army, the Kriegsmarine, the Luftwaffe and the Waffen-SS within the area of the Netherlands, Friesland including West and East Friesland Island and Heligoland, Schleswig-Holstein and Denmark. To be made known to all subordinate troops immediately. Check reception of orders, troops remain in their positions with their weapons. Transport operations by the Kriegsmarine at sea to be continued. Strictly no destructions, scuttling and demonstrations. Securing of all stocks, obedience and discipline to be maintained with iron strength. Further orders to follow.[8]

In respect of the timing of this instruction which made no specific mention of 'Regenbogen' there are several clues indicating that it was despatched either very late on 4 May or very early on 5 May – most probably the latter. For example, as revealed in a message found in the war diary of the light cruiser *Leipzig*, which was being used as an accommodation ship in the Danish port of Aabenraa, from Vice Admiral Hans-Heinrich Wurmbach who was Admiral (Skagerrak) and who was responsible for the coastal defence of Denmark, its contents were not forwarded to the Kriegsmarine units in his area of responsibility until 0145 on 5 May.[9]

Also, there is an entry in the OKM War Diary on 5 May which shows that despite Keitel's message bearing the very highest transmission priority, it was apparently only passed-on to the OKM/Skl staffs at 0425 on 5 May.[10]

Additionally, another high-priority message sent at 0517 on 5 May to the Admirals commanding the Kriegsmarine's Naval Command West and Naval Command North reinforced the Keitel message, saying: 'The cessation of hostilities viz-a-viz Field Marshal Montgomery's troops, which comes into force at 0800/5/5, applies to the area of the Netherlands, Friesland (including the Western and Eastern Friesland Islands and Heligoland), Schleswig-Holstein and Denmark.'[3] But even this did not entirely clarify the situation and as a result Admiral (Netherlands) responded to the Skl at 0815 on 5 May saying: 'Query. Is freedom of independent action for Admiral Netherlands with regard to key-word Regenbogen cancelled by the order concerning the truce?'[3]

All this suggests that there were major communication difficulties, that the instruction about 'no scuttling' was only slowly making its way down through the various levels of the chain of command, but more especially that even the Kriegsmarine's senior officers were unclear as to whether or not the Keitel message formally overrode the 'Regenbogen' order.

Also, the wording of Keitel's message concerning the timing of the 'ceasefire' seemed to have created an opportunity for its recipients to make their own choice as to when the order about 'no scuttling' was to take effect. Thus, during the night of 4/5 May the news that no U-boats were to be destroyed or scuttled in lieu of surrender was followed by much concern and misunderstanding within the OKM and the Skl, as well as in U-Boat Headquarters (BdU), about the exact meaning and implications of the message. For instance, did it apply immediately or only after 0800 on 5 May?

By then Dönitz was no longer the C-in-C of the Kriegsmarine and Admiral U-Boats, and during the evening of 4 May his successor in both appointments, Admiral von Friedeburg, was on his way to Reims to meet General Eisenhower to negotiate the complete capitulation of the German State on Dönitz' behalf. Additionally, Admiral Godt who was the BdU's Chief of Staff was on his way to Norway. There may therefore have been a temporary lack of effective leadership amongst the Kriegsmarine's senior OKM, Skl and BdU staff, which conspired to create a decision vacuum.

Neither the OKM, the Skl staff, the BdU staff nor several U-boat COs at the new HQ location in Flensburg could believe that Dönitz would have rescinded the 'Regenbogen' order voluntarily and that if he had done so the decision must have been made under duress and against his better judgement. There were attempts to speak directly to the Admiral late in the evening of 4 May but by then he was sleeping and unavailable to clarify the situation.

In the absence of such clarity the BdU staff therefore took matters into their own hands and in what could be interpreted as a direct contravention of the OKW's Keitel order they despatched a message early on 5 May which said, according to an ULTRA intercept which said:

New situation.
If possible U-boats which at 0800/5/5 are in German or Danish ports, roads or bays or are south of latitude 55.10 north will carry out 'Regenbogen', i.e. scuttle in as deep water as possible.[5]

It was not until around midday on 5 May that this order was belatedly rescinded by the BdU in a message sent to all U-boat COs in German and Danish waters saying: 'Do not carry out any further Regenbogen after 0800/5/5.'[5]

There is no evidence which establishes the precise time of release of this latter message but the use of the word 'after' in the message implies that as far as the BdU was concerned it was acceptable for the commissioned but non-operational U-boats located in German and Danish ports or at sea south of latitude 55.10 degrees N to be scuttled prior to 0800 on 5 May but not later.

It was also by then too late to reverse the many local actions which had been initiated in the early hours of 5 May. As a result, a further ninety-five U-boats were scuttled out of sight of any Allied forces during 5 May mostly from Kiel, Flensburg, Wilhelmshaven and Wesermunde and mostly, it may be assumed, in the early hours of the morning prior to the deadline of 0800 imposed by the 21st Army Group's 'Instrument of Surrender'.

Several examples of the reaction to the activation and the subsequent cancellation of 'Regenbogen' were intercepted by ULTRA on 5 and 6 May:

On the morning of 5 May, the 26th U-Boat Flotilla at Warnemunde reported: Measure 'Regenbogen' completed.[3]
On the evening of 5 May, the 4th U-Boat Flotilla reported that 2 U-boats had been: Sunk in Flensburg.[4]
On the evening of 5 May, the 8th Defence Division reported: The Commanding Officer of U-2544 reports 'Regenbogen' carried out.[5]
On the evening of 5 May, Captain (U/B) Baltic reported that 2 U-boats were: Blown up as the last U-boats in the [Kiel] canal.[4]
Late on 5 May, the U-Boat base at Wesermunde reported: Cancellation of 'Regenbogen' received too late. 'Regenbogen' carried out.[4]

Early on 6 May, the U-Boat base at Wilhelmshaven reported: Wilhelmshaven is being occupied. Secret matter destroyed. 'Regenbogen' carried out.[3]

There were major communication difficulties in North Germany on 4 and 5 May and so the dates and times of these ULTRA intercepts do not necessarily indicate exactly when the various messages were first originated and/or transmitted. For instance, in respect of the message from Wilhelmshaven on 6 May, its veracity was confirmed by the CO of the RN's local Submarine Party which had arrived at Wilhelmshaven in early May and whose Report of Proceedings stated without any seeming concern: 'All U-boats in Wilhelmshaven, some 26 in number, were found to have been sunk, three by recent air attacks and the remainder by order of the German Admiral von Friedeburg some days previous to our arrival.'[11]

Despite the considerable confusion about the scuttling of the U-boats that had arisen because of the series of orders and counter-orders which led to the scuttling of the ninety-five U-boats on 5 May, there were nevertheless a small number of U-boat COs who complied with Keitel's 'No scuttling' interpretation of the 21st Army Group's 'Instrument of Surrender' and so chose or were instructed not to scuttle their boats in accordance with the extant 'Regenbogen' order.

By the end of the day on 5 May, nineteen U-boats had surrendered in port as instructed: sixteen in the German ports of Heligoland, Cuxhaven and Flensburg, and three near Fredericia in Denmark. Subsequently two more U-boats arrived from sea to surrender in ports which either had already been or were about to be taken over by the Allies. Of the fourteen U-boats which surrendered in port on 5 May, two were the Type XVIIB 'Walter' U-boats *U-1406* and *U-1407* in Cuxhaven, which were subsequently scuttled on 6/7 May, and all but one of the others were also located in Cuxhaven and Heligoland. In these two locations, in contrast to the actions that took place in almost all the other ports and anchorages, and although neither had at that stage been captured by the Allies all the U-boats surrendered rather than being scuttled by their COs.

The surrender of the U-boats in Cuxhaven rather than being scuttled in accordance with the 'Regenbogen' order was due to the personal intervention of Vice Admiral Gustav Kleikamp, the Coast Commander German Bight, who was based in Cuxhaven. The Admiral was not directly responsible for the operational control of the U-boats in the harbour at Cuxhaven, but early in the morning of 5 May he and his staff had become aware of the requirement in the 'Instrument of Surrender' as set out in Keitel's message that no warships were to be scuttled.

The Admiral and his staff had also been alerted to the situation by a message in the early morning of 5 May from the COs of the two 'Walter' U-boats, *U-1406* (Lieutenant Klug) and *U-1407* (Lieutenant Heitz) which had only recently arrived from Kiel, saying: 'We request order to scuttle for "Walter" front-line boats in event of seizure by the enemy being imminent.'[3]

In response, rather than allowing any scuttling to proceed, it was made clear to the COs of all the U-boats in Cuxhaven that despite the extant 'Regenbogen' order they were to surrender their charges. The chain of events during 5/6 May including the precise reasons why the surrenders took place is set out in the RN's Interrogation Report of Lieutenants Klug and Heitz, viz:

> At 0400 on 5 May the order 'Regenbogen für U-Boote' which meant 'All U-boats within certain latitudes should be scuttled' [was received]. This order included Cuxhaven. We thereupon called Korv. Kapt. Stollte aboard the 'Heligoland' informing him that we were going to put out to sea to carry out the order.
>
> Stollte told us that Admiral Kleikamp had phoned him instructing him that the order was cancelled. We told Stollte that we had not 'heard' the [latter] order and would go out just the same. Stollte said to us 'what I am telling you now is an order from me, and you are not to sail'. We thereupon returned to our ships to await further orders which never came.
>
> During the morning at about 1100 we met Lt. Grumpelt in the harbour and made an appointment with him to sail, in the company of other U-boats, to scuttle our craft. Kapt. Thoma probably got to hear of this scheme, because he came to contact us and again gave us an order that we were not to sail. Grumpelt evidently got to hear that Thoma had forbidden us to sail, and new arrangements were made to run out at 2200 that evening.
>
> At about 2000 we received a signal that we were to report aboard the 'Heligoland' where we met all the other U-boat commanders based at Cuxhaven. When we were all there, we were driven out to Kubelbake to Admiral Kleikamp's headquarters. We assembled there, the Admiral came in, made a speech, and we each of us, individually, had to give our word of honour to the Admiral and seal it with a handshake, that we would not scuttle our craft.[12]

In respect of the U-boats which surrendered in Heligoland on 5 May, they like those in Cuxhaven were under the operational control of No.

34 U-Boat Flotilla based in Wilhelmshaven. They were also under the administrative control of Vice Admiral Gustav Kleikamp, as well as his subordinate Rear Admiral Rolf Johannesson, the Commander of the Elbe-Weser Naval Defence Region, which included both Cuxhaven and Heligoland.

Though still a U-boat training base in early May Heligoland was in the process of being converted into an operational base, and Captain Alfred Roegglen who was both the fortress commander and the senior German Naval Officer was aware of the general requirement for the destruction of the Island's facilities and weapons prior to any possible capture by the Allies. However, despite this a message originated at 0135 on 5 May was received from Admiral Johannesson which passed on the contents of the OKW order from Field Marshal Keitel containing the 'no scuttling' instruction.[13]

As a result, and despite Heligoland having not yet been captured by Allied forces, the seven U-boats based there were not scuttled in accordance with the 'Regenbogen' order. Instead, they surrendered, and their COs awaited their fate until a party of Royal Marines arrived from Cuxhaven on 8 May.

Of the remaining six U-boats which surrendered to the Allies on or after 5 May as required by the 'Instrument of Surrender' rather than being scuttled by their COs in accordance with their 'Regenbogen'-related orders:

U-2351 had departed Flensburg on 4 May en-route to Norway but had been attacked by aircraft and re-entered Flensburg the same day. Unable to sail again it surrendered on 5 May.

U-155, *U-680* and *U-1233* had departed Flensburg on 4 May en-route to Norway but had been attacked by aircraft and taken shelter in Baring Bay on the same day. They surrendered on 5 May after receiving advice about the cessation of hostilities from the local Danish harbourmaster.

U-806 had departed Kiel on 3 May en-route to Norway but had been damaged after grounding on 5 May. This caused it to enter Aarhus in Denmark on 6 May which by then had been occupied by British troops to whom it surrendered.

U-1198 had departed Cuxhaven on 4 May en-route to Norway and was about 100 miles north of Cuxhaven on 6 May when it received news of the need to surrender. As a result it returned to Cuxhaven, arriving on 8 May where it surrendered.

Despite the limited number of U-boats which surrendered to the 21st Army Group in the geographical area of North Germany and southern Denmark, the war was by no means over on 5 May, and the remaining U-boats were still considered to be part of the Kriegsmarine's operational force. This was the case even though Dönitz had ordered that attacks against British and American targets were to cease and that all the U-boats at sea were to return clandestinely to Norwegian bases.

The BdU message on 4 May saying that 'The U-boat war goes on' was still valid, and a whole series of Admiralty and RAF Coastal Command messages originated between 4 and 7 May made it clear that the surrender to Montgomery's 21st Army Group did not signal the end of the U-boat war:

> 4 May – from RAF Coastal Command: All attacks to cease immediately except within 20 miles of Norwegian coast. This does not repeat not apply to U-boats at sea against which operations are to continue.

> 4 May – from the Admiralty: Attacks on U-boats and escorting vessels at sea should be continued.

> 5 May – from RAF Coastal Command: Personal from AOC-in-C. In spite of surrender of German forces on the continent there is as yet no indication that they contemplate surrender in Norway. We may therefore expect the continuance of intensive U-boat operations from Norwegian bases. All ranks must realise that for Coastal Command the war goes on as before. We started first, we finish last. I call upon all Squadrons for a great final effort against our old enemy. It falls to Coastal Command to strike the final blow against the enemy's one remaining weapon.

> 5 May – from the Admiralty: Enemy shipping in the Skagerrak north of 58 degrees (N) and proceeding towards Norway may be attacked pending further instructions.

> 7 May – from RAF Coastal Command: Normal operations against U-boats to be continued until 0001 9 May.

> 7 May – from the Admiralty: Attacks on U-boats should continue as heretofore.[14]

Thus, there is no evidence to suggest that the U-boat war ceased after the Montgomery surrender in North Germany came into force at 0800 on 5 May. Rather, it did not formally end until just after midnight on 8/9 May when the British Vice-Chief of Naval Staff at the Admiralty in

London issued the instruction 'Carry out Operation Adieu' so signifying the formal end of the war at sea.[15]

In the meantime, U-boats continued to attempt the transit passage from North Germany to Norway, and the British and Americans continued their air attacks on these U-boats, many of which were forced to make the voyage on the surface whilst finding their way through the British and German minefields. Thus it was not surprising that additional scuttlings took place between 6 and 9 May, two of which were directly related to damage from air attack whilst in transit to Norway, but others were clearly contrary to both the Kriegsmarine's 'Cancel Regenbogen' message and the British orders as set out in the 21st Army Group's 'Instrument of Surrender', albeit that it is possible that the on-going communication difficulties might have contributed to the confused situation.

Although 'Regenbogen'-related, the scuttling of *U-1406* and *U-1407* on the night of 6/7 May 1945 after they had surrendered on 5 May was a one-off special case, the details of which were described in 'The Case for the Prosecution' against Lieutenant Grumpelt at his Court Martial in February 1946, which included the information that:

> After a day of discussion as to whether the U-boats were to be scuttled on the next night, Grumpelt went aboard these two U-boats with a rating, and scuttled them. He did it, according to his statement, of his own volition, quite openly and in a sane mind, because he wished to deprive the Allies of the use of those two submarines, which were of the very latest type and capable of giving a great deal of information to the Allies.[16]

It is apparent from the evidence presented at Lieutenant Grumpelt's trial that despite all the very many German messages, instructions and counter-instructions that were originated on 4 May and in the early hours of 5 May, the British authorities' understanding of the conditions set out in the 'Instrument of Surrender' was that no 'Regenbogen'-related scuttlings were permitted after 0800 on 5 May. Thus, all the scuttlings which took place on that day mostly probably before or around 0800 were accepted as legal within the terms of the 21st Army Group's 'Instrument of Surrender'.

The scuttling of *U-1008* and *U-3503* after being attacked from the air and damaged whilst in transit from the Baltic to Norway could more properly be regarded as 'war losses' rather than 'Regenbogen'-related scuttlings. In contrast, there is good cause to believe that the scuttling of *U-2365*, *U-2367*, *U-2512*, *U-2538* and *U-3030* were contrary to both the extant Kriegsmarine and Allied orders and were, strictly speaking, examples of deliberate disobedience. Each of their COs was undoubtedly aware of the orders pertaining after 0800 on 5 May but despite this they each decided to deny their U-boat to the Allies.

On the other hand, the U-boat war was still underway and any submarine at sea in the Baltic was at serious risk of being attacked from the air and sunk with the total loss of the crew irrespective of its CO's intentions, especially in the absence of any formal surrender procedure (as happened as part of the main capitulation several days later). The circumstances which led to the – perhaps not so unreasonable – late scuttling of these five U-boats were:

a. *U-2365* was scuttled in the Kattegat off the Danish Island of Anholt on 8 May. After an air attack on 5 May whilst on passage to Norway the CO continued north towards the Norwegian U-boat base at Kristiansand-South, but then learned that the German forces had capitulated. *U-2365* immediately turned south and headed for Germany until 1700 on 8 May when it encountered a Kriegsmarine guardship in the vicinity of Anholt. Although the CO knew by then that scuttling was forbidden, he went ahead with it and he and the crew transferred to the guardship.

b. *U-2367* was in Kiel on 3 May when the British forces arrived but rather than scuttling his U-boat the CO moved it to Flensburg where he should have surrendered. Instead, he left the harbour in company with a coastal patrol boat and headed for Schleimunde which had not yet been taken over by British forces. After lying submerged off Schleimunde for the next two days *U-2367* entered the port and disembarked most of the crew before being scuttled in the Baltic four miles south-east of Schleimunde lighthouse on 9 May.

c. *U-2512* arrived in Kiel on 3 May en-route to Norway and at midnight the CO received orders to leave the harbour and scuttle his U-boat. Despite this he decided to head for Flensburg to pick up some of his crew who he had allowed ashore. *U-2512* was then moved to Eckernförde where the Engineer Officer and two members of the crew were put ashore to check the military situation whilst the rest of the crew prepared the U-boat for scuttling. During the next two days *U-2512* was twice ordered to surrender, first by the CO of the local No. 33 U-Boat Flotilla and then by the CO of the Torpedo Trials School, but the U-boat's CO disagreed. Instead, he proposed to decommission his U-boat and hand it over to the CO of the Torpedo Trials School. The local informal decommissioning ceremony took place on the evening of 7 May but shortly after midnight eight members of the crew re-boarded *U-2512* and scuttled it in Eckernförde Bay in the early hours of 8 May.

d. *U-2538* escaped from Swinemünde at the beginning of May and arrived off Travemünde on 3 May to find that all other U-boats there had been scuttled on 2 May. It was ordered by the CO of No. 25 U-Boat Flotilla to scuttle in the open Baltic but before it was able to do so a group of four other U-boats, which included *U-2538*, were attacked by aircraft on 3 May. Of these, one was sunk but the other three escaped towards the western Baltic. Soon afterwards the CO learned of the capitulation from an Allied radio message, but he was not prepared to surrender his U-boat. Although he knew that it was contrary to his orders, he decided to sail north-west until he arrived off the Danish coast near the small island of Aero where *U-2538* remained mostly submerged until the U-boat was scuttled at 0445 on 8 May after the weather conditions had allowed the crew to go safely ashore.

e. *U-3030*, in company with *U-2538*, also escaped from Swinemünde at the beginning of May and arrived off Travemünde on 3 May to find that all other U-boats there had been scuttled on 2 May. Like *U-2538* it was then ordered by the CO of No. 25 U-Boat Flotilla to scuttle in the open Baltic but before it was able to do so a group of four U-boats, which included *U-3030*, were attacked by aircraft on 3 May. Of these, one was sunk but the other three escaped towards the western Baltic. *U-3030* arrived in Eckernförde on 4 May and the CO went ashore to reconnoitre the situation. After he returned, he moved *U-3030* near to the small fishing village of Noer where one of the crew knew a local farmer and the U-boat remained submerged there for three nights until after unloading all their provisions with the help of local fishermen the crew went ashore, and the CO scuttled his U-boat on the morning of 8 May

Thus, the only scuttlings which might have been of concern to the British authorities were those which took place on 6 May and thereafter but, other than in the case of *U-1406* and *U-1407*, any evidence that might have been available about any U-boats which were scuttled later than the deadline was ignored. It seems that the COs of only five U-boats contravened the agreed surrender conditions, but that the confusion and fog-of-war pertaining at the time enabled them to avoid any sort of censure or other disciplinary action.

There are several good secondary sources of information relating to 'Regenbogen', four of which were written shortly after the war by officers directly associated with the 21st Army Group's surrender negotiations and which, with the advantage of hindsight, shed extra light on what were obviously the confused conditions in Flensburg on 4 and 5 May 1945. The first was written by Admiral Dönitz himself, and others by three Kriegsmarine officers: Korvettenkapitän (Commander) Walter Ludde-Neurath, Fregattenkapitän (Captain) Gunter Hessler and Oberleutnant zur See (Lieutenant) Dr Wolfgang Frank.

Admiral Dönitz' book *Memoirs*, first published in Germany in 1958 under the title *Zehn Jahre und Zwanzig Tage* ('Ten Years and Twenty Days'), was published in England in 1959, and in it he records, perhaps somewhat naively and maybe with a slight lapse of memory:

> Except for a few U-boats which were blown up by their captains in the night of May 4-5 before the armistice came into force, no warships of the German Navy were sunk. The U-boats in question had already been prepared for scuttling before the Naval Staff's orders to the contrary had arrived. Their captains were sure that in sinking their boats they would be acting in accordance with my wishes, since they could not believe that I would have issued orders to surrender except under compelling pressure.[1]

Commander Walter Ludde-Neurath was Dönitz' Flag Lieutenant (Adjutant) from September 1944 until the end of the war, and he was very closely associated with the events that occurred in the first week of May 1945. The first German-language edition of his book *Unconditional Surrender* was published in 1950, having been written in 1948 when the memory of events in 1945 was still relatively fresh in his mind. The latest English-language edition was published in 2010, and includes the information:

> At 1940 hrs the same evening [4 May] we received a signal confirming the signing at Montgomery's HQ and at 0800 hrs on 5 May the guns fell silent. Following Dönitz' order, OKW ordered that no weapons were to be destroyed and with a brief explanation ordered them to be surrendered to the enemy.
>
> It was obeyed almost without exception. Only the U-boat arm, loyal to Dönitz in a special way, declined the order in the Homeland. Dönitz had already left when [Heinrick] Liebe [ex *U-38*] and [Martin] Duppel [ex-*U-959*], both veteran U-boat commanders, stormed into my office. Both were attached to the BdU staff [and] had now received the incomprehensible order not to scuttle the U-boat fleet. They would only obey this order if they heard it from Dönitz' own mouth.
>
> I was certain that Dönitz would not go back on his decision. Therefore I refused them an interview with Dönitz with the observation that I knew what I would do as a commander. Both understood.

U-boats that received the order were scuttled on the night of 4 May. Dönitz himself was at first very surprised by the mass scuttling. None of the feared reprisals followed. On the contrary, we later gained the impression that this destruction was approved by the Western Allies.[17]

Captain Gunter Hessler, who was Dönitz' son-in-law, was a staff officer in the Operations Branch of the BdU from 1942 until the end of the war, who at the request of the Admiralty was given free access to the surviving war diaries and primary sources of the German Navy and in 1950 wrote what was initially a classified Admiralty document before it was published by HMSO in 1989 under the title *The U-Boat War in the Atlantic 1939-1945*. In it, in relation to 'Regenbogen' and the actions that took place during the first week of May 1945 and the surrender to Field Marshal Montgomery's 21st Army Group, Hessler records:

> Details of the surrender terms were transmitted to all German forces late on 4 May. However, the commanders of U-boats in the Western Baltic, who had already prepared their boats for scuttling in accordance with the orders for Regenbogen and were of the opinion that the order forbidding the sinking of their ships was contrary to Dönitz' intention and given under duress, scuttled their U-boats that night, just before the armistice.[18]

Lieutenant Dr Wolfgang Frank was a Public Relations Officer on the BdU staff in 1945 who described his memories of the activities in early May in relation to the 21st Army Group surrender in his 1953 book *Die Wölfe und der Admiral*, an English version of which was published in 1955 under the title *The Sea Wolves: The Story of the German U-Boats at War*. In it he confirms Ludde-Neurath's version of events, albeit using somewhat more flamboyant and exaggerated language, saying:

> The order to cancel 'Rainbow' loosed a flood of questions and protests. Had the Grand Admiral really given the order? If he had it could only have been given under duress. Ludde-Neurath's telephone never stopped ringing; he could only repeat the same answer over and over again. That is the truth, 'Rainbow' has been cancelled.
>
> Late that night a group of officers stormed in. Where is the Grand Admiral? We must speak to him at once. The capitulation doesn't come into effect until tomorrow. Suddenly one of them now realised what was needed. There was unanimity of feeling, [and] within a very short time the U-boat wireless transmitters began to buzz throughout North Germany: Rainbow, Rainbow, Rainbow.
>
> All along the coast, at Flensburg, Eckernförde and Kiel, in Lubeck-Travemünde, at Neustadt, Hamburg and at Wilhelmshaven, [the U-boats] slid away from the jetties for the very last time.[19]

Another commentary on the confusing situation in early May 1945 was recorded by Commander Peter Cremer in the 1987 English-language version of his book *U-Boat Commander*, who at that time was in charge of Dönitz' bodyguard and therefore in close personal contact with the Admiral. Although his own U-boat (*U-2519*) had been scuttled in Kiel on 3 May, and despite some memory lapses regarding the timing of the various 'Regenbogen'-related scuttlings, he recorded: 'When these incidents were reported to him, I was personally present. The Grand Admiral looked very surprised and at first disapproving, then a slight smile crossed his face. And we commanders also got away with it, for the Allied reprisals which we had expected did not occur.'[20]

It had been hoped that the recollections of Count Schwerin von Krosigk, who was present at Dönitz' meeting at 0900 on 4 May, would shed additional helpful light on the discussions that took place about the implication of the proposed terms and conditions of the surrender to Montgomery's 21st Army Group, but his version of the story is equivocal to say the least. He says that the meeting took place on 3 May (which is incorrect), and the words used in his 1977 *Memoirs* follow very closely those of Ludde-Neurath. Indeed, they seem to have been based directly on the latter's version of events, they add nothing to the information that is already available from other sources and they therefore add nothing substantive to the debate.

Because of the fog-of-war surrounding events in North Germany in early May 1945, it is difficult to establish the precise dates and times at which the various orders relating to 'Regenbogen' were initiated and received, and this is exacerbated by the fact that no version of the May 1945 BdU War Diary exists. There are, however, other secondary sources which purport to specify the exact dates and times of the 'Regenbogen' executive instruction and its withdrawal.

First, in the British naval historian Dan van der Vat's book *The Atlantic Campaign* published in 1988 he recorded:

> Confusion now reigned in the residual submarine command. The code word 'Regenbogen' was transmitted at 1.34 a.m. on May 5. The German word for rainbow was the predetermined message indicating that submarines should scuttle themselves rather than surrender. At 1.42 a.m. however there came another message from Headquarters, now in Flensburg in Schleswig-Holstein, which ordered that 'no scuttle or destruction should be undertaken'.[21]

Second, the American naval historian Clay Blair in his book *Hitler's U-Boat War* published in 1998 somewhat cautiously recorded, in what seems to be an echo of Dan van der Vat's commentary, that:

According to some sources, the codeword 'Regenbogen' (Rainbow), the directive to initiate scuttling, was transmitted from Flensburg at 1.34 a. m. on May 5, German time, but rescinded by Dönitz or an aide eight minutes later. Whether this is true or not, it is certain that ambiguous orders of some kind regarding scuttling reached the U-boats. As a result, some skippers or surrogates commenced scuttling on May 5, but others did not.[22]

Third, in an e-mail message in December 2013, the late Herr Horst Bredow – the authoritative German creator and mastermind of the Cuxhaven U-Boat Museum and Archive – stated:

The official 'Regenbogen' message was transmitted at 01.34 hrs (German Summer Time) on 5 May 1945, to be followed by a second message at 01.42 hrs on 5 May 1945 signed by Field Marshal Keitel himself informing all stations about the partial surrender to Montgomery and the strict order not to scuttle.[23]

However, none of these three secondary sources gives any precise indication of the primary sources from which the authors apparently discovered the specific date/times that they quoted. Instead, the two latter versions might well be based on Dan van der Vat's 1988 version. There is therefore a need to seek proof concerning the two quoted messages: The first apparently sent at 0134 on 5 May and the second apparently sent at 0142 on 5 May.

There is no question that the BdU's 'Regenbogen' implementation message was the one intercepted by ULTRA at 0150 on 5 May and which suggests that its time of origin was 0134 on 5 May. However, there is no evidence concerning any closely following specific 'Regenbogen' cancellation message from the BdU. The message saying 'Do not carry out any further Regenbogen after 0800/5/5' was not intercepted by ULTRA until 1336 on 5 May, although that does not prove its time of origin.

Dan van der Vat says that the cancellation message was timed at 0142 on 5 May and contained the words 'no scuttle or destruction should be undertaken', and Horst Bredow stated that it was 'signed by Field Marshal Keitel himself informing all stations about the partial surrender to Montgomery and the strict order not to scuttle'.

The OKW's Keitel message, for which there is no evidence as to its exact date/time of origin, except that according to both Walter Ludde-Neurath and Gunter Hessler it was sent late in the evening of 4 May, contained the words 'strictly no scuttling', so it would seem likely that a version of this which was transmitted to the lower formations may be the alleged cancellation message quoted by both Dan van der Vat and Bredow. However, this is not substantive evidence that it was the formal cancellation of the 'Regenbogen' implementation message sent at 0134 on 5 May, nor does it answer the question as to exactly when the 'Do not carry out any further Regenbogen after 0800/5/5' message may have originated.

This lack of sound evidence concerning the precise details and timing of the cancellation of the 'Regenbogen' order is also confirmed – by omission – in the Canadian naval historian Dr Chris Madsen's comprehensive and exceptionally well-researched 1998 book *The Royal Navy and German Naval Disarmament 1942-1947*, when all he had to say on the matter was:

> Some German captains and crews decided to scuttle their warships and submarines before formal implementation of the surrender to 21st Army Group. Whether Dönitz and the German naval staff sanctioned these actions is unclear.
>
> The German naval staff originally intended to leave as few submarines as possible to the British. Early on 5 May British intelligence staffs intercepted a wireless message from the German naval high command [saying carry out 'Regenbogen'].
>
> There is some suggestion that Dönitz later countermanded the order.[24]

Dr Madsen had obviously not been able to locate any specific 'Regenbogen' cancellation message that had been originated in the early hours of 5 May, but at least he did not attempt to conflate it with the Keitel message. Thus, the exact timing of any formal cancellation messages from the BdU in the early hours of 5 May, if indeed there ever were any, remains a mystery. All that is known is that they might have originated sometime after 0001 and before 0800 on 5 May.

A more likely explanation of this 'Regenbogen'-related order/counter order conundrum is that it stems from the coincidental overlap between the BdU's orders which followed the operational chain of command and the OKW's Keitel message relating to the Montgomery surrender which followed the Kriegsmarine's administrative chain of command. Thus, the 'Regenbogen' implementation message sent out by the BdU in the early morning of 5 May never was specifically rescinded several minutes later. Rather, several versions of the Keitel message were received at around the same time and shortly after but they did not specifically mention the cancellation/withdrawal of 'Regenbogen', even though they forbade scuttling after 0800 on 5 May.

The operational U-boat authorities and COs were therefore faced with two separate but related messages: one from the BdU timed at 0134 on 5 May saying 'scuttle' and the other from their administrative commanders in the early hours of 5 May (of which those from Admiral (Skagerrak) at 0145 on 5 May and Sea Commander Elbe-Weser at 0135 on 5 May are but two examples) saying 'do not scuttle'. No wonder there was confusion!

This confusion was well illustrated by the CO of *U-999*, Lieutenant Wolfgang Heibges, who scuttled his U-boat in Flensburg Fjord in the early morning of 5 May:

> The hours passed without the password Regenbogen being initiated. Instead, we received a counterorder from the Naval Staff, which forbade scuttling. I was clueless and now totally uncertain.
>
> Was this counter order really in line with Dönitz' mind? What were the reasons for it?
>
> The uncertain situation did not relax when the partial surrender in the west was communicated during the night of 4/5 May, which was to come into effect on 5 May at 0800 hours.
>
> We still dealt with the question: should we, may we, or must we scuttle our boat or not?
>
> Just one thing was totally clear: scuttling after the time of partial surrender would have been a violation of the surrender conditions, no longer allowed within a few hours time.
>
> I was relieved from this fateful decision, when the upper deck lookout reported that the first boats were being scuttled.[25]

A further piece of the puzzle is provided by the German naval historian Michael Salewski who, in Volume II of his 1975 book *Die Deutsche Seekriegsleitung 1935-1945* (*The German Naval War Command 1935-1945*) suggested that the confusion surrounding 'Regenbogen' might have resulted from Admiral Dönitz deliberately turning a blind eye to the final tranche of the scuttling of the U-boats in the early hours of 5 May, saying:

> In the night from 4 to 5 May 1945 all German U-boats which could be reached somehow sank themselves without the keyword Regenbogen ever having been transmitted [which is clearly incorrect]. Dönitz – allegedly surprised – could congratulate himself: Without proof of violating the ceasefire agreements, a matter of heart for the BdU had been fulfilled. As had been hoped there occurred no Allied reprisals, no

doubt that the Western Allies were not discontent with this course of events.[26]

In the interests of rescuing troops and refugees from the eastern Baltic it was essential that no surface warships were scuttled, but this was not so important in the case of the U-boats. Salewski implies that whilst Dönitz ensured that Field Marshal Montgomery was made aware of the order on 4 May that all U-boats were to cease combat operations and return to their bases, he deliberately chose to stay silent about the implementation of 'Regenbogen' as far as the U-boats were concerned. Instead, he left the matter in the hands of the BdU and thus (by omission) allowed the 'Regenbogen' order to be transmitted in the knowledge that its subsequent cancellation would be received too late to stop the related scuttling actions.

In what may well be the most accurate version of the events and their timing, there is Major Joachim Schultz-Naumann's 1991 book *The Last Thirty Days: The War Diary of the German Armed Forces High Command from April to May 1945*, the German edition of which (*Die Letzten Dreissig Tage*) was first published in 1951. This is an informal version of the OKW War Diary that had formally ceased being recorded on 19 April 1945, and in it the diary entry at 0045 on 5 May records: 'The order concerning the beginning of the armistice at 0800 hours German Summer Time, May 5, is sent to Commander in Chief North, Wehrmacht Commander Denmark, Naval High Command and the Luftwaffe High Command.'[27]

It would seem therefore that this was most probably the first version of the Keitel message to be despatched, albeit that the diary entry at 0445 then states, presumably in reinforcement of the earlier (0045) message:

> Telexes are sent to Commander in Chief North, Wehrmacht Commander Denmark, Commander in Chief Netherlands, Naval High Command, Luftwaffe High Command and various departments of the Reich, explaining why there was an armistice in the Northern Zone while fighting continues in the east.[27]

The OKW diary also sheds some light on the timing of any possible separate specific instruction concerning the scuttling of the Kriegsmarine's warships. On the one hand, and despite Dönitz being asleep at the time, in the entry made at 0028 on 5 May, Schultz-Naumann records: 'The Grand Admiral wishes that no demolitions or scuttling of ships be undertaken.'[27]

However, in the diary entry made at 1910 on 5 May, well after the formal cancellation of 'Regenbogen' by the BdU, Schultz-Naumann says:

'In the evening, the Grand Admiral cancels all orders concerning the scuttling of ships. There is evident desire to ensure a smooth transition as demonstrated by the sequence of events and the manner in which they have been handled by both Germans and Allies.'[27]

There is no specific mention of 'Regenbogen' in this sole remaining version of the OKW War Diary. It is therefore possible to conclude that whilst Dönitz was keen to ensure that no warships were scuttled in the light of the terms of the ceasefire/surrender to Montgomery's 21st Army Group, there was a failure in the follow-up staff actions designed to transmit that message with sufficient clarity to ensure that all recipients fully understood that it also withdrew the extant 'Regenbogen' order.

There is no evidence of any British adverse reaction to the many U-boat scuttlings that took place on 5 May or shortly thereafter, nor is there any evidence that these scuttlings were considered to have been made in contravention of the 21st Army Group's 'Instrument of Surrender'. That early surrender took effect at 0800 on 5 May, and it seems to have been accepted by the British authorities that all the scuttlings that took place before or around that time were, by definition, legal or at least acceptable.

As it happened, the 'Regenbogen'-related U-boat scuttlings were a blessing in disguise. This was because, although Field Marshal Montgomery required all the German warships in North Germany to surrender, the Admiralty wished to see the earliest possible destruction of the U-boats. Without 'Regenbogen', more than 350 would have been available to surrender, so it was perhaps no wonder that the Royal Navy raised no objection to its implications.

There are many different versions of the number of U-boats that were scuttled in early May in accordance with 'Regenbogen'. Some versions are restricted to just those U-boats which were still operational, whilst others include U-boats which were either non-operational, awaiting commissioning or which had already been decommissioned. For instance, Roskill's official *History of the War at Sea* published in 1961 quotes a figure of 221, although he does not list the U-boats concerned.[28]

As a general guide, and to avoid endless discussion as to which figures were or were not correct and which U-boats were or were not involved, possibly the most accurate figures are those published in Dr Axel Niestlé's 2014 book *German U-Boat Losses during World War II*. This indicates that three U-boats were scuttled on 1 May, 32 on 2 May, 46 on 3 May, five on 4 May, 95 on 5 May and nine thereafter – a total of 190.[29]

CHAPTER 6

The Assembly of U-Boats in the UK in May, June and July 1945 – Operation 'Pledge'

THE ROYAL NAVY'S OPERATION 'Pledge' filled the gap between the surrender of the U-boats in Europe and the Eastern Atlantic in May 1945 and their ultimate disposal. The operation covered the reception of the U-boats which had surrendered at and from sea in the UK, as well as the transfer of those and the many others which had surrendered in European ports to Lisahally and Loch Ryan in May, June and July 1945.

The detailed arrangements were set out by Admiral Sir Max Horton, the C-in-C WA, on 19 April in his 'Pledge One' Operation Order[1] which indicated that the surviving U-boats would be dealt with in two phases, although these very quickly merged into one continuous process. First, the surrender of the U-boats which were still at sea and, second, the disposal of the U-boats remaining in the German and German-controlled ports.

The Operation Order emphasised that there would be three elements to the reception of the U-boats which surrendered either at or from sea:

a. A preliminary examination and the placing of RN armed guards on board, primarily in Loch Eriboll.
b. A final inspection in Loch Alsh to check for the presence of booby traps, and to ensure that each U-boat was innocuous. At the same time, the German crews would be removed, except for a minimum steering party.
c. The berthing of the U-boats at one of the two laying-up ports of Lisahally and Loch Ryan, and a further reduction of the German crews, leaving only those necessary for maintenance duties.

It also set out details of the preliminary actions to be taken to establish the necessary organisations in Loch Eriboll, Loch Alsh, Loch Ryan and Lisahally to enable them to be ready for action on receipt of the order 'Carry out Pledge One':

a. The Flag Officer-in-Charge, Greenock was instructed to arrange for two submarine parties to proceed to Loch Alsh. One party was to remain embarked in HMS *Philante*, and the other was to be accommodated at Loch Alsh. HMS *Philante* was then to proceed to Loch Eriboll.

b. The anchorage at Loch Eriboll had no permanent RN port facilities, and so on 6 May the 21st Escort Group (21 EG), comprising HMS *Conn*, HMS *Fitzroy*, HMS *Rupert*, HMS *Deane* and HMS *Byron*, was ordered to proceed to Loch Eriboll to secure the anchorage and to prepare to receive a then-unknown number of U-boats. Additionally, four ex-civilian trawlers, HMT *Harlech Castle*, HMT *Grosmont Castle*, HMT *Walwyns Castle* and HMT *York City*, were ordered to carry out patrols outside the entrance to the Loch. On 9 May, 21 EG was joined by HMS *Philante* carrying Captain Martin Evans, who assumed command of the Loch Eriboll Force.

c. The Naval Officer-in-Charge (NOIC) Loch Alsh was to be responsible for the organisation there, and an Escort Group would be provided. After the removal of most of the German crews and any torpedoes, the U-boats were to be sailed to their laying-up ports. The general rule was that U-boats with a draught of 14ft or more were to be sailed to Lisahally, and those with a draught of less than 14ft were to be sailed to Loch Ryan, although this could not happen until after Loch Ryan became operational.

d. HMS *Sandhurst* was nominated to be the HQ ship in Loch Ryan. However, these arrangements could not be activated until 1 June, with the result that initially all the U-boats processed in Loch Eriboll and Loch Alsh were to be moved to Lisahally despite the intention to assemble the smaller U-boats at Loch Ryan and only the larger ones at Lisahally.

e. The Flag Officer-in-Charge, Northern Ireland was instructed to bring all preparations at Lisahally to immediate readiness.

f. For those U-boats which might arrive elsewhere in the UK such as Portland and Dundee, the C-in-C Plymouth was requested to sail any U-boats after their preliminary examination at Portland to either Loch Alsh, Lisahally or Loch Ryan depending on whether it had been possible to remove their torpedoes and ammunition. The C-in-C Rosyth was asked to sail any U-boats after their preliminary examination at Dundee to Loch Eriboll.

Immediately after the German capitulation, the C-in-C WA issued the order 'Carry out Pledge One'. This was the instruction to execute Operation 'Pledge' and it formally initiated the reception and processing arrangements for the surrendering U-boats. In respect of those which were still at sea, the German capitulation document dealt with the arrangements in considerable detail, and the surrender instructions were set out in the 'Special Orders by the Supreme Commander Allied Expeditionary Force (SCAEF) to the German High Command relating to Naval Forces'.[2]

In accordance with these orders the U-boats at sea in the Eastern Atlantic, the Western Approaches, the Barents Sea and the North Sea began to surrender on 9 May and to be directed and/or escorted by Allied warships and aircraft to one or other of the initial examination locations, with the main UK surrender port being Loch Eriboll. Most of the thirty-eight U-boats which surrendered at sea in the environs of the UK were therefore directed to Loch Eriboll, but others were either directed to or arrived at Portland and Dundee in the UK, Gibraltar, Bergen, Narvik and Stavanger in Norway, and Cuxhaven, Kiel, Hohwacht Bay (near Kiel), List (in Sylt) and Emden in Germany.

The initial element of Operation 'Pledge' came into effect when *U-1009* became the first U-boat to surrender from sea, arriving in Loch Eriboll on the morning of 10 May. Between then and 18 May, a further seventeen U-boats arrived:

10 May   *U-1009, U-1058, U-1105* and *U-1305*
11 May   *U-293, U-802* and *U-826*
12 May   *U-1109*
13 May   *U-532, U-825, U-956* and *U-1231*
14 May   *U-244, U-516, U-764* and *U-1010*
17 May   *U-255*
18 May   *U-2326* (which had previously arrived at Dundee on 14 May)

None of these eighteen U-boats spent long in Loch Eriboll. Instead, with RN armed guards on board they were moved under escort by ships of 21 EG to Loch Alsh where their torpedoes were removed and where most of the German crews were taken into captivity. The pattern of the departures of the U-boats from Loch Eriboll to Loch Alsh generally followed the pattern of arrivals and illustrates the short time that any of the U-boats spent in Loch Eriboll:

10 May   *U-1009* and *U-1305* (HMS *Byron*)
11 May   *U-293* and *U-826* (HMS *Fitzroy*), *U-1058* and *U-1105* (HMS *Rupert*)
12 May   *U-802* (HMS *Deane*) and *U-1109* (HMS *Conn*)
13 May   *U-532* and *U-1231* (HMS *Rupert*), *U-825* and *U-956* (HMS *Byron*)

14 May   *U-1010* (HMS *Fitzroy*)
15 May   *U-244, U-516* and *U-764* (HMS *Deane*)
17 May   *U-255* (HMS *Byron*)
18 May   *U-2326* (HMS *Fitzroy*)

On 19 May, the day after *U-2326* had departed Loch Eriboll, action began in accordance with what was essentially Phase 2 of Operation 'Pledge' when fifteen U-boats which had surrendered in Narvik on 9 May arrived at Loch Eriboll. These were: *U-278, U-294, U-295, U-312, U-313, U-318, U-363, U-427, U-481, U-668, U-716, U-968, U-992, U-997* and *U-1165*

There were no Allied forces in Narvik at the time of the German capitulation on 9 May, and so the surrender arrangements for the German naval vessels there were implemented by the Kriegsmarine's commander in Narvik, Captain Reinhard Suhren, who was Captain (U/B) Northern Waters, acting under the orders of the Kriegsmarine's 'Naval Chief Command Norway' (NCCN), which was itself acting under Allied orders.

After completing the surrender orders, Suhren became worried about the security situation in Narvik, his description of the local situation being that:

> The German fleet was widely scattered at the time, and as part of the surrender process the Allies gave orders for [the vessels] to meet at fixed collection points and to be handed over there. We in Narvik felt that we were situated a bit too close to Murmansk, and that the Soviets might decide to occupy Narvik and take us over too. As a precaution I appealed to [the] Allied Command and suggested that as regards getting all the submarines together, we could bring them and all their attendant ships to Trondheim.[3]

On 11 May, the NCCN staff approved Suhren's proposal to move the U-boats from Narvik to Trondheim, although on 12 May they were moved to the anchorage in Skjomenfjord 30 miles south of Narvik in order to avoid conflicts with Norwegian and other forces, including ex-POWs.

Suhren signalled NCCN on 13 May saying:

> In accordance with Naval Chief Command Norway's message of 11 May intend to transfer on 13 May eight U-boats of the 13th U/B Flotilla and seven U-boats of the 14th U/B Flotilla to Trondheim. Accommodation in Narvik has so far been almost exclusively afloat, which can no longer be reckoned with. Accommodation ashore in the Narvik area is impossible owing to the general lack of space, whereas in

Trondheim the 13th Flotilla's Depot can accommodate Captain (U/B) Northern Waters' entire unit.[4]

With the consent of the Allied Commission in Oslo, the U-boats therefore departed from Skjomenfjord en route to Trondheim on 15 May. Under the command of Suhren in the yacht *Grille*, they sailed on the surface in accordance with the surrender orders and all were flying a black surrender flag. Also, before departing all ammunition and mines had been landed and all torpedoes had been rendered harmless.

On the morning of 16 May the circumstances changed dramatically when the Royal Norwegian Navy destroyer HMNoS *Stord*, which was transporting the RNoN's Rear Admiral E C Danielsen to Tromso, sighted the German convoy in Vestfjord en route to Trondheim. At that stage, the UK naval authorities knew nothing about the surrender arrangements for these fifteen U-boats and as recorded in the Admiralty War Diary a flurry of signal messages followed:

a. Stord to Flag Officer Norway: Have met German convoy in Vestfjord. They say they are sailing from Narvik to Trondheim. Is this in order?

b. Assistant Chief of Naval Staff to Flag Officer Norway: Admiralty is taking action on Stord's [message].

c. Assistant Chief of Naval Staff to Stord: U-boats are to be escorted to Loch Eriboll.

d. Flag Officer Norway to Stord: Yes, German submarines have been in touch with Trondheim.

e. Assistant Chief of Naval Staff to Flag Officer Norway: Request report whether convoy referred to in Stord's [message] was ordered by you to sail from Narvik to Trondheim or whether it sailed under German orders. This is not clear from your 161340.

f. Flag Officer Norway to Admiralty: Permission for German Naval Command to sail convoy from Narvik to Trondheim was granted by disarmament Heralds who preceded joint force Commanders to Norway. Reason for request was shortage of stores and of accommodation for personnel landed after disarmament at Narvik.[5]

The last Arctic convoy, JW 67, which was on passage to Murmansk, was in the vicinity, and so the 9th (Canadian) Escort Group (9 EG), comprising HMCS *Matane*, HMCS *Loch Alvie*, HMCS *Nene*, HMCS *St Pierre* and HMCS *Monnow*, was detached from JW 67 on 16 May to intercept the U-boats. Also, as discussions were already underway with the US Joint Chiefs of Staff in Washington about a British proposal to transfer all the seaworthy U-boats in Norway, Germany and Denmark to the UK the Admiralty took an immediate unilateral decision that the fifteen U-boats should be moved to Loch Eriboll.

The Canadian Escort Group sighted the German convoy off the Norwegian coast on the morning on 17 May and a boarding party from HMCS *Matane* was put aboard *Grille*. At the same time the other RCN escort vessels were ordered to approach the two lines of U-boats to ascertain whether or not they had complied with the surrender terms. As a result and as described by Commander Frank Layard, the Senior Officer of 9 EG in his Report of Proceedings (ROP): 'Boats were lowered and several U-boats were boarded and the reports which I received satisfied me that the surrender terms had been complied with and that we were unlikely to experience any trouble or hostilities.'[6]

In the meantime on board *Grille* Suhren was having some difficulty in accepting the new instruction that the U-boats were to be diverted to Loch Eriboll. As recorded in 9 EG's ROP:

> He [Suhren] explained that his reluctance was due to the fact that he was proceeding to Trondheim under German High Command orders in co-operation with the Allied High Command. [However] he was informed that he was to comply with all orders given by Boarding Officer [and that] his High Command would be informed, if necessary, by the Allied High Command. At that, he surrendered his command of the U-boats and ordered [the CO of] *U-278* to assume command under Senior Officer 9EG, forming up and proceeding in accordance with instructions.[6]

The fifteen ex-Narvik U-boats arrived at Loch Eriboll on 19 May for initial processing. At 1400 on the same day, the C-in-C WA ordered the 30th Escort Group (30 EG), comprising HMS *Pevensey Castle*, HMS *Caistor Castle*, HMS *Launceston Castle* and HMS *Kenilworth Castle*, to move to Loch Eriboll to assist 21 EG with the processing arrangements. 30 EG arrived in Loch Eriboll in the late morning of 20 May and immediately began to deploy armed guards on the U-boats. After that the fifteen U-boats were quickly transferred to Loch Alsh sailing south in three separate batches of five:

a. The first batch comprised *U-294*, *U-481*, *U-716*, *U-968* and *U-997* and they were escorted from Loch Eriboll by four ships from 9 EG (HMCS *Matane*, HMCS *Loch Alvie*, HMCS *Nene* and HMCS *Monnow*) on 20 May.

b. The second batch comprising *U-278*, *U-427*, *U-668*, *U-992* and *U-1165* left Loch Eriboll on 21 May escorted by two ships from

21 EG (HMS *Conn* and HMS *Fitzroy*) and one from 30 EG (HMS *Caistor Castle*).

c. The third batch comprising *U-295*, *U-312*, *U-313*, *U-318* and *U-363* escorted by three ships from 21 EG (HMS *Rupert*, HMS *Deane* and HMS *Byron*) also left Loch Eriboll on 21 May.

The designation of Loch Alsh as a 'Port for Final Examination', the principal role of which was to remove the U-boats' torpedoes, as well as to take most of the German crews into captivity, was influenced by the fact that it was already a formal naval anchorage. However, it had insufficient facilities to process the number of U-boats that were expected to pass through in transit to Lisahally. As a result, the 5th Escort Group (5 EG), comprising HMS *Aylmer*, HMS *Tyler*, HMS *Bligh*, HMS *Grindall*, HMS *Keats* and HMS *Kempthorne*, was ordered to Loch Alsh to organise this intermediate part of the surrender process. 5 EG arrived at Loch Alsh on 10 May and the Naval Officer-in-Charge (NOIC) there asked the CO of 5 EG to assume the responsibility for berthing, disarming and the custody of the U-boats and their crews before they were escorted to Lisahally.

It had originally been intended to berth the U-boats singly alongside the Loch Alsh railway pier where with the aid of its steam crane torpedoes were to be off-loaded. However, it soon became clear that the rate of arrival of the U-boats from Loch Eriboll, the lack of onshore accommodation at Loch Alsh, and the general shortage of personnel would result in a very slow turnover. Fortunately, there were two ex-seaplane carriers, HMS *Engadine* and HMS *Athene*, moored in Loch Alsh which were awaiting disposal by the RN. These two ships were well suited to the U-boat-related task especially as each possessed an electric crane and was able to provide temporary accommodation for the German prisoners.

Early on 11 May *U-1009* and *U-1305* arrived from Loch Eriboll for processing. This began with the removal of the officers and men from each U-boat, except for a small residual steaming party. The RN submarine inspection party then commenced a formal inspection of each U-boat and as soon as the torpedo compartments were pronounced clear the removal of the torpedoes commenced. Within the first 54 hours, eight U-boats had been cleared, 54 torpedoes had been removed, and 23 German officers and 260 ratings had been searched and landed prior to being despatched into POW captivity.

This routine resulted in a rate of clearance of four U-boats per day and by midday on 12 May the NOIC Loch Alsh was able to advise the

C-in-C WA that: 'Following U-Boats available to sail for Lisahally p.m. 13 May: *U-1305*, *U-1009*, *U-1105*, *U-1058*, *U-826*, *U-293*. Two others [*U-802* and *U-1109*] may also be ready. Owing to requirements at Loch Alsh only 2 escorts are available.'[7]

The prospect of up to eight U-boats being transferred to Lisahally so quickly after the German capitulation provided an ideal opportunity for Admiral Sir Max Horton to stage a public multi-national surrender ceremony to celebrate the successful end of the U-boat war in the North Atlantic. He therefore ordered more than a dozen representative vessels to Loch Alsh to form an escort for the movement of these eight U-boats to Lisahally, and on the evening of 12 May he issued instructions for what he called Operation 'Commonwealth':

> Eight U-boats are to be sailed from Loch Alsh northabout Skye to Lisahally, Lough Foyle.
>
> Sailing is to be adjusted so that U-boats pass Foyle Buoy at 1300B/14 May.
>
> The escort under the command of Commander R A Currie (S.O. 14 EG in *Hesperus*) is to consist of *Hesperus*, *Havelock*, USS *Paine*, HMCS *Thetford Mines*, FS *Commandant Drogou*, 5 ships of 31 EG, *Bentley*, 1 ship of 5 EG (name to be reported), A/S trawler *Guardsman* and rescue ship *Goodwin*.
>
> Aircraft will co-operate for photographic purposes.
>
> From time of passing Foyle Buoy, Cdre (D) WA is requested to take control of movements and to arrange pilotage and berthing of all vessels.[7]

In response, the NOIC Loch Alsh advised Commander (D), Western Approaches that the eight U-boats and their escorts had departed Loch Alsh en route to Lisahally on 13 May. However, the weather in the vicinity of Skye was particularly bad and a south-westerly gale impeded progress during the night of 13 May. Nevertheless, once it had passed the island of Tiree the escort force and the U-boats were lined up prior to the arrival of photographic aircraft. Speed was increased and the convoy arrived off Loch Foyle at 1400 on 14 May.

The U-boats were manned by their skeleton German crews under the supervision of RN personnel and, as they sailed up Lough Foyle towards Lisahally they were escorted by vessels representing the RN, the RCN, the USN and the French Navy. Overhead, there was a close escort of Liberator, Sunderland and Wellington aircraft from RAF Coastal Command.

When the U-boats arrived at Lisahally their senior officers, led by the CO of *U-1009*, made a formal ceremonial surrender to Admiral

Horton as a token force on behalf of the German U-boat fleet. As well as Admiral Horton the official party at Lisahally included representatives of the Canadian and US Navies as well as personnel from Lisahally, RNAS Eglinton, RNAS Maydown, RAF Ballykelly and the British Army. There was also a representative of the Irish Defence Forces. Unfortunately this staged ceremony which was given extensive press coverage was responsible for the long-held but incorrect belief that some of the U-boats had surrendered directly in Lough Foyle.

After clearing these eight U-boats from Loch Alsh, the process there settled down and ran smoothly. German prisoners were cleared every other day so that there were never more than 180 men in either depot ship at any one time. The later U-boats had few torpedoes and many had none, so the rate of handling went up to six per day at times.

U-532 had arrived at Loch Alsh from Loch Eriboll on 14 May and aroused considerable interest because of its cargo of strategic materials from the Far East, and it was then sailed to Liverpool on 15 May, escorted by HMS *Grindall*. The U-boat arrived in Liverpool on 17 May for its cargo to be unloaded. However, this did not prove possible and so *U-532* was moved to Barrow-in-Furness on 25 May for completion of the unloading process. In the meantime, whilst in Liverpool the U-boat was inspected by Admiral Horton amid considerable publicity, giving rise to the often repeated but erroneous story that it had surrendered there.

The movement of the remaining U-boats from Loch Alsh to Lisahally went equally smoothly, with the U-boats and their escorts departing regularly especially after the Loch Alsh Force had been reinforced by the three ships of 12 EG (HMS *Loch Tarbert*, HMS *Cayman* and HMS *Barbados*) which arrived there on 19 May:

15 May	*U-825* and *U-956* (HMS *Bligh*)
15 May	*U-1010* and *U-1231* (HMS *Kempthorne*)
16 May	*U-516* and *U-764* (HMS *Keats*)
18 May	*U-244* and *U-255* (HMS *Bligh*)
19 May	*U-2326* (HMS *Kempthorne*)
21 May	*U-294* and *U-968* (HMS Loch *Tarbert*)
21 May	*U-481* and *U-997* (HMS *Keats*)
22 May	*U-312*, *U-716*, *U-992* and *U-1165* (HMS *Conn*, HMS *Fitzroy*, HMS *Rupert* and HMS *Deane*)
23 May	*U-313*, *U-318*, *U-363* and *U-427* (HMS *Cayman* and HMS *Barbados*)

On 24 May HMS *Aylmer* and HMS *Tyler* sailed from Loch Alsh with the last three U-boats (*U-278*, *U-295* and *U-668*) bound for Lisahally. Thus, as stated in HMS *Aylmer*'s ROP:

> The operation at Loch Alsh was completed.
> Thirty three U-boats had passed through in twelve days [32 en-route to Lisahally and one to Liverpool], 92 torpedoes were removed and disposed of, and in nearly all cases the warhead had been parted from the torpedo. 1627 Huns and their personal gear were searched, and 1,073 of them were landed for transfer to POW Camps.
> The conclusion of the operation, facetiously known in the Group as 'Operation ANY OLD IRON', brought to an end the 5th Group's part in the European war and we face our disbandment with dismay and sorrow.[8]

Loch Alsh was therefore no longer needed as a 'Port for Final Examination' and in his Fortnightly Diary of Events dated 31 May, the Flag Officer-in-Charge Greenock reported to the C-in-C WA that:

> Arrival of surrendered U-boats [at Loch Alsh] continued until 22 May. Seventeen arrived during the period under review, making a total of 33 in all.
> The organisation already in existence for removal of torpedoes, stores and surplus German personnel continued to function. A further 828 prisoners were handed over to the Army up to 25 May, after which date no more have been handled.
> Instruments and stores removed from the U-boats have been stored in HMS *Athene* and *Engadine*. Torpedoes have been sent to Greenock, and warheads to Crombie as ordered, and surplus heads and bodies have been dumped at sea.
> In view of the completion of PLEDGE ONE so far as Loch Alsh is concerned, preparations are now being made for return of extra personnel, and craft supplied for the operation.[9]

The three U-boats that had surrendered from sea in Portland on the south coast of England in mid-May had all had been operating at the western end of the English Channel. *U-249* had surfaced and reported its position on 9 May before being escorted into Weymouth Bay early on 10 May. *U-1023* had surfaced and reported its position early on 10 May and was escorted into Weymouth Bay later the same day. Finally, *U-776* had surfaced and reported its position on 14 May and it too was escorted into Weymouth Bay arriving on 16 May.

All three were processed at the RN base at Portland, most of their crews were removed and sent to POW camps and their ammunition and torpedoes were also removed. There was therefore no need to transfer them to Loch Alsh as had been envisaged. Instead, they were moved directly to Loch Ryan, though not immediately. *U-249* was retained at Portland to conduct search-radar trials off Weymouth Bay on 24, 25 and 27 May before sailing for Loch Ryan on 3 June arriving there on 5 June. The other two U-boats were earmarked for publicity and fund-raising tours of UK ports. *U-776* sailed from Portland on 21 May for an extensive tour of British east coast ports and arrived in Loch Ryan on 22 August. *U-1023* sailed from Portland on 25 May for an equally extensive tour of British west coast ports and arrived in Loch Ryan on 14 August.

By the time the war in Europe ended, the RN's First Sea Lord, Admiral of the Fleet Sir Andrew Cunningham, and the other members of the UK/US Combined Chiefs of Staff (CCS) had become very suspicious of the Russians and one of the principles adopted by the CCS was that no advanced technology should be allowed to go to the Soviet Union. Thus, the First Sea Lord took early action to ensure that where possible all advanced U-boat technology should remain firmly in British and/or American hands. Almost the first example of the application of this principle occurred in mid-May when plans were formulated to transfer the U-boats which had surrendered in Norway to the UK.

This action was initiated by the UK Chiefs of Staff (COS) in a paper (*COS (45) 338*) dated 15 May in which the First Sea Lord, under the heading 'Disposal of the German Fleet', said:

> It is expected that over 100 U-boats will be found in Norwegian bases. The disposal of these U-boats raises an immediate practical problem and an important issue of long-term security.
>
> I consider that U-boats in Norwegian waters should, as a first step, be brought over as quickly as possible to the United Kingdom.[10]

The First Sea Lord's proposal was considered at the COS Meeting on 16 May, where it was agreed that subject the Prime Minister's approval the suggestion should be forwarded to the USN on the basis that:

> The orders given to the German Navy instruct shipping in harbour to remain there and shipping at sea to proceed to the nearest German or Allied port. These orders were agreed with the Russians and require shipping once in harbour to remain there pending further direction from the Allied representatives.
>
> The 100 U-boats in the Norwegian bases present a difficult problem requiring immediate decision. They are concentrated in five main Norwegian ports, but guarding and maintenance constitutes a

considerable manpower commitment. This could be better undertaken in United Kingdom ports.

If the Russians are not consulted about the movement they may make a complaint. If, however, they are consulted, they will almost certainly cause delay and will probably ask for a large number to be sailed to North Russia, which would not suit our book. We therefore propose that the U-boats should be sailed from Norway without prior reference to the Russians, and that this action should, if necessary, be justified on the practical grounds of maintenance and security.

[Also,] the sailing of the U-boats in Norwegian waters to the United Kingdom will strengthen the position of the United Kingdom and the USA in future discussions [with the Russians] concerning their ultimate disposal.[11]

The proposed action was approved by Churchill on 17 May and as a result and without any prior notification to the Russians Admiral Cunningham sent a message to the USN's Admiral Harold Stark, the Commander of US Naval Forces in Europe (ComNavEu), on 17 May which said:

I enclose for your private information a copy of a signal which the British COS have sent to our JSM in Washington concerning the disposal of the German U-boats in Norwegian ports.

The policy set out therein has the approval of the Prime Minister. If you are in agreement perhaps you would support it with Admiral King [the US Navy's CNO]. You will realise the urgency as the sooner we get these 100 or so U-boats under our control in ports in the British Isles before our Russian allies start to ask questions the better. Perhaps I should also point out that bringing them over here constitutes an infraction of the rules, but I think we can get away with that.[12]

After the proposal was agreed by the USN and the CCS, A V Alexander, the First Lord of the Admiralty, still fearing that a diplomatic row was possible, wrote to the Prime Minister on 25 May saying:

You recently approved the despatch of a telegram from the Chiefs of Staff (COS (W) 877) to the JSM proposing that all the U-boats in Norwegian bases should be removed to the United Kingdom for laying up pending a decision concerning their disposal at the Peace Table. Further reports concerning the situation at Bergen, where there is a large number of U-boats, have emphasised the serious security risk if the U-boats remain in Norway. The Combined Chiefs of Staff have now agreed with our proposal and have directed General Eisenhower to arrange with the Admiralty for the sailing of all the U-boats to the United Kingdom.

The Foreign Secretary has suggested that in view of the possible Russian objections to this move, the Cabinet should be informed. If you agree, I suggest that the attached memorandum should be circulated.[12]

The First Lord's memorandum explained the situation and emphasised that the action had been initiated without either the agreement or knowledge of the Russians. It included:

All important surviving German naval units including the U-boat fleet are believed to be under the control of the British and United States Navies. None appear to have fallen intact into Russian hands. There are 22 [U-boats] in North West Germany, five in Denmark and 80 are distributed in five Norwegian bases.

The orders given to the German Navy instruct ships in harbour to remain there. These orders were agreed with the Russians and require ships to remain there pending further instructions from the Allied Representatives. Meanwhile the guarding and maintenance of the U-boats constitutes a considerable undertaking which could be more easily managed in United Kingdom ports where berths have been prepared for nearly 200 U-boats.

The obvious course was therefore to sail the U-boats to the United Kingdom for laying up pending a decision at the Peace Table concerning their disposal.

It was considered that to consult the Russians could only lead to delay. General Eisenhower has been instructed by the Combined Chiefs of Staff to arrange with the Admiralty for the sailing of the U-boats.[12]

Once 21 EG at Loch Eriboll had processed the fifteen U-boats from Narvik on 21 May and had despatched them to Loch Alsh, it seemed likely that no more U-boats would arrive at Loch Eriboll. The C-in-C WA therefore proposed to the Admiralty on 22 May:

In view of the smaller number of U-boats now expected to surrender from sea, it is considered that the Loch Eriboll Force can be reduced. The following are my intentions:

At 0001 24 May a force of 4 trawlers from Aultbea is to be at Eriboll. Incoming U-boats are to be met and escorted towards Loch Alsh until relieved by an escort vessel as arranged by NOIC Loch Alsh.
Procedure now carried out at Eriboll is to be undertaken at Loch Alsh, in addition to the existing routine.
When the new organisation comes into force *Philante* [is to proceed] to Greenock to disembark submarine party and lay over at 8 hours notice for sea.[13]

As a consequence of the CCS' decision to transfer all the remaining U-boats in Norway, Germany and Denmark to the UK, this proposal was quickly overtaken by events. On 24 May the Admiralty issued the executive order for all the seaworthy U-boats to be moved to the UK as soon as possible and this was reinforced by a similar instruction from Allied Naval HQ in Germany on 25 May saying that the sailing of these U-boats was to be given the highest priority. So, in the midst of the rundown of the 'Pledge One' reception arrangements at Loch Eriboll the dispersal arrangement planned for the Loch Eriboll Force had to be changed, but there was no new formal Operation Order. Instead, the Admiralty issued an executive instruction on 25 May saying:

> C-in-C Rosyth is requested to order routes and control the passage of these U-boats from the time of sailing from Norwegian ports until arrival off Loch Eriboll, after which C-in-C Western Approaches is requested to assume control.
>
> If necessary arrangements should be made with C-in-C Home Fleet for the temporary berthing of U-boats at Scapa if they cannot be immediately received at Loch Eriboll.[13]

The hint in the Admiralty instruction that the reception arrangements at Loch Eriboll had changed as had those at Loch Alsh was by then a fact. Thus, in order to process the U-boats that had surrendered in the Norwegian, German and Danish ports it was decided on 27 May that HMS *Philante* should sail to Scapa Flow in the Orkney Islands to continue the process. The 'Pledge One' reception organisation was therefore moved to the RN base at Scapa Flow.

Initially it was thought that Scapa would need to replicate the activities at Loch Eriboll and that the U-boats would still need to be transferred to Loch Alsh for the removal of many of the crews and all their torpedoes. However, as advised by C-in-C WA on 29 May:

> It appears that all U-boats coming from Norway are likely to arrive without torpedoes and with crews already reduced. Their call at Loch Alsh will consequently become unnecessary.
>
> NOIC Loch Alsh is requested therefore to sail HMS *Aylmer* and HMS *Bligh* to Scapa as soon as submarine parties, interpreters and other specialists have been embarked.
>
> Intention is that subject to concurrence of C-in-C Home Fleet preparation of U-boats for laying-up should now be completed at Scapa and that U-boats should sail from there direct to Lisahally or Loch Ryan.[13]

In effect, Operation 'Pledge Two' was now implemented, albeit that there was neither the time nor need to publish a separate Operation Order to mirror the earlier one issued on 19 April. A total of ninety-six U-boats had surrendered in Norwegian ports and after the transfer of the fifteen U-boats from Narvik, eighty-one remained:

Bergen	32
Kristiansand (S)	17
Trondheim	13
Horten (Holmstrand)	10
Stavanger	9

Similarly, twenty-seven U-boats had surrendered in German and Danish ports, mostly on 5 May after their surrender to General Montgomery's 21st Army Group:

Cuxhaven, Germany	10
Heligoland, Germany	7
Baring Bay, Denmark	3
Kiel, Germany	2
Flensburg, Germany	1
Aarhus, Denmark	1
Emden, Germany	1
Hohwacht Bay, Germany	1
List (Sylt), Germany	1

The first group of twelve U-boats from Norway comprising four from Oslo (ex-Horten) and eight from Stavanger arrived at Scapa Flow on 30 May and between then and 5 June a further fifty-two arrived from Norway:

30 May – Oslo:	U-170, U-874, U-975 and U-1108
30 May – Stavanger:	U-637, U-901, U-1171, U-2322, U-2324, U-2329, U-2345 and U-2348
31 May – Trondheim:	U-483, U-773, U-775, U-861, U-953, U-978, U-994, U-1019, U-1064 and U-1203
31 May – Bergen:	U-245, U-298, U-328, U-868, U-928, U-930, U-1002, U-1022, U-1052, U-1061, U-1104, U-1272 and UD-5
1 Jun – Kristiansand (S):	U-281, U-299, U-369, U-712, U-1163, U-2321, U-2325, U-2335, U-2337, U-2350, U-2353, U-2354, U-2361 and U-2363
2 Jun – Stavanger:	U-3035

| 4 Jun – Bergen: | *U-218, U-539, U-778, U-875, U-907,*
U-991, U-1004, U-1005, U-1057, U-1271,
U-1301, U-1307 and *U-2328* |
| 5 Jun – Kristiansand (S): | *U-2334* |

As had happened with the thirty-three U-boats which had been processed in Loch Eriboll and Loch Alsh, the sixty-four U-boats processed at Scapa only remained there for a short time especially because they did not need to disembark either torpedoes or German crew members. The U-boats were then moved directly either to Lisahally (fourteen) or Loch Ryan (fifty), the latter having become operational on 1 June, departing Scapa as follows:

30 May	Lisahally:	*U-874, U-975* and *U-1108*
31 May	Lisahally:	*U-637, U-901* and *U-1171*
	Loch Ryan:	*U-170, U-2322, U-2324, U-2329, U-2345* and *U-2348*
1 Jun	Lisahally:	*U-861, U-928, U-930, U-1002, U-1022* and *UD-5*
2 Jun	Lisahally:	*U-3035*
	Loch Ryan:	*U-245, U-298, U-328, U-483, U-773,* *U-775, U-868, U-953, U-978, U-994,* *U-1019, U-1052, U-1061, U-1064,* *U-1104, U-1203* and *U-1272*
3 Jun	Loch Ryan:	*U-281, U-299, U-369, U-712* and *U-1163*
4 Jun	Loch Ryan:	*U-2321, U-2325, U-2328, U-2335,* *U-2337, U-2350, U-2353, U-2354,* *U-2361* and *U-2363*
5 Jun	Lisahally:	*U-875*
	Loch Ryan:	*U-991, U-1057, U-1271, U-1301* and *U-1307*
6 Jun	Loch Ryan:	*U-218, U-539, U-778, U-907, U-1004* and *U-1005*
7 Jun	Loch Ryan:	*U-2334*

U-2334, which arrived in Loch Ryan on 7 June, had originally been part of the large group of U-boats from Kristiansand (S) which arrived at Scapa on 1 June. However, it broke down on 31 May whilst on passage across the North Sea and had to be towed into Dundee by HMS *Barbados*. It was then repaired and sailed to Scapa on 5 June. After the last of these U-boats left Scapa on 7 June the Operation 'Pledge' reception force was formally disbanded and the remaining U-boats to be transferred from Norway as well as those from Germany were all moved directly to either Lisahally or Loch Ryan.

At the beginning of June there were still thirty-five seaworthy U-boats in Norwegian (ten) and German (twenty-five) ports. Of the former the six Type XXI U-boats which had surrendered in Holmstrand (Horten) had been moved to Oslo on 18 May. The ten serviceable U-boats remaining in Norway were then transferred directly to Lisahally departing between 3 June and 17 June:

3 Jun	Oslo:	*U-2513, U-2518, U-3017* and *U-3041* (arrived at Lisahally on 7 Jun). *U-2502* and *U-3515* (arrived at Lisahally on 9 Jun)
3 Jun	Kristiansand (S):	*U-2529* (arrived at Lisahally on 6 Jun)
6 Jun	Bergen:	*U-3514* (arrived at Lisahally 8 Jun)
17 Jun	Bergen:	*U-2506* and *U-2511* (arrived at Lisahally on 21 Jun)

To assist with the clearance of the harbours in north-west Germany and despite no U-boats having surrendered there the twenty-five serviceable U-boats located in Germany and Denmark were transferred to Wilhelmshaven on instructions from the Allied Naval Commander Expeditionary Forces (ANCXF) on 8 June. Then, on 13 June after all the transfers from Norway had been completed ANXCF sent a message to the Admiralty saying:

All seaworthy U-boats have now been sailed from Norway to UK. In order to relieve congestion and for security reasons, suggest seaworthy U-boats now at Wilhelmshaven should be sailed for UK.[14]

The Admiralty agreed with this proposal saying on 14 June:

Approved to sail all seaworthy U-boats at Wilhelmshaven to UK to be laid-up at Lisahally or Loch Ryan.

ANCXF is requested to report total number of each class of U-boat and is to arrange for all ammunition and torpedoes to be removed before sailing. U-boats are to be sailed with reduced German crews.[14]

Without telling the Russians these twenty-five U-boats were transferred directly to either Lisahally or Loch Ryan departing between 21 and 30 June:

21 Jun	Wilhelmshaven:	*U-883, U-2336, U-2341, U-2351, U-2356* and *U-3008* (arrived at Lisahally on 27 Jun)
22 Jun	Wilhelmshaven:	*U-155, U-806, U-1230* and *U-1233* (arrived at Loch Ryan on 26 Jun)

23 Jun	Wilhelmshaven:	*U-368, U-1102, U-1103, U-1110* and *U-1194* (arrived at Loch Ryan on 27 Jun)
24 Jun	Wilhelmshaven:	*U-291, U-680, U-720, U-779* and *U-1198* (arrived at Loch Ryan on 28 Jun)
30 Jun	Wilhelmshaven:	*U-143, U-145, U-149, U-150* and *U-739* (arrived at Loch Ryan on 6 Jul)

All thirty-five U-boats were moved to Lisahally and Loch Ryan via the Pentland Firth sea route to the north of Scotland and in many cases were escorted by the RN ships which had been part of the Scapa reception force. Evidence of the transfers was recorded in *The Scotsman* newspaper in June 1945 which also reported that two of the RN-crewed Type XXI U-boats from Bergen (*U-2506* and *U-2511*) had been diverted into Lerwick on 18 June for an overnight stay because of a gale warning. The remaining Type XXI, *U-3008*, was in the first batch to be transferred from Wilhelmshaven. It was escorted by HMS *Hargood*, but in contrast to the other eleven Type XXIs from Norway it was manned by its German crew.[15]

The two U-boats that had surrendered from sea in Gibraltar (*U-485* and *U-541*) left there on 23 May en-route for the UK and arrived at Lisahally on 28 May, although *U-485* was subsequently transferred from Lisahally to Loch Ryan on 24 June.

For completeness, mention needs to be made of the ten U-boats which had surrendered in continental ports, but which were not moved to the UK under the Operation 'Pledge' arrangements.

First, there were the two Type XVIIB 'Walter' U-boats *U-1406* and *U-1407* which had surrendered in Cuxhaven on 5 May and then been scuttled on 7 May making them unavailable for transfer. Second, there were eight U-boats which were insufficiently seaworthy for transfer to the UK. One was in France (*U-510*) and seven were in Norway (*U-310, U-315, U-324, U-926, U-995, U-1202* and *U-4706*). These latter eight U-boats were never transferred either being scrapped in-situ or eventually being repaired and taken into use by their host Nations. Additionally, the unserviceable *U-760* which had been interned in Spain since September 1943 and which was not part of the formal surrender process, was transferred from Vigo in north-west Spain on 23 July arriving under tow in Loch Ryan on 3 August.

Extracts from Captain Martin Evans' Report of Proceedings dated 9 June 1945 give a good flavour of the activities at Loch Eriboll and

Scapa Flow for the four-week period in May and June when the two anchorages were used as part of the process for accepting the surrender of U-boats from sea, as well as the transfer of others from the ports in Norway where they had surrendered:

I have the honour to submit the following report of proceedings of HMS *Philante* and the Loch Eriboll Force at Loch Eriboll and Scapa between 9 May and 6 June 1945 in connection with 'Operation Pledge'. The following brief narrative and remarks together with its appendices is not necessarily of immediate interest, but may perhaps serve a similar purpose and provide a helpful document of reference to the officer charged with accepting the surrender of German U-boats after the next War.

At 1505 9 May, *Philante* arrived at Loch Eriboll and at 0713 the next morning, 10 May, *Harlech Castle*, on patrol outside Loch Eriboll, reported sighting a U-boat coming in to surrender. This proved to be *U-1009* who had an armed guard on her by 0815 thus becoming the first U-boat to surrender after the war. Thirty one minutes later, *U-1305* was sighted and the routine for boarding and inspection was carried out. By 18 May, 18 U-boats had been boarded, inspected and escorted to Loch Alsh.

On 19 May, 15 U-boats escorted by EG 9 arrived from Norway. Small anchorage parties were put on board at the entrance to Loch Eriboll and U-boats were then ordered to anchor or berth on escorts as necessary. By 2325 on 21 May all the U-boats, 33 in all, had sailed for Loch Alsh. After this there was a pause with no sign of any more coming in from sea.

It was decided on 27 May that the Loch Eriboll link was unnecessary and *Philante* therefore sailed at 0230 on 28 May for Scapa, where the arrangements were made for boarding, inspecting and the onward escort of the remaining U-boats, which were all to come escorted from Norway. At 0900 on 30 May, 4 U-boats arrived from Oslo followed at 1400 by 8 – including 5 Mark XXIIIs – from Stavanger. On 31 May 10 U-boats were expected from Trondheim and 13 from Bergen, whilst 14 from Kristiansand were due to arrive on 1 June. The last six of the 64 U-boats to arrive at Scapa from Norway sailed for Loch Ryan at 1800 on 6 June and at 2030 *Philante* herself left Scapa having boarded, inspected, guarded and despatched 97 U-boats in 28 days.

As a reception base Loch Eriboll has the advantages of accessibility and space and also a complete absence of important shipping or installations which would have been open to attack had the Germans decided to bring their careers to a suicidal but offensive finish. On the other hand the absence of buoyage, the fierce and unpredictable winds and the poor holding ground in most of the Loch were severe disadvantages.[8]

Good planning, hard work and effective co-operation between the RN and the German U-boat crews had ensured that the arrangements at Loch Eriboll, Loch Alsh and Scapa Flow in support of Operation 'Pledge' were slick and successful, and the concerns that there could be some rogue U-boat COs who might be inclined to cause various sorts of trouble were misplaced.

As a result of the extended Operation 'Pledge':

a. Thirty-three U-boats were processed in Loch Eriboll: seventeen direct from sea, fifteen from Narvik and one from Dundee
b. Thirty-three U-boats were processed in Loch Alsh ex-Loch Eriboll
c. Thirty-two U-boats arrived at Lisahally ex-Loch Alsh (except *U-532*)
d. One U-boat arrived in Loch Ryan ex-Loch Alsh via Liverpool and Barrow (*U-532*)
e. Sixty-four U-boats from Norway were processed in Scapa Flow: fourteen were transferred to Lisahally and fifty were transferred to Loch Ryan
f. Ten U-boats were transferred directly from Norway to Lisahally
g. Twenty-five U-boats were transferred directly from Germany: six to Lisahally and nineteen to Loch Ryan
h. Three U-boats were transferred from Portland to Loch Ryan
i. Two U-boats were transferred from Gibraltar to Lisahally
j. One U-boat was transferred from Spain to Loch Ryan

There is no doubt that Operation 'Pledge' made a unique contribution to British naval history, especially because it was a model of effective co-operation during a chaotic time. Perhaps the best person to articulate the overall result is the C-in-C WA, Admiral Sir Max Horton, who in a letter to the Secretary of the Admiralty on 7 July 1945 after the dispersal of the naval forces involved brought to the attention of the Admiralty Board his pleasure about a job well done:

> I would bring to the notice of their Lordships that this operation was carried out in a highly satisfactory manner, and reflects the greatest credit on all those actually concerned.
>
> It is desired to place on record the fact that in all its aspects this difficult task, calling for arduous work and a high degree of tact, was performed with efficiency and zeal. There was no hitch whatsoever, and in an operation which must necessarily be beset with many difficult situations, this could only have been achieved by a general standard of efficiency and discipline which is worthy of high praise.

It is also desired to mention that the Admiral (Submarines) was called upon to supply crews at what was often exceedingly short notice. This he unfailingly did, and the complete absence of delay in this most important aspect undoubtedly contributed very considerably to the success of the operation.[8]

CHAPTER 7

The Hunt for the 'Walter' U-Boats

THE USN AND THE RN had known about the German development of the high-tech Type XVII and XVIIB 'Walter' U-boats before the end of the war, and the searches for these U-boats and their development facilities began as soon as hostilities ceased. Nine 'Walter' U-boats had been built, of which seven were commissioned.

There were four Type XVIIs, comprising two Wa 201s (*U-792* and *U-793*) built by Blohm and Voss in Hamburg and two Wk 202s (*U-794* and *U-795*) built by Germaniawerft in Kiel. *U-792* and *U-794* were commissioned in November 1943 and *U-793* and *U-795* were commissioned in April 1944 but all four were intended for experimental purposes only.

There were five Type XVIIBs, all of which were built by Blohm and Voss in Hamburg and all of which were intended for operational use. *U-1405* was commissioned in December 1944, *U-1406* in February 1945 and *U-1407* in March 1945. Construction on the other two (*U-1408* and *U-1409*) was abandoned in March 1945 before being completed and both suffered bomb damage during an air attack on the shipyard on 8 April. *U-1408* had been 90 per cent complete and *U-1409* had been 80 per cent complete when construction ceased.

Eight of these U-boats were powered by an air-independent 'Walter' gas turbine using high-test peroxide (HTP) as its fuel which enabled them to achieve higher underwater speeds than conventionally powered submarines. The remaining one, *U-794*, was powered by a closed-cycle oxygen plant although this was not realised until after it had been found.

Though intended for wartime operations, *U-1405*, *U-1406* and *U-1407* were still engaged in working-up trials as the end of the war approached. *U-1406* had only used its 'Walter' unit once and *U-1407* had not used its one at all. During April all three of these Type XVIIB

U-boats were carrying out trials in the Kiel area and towards the end of the month they were based at Rendsburg to the north of Kiel. After that *U-1406* and *U-1407* transferred to Cuxhaven via the Kiel Canal and *U-1405* returned to Kiel to have its schnorkel fitted.

The British and the Americans were determined to ensure that where possible the 'Walter' submarine technology should be denied to the Russians at the same time as it was being exploited by the RN and USN. Thus, there were two linked activities that needed to be undertaken in early May relating to the 'Walter' U-boats. The first was to capture the 'Walterwerke' at Kiel before it could either be sabotaged by its German staff or captured by the Russians and the second was to locate the U-boats themselves and ensure that they remained in British and American rather than Russian custody.

The results of this planning meant that the British and American ground forces which were advancing into north-west Germany in 1945 included amongst their formations a special British unit (T-Force) which amongst its many tasks was charged by Naval Intelligence with capturing and preserving equipment and facilities connected with the very latest U-boat technology. There was very close liaison between T-Force, the USN's Technical Mission in Europe (NavTecMisEu) and the USN's Submarine Mission in Europe (SubMisEu), all of which had similar albeit overlapping interests in locating examples of the 'Walter' U-boats, thus ensuring their early availability for the planned assessments by both the RN and the USN.

As far as the 'Walterwerke' was concerned the British and American intelligence staff knew well before the end of the war that gas turbine engines powered by HTP were being developed there for use in U-boats. Therefore, the capture of the factory and its staff in Kiel on 5 May, even before any of the formal surrender arrangements had taken effect in the city, was the result of a carefully planned and orchestrated joint UK/US intelligence-led process.

Though urgent, it was dangerous work especially because the British and Americans were worried that the Russians might not as had been agreed halt their westward advance on the east bank of the River Trave, but instead would attempt to advance to Lubeck, Kiel and the rest of Schleswig-Holstein, and perhaps even into southern Denmark. To counter this possibility British forces concentrated on reaching the Baltic coast at Wismar near Lubeck arriving there on 2 May. However, at the time of the surrender in north-west Germany on 5 May there was a large area of territory to the north of Lubeck and Hamburg but to the south of the Danish border which was not occupied by British troops and this included Kiel which was some 60 miles to the north of the front line.

When the surrender of German forces and facilities in the Kiel area came into effect, T-Force was still behind the front line of the British Army. Elements of T-Force, including the RN No. 30 Assault Unit (30AU) therefore took steps to move to Kiel as a matter of urgency. T-Force had a list of some 150 British and American targets in the Kiel area of which the most important was the 'Walterwerke' factory and there was considerable concern that the Russians might even attempt a seaborne operation to capture the city. Its capture involved travelling through territory that had yet to be occupied by the British Army but despite the dangers T-Force began its move north at 0800 on 5 May and some three hours later had informally assumed control of Kiel and accepted the surrender of the German naval forces in the city. At the same time an RN team from 30AU made haste to Tannenberg just to the north of Kiel and near the eastern entrance of the Kiel Canal where the 'Walterwerke' factory was located capturing not only the works intact but also Dr Helmut Walter and his senior staff.

The 'Walterwerke' was therefore under British control and a message from SHAEF to the Admiralty on 7 May confirmed that: 'Walter Research Works in Kiel intact. Dr Walter and staff available for interrogation. Development machinery set up for submarine high underwater speed partially complete.'[1]

There was nevertheless a great deal of concern about the security of the project and the need to exclude the Russians and this was emphasised in another message on 7 May from the British Director of Naval Intelligence (DNI) at the Admiralty in London to the Allied Naval Commander-in-Chief Expeditionary Force (ANCXF) in Germany, which said: 'It is requested that the secrecy of Walter-boats Type XVII and XXVI, particularly of the turbine propulsion units, should be preserved and not disclosed except to authorised Anglo-American personnel. This should apply also to component parts, drawings, plans, etc.'[1]

This was followed by a further message from the DNI to ANCXF on 21 May which particularly reflected American concerns stating:

Following received from ComNavEu: Following dispatch received from NavTecMisEu – German submarine units 1405 to 1407 inclusive have Walter propulsion plants of great technical value. Were to have become operational 5 May 1945 and may be at sea or sunk. Request special guarding and notification location if surrendered. ComNavEu please advise Admiralty. Comment: It is reported that these three boats left Kiel on or about 5 May but their subsequent movements were not known. They may have been sunk or scuttled in the Denmark area.[2]

In late April the three operational Type XVIIBs (*U-1405*, *U-1406* and *U-1407*) had been based in Rendsburg near the eastern end of the Kiel Canal. However, after *U-1405* had returned to Kiel to have its schnorkel fitted the other two left Rendsburg on 1 May and sailed via the Kiel Canal to Cuxhaven where they arrived on 3 May. This was followed by the surrender agreement which came into effect on 5 May and required the German armed forces in north-west Germany including all naval vessels and thus the U-boats at Cuxhaven to surrender unconditionally. Despite this the COs of *U-1406* and *U-1407* jointly sent a message to their local Headquarters at 0508 on 5 May saying: 'We request order to scuttle for Walter front line boats in the event of seizure by the enemy being imminent.'[3]

However, whilst there were local discussions about the possibility of scuttling the several U-boats that were moored in the harbour at Cuxhaven, all the U-boat COs were forbidden by the senior local Kriegsmarine officers to scuttle or otherwise sabotage them, being threatened with shooting in the event of disobedience. The surrender arrangements at Cuxhaven were duly completed during 5 May. Thereafter *U-1406* and *U-1407* ceased active duty and the COs and crews of both these U-boats were interned in one of the fish-processing halls at Cuxhaven. On 6 May the then unmanned *U-1406* and *U-1407* were towed to the New Fishery Haven in Cuxhaven port where all the surrendered U-boats in the harbour were left in the custody of two guard ships. The latter were moored alongside *U-1406* and *U-1407* to ensure that no unauthorised personnel should gain access to the U-boats.

Nevertheless, on the night of 6/7 May Lieutenant Gerhard Grumpelt, who was an experienced U-boat engineer, decided to scuttle the two U-boats on his own authority. He was not a member of the crew of either *U-1406* or *U-1407* but he was temporarily accommodated in one of the guard ships. He therefore went on board *U-1406* and *U-1407* and scuttled each of them by opening the main vents and other flooding valves and leaving the conning tower hatches open an action for which he was subsequently court-martialled, found guilty and sentenced to imprisonment.

Whilst the two incomplete and damaged 'Walter' U-boats *U-1408* and *U-1409* had been found in the Blohm and Voss Shipyard in early

May after the capture of Hamburg, the prime objective for the UK and US intelligence teams was to find *U-1405*, *U-1406* and *U-1407*. Their locations were not known and it was neither a quick nor easy task to find them. The initial search was made by the RN's Captain Gilbert Roberts, who had been sent to Germany by the C-in-C WA. Captain Roberts' optimistic report to his Commander-in-Chief on 30 May stated that he had carried out a search for *U-1405*, *U-1406* and *U-1407* on 26 May and that he had discovered them in the Rendsburg area of the Kiel Canal – all scuttled. As described by Captain Roberts it had not been an easy search but it seemed to him to have produced the desired results, viz:

> It has been reported that three U-Boats of this type, which are experimental prototypes of Type XXVI, were ready to be operational and that they were considered satisfactory. Very vague reports placed these three, *U-1405*, *U-1406* and *U-1407*, in the Kiel Canal, but no German officers knew where they were, or if they did, they evaded reply to questioning.
>
> Evidence was pooled to four Interrogators, including Commander Gheradi, USN, at a meeting on 25 May, and it was decided to make a search for these three U-Boats on 26 May. It was felt that even though all details of Walter propulsion were known it was important to see the shape of these U-Boats even though they might be found scuttled.
>
> After long and difficult interrogation of local inhabitants in a probability area in the Kiel Canal, these three U-Boats were traced with reasonable certainty to positions as follows:
>
> a. Point 71. Kiel Canal, north bank. Small red buoy marks the spot where the U-Boat is sunk in about 8 fathoms.
> b. Point 67. In a backwater off the Kiel Canal near the jetty of a small signal station. Two small red buoys mark the spot where the U-Boat is sunk in about 8 fathoms. Bubbles and a small quantity of oil are rising to the surface, two yards from the southern buoy.
> c. Point 64. In the Eiderhaven of Rendsburg town. The top of a conning tower was stated to be just awash, but it was not sighted. This position was not found by ourselves but it had been sighted by a Sgt, RA, in a British Army patrol boat, and local evidence confirmed this.[4]

Unfortunately, Captain Roberts' information turned out to be incorrect and salvage operations produced only *U-792* and *U-793* plus a Type VIIC U-boat. Thus, by the end of May, despite all the intense interest in the 'Walter' U-boats especially the Type XVIIBs, the British and Americans had still not located *U-1405*, *U-1406* or *U-1407*. Two of the Type XVII boats (*U-792* and *U-793*) were nevertheless recovered and taken to Kiel for possible restoration and the search for the two other Type XVIIs and the three remaining Type XVIIBs continued. Conditions in and around the heavily damaged ports and shipyards of north-west Germany were chaotic in May and June, and it was not easy to pinpoint the location of any specific U-boats. Thus, in mid-June ANCXF sent Rear Admiral Eberhard Godt who was the ex-Chief of Operations in the U-Boat High Command on a tour of investigation with the specific task of locating the three missing Type XVIIBs.

After his tour Admiral Godt returned to the ex-Kriegsmarine Headquarters at Flensburg and on 24 June reported that whilst he had been unable to trace *U-1405* he had located *U-1406* and *U-1407* at Cuxhaven where they had been scuttled after first surrendering. The results of the admiral's investigations as well as the interrogations of the COs of *U-1406* and *U-1407* which took place on 29 June are recorded in an ANCXF report to the Admiralty on 12 July which included the information that:

> Early information gave them as scuttled in the Kiel Canal [though this had proved to be incorrect].
>
> The actual finding of *U-1406* and *U-1407* was a direct result of sending Admiral Godt on a tour of investigation.
>
> [Admiral Godt] reported that he had reliable information that *U-1406* and *U-1407* were scuttled in the New Fishery Haven, Cuxhaven. He had no knowledge of *U-1405*.
>
> *U-1405*, *U-1406* and *U-1407* were in company and carrying out trials during April. Towards the end of that month they were at Rendsburg together. *U-1405* returned to Kiel to have [a] schnorkel fitted, and it is the opinion of the [COs] of *U-1406* and *U-1407* that *U-1405* was scuttled either in Kiel or Eckernförde. *U-1406* and *U-*1407 proceeded to Cuxhaven about 1 May and on 3 or 4 May the German Senior Naval Officer at that port sent for the Commanding Officers and made them promise not to scuttle or sabotage their ships.
>
> On the night of 7 May *U-1406* and *U-1407* [were] scuttled by opening main vents and certain flooding valves and leaving the conning tower hatch open. No scuttling charges were fitted and no damage was done except by flooding. The two COs admitted removing one or two parts of the Walter Unit before their departure on 4 May.
>
> Arrangements have been made for *U-1406* and *U-1407* to be taken from Cuxhaven to Kiel in order to receive expert assessment and attention preparatory to their departure for United Kingdom.

Information has now been received that *U-1405* is almost certainly scuttled in Geltinger Bight and steps are being taken to confirm this. If found the vessel will be salvaged and taken to Kiel.[5]

As a result of this information, arrangements were made to start salvage operations on 29 June, and the Naval Officer in Charge (NOIC) Cuxhaven sent two messages to ANCXF on 30 June concerning the progress of this activity:

301614 June: Salvage operations in progress on *U-1406* and *U-1407*. On completion of salvage propose U-Boats be towed to Kiel in order the Walterwerke personnel may assess damage and take action to combat corrosion.

301721 June: *U-1407* on surface in Fischerei Hafen and pumped out except diving tanks. Intend to make ship seaworthy for towing to Kiel. Some structural damage to superstructure and one hatch distorted. Recommend examination of vital parts by expert before she sails to another port. Estimated time for temporary repairs one week.[6]

Thus, the two Type XVIIBs *U-1406* and *U-1407* were raised in great haste and moved to the Howaldt-Werke Shipyard in Kiel at the beginning of July, though this was not before a fire had started in *U-1406* causing it to be temporarily re-immersed in Cuxhaven harbour.

At the same time as this was taking place, USN officers from NavTecMisEu and SubMisEu were also searching for the Type XVII and Type XVIIB U-boats, and especially for an example of the Type XVIIB. They quickly became aware that the British had located *U-1406* and *U-1407* and on 26 July advised the Commander of the USN in Europe (ComNavEu), and through him, the Commander-in-Chief United States Fleet (Cominch) that in their opinion just one Type XVIIB (*U-1406*) would be sufficient for the USN's research purposes.

As far as the Type XVIIs were concerned, the two that had been found in the Kiel Canal (*U-792* and *U-793*) had been scuttled by their crews on 4 May and were lying in 11m of water and both were holed. They were nevertheless raised and taken to Kiel: *U-792* on 26 May and *U-793* on 15 June. Of the other two, *U-794* had been scuttled by its crew in Gelting Bay on 5 May and *U-795* had been blown up in the Germania Werft shipyard in Kiel on 3 May after being decommissioned and laid-up on its slipway.

On 4 and 5 August Captain L V Honsinger from the USN's NavTecMisEu and Commander F Beltz from the SubMisEu jointly reviewed what was known about the Type XVII and Type XVIIB U-boats, five of which had by then been assembled on the dockside at Kiel albeit that four of them had previously been scuttled and then salvaged and all of which were damaged and non-operational. Their report on 5 August, which included some inconsistency especially in relation to *U-794*, stated:

[We] have looked over all XVII U-Boats during past day and a half:

U-792	Kiel	internally blown – British originally requested
U-793	Kiel	internally blown – worse than above
U-794	Kiel	satisfactory, but closed cycle oxygen plant
U-795	Kiel	school boat – 10 foot hole in Walter engine room
U-1405	Kiel	still sunk in Kiel Canal
U-1406	Kiel	satisfactory – sunk, raised, burned, sunk, raised
U-1407	Kiel	good – but British are taking
U-1408	Hamburg	no good, but can cannibalise
U-1409	Hamburg	blown in two but can cannibalise[7]

They then drafted a memo and signal message on 5 August which discussed the way ahead especially in respect of *U-1406*, and Captain Honsinger's memo included the information that:

Most people believe *U-1406* is best [for the US Navy]. I think *U-795* best. However, have decided no change. Will take *U-1406*.

U-1406 needs everything stripped out of it and then the parts preserved and reinstalled plus a new Walter engine plus a few other missing parts. Work of tearing out and preserving to be done by German labour. I've started all above work.

Commander Beltz and [Commander] Loughan are most anxious for us to have Germans rebuild *U-1406* alongside *U-1407* per request of British. I don't agree. I think we should be satisfied to take home the Walter machinery only and build up from there back home.[7]

Commander Beltz's rather more comprehensive draft message, which was to be sent from NavTecMisEu to Cominch, stated:

Type XVII submarines with Walter engines *U-1406* and *U-795* best available to United States. *U-1406* now on quay wall at Deutschewerke Kiel was scuttled by Germans and critical elements of regulator, combustion chamber, and switchboard destroyed. When vessel was raised [HTP] fire developed and got beyond control necessitating immersion again. Finally raised after considerable interior damage due to fire and immersion. Hull in excellent condition. *U-795* on quay wall at Kiel Germania prototype of XVII used as school boat and experimental depth charging, never flooded or scuttled. Demolition charge in Walter engine room wrecked engine and blew hole 10 feet by 10 feet on port side of engine room. After needs of NavTecMisEu with Type XVII engine for Engineering Experimental Station and British equipments are satisfied it is believed one XVII can be made operational with limited reserve of critical spares. Two alternatives possible. Alternative one – sectionalize for shipboard shipment to States *U-1406* or *U-795* with all available parts for assembly. Alternative two – in German shipyard, preferably Blohm and Voss builders at Hamburg, demand Germans to place submarine in satisfactory operational condition under United States Naval inspection. Advise desires.[7]

Commander Beltz then submitted a comprehensive 'Material Report on U-Boats Under Cognizance of Commander Submarine Mission Europe' to the Commander Submarines, Atlantic Fleet (ComSubLant) on 17 August which, in relation to the 'Walter Turbine Boats' and reflecting some errors stemming from the obvious confusion of the time, said:

There were eight Walter boats built or in the process of being built by Blohm and Voss, Hamburg. The *U-792, U-793* and *U-795* were built as experimental boats to test out the Walter engine and to be used for training purposes. The German Admiralty ordered 12 more built, *U-1405* to *U-1416* as operational boats, [but] after 'D' Day and the emphasis on Type XXI boats, construction of Walter boats was only continued on *U-1405* to *U-1409*.

U-792, U-793 and *U-795* are on the quay wall at Germaniawerft, Kiel. At the time of the German surrender these vessels were wrecked by demolition bombs spotted in the Walter engine room. *U-1405, U-1406* and *U-1407* were sunk at the entrance of Kiel Canal after critical elements of the Walter engine and its controls had been thrown over the side. *U-1408* and *U-1409* were in the process of completion on the builders skids at Hamburg. They were also demolished by demolition charges.

Hamburg and Kiel are at present in British zone of influence. As consequence the British have made the first demand on all German material in those areas. The British have relinquished rights for the Walter engine on the test stand to United States provided they can participate [in] the tests at Experimental Station, Annapolis. The present tentative plans of the British are to make *U-1407* operational at Kiel. Of the remaining Walter boats *U-1406* and *U-795* appear to be the best.

The purpose of this dispatch is to advise Cominch that there are possibilities of obtaining a Walter Type submarine for operational purposes in the United States. We [feel] that the best recourse to assemble an operating submarine would be either at Hamburg, Germany or in the United States. We were advised on account of British political reasons, efforts to place a ship in operating condition at the builders yard, Blohm and Voss, would meet with some resistance.

We were informed by the British at Kiel that the British Government was determined that for economic reasons Blohm and Voss would never be allowed to turn over another wheel. We also had information that the Russians who [might] fall heir to the Kiel area have had no information on the Walter engine, as a consequence consideration was being given by United States and the British to evacuate from Kiel all equipment that pertained to the Walter engine and Walter boat and move it on to Hamburg, United Kingdom or United States.

If Cominch desires an operating Walter boat, I personally would recommend that we should first investigate the possibility of persuading the British to allow Blohm and Voss to complete one boat to our satisfaction. Failing this proposal, I would recommend that we require Deschimag at Bremen in the American zone of influence to complete one boat. As a last resort I would recommend the assembly of parts of a Walter boat and ship them to United States for assembly at Navy Yard Portsmouth.

However I feel if we are to get the full benefits from the Walter design we should utilise the facilities, talent and technique of the Germans and do the job in Germany. This would probably be the quickest and cheapest method of getting an operating Walter boat and would give us the fullest opportunity to evaluate the German technique.[7]

By early August it was clear, despite any possible Russian aspirations, that *U-1406* had been earmarked for the Americans and that *U-1407* had been earmarked for the British. All that remained to be done was to ensure that these two severely damaged U-boats now located at Kiel were formally allocated to the US and the UK. Also, decisions needed to be taken about where and how they were to be repaired, especially as both had previously been scuttled. Finally, steps needed to be taken to ensure that the remaining Type XVII and Type XVIIB U-boats were put beyond any prospect of their acquisition by the Russians.

Of the remaining seven Type XVII and XVIIB U-boats, the building of *U-1408* and *U-1409* had ceased in March 1945 before they were complete, and both had sustained irreparable bomb damage during an air attack on 8 April. Their hulks were therefore scrapped. The other 'Walter' U-boats, *U-792*, *U-793*, *U-794*, *U-795* and *U-1405*, were subsequently defined by the TNC as having been 'scuttled in shallow water' despite *U-792*, *U-793* and *U-795* having been located, raised and made available for inspection at Kiel. This meant that they were to be destroyed in accordance with the TNC's recommendation that:

> Ships and craft sunk in shallow water, not in obstruction of normal shipping, should be destroyed in such a manner that the possibility of salvage and partial or full use for naval purposes is precluded.
>
> The Power in whose zone of occupation the[se] ships and craft are located shall be responsible for executing the stipulated destruction.[8]

U-794 had been located after scuttling in Gelting Bay and raised, but its hull and machinery had been so seriously damaged that after a brief inspection it was re-scuttled in the same position. Nevertheless, on 8 September 1945 the Admiralty advised the RN's C-in-C Germany that the U-boat was to be demolished after the TNC Inspection Party had visited Kiel. The same message also contained the Admiralty's agreement to the demolition of *U-1405* which had been discovered in Gelting Bay in late August. It had sunk on 3 May after the explosion of its scuttling charges and the wreck was finally demolished in September by a depth charge. The last three Type XVIIs, *U-792*, *U-793* and *U-795*, which had been raised and made available for the TNC inspection visit to Kiel in early September were due for destruction no later than 15 February 1946. These actions were completed by the British and this was confirmed by the British Army of the Rhine (BAOR) Controller of Salvage on 25 February 1946.[9]

Therefore, of the Type XVII and XVIIB U-boats only *U-1406* and *U-1407* were, despite their unserviceable condition, candidates for allocation to the Allies. These two had (in effect) the Stars and Stripes painted on the side of one and the Union Jack painted on the side of the other and for whatever reason the Russians agreed to their allocation to the USA and UK without demure. Either the secrecy that the Admiralty had requested on 7 May had been maintained or the Russians already knew enough about the 'Walter' turbines to satisfy their own needs. It was probably the latter.

CHAPTER 8

Potsdam – Pre-Conference Proposals

AT THE SAME TIME as the British and American intelligence teams were scouring Germany in search of U-boat related technology, Marshal Stalin sent a message to President Truman and Prime Minister Churchill on 23 May 1945 making it clear that, despite no German naval vessels having surrendered to Soviet forces, he expected at least one-third of Germany's surviving warships to be allocated to the Soviet Union, saying:

> According to information of Soviet Naval Commandant, Germany by act of capitulation surrendered her whole Navy and Merchant Marine to the English and Americans. I have to state that the Germans refused to surrender a single naval or merchant vessel to the Soviet armed forces, having arranged the surrender of her whole fleet and merchant marine to Anglo-American armed forces.
>
> Under these circumstances question naturally arises of apportioning to the Soviet Union her share of German naval and merchant vessels, in accordance with earlier example of Italy. The Soviet Government consider that it can, with full reason and justice, count on a minimum of one-third of the navy and merchant marine of Germany. I also consider it necessary that representatives of the Navy of U.S.S.R. should be given an opportunity of acquainting themselves with all particulars of the surrender of Germany's Navy and Merchant Marine, and also with the actual condition of the surrendered vessels.
>
> For its part, the Soviet Naval Command has appointed for this purpose Admiral Levchenko and a group of assistants.[1]

Whilst Stalin's message stated that no German naval vessels had surrendered to the Soviet armed forces, he neglected to mention that after the capture of Danzig on 30 March 1945 a Sovinformburo (the Soviet News Agency) Press Release[2] describing the capture of Danzig had included the incorrect information that forty-five submarines had been captured. Indeed, this Press Release had already been the subject of a written question and answer in the UK House of Commons on 17 April under the heading 'U-Boats (Russian Captures)'.[3]

The question by Colonel William Carver, the Member of Parliament for Howdenshire, asked the First Lord of the Admiralty: 'Whether he had any information as to the capture of 41 [*sic*] U-Boats by the Russians when they captured Danzig; whether these boats were fit for use or whether they were in an incomplete stage; and what is going to be done with them?'[3]

The answer from the First Lord of the Admiralty, A V Alexander, was:

Marshal Stalin's Order of the Day [*sic*] dated 30 March announced the capture of 45 U-Boats at Danzig and a subsequent Soviet announcement stated that eight of the captured U-Boats were large [presumably Type XXIs]. A request has been addressed to the Soviet authorities for further details. I have no details as yet about the last part of the question.[3]

Churchill's reply on 27 May to Stalin's message thanked the latter for his telegram and said: 'It seems to me that these matters should form part of the general discussions which ought to take place between us and President Truman at the earliest possible date, and I thank you for giving this outline of your views beforehand.'[4]

Truman, after first assuring Winston Churchill that they were in general agreement on the matter, replied to Stalin in similar vein on 29 May saying:

Thank you for your suggestion regarding surrendered German ships contained in your message dated 23 May 1945. It appears to me that this is an appropriate subject for discussion by the three of us at the forthcoming meeting at which time I am sure a solution can be reached which will be fully acceptable to all of us.[4]

In the meantime, Stalin raised the matter on 27 May with Harry Hopkins during the latter's informal mission to Moscow on President Truman's behalf. The notes of the meeting record that Stalin said:

As regards to the German fleet which had caused so much damage to Leningrad and other Soviet ports not one [vessel] had been turned over to the Russians despite the fact the fleet had surrendered. He added that he had sent a message to the President and Prime Minister [Churchill] suggesting that at least one-third of the German Navy and merchant marine thus surrendered be turned over to the Soviet Union. The rest could be disposed of by Great Britain and the United States as they saw fit. He added that if the Soviet Union had been entitled to a part of the Italian fleet they certainly had more right to their fair share of the German fleet, since they had suffered five million casualties in this war. He said that the Soviet Government had certain information leading it to believe that both the United States and England intended to reject the Soviet request and he must say that if this turned out to be true, it would be very unpleasant.[4]

In response, Hopkins assured Stalin:

From conversations he had had with Admiral King [the US Navy's Chief of Naval Operations] he was able to state that the United States had no desire to retain any portion of the German fleet and merely wished to examine the vessels for possible new inventions or technical improvements. After that we were prepared to sink the share turned over to us. He also said that he had always understood that the fleet was to be divided between the United States, the Soviet Union and Great Britain and that insofar as the United States was concerned there was no objection to whatever disposition the Soviet Government wished to make with its share. He added that he thought that this matter could be definitely settled at the forthcoming meeting of the three Heads of Government.[4]

The matter was raised again during Hopkins' visit when at their meeting on 30 May Stalin said he had received a suggestion from General Eisenhower saying:

That a naval commission composed of the four countries [USA, USSR, UK and France] should be set up to consider the disposal and division of the German fleet; that the American representative on this commission would be Admiral Ghormley and that he would name Admiral Levchenko as the Soviet representative.[4]

Whilst Stalin was intent on making the running concerning the division of the German fleet, such an approach was not unexpected by either the USA or the UK. It was therefore agreed that the topic should be discussed at the forthcoming Potsdam Conference (code-named 'Terminal') and that a mutually acceptable decision was the desired outcome. However, whilst the British were hoping to use their agreement to the division of the surviving German naval vessels between the Allies as a bargaining chip their position had been somewhat undermined by the unilateral assurances given to Stalin by Hopkins as well as by General Eisenhower's proposal concerning a naval commission to consider the details. To facilitate this the UK advised the US Acting Secretary of State on 1 June:

Mr Eden [The British Foreign Secretary] has asked me to tell you that in view of Marshal Stalin's message about surrendered German naval and merchant ships, His Majesty's Government propose the addition of the following item to Section 2 of the Agenda for the forthcoming meeting of Heads of Governments: 'Disposal of German Fleet and Merchant Ships'.[5]

As the issue of the German naval fleet was to be an agenda item at the Conference which was due to start on 17 July, both the US and the UK staffs produced Briefing Notes for their respective delegations, with the USA's paper being written by the Joint Chiefs of Staff because it was considered to be a military matter.

The US Joint Chiefs of Staff advice to President Truman dated 10 July stated in relation to the disposition and distribution of the German fleet that their preferred solution which reflected the approach taken earlier in their EAC/44/34 proposal remained:

a. Except for a limited number of ships for experimental and test purposes, all naval vessels should be destroyed, i.e. sunk on the high seas or scrapped.

b. Failing agreement by the nations represented on the European Advisory Commission as to this disposition, then the United States should press for:

   (1) Agreement that all capital ships, and also submarines be destroyed while smaller craft and more lightly armed vessels be shared equally by the United States, Union of Soviet Socialist Republics, United Kingdon, and France, or failing this

   (2) Agreement that one-fourth share of each category of ships in the German flet be assigned to each of these four major powers.

c. In any event, the United States should press for the sinking of German submarines.[4]

This final piece of US military advice to the President concerning the U-boats which had surrendered had been strongly emphasised in an earlier JCS Report dated 5 July which had highlighted the US view that: 'The German surface ships are not a particular menace, whereas the German submarines are a considerable potential menace to world peace. The United States should endeavour to obtain agreement to sinking these.'[4]

The JCS suggestion that France should be allocated a share of the German Navy's surviving surface fleet was not a new idea especially as the French had been lobbying the Americans and British on the topic since mid-1944. Whilst France had become a member of the European Advisory Commission in November 1944 it was neither invited to join the 'Big Three' nor to participate in the Potsdam Conference. This did not please the French and had a direct impact on the later debates about the possible allocation to France of surrendered German surface warships and U-boats.

As had become apparent during Hopkins' meeting with Stalin in May, the US military authorities were nevertheless sympathetic to the French being allocated a share of the surviving German naval vessels, a position which had been reinforced by General Eisenhower's early suggestion that France should be allocated a seat on the naval commission which would eventually consider the disposal and division of the German fleet.

This suggestion was re-emphasised on 22 June when a message from the US Political Advisor in Germany to the Acting US Secretary of State in Washington included the statement:

> With reference to the division by agreement between the US, UK, USSR and France of the naval and merchant fleets of Germany, Ambassador Pauley has informed General Eisenhower that it is his view that as long as the US is at war with Japan the division of both the German naval and merchant fleets is strictly a military matter.[4]

Stung by his exclusion from the earlier Yalta Conference in February 1945, General de Gaulle was very keen that France should be included as a full member of the Potsdam Conference, but rather than challenging the three Heads of State concerning the allocation of German naval vessels, he chose to argue for France's place at the conference table with the new American President via diplomatic channels.

Despite a great deal of pressure and despite the US State Department's sympathetic views, the question of French participation was never formally raised during the preliminary negotiations about the forthcoming Conference between Truman, Churchill and Stalin. Indeed, Churchill took successful steps to discourage Truman from a possible face-to-face meeting with de Gaulle before the Conference as neither he nor Stalin would have welcomed de Gaulle's participation. Thus President Truman did not pursue the matter particularly as he was in no doubt about Churchill's views after the visit to London in late May of Mr Joseph Davies, the President's personal representative, whose report dated 12 June recorded: 'As to France, he [Mr Churchill] was bitter. He was completely fed up with de Gaulle and out of patience. He [General de Gaulle] ought to be "brought up" sharply and given to understand clearly that he cannot act arbitrarily and inconsiderately.'[4]

Despite de Gaulle's efforts to the contrary, the Potsdam Conference did not include France, and thus the leaders' discussions about the division of the surviving German naval vessels and particularly the specific allocation of the surface ships and submarines took place between just the Three Allies.

The US position relating to the surface fleet as well as to the possibility of an allocation to France was modified during the discussions that took place on board the cruiser USS *Augusta* which between 7 and 14 July transported Truman and his party from the USA to Europe when he agreed that the 'line-to-take' with respect to the 'Disposition of Captured German Ships' was: 'He believed that captured German war vessels should be divided as equally as possible among the Three Powers [USSR, UK and the USA] at the earliest practicable date.'[6] A file note to that effect written by Admiral Leahy the President's Chief of Staff includes the notation: 'To be used only if brought up by Stalin or Churchill.'[6] As a result this was the position that Truman adopted at Potsdam and it effectively ended the previous US desire to ensure that France was allocated a share of the surviving vessels of the German Navy.

As far as the British were concerned there were two important papers relating to the future of the German naval vessels. The first of these was the Foreign Office's 'Brief for the United Kingdom Delegation to the Conference at Potsdam' dated 6 July which stated:

> It would clearly be in the interest of this country, and in the interest of the World as a whole, to scrap the entire German fleet. While there is unfortunately little chance of the Russians agreeing to scrap as a general policy it is suggested that we ought, if only for technical reasons, to support strongly any American initiative proposing the scrapping of the entire fleet.
>
> The French claim to a share in the German fleet, which has already been put forward semi-officially to the Admiralty, is weak in equity. But it is in our interest to preserve good relationships between the Royal Navy and the French Navy. Accordingly, it is submitted that we should allow the French a few ships.[7]

However, this latter statement was not supported by the new First Lord of the Admiralty, Brendan Bracken, when he wrote on 7 July saying: 'The Russian contribution at sea does not justify claim to one third of fleet, and the French claim to German warships has few merits.'[4]

The second major British pre-conference statement of policy was the Admiralty's paper 'Disposal of the German Fleet', which was submitted to the Cabinet by Brendan Bracken on 7 July and which included:

> The Admiralty consider the scrapping of the combat units of the German Fleet to be in the best interests both of the Royal Navy and of world peace.
>
> Marshal Stalin bids for a minimum of one-third on the grounds of reason and justice. The exertions and losses of the Red Navy give no foundation for a claim to one-third. The Russian contribution at sea has been almost negligible. The Russians must therefore justify their claim on the general, not the naval contribution of the USSR to the common victory.
>
> The disposal of the surrendered German ships is a matter on which the French, who will be absent from 'Terminal', will presumably claim a right to speak. They have unofficially intimated that they will ask for some destroyers and U-boats. On the other hand, a French claim to German warships has few merits since the parlous state of the French Fleet today is largely due to their own defaults.
>
> The Admiralty's aim is to satisfy British requirements and to keep U-boats out of undesirable hands, particularly Russian hands. It is believed that the Americans, also, will have the latter objective. As the German warships are all in our hands, our bargaining position is extremely strong.
>
> If the Russian desire for a division has to be met, we should claim our full share. The Russians, for reasons of prestige, are likely to be tempted by the offer of cruisers and destroyers. We do not covert the surface combat ships and should insist on taking our share primarily out of the U-boat fleet.[8]

The Admiralty Cabinet Paper then suggested that whilst the Russians should be allocated only ten U-boats, the British and Americans should be allocated sixty-five each and, contrary to the views of the First Lord, that six should be allocated to France. The stated British requirement was for a large number of U-boats for experimental purposes most of which would be used in extended explosive trials an action which it was hoped would be seen as tantamount to scrapping them. It was assumed that the US would require the same number for the same purpose and that this somewhat speculative suggestion would attract American support. The Cabinet Paper also stressed that if the Russians contested the allocation of sixty-five U-boats each to Britain and America they should be reminded about the Red Army's press release in March which had announced the capture of forty-five U-boats in Danzig. It was expected that the Russians might find it embarrassing to retract the announcement.

The Cabinet Meeting on 12 July considered the Admiralty proposals and although no red line was formally put through them at the meeting the suggested U-boat allocation figure of sixty-five each for the USA and the UK did not survive and never re-appeared. The more important point that was agreed by the Cabinet was:

> So far as concerned the German fleet, we should strongly support the American view that there should be a wholesale scrapping of combat units with the exception of vessels which were required for experimental or immediate operational purposes. If, however, the Russians refused to accept this proposal, we should suggest a division of the German fleet on the lines indicated, the main effect of which was to give the Russians the minimum number of U-boats.[9]

The formal conclusion of the Cabinet meeting was that the proposal with regard to the disposal of the German fleet should be adopted by the UK as a basis for any negotiations at the forthcoming conference and that in respect of the surviving U-boats the UK and the US would be adopting similar negotiating positions.

CHAPTER 9

The Potsdam Conference and Agreement – July/August 1945

WHILST THE POTSDAM CONFERENCE was about far more than the future of the Kriegsmarine and the remaining U-boats, which was just one small part of a whole series of momentous topics to be considered at what was essentially a peace conference, it nevertheless established the way ahead for the 156 U-boats that had surrendered at the end of the European war. There was no question of the survival of most of them. The question was how this was to be achieved.

The 1st Plenary (Leaders) Meeting of the Conference was held on 17 July and to emphasise his concerns as well as to rile Churchill, Stalin immediately raised the question of the division of the German naval fleet which, he said, the UK and the USA had agreed would be discussed. There are three slightly different records of the debate at the Meeting.

The US 'Thompson Minutes' record that:

Stalin asked why does Churchill refuse to give Russia her share of the German fleet?

Churchill exclaimed 'Why?' and went on to say that he thought that the fleet should be destroyed or shared.

Stalin said, let's divide it. If Mr Churchill wishes, he can sink his share.[1]

The US 'Cohen Notes' record that:

Stalin: If you are in such an obedient mood today, Mr Prime Minister, I should like to know whether you will share with us the German fleet. Churchill: We will share it with you or sink it.[2]

The UK Minutes record that:

Premier Stalin asked why Mr Churchill did not agree that Russia should have a third of the German Fleet.

Mr Churchill said that this was not the position. It was, however, for consideration whether the German Fleet should be divided up, or whether it would be sunk.

Premier Stalin said that in his view the German Fleet should be divided up. If other countries wished to sink the ships which made up the share allotted to them they could do so, but he did not intend that the ships allotted to Russia should be sunk.[3]

The parallel 1st Meeting of Foreign Secretaries was held on 18 July and Molotov, the Soviet Foreign Minister, suggested that the disposal of the German fleet should be added to the agenda of the forthcoming 2nd Plenary Meeting. In response Anthony Eden, the British Foreign Secretary, said: 'That this was not a particularly difficult issue and could conveniently be left until later in the Conference.'[4] Molotov replied that if the issue was simple there was much to be said for disposing of it without delay. It was, however, agreed that it would not be included in the 2nd Plenary but at one soon after.

On the same day Churchill had lunch with President Truman and the former's note of their conversation records that:

> The President asked how I thought we should handle the Russian request for the division of the German Fleet. I said I found it hard to deny the Russians the right to keep their third of the Fleet afloat if they needed it. We British should not have any use for our third of the warships. The President said that the Americans would take their share, but it would be of no use to them. I made it clear that the case of the U-boats must be considered separately, as they were nasty things to have knocking about in large numbers. He seemed to agree.[5]

The 2nd Meeting of Foreign Secretaries was held on 19 July, one of the purposes of which was to agree the agenda for the 3rd Plenary to be held later that day. Molotov was keen for an early discussion of the paper he had produced about the future of the German Navy and James Byrnes, the US Secretary of State, and Eden both agreed that it should be included in the agenda for the Plenary. The Soviet paper was short and to the point and included the proposal: 'One third of the total German Navy shall be handed over to the Soviet Union.'[6]

The 3rd Plenary Meeting was held on the evening of 19 July and under Agenda Item No. 6 the Minutes included a long debate between the three leaders, primarily Stalin and Churchill, about the future of the German fleet. Stalin opened the discussion with a reference to the Molotov paper and Churchill, who was determined to take a hard line, assured him that although he had no objection to the Soviet proposal that the German fleet should be shared, he linked this to the need for a satisfactory outcome to the Conference as a whole:

> He did not want to approach the question of the German Fleet from any judicial standpoint with exact definitions, but rather to try and reach a fair and friendly agreement between the three Powers as part of a general settlement of the problems before them. The major part of the German Fleet was now in British hands; and, assuming that the Three Powers came to a friendly general settlement of the affairs before the Conference, he would not oppose a fair division of the German Fleet.[7]

Mr Churchill then turned his attention specifically to the subject of the U-boats, saying:

> It seemed to him that the disposal of the German U-boats was in a rather different position from the other vessels. U-boats had a limited war use. He considered that the U-boats should be destroyed or sunk. However, some of the most modern U-boats had devices of interest to all Three Powers, and these should be shared. He therefore suggested that as part of a final settlement, most of the U-boats should be sunk, and the small balance required for research should be shared.
>
> As regards the other units of the German Fleet, if the Conference came to a friendly general settlement of their problems, he was prepared to divide them equally, for he would welcome the appearance of the Russians on the seas of the world.
>
> He had made a distinction which he regarded as important between the German surface fleet and the U-boats. He knew that Premier Stalin would appreciate the sensitivities of the people of an island like Great Britain, which grew far less than two-thirds of its food. We have suffered greatly from U-boats in two wars, in a way that no other nation had suffered. Twice we had been brought to the brink of disaster by U-boat campaigns, and the U-boats were not a popular weapon with the British people.
>
> He would strongly urge that a considerable portion of the U-boats should be sunk, and that the rest should be shared alike: the number kept by the Three Powers should be a token; more in order to spread technical knowledge than to keep large numbers in existence. As Great Britain had been subjected to terrible assaults by U-boats, we did not welcome any nation expanding in this form of naval construction. He hoped that Premier Stalin and President Truman would pardon his emphasising our special position in this matter.[7]

In response, and in a major breakthrough in the debate about the future of the remaining U-boats during the course of which Churchill had reminded him about the Red Army's boast that they had captured forty-five U-boats in Danzig, Stalin for the very first time and in a significant Soviet policy about-turn, said: 'He too also favoured sinking a large proportion of the German U-boats and was in agreement with this view.'[7]

Truman confirmed that he too was agreeable to a three-way division of the German naval surface fleet as well as the sinking of a large proportion of the U-boats.

Once the principle of the need for a three-way split of the surface fleet had been recognised by Truman and Churchill, Stalin agreed that the details should be settled at the end of the Conference. As a result the question was put on hold although the need for progress was briefly mentioned by Molotov at the 5th Meeting of Foreign Secretaries on 22 July:

> Mr Molotov referred to other subjects on which the Soviet Delegation wished to see some further progress made at an early date. It was pointed out that the question of the German Fleet was one for discussion for the Plenary Meeting, and Mr Byrnes indicated that the United States Delegation intended to put forward proposals on this subject.[8]

The topic was next raised at the 9th Plenary Meeting on 25 July. However, Churchill and Truman stated that their staffs were still working on their detailed proposals and Stalin agreed that the matter could be postponed. The Minutes record: 'It was agreed that further consideration of this matter should be deferred until detailed proposals were available.'[9]

Action concerning the disposal of the German naval fleet then accelerated as the Potsdam Conference approached its close, and the staffs of each of the three delegations produced their final position papers.

The US Delegation's Working Paper of 29 July stated: 'It is agreed that the German fleet shall at once be divided equally among the USSR, the UK, and the US. A large proportion of the German submarines shall be destroyed, a small number being retained for experimental and training purposes.'[10]

The paper by the Soviet Delegation of 30 July, which for the first time dealt with the surface vessels and submarines separately, proposed:

> One third of the total strength of the German surface navy shall be transferred to the Soviet Union.
> A larger part of the German submarine fleet shall be sunk. A part of the submarine fleet viz. submarines presenting the greatest interest

from the technical standpoint shall be preserved and divided between
the USSR, Great Britain and the USA.[11]

The paper by the British Delegation of 30 July took a more detailed
approach and again raised the issue of allotting surface vessels and U-boats
to France. This was a topic which had been discussed between the new
British Prime Minister Clement Attlee, the new British Foreign Secretary
Ernest Bevin, and senior Foreign Office officials on the previous day
when: 'The Foreign Secretary asked whether difficulty would arise later if
a decision was taken at this Conference about the disposal of the German
Fleet, without providing for the French to have some share of it.'[12]

In response and in a statement that was slightly economical with the
truth: 'It was pointed out that the distribution which had been suggested
by the Admiralty, and approved by a Cabinet decision of the late
Government, had made provision for a share to be given to the French.'[12]

Whilst the Admiralty was equivocal about the question of allocating
German warships to the French, the Foreign Office took a far more
positive line. having advised Bevin on 28 July:

> The French claim to a share of the German warships was not mentioned
> at the Plenary discussion and the British Delegation consider it
> impractical to raise it now. It seems to be deliberate Russian policy to
> ignore the French. Conversely it seems to be in our interests to ensure
> that France plays her full part as fourth partner in German affairs. The
> Foreign Office would therefore suggest that we should try to obtain
> some German warships for the French.[13]

In the light of this, the British proposal which alluded to the discussions
between the three leaders on 19 July stated:

> It was agreed on the 19th July that the German surface ships should
> be shared equally between the Three Powers. The British Delegation
> suggest that consideration should now be given to allotting a share to
> France which is an equal party to the terms of surrender for Germany
> and is a full member of the Control Council for Germany.
>
> At the same time it was agreed in principle that the German U-boats
> should be dealt with separately, the greater part being destroyed. A
> token number would be retained for equal division among the Three
> Powers for purposes of research. The question of a French share of the
> retained U-boats should also be considered.[14]

The 10th Meeting of Foreign Secretaries was held on 30 July and in
the light of the three slightly differing final position statements from

each of the Allies, 'It was agreed that a Technical Sub-Committee should be established to examine the questions raised and to report to an early meeting of Foreign Secretaries'.[15] This Technical Sub-Committee was led by three senior Allied naval officers, the British Rear Admiral Edward McCarthy, the American Vice Admiral Charles Cooke and the Russian Admiral of the Fleet Nikolai Kuznetsov. The latter, who out-ranked his colleagues, was Commander-in-Chief of the Soviet Navy and his presence showed how seriously the USSR was approaching the question of the final disposal of the surviving German naval vessels.

At the 11th Plenary Meeting held on 31 July Stalin, who was becoming increasingly impatient, urged that a definite decision should be made about the question of the German fleet. Even though the report of the Technical Sub-Committee was not yet available Stalin again stated his view that it had already been agreed that Russia would get one-third of the German fleet except submarines, the majority of which should be sunk.

In response the US Secretary of State advised: 'The Committee which had been set up to study this question were meeting later that evening and hoped to reach agreement. He thought it would save time to await their Report.'[16]

The meeting of the Technical Sub-Committee took place on 31 July with Admiral Kuznetsov as its Chairman and the Minutes record a lively discussion about the division of the German fleet. There was a lengthy debate about the surface warships which initially became bogged down in unnecessary detail and yet again the British view that some should be allocated to France was emphasised. Predictably this did not find favour with the Soviet Delegation, with the Minutes recording:

> Considerable discussion followed on this point. The Soviet Representatives pointing out that at the Plenary Meeting [on 19 July] it was decided that one-third of the German surface warships should go to the Soviet Union and that this Sub-Committee is conferring on that basis alone. The question of giving a share to France was not connected with the agreement for transferring one-third to the USSR. There were no reasons for becoming involved in this question today as full agreement had already been reached on this division of one-third.[17]

As far as the U-boats were concerned the British Delegation once again raised the issue of allocating a share to France. Fortunately the sting was taken out of the debate by it being agreed that the principle of any allocation of warships to France would be raised in the Sub-Committee's final report. This was then followed by a discussion focussed on the number to be retained.

Admiral McCarthy, supported by Admiral Cooke, suggested that the Three Powers should each retain just six which, with a possible allocation of two to France, would give a total of twenty. Whilst ignoring the question of any U-boats being allocated to France with which he disagreed, Admiral Kuznetsov said that there were three interesting types of U-boat (presumably Types XVII, XXI and XXIII) and that the Soviet Union would like to have ten of each, giving them a total of thirty. The reasons he gave for this proposal were:

> That it would be necessary for experimenting with these submarines that some of these types should be delivered to industrial enterprises to be taken to pieces and examined.
>
> Others would be required for operating tests, sending some to the north and some to the south to see how they react to conditions.
>
> One type would not guarantee results as any accident would destroy the value of the test.[17]

The Soviet proposal did not attract support from the American and British admirals, especially the latter. Counter arguments were that this would involve some 60 per cent of the surviving seaworthy U-boats which was contrary to the agreements already made during the Conference, that there were insufficient numbers of the 'three interesting types' and that there would be major problems concerning the supply of spare parts. The Foreign Office representative on the British Delegation stressed:

> We should base ourselves on what was said on 19 July when Mr Churchill made a very forceful appeal for the destruction of the greater part of the U-boats. He explained the extreme sensitiveness of the British people towards this weapon which had twice brought Britain to the brink of disaster. Generalissimo Stalin said at the same time that he agreed and favoured sinking a large proportion of the German submarines. The British Government had never contemplated that the Sub-Committee had authority to propose the retention of anything like half of the German U-boat fleet, and that in following the basis of Mr Churchill's remarks we should only maintain a number of something in the nature of 10 per cent.[17]

There was no meeting of minds amongst the admirals as to how many U-boats should be retained and to break the deadlock Admiral Kuznetsov suggested that the question should be remitted to the Allied leaders for a final decision on the basis that: 'The British Delegation suggested that the number of submarines left should not exceed 20 per cent, while the Soviet representative did not consider this enough, the final decision being left to the Big Three.'[17]

The Technical Sub-Committee's Report which was submitted on 1 August included the recommendations that:

The total strength of the German surface navy shall be divided equally among the USSR, UK and US.

The British representatives expressed the view that a portion of the German Navy should be allotted to France and that, therefore, full agreement with the above principle must be subject to final decision of the Plenary Conference.

The larger part of the German submarine fleet shall be sunk.

The Committee are not able to make a recommendation as regards the number of submarines to be preserved for experimental and technical purposes.

It is the opinion of the British and American members that not more than 30 submarines shall be preserved and divided equally between the USSR, UK and US for experimental and technical purposes.

It is the view of the Russian members that this number is too small for their requirements and that USSR should receive about 30 submarines for its own experimental and technical purposes.[18]

The Report was considered at the 11th Meeting of Foreign Secretaries held on 1 August and in an unexpected meeting of minds there was no debate whatsoever about the allocation of either surface warships or submarines to France. In respect of the surviving surface warships the Minutes of the Meeting recorded:

Mr Byrnes said that the first question on which agreement had not been reached in the Committee was the distribution of warships.

Mr Molotov recalled that it had already been decided at a Plenary Meeting that the German warships should be divided into three parts.

Mr Bevin said that, as regards the warships, he was prepared to agree a division into thirds.[19]

The debate concerning the submarines was not quite so simple, with Bevin making a very strong statement on behalf of both the UK and the USA:

On submarines, Mr Bevin said that the question was how many should be destroyed. Mr Churchill had said that only a token number should be retained. The British and United States Delegations suggested that only 30 submarines should be preserved. This was a matter on which the British people felt very strongly, since no less than 30,000 British seamen had lost their lives during the war by U-boat warfare alone while carrying supplies by sea to Russia and elsewhere. On this point the British and United States Delegations were not prepared to make any concession. No German submarines should be retained except for experimental purposes, and in his opinion 30 was adequate for those purposes.

Mr Molotov said that he was prepared to agree.[19]

As a result, after all the debates about the future of the German Navy since the end of the war in Europe in May 1945 the three Foreign Secretaries finally agreed: 'That thirty submarines should be retained for distribution among the Three Powers, and the remainder destroyed.'[19]

At the 12th Plenary Meeting also held on 1 August and without further debate the three Leaders endorsed the conclusions that had been reached by their respective Foreign Secretaries earlier that day concerning the disposal of the surface vessels and submarines of the German naval fleet.

Immediately after this Attlee wrote to Churchill, saying:

> The Conference is ending tonight in a good atmosphere. I would like you to let you know the broad results before the communiqué is issued. We have, of course, been building on the foundation laid by you, and there has been no change of policy.[20]

The letter ended with a postscript which said:

> We have reached a satisfactory agreement on the German Fleet, especially on U-boats. Of these all are to be sunk except 30 which are to be divided equally between the Three Powers for experimental and technical purposes.[20]

The result of these high-level discussions was the production of the Proceedings (Minutes) of the Potsdam Heads of State Conference which took place in Berlin between 17 July and 2 August 1945. In respect of the U-boats the Proceedings said that the UK, the USA and the USSR had concluded that:

> The larger part of the German submarine fleet shall be sunk. Not more than thirty submarines shall be preserved and divided equally between the USSR, UK and USA for experimental and technical purposes.
>
> The Three Governments agree to constitute a Tripartite Naval Commission to submit agreed recommendations to the Three Governments for the allocation of specific German warships.
>
> The Three Governments agreed that transfers shall be completed as soon as possible, but not later than 15 February 1946.[21]

Thus, by the end of the Conference each of the Allies had achieved what they wanted. The German Navy had been eliminated, no vessels had been allocated to France, and Stalin who had raised the issue had achieved his requirement for the USSR to be allocated one-third of the surface ships, although he had made a major concession in respect of the U-boats.

The Allies had each been allocated similar shares of the surviving German fleet albeit that the UK and the US had no great aspirations to be allocated any surface vessels. The US proposal to sink almost all the U-boats had been achieved as had the UK's similar proposal. It would however be wrong to believe that the destruction of the German Navy was a one-sided view espoused by any one of the Allies. Their stated objectives were similar even if their motivation differed and even if the means whereby the objectives were achieved varied in detail.

It is interesting to speculate why Stalin was prepared to compromise in respect of his claim to a one-third share of the surviving U-boats. Perhaps it was because he recognised that almost all the U-boats which had surrendered were by then located in the UK or that he realised that Churchill and the British Government held very strong views about the need for their destruction or that there were other more important matters on which agreement was necessary. However, the explanation may be much simpler because, despite the earlier exaggerated statement that the Red Army had captured forty-five U-boats in Danzig in March 1945, the Russians had captured eight almost-complete Type XXI U-boats and had already taken steps to incorporate them into the Soviet Navy's Baltic Fleet.

Additionally, although the British and Americans did not become aware of the full details until early 1946 the Russians had completely dismantled the Schichau shipyard in Danzig in 1945 and had moved everything to the Soviet Union as war reparations. During that process they had gained access to a large number of pre-fabricated Type XXI U-boat sections which though earmarked for specific U-boats had not yet reached the keel-laying/assembly stage. This meant that the Soviet Navy had sufficient pre-fabricated sections and other parts as well as the assembly jigs and facilities to complete at least another twelve Type XXI U-boats, the plans for the final keel-laying and building of which had been underway before Danzig was captured.

One of Stalin's priority post-war interests was to create a blue-water navy and the large, high-speed, ocean-going, high-tech German Type XXI U-boat was therefore a prime attraction for the Soviet Navy. He secretly already had in his possession sufficient examples of this type of

U-boat and it is most probable that it was this fact that enabled him to compromise during the debates about the number of U-boats to be retained. It was now up to the Tripartite Naval Commission (TNC) to decide the detailed fate of the 156 surviving U-boats.

CHAPTER 10

The Tripartite Naval Commission

THE TRIPARTITE NAVAL COMMISSION (TNC) which had been established by the Potsdam Agreement was charged with the apportionment between the Allies of more than 2,000 surviving German warships, including the 156 U-boats which had surrendered. It comprised representatives of the UK, the USA and the USSR, the senior members of the respective delegations being the British Admiral Sir Geoffrey Miles, the American Admiral Robert Ghormley and the Russian Admiral Gordei Levchenko. They were supported by the Royal Navy's Rear Admiral William Parry, the US Navy's Commodore Herbert Ray and the Soviet Navy's Rear Admiral N Alekseev.

The Terms of Reference (ToRs) for Admiral Ghormley were brief and to the point. They were issued on 13 August 1945 by the USN's CNO, and said that the general principles for the distribution of the German Navy as agreed at the Potsdam Conference were being provided to the US delegation. The message then went on to say:

> In addition to the general principles, the following detailed directives are issued for the guidance of the US members of the TNC ... Submarines: The US desires its proportionate share (10) of the thirty submarines to be preserved. These to be types embodying latest German developments including at least one Type 17B.[1]

Significantly, whilst the CNO's message included details of the U-boats already in USN custody, it failed to mention that two of the high-tech Type XXI U-boats which had surrendered in Europe, *U-2513* and *U-3008*, were at that precise time being covertly sailed across the Atlantic from Lisahally by USN crews behind the backs of the Russians.

This initial message from Washington was followed a day later by another to Admiral Ghormley from the US Joint Chiefs of Staff which, as promised by the CNO, emphasised the decisions of the Potsdam

Conference in relation to the distribution of the surviving ships of the German Navy, including the U-boats.

In contrast to the brief general guidance given by the USN, the British Admirals on the TNC were given a long and detailed Admiralty Directive on 13 August which made clear the hard line which HM Government wished them to take with the Russians:

> You should be aware that the Admiralty and other Departments of HMG have learnt by bitter experience that it is useless to negotiate with the Russians in a spirit of reasonable compromise. The Russian Delegation may be expected to drive the hardest possible bargain and concede nothing unless forced to do so. It is recommended that your tactics should be generally to hold out, so far as possible, on all points of importance to the Russians until essential British requirements have been met. Concessions made in advance by way of inducement have not, in the past, been found effective in obtaining countervailing concessions from the Russians.[2]

It also included mention of the Type XVIIB U-boats, stressing that the Russians were to be denied access to the 'Walterwerke' in Kiel, specifically saying:

> It is desired to exclude the Russians from acquiring any of these special types of U-Boat [and] pending further instructions your case should be:
> a. To maintain that *U-1406* and *U-1407* are the only boats of this type available for disposal within [the] Protocol.
> b. To insist in concert with your USA colleague, that *U-1406* and *U-1407* are to be allocated to the USA and UK respectively.[2]

The 1st TNC Meeting took place on 15 August when it was decided that an initial action should be to produce an Agreed List of all the German warships which were to be considered by the Commission. A Technical Sub-Committee was set up to undertake this task, it was to meet on 16 August, and it was expected to finish its task within 48 hours. Predictably, Admiral Levchenko stated that he wished to discuss the division of the U-boats immediately, but Admiral Miles insisted that this could not be done until the Agreed List had been produced.

The 2nd TNC Meeting took place on 16 August, the main business of which was the initiation of arrangements for the inspection of all the German warships which had surrendered, including the U-boats most of which had by then been assembled in the UK. The Minutes of the Meeting record that:

The Commission agreed that a combined inspection should be made simultaneously by Russian, British and American representatives. This Inspection should be carried out by two parties; one for German naval ships located in the United Kingdom and one for German naval ships on the Continent.

Inspection of German naval vessels in the Western Hemisphere will be carried out by representatives of the three nations present in that area.[1]

The TNC's Technical Sub-Committee was given the responsibility for appointing the Inspection Parties (also called Tripartite Naval Boards) to undertake the detailed work involved in recommending which ships and U-boats should be retained, their allocation between the Allies, and the disposal arrangements for the remainder.

Thereafter, the TNC meetings took place on a regular basis, with most of their time being taken up by discussions about vessels other than the U-boats. Clear decisions about the latter had already been taken at the Potsdam Conference, and the Admirals therefore had little leeway for disagreement which was not always the case when it came to the division of the other vessels.

The initial version of the Agreed List of U-boats was approved by the TNC at their 3rd Meeting on 18 August, but that was superseded by an updated version on 25 August which included several U-boats which had not formally surrendered. That version of the Agreed List therefore came with the proviso that it would need to be amended yet again depending on the findings of the Inspection Parties. The 25 August version comprised 176 U-boats, as follows:

Serviceable U-boats (mostly in the UK)	146
Unserviceable U-boats in Continental Ports	12
U-boats in Japanese Hands	5
U-boats in Russian Ports	13 (all unserviceable)

Compared with the challenge of dividing up more than 2,000 naval vessels of a whole variety of classes, the task of the TNC as far as the Kriegsmarine's submarine fleet was concerned was relatively easy, being primarily to select from the U-boats which had surrendered just the 30 that were to be retained and transferred to the Allies for experimental and technical purposes, i.e. the allocation lists. The most important decision at the 3rd Meeting was that, after their inspection, all the German naval vessels (including U-boats) would be assigned one of three categories:

Category A: Operable
Category B: Capable of completion or repair within agreed timescales
Category C: All other vessels. These to be scrapped or destroyed

Two significant points were recorded in the Minutes of the 5th TNC Meeting on 22 August:

> It is estimated that about one month will be required to complete inspections.
>
> Admiral Ghormley's suggestion that additional information of sunk or damaged ships should be obtained after inspection in order to give a complete account of all German naval vessels, was put forward and agreed.[3]

The latter decision was an important extension to the TNC's ToRs, especially because the Norwegian and German ports and anchorages contained a great many scuttled, scrapped and otherwise unserviceable U-boats, all of which would now need to be identified and then recommended for disposal in such a way as to preclude their future use.

Arrangements for the various Inspection Parties were discussed at the 6th Meeting of the TNC on 24 August. There were to be four Parties:

a. United Kingdom
b. Western Hemisphere
c. Norway and Denmark
d. Continental Ports (in the Baltic and North Germany)

The Inspection Parties visited Britain, America, Canada, Trinidad (to inspect the two U-boats that had surrendered in Argentina and which were en route to the USA), Germany, Denmark and Norway, as well as Poland and the USSR, in August and September. They then submitted their reports to the TNC's Technical Sub-Committee, which had the task of recommending to the TNC itself the initial allocations to each of the Allies.

The UK Inspection Party was required to review the 135 U-boats held in the UK, primarily in Loch Ryan and at Lisahally, and the Western Hemisphere Inspection Party had to review the 11 U-boats in the Western Atlantic area. These included the five which had surrendered in America, the two which had surrendered in Canada, the two which had surrendered in Argentina, as well as the two which had been covertly moved to the USA.

The task of the Continental Inspection Party was more difficult because, as well as inspecting the U-boats already identified in the Agreed

List, it found a large number of U-boats – particularly in the German Baltic ports – which had been scuttled or scrapped before the end of the war, the fate of which now needed to be considered by the TNC, albeit that this action was outside the latter's ToRs.

After the 6th TNC Meeting on 24 August, and whilst the inspections were underway, there was a break in the meeting schedule, and the 7th Meeting did not take place until 12 September. As far as routine business was concerned, the main item of significance was the decision to amend the Agreed List of U-boats in the light of the inspection reports. There was also a major query as a result of the inspection visit to Danzig, where the Baltic and North Germany Inspection Party had discovered that the Russians had launched and towed away eleven U-boats (three Type VIICs and eight Type XXIs) to the Soviet-controlled port of Libau in Latvia. They had not been declared to the TNC and they had not been included in the Agreed List of U-boats to be inspected.

In addition, after removing these U-boats from Danzig, the Russians had completely dismantled the local shipyards and moved everything to the Soviet Union as war reparations. Thus, during the course of this process, they had gained access to a large number of pre-fabricated Type XXI U-boat sections which, though earmarked for specific U-boats, had not reached the keel-laying/assembly stage. The result was that if they wished to do so the Soviet Navy had sufficient pre-fabricated sections and other parts, as well as the assembly jigs and facilities, to complete at least another twelve Type XXI U-boats, the plans for the final keel-laying and building of which had been underway before Danzig was overrun.

The 8th (18 September), 9th (20 September) and 10th (24 September) TNC Meetings all indicated the progress of the Inspection Parties, but the Minutes contained no specific U-boat-related information. There was, however, some debate at the 9th Meeting about the action to be taken in respect of the allocation of Category C vessels, with Admiral Miles making clear his view that: 'It was against the whole spirit of the protocol to divide ships which would have to be towed.'[3]

Progress concerning the division of the U-boats was evident at the 11th TNC Meeting on 5 October, with the Minutes recording:

Captain Graubert [one of the US Navy Delegation's staff officers] requested that each delegate on the Sub-Committee should make a list of the 10 submarines that his country required, to facilitate the task of allocating these vessels. Both the Soviet and British member of the Sub-

Committee promised to do this, although Admiral Miles pointed out that the submarines at Libau had still to be inspected.[3]

This was raised again at the 12th TNC Meeting on 6 October when Admiral Ghormley asked that lists of the ten submarines which were desired by the USSR and the UK should be presented to the Sub-Committee. Admiral Miles responded to this request, but whether or not such action was ever taken by Admirals Ghormley and Levchenko is unclear. The wholesale changes subsequently effected to the initial US allocation suggest that the USN probably failed to react to this request.

What is clear is that each of the Allies had different interests. The USN was primarily interested in the Type XXI and the Type XVIIB 'Walter' U-boats and, after covertly transferring the two Type XXI U-boats (*U-2513* and *U-3008*) to the USA in August, was largely content to accept its allocation from the other U-boats which had surrendered in the Western Hemisphere, three of which were already undergoing minor refits in USN shipyards. On the other hand, the Russians viewed the allocation process as an important contribution to their plan to create a blue-water navy, and they were keen to obtain good examples of the Type VIIC and Type XXI U-boats. Surprisingly, the Russians never expressed any specific interest in the Type XVIIB 'Walter' U-boats, possibly because they had captured some of the 'Walter' technology in the Soviet Zone of Germany and because they had no desire to share it with the British and Americans.

The Admiralty initially advised Admiral Miles on 13 August of the 'Provisional Requirements of the Royal Navy' for German naval vessels, including U-boats and at that stage the RN's first preference was for two Type VIICs, one Type XVIIB, two Type XXIs and six Type XXIIIs. However, this provisional requirement was reviewed in the light of the trials that the RN was covertly conducting on some of the U-boats in the UK, as well as its absolute requirement to obtain *U-1407*. The Admiralty's revised response on 25 September stated that:

The U-Boats required are:

1 Type XVIIB	*U-1407*
5 Type VIIC	to include *U-1105* and *U-1171*
2 Type XXI	any two except *U-2506*
2 Type XXIII	to include *U-2326*.[4]

The 13th Meeting of the TNC on 10 October was the decisive one as far as the division of the surviving U-boats was concerned. Agreement had already been reached at Potsdam on the principle of retaining and dividing just thirty U-boats between the Allies, and thus the number to be allocated to each of them was accepted by the TNC without demur. That said, the TNC agreed that there should be some flexibility of choice and that providing the number allocated to each country did not exceed ten, bi-lateral exchanges of individual U-boats could be made subject to formal TNC approval.

There was nevertheless an important supplementary point recorded in the Minutes of the 13th Meeting, viz: 'Admiral Miles raised the question of ensuring that all other submarines other than the 30 allocated to the three Powers were in actual fact sunk, in accordance with the Potsdam Agreement.'[3]

The initial U-boat allocations made to the Allies on 10 October were as follows:

UK   Five Type VIICs, two Type XXIs, two Type XXIIIs and one Type XVIIB, comprising: *U-712, U-953, U-975, U-1108, U-1171, U-1407, U-2326, U-2348, U-2518* and *U-3017*

USA   Two Type VIICs, two Type XXIs, two Type XXIIIs, one Type XB, one Type IXC, one Type IXD and one Type XVIIB, comprising: *U-234, U-873, U-889, U-1105, U-1023, U-1406, U-2351, U-2356, U-3041* and *U-3515*

USSR   Four Type VIICs, four Type XXIs, one Type IXC/40 and one Type XXIII, comprising: *U-1057, U-1058, U-1064, U-1231, U-1305, U-2353, U-2502, U-2529, U-3035* and *U-3514*

Of these thirty U-boats, twenty-six were in the UK, three were in the USA, and one was in Canada. As to their categories, sixteen were Category A, twelve were Category B (including all the Type XXIs), and two (the Type XVIIB 'Walter' U-boats *U-1406* and *U-1407*) were Category C. The latter according to its own rules should have been earmarked for scrapping or destruction, but the TNC turned a blind eye to this requirement.

These initial lists indicated that the RN and the Soviet Navy were each allocated most of the U-boats that they wanted. On the other hand, the allocation to the USA was totally contrary to the USN's U-boat policy. It comprised just three of the U-boats already in the USA, one that was in Canada and six that were in the UK. It even failed to include the two Type XXIs which had been transferred to the USA, and it also failed to include one of the Type IXDs that was already being refitted by the USN. Despite the specific request at the 11th TNC Meeting, the USN had failed to advise its requirements for U-boats before the initial allocations were made.

The Minutes of the 13th TNC Meeting on 10 October were, as were the Minutes of all the TNC meetings, security classified as Top Secret, and the associated messages notifying the Allies of the proposed allocations were classified Secret. But despite this there was a blatant breach of security when on 9 October *The Times* filed a story from Hamburg (published on 10 October) which stated:

> Provisional agreement, subject to ratification of the Powers concerned, has been reached on the disposal of the former German U-Boat fleet, it is understood here. Under the terms of the decisions taken by the naval representatives of Great Britain, Russia and the United States, each one of these three Powers will receive six [*sic*] boats for experimental purposes. The remainder of the fleet, totalling approximately 150 submarines, will be scrapped.[5]

After receipt of the reports of the Inspection Parties, and just before the TNC formally started the division and allocation process, the Russians decided to take exception to the hard line that Admiral Miles, in accordance with his Directive, was taking in the TNC discussions in relation to the demands of the Soviet Navy. This precipitated a strong letter from the Soviet Foreign Minister Molotov to his British and American counterparts on 28 September beginning with the statement:

> The Soviet Government consider it necessary hereby to draw the attention of the Government of the United States of American and of the Government of the United Kingdom to irregularities which are occurring in implementing the decision of the Berlin Conference on the partition of the German Navy and Merchant Marine. So far the Commission, which consists of representatives of the United Kingdom, the United States of America and the Soviet Union, and was set up in accordance with the decision of the Berlin Conference in order to give practical effect to the above-mentioned decision of the Berlin Conference, has failed to achieve substantial results in its work. The chief reason for this situation is the attitude adopted by the United Kingdom representatives on this Commission.[6]

It went on to highlight seven separate complaints and, though most of them were concerned with matters which did not relate to the division of the U-boats, two were directly relevant:

> Difficulties met with by Soviet representatives in the inspection of ships in British ports.

Employment of German vessels subject to partition without prior agreement with the Soviet authorities.[6]

The Foreign Office viewed this letter from Molotov as 'a typical Soviet production', and initially suggested that 'we might imitate Mr Molotov's procedure and prepare an equally tart memorandum which Mr Bevin could send to Mr Gousev [the Soviet Ambassador in London]'.[6]

The Admiralty's view of Molotov's 'offensive' letter was that it was:

> A typical Russian device intended to make us more accommodating over 'marginal' equipment
>
> The Russian note is obviously a manoeuvre designed to shake Admiral Miles' confidence, particularly when they [the TNC] are about to get down to the real business of allocating warships
>
> We should not attempt to give them a full answer.[6]

Thus, whilst producing a robust response, the Foreign Office decided to take the heat out of the matter, and a reply was sent at official level to Gousev on 16 October, with the covering letter saying:

> Mr Molotov's aide-memoire made a number of strong criticisms of the alleged attitude and conduct of the British representatives on the Commissions and of the other responsible British authorities concerned with these matters. These criticisms have been carefully examined by His Majesty's Government whose comments are contained in the memorandum which I am sending you.[6]

The memorandum dealt with almost all the detailed Soviet points, but nevertheless started with the statement that:

> His Majesty's Government cannot accept the suggestion in Mr Molotov's Memorandum of 27 September that the British Representatives on the Tripartite Commissions for the disposal of the German Fleet and Merchant Marine are preventing the respective Commissions from achieving substantial results.[6]

Again, most of the details in the rebuttal related to the points that had nothing to do with U-boats. However, two were relevant. One, by its emphasis was designed to embarrass the Soviets, and the other by its omission might well have been a covert admission of guilt.

First, the Soviet Union was forcefully reminded about its failure to notify the British and Americans about the eleven U-boats that had been removed from Danzig after its capture by the Red Army. Second, the valid point about the employment of German vessels subject to partition without prior Allied agreement was completely ignored.

The facts were that the Canadians were using two of the surrendered U-boats for trials, the Americans were already refitting three of the U-boats that had surrendered in the USA, the USN had covertly transferred two Type XXI U-boats from the UK to the USA, one of which was already being overhauled and refitted, and the British were using five U-boats for trials. All this had taken place without prior notification of or approval by the Russians, though maybe not without their informal knowledge. It was not therefore surprising that neither the Admiralty nor the Foreign Office wished to address this Russian complaint, though it is perhaps more surprising that the Russians did not press the point.

Whether this complaint from Mr Molotov was, as suggested by the Foreign Office and Admiral Miles himself, simply the application of Russian pressure in order to achieve the decisions that they required, whether it was the result of the implementation of Admiral Miles' Directive from the Admiralty, whether it was as a result of Miles' visit to Danzig with the Inspection Party on 28 August where he had uncovered the story that the Soviet Navy had launched and towed away the eleven U-boats, or whether it was a valid criticism of Miles himself, is difficult to discern. Whatever the motivation, it eventually had no impact on the process for dividing and allocating the U-boats, an action which was agreed without difficulty 14 days later.

Once the U-boat allocations had been decided by the TNC, a series of actions began involving, first, several mutually-acceptable variations to the allocation lists, second, decisions as to what was to become of the unallocated U-boats, especially the long list of unserviceable and scuttled U-boats identified by the Inspection Parties and, third, the production of the TNC's final report.

After the decisive 13th Meeting of the TNC on 10 October, the Minutes of several of the following meetings contained little relating to the U-boats. However, the 18th Meeting on 29 October turned out to be important because the admirals discussed not only the time limit for the sinking of the unallocated U-boats, but also the action that was to be taken in respect of the scrapped and scuttled U-boats:

> Admiral Miles considered that there should be a date named by which all unallocated German submarines should be sunk in accordance with paragraph 3 of Part A of the Potsdam Protocol. Admiral Levchenko proposed that this should be 15 February 1946, and this was agreed.

Admiral Ghormley raised the point that in various ports, notably Bremen [which was in the US Zone], there were unallocated German submarines which were unable to float, and which were, in fact, hulks on the beach. It was agreed that these hulks should also be destroyed by 15 February 1946, and Admiral Levchenko suggested that they should be used for scrap, to which the other representatives raised no objection.

Admiral Miles proposed that a recommendation should be made that each of the three Governments concerned should exchange reports by 15 February 1946 of the unallocated German submarines which have been destroyed.[3]

At the 19th TNC Meeting on 31 October, two significant points related to U-boats were recorded in the Minutes:

Admiral Ghormley reported that he had received a despatch from Washington requesting that certain submarines allocated to the United States could be exchanged for submarines in the United States.

Admiral Ghormley asked if it was the intention of the Soviet delegation to exchange [the eleven ex-Danzig] submarines located in the Soviet zone for submarines based in the United Kingdom and allocated to the USSR. Admiral Levchenko replied that there were no submarines in good condition in the Soviet zone and that it was not his intention to effect such changes.[3]

Further to the second of these two points, Admiral Ghormley was predictably able to advise the CNO on 5 November that this challenge had not been well received, and that: 'Soviet representatives state U-Boats in their zone are not completed and they do not desire to accept them in place of U-Boats located in United Kingdom.'[1]

With regard to the first point about the need to amend the US allocation, action between Washington and Admiral Ghormley had been underway since 11 October. The USN had immediately realised the implications of what appears to have been its poor staff work and had advised Admiral Ghormley that it wished to retain *U-805*, *U-530*, *U-858*, *U-977*, *U-2513* and *U-3008*, all of which were already in US custody. The message from Washington also said that the USN had no requirement for the Type VIICs (*U-1023* and *U-1105* – with its anti-sonar rubber coating), the Type XXIIIs (*U-2341* and *U-2356*) and the Type XXIs (*U-3041* and *U-3515*), all of which were held in the UK.

The US proposal was discussed by the TNC Sub-Committee, when both the Soviet and British representatives noted that the rubber-covered *U-1105* was apparently no longer required by the USN, and this caused a flurry of interest and an urgent exchange of messages, including one from Admiral Levchenko, who advised his TNC colleagues on 1 November that:

> In accordance with the desire of Vice Admiral Ghormley to take all ten submarines allotted to the USA from the number located at present in the USA, I am asking your consent to exchange allotted to the USSR submarines of the XXI type No. 2502 and of the VII type No. 1305 for the submarines XXI type No. 3041 and VII type No. 1105 which USA at present wish to release.[1]

The USN quickly realised its error in respect of *U-1105*, and the CNO advised Admiral Ghormley on 1 November that he wished to retain it rather than *U-805*. Thus, on 3 November, Admiral Ghormley closed the matter with a formal application to his TNC colleagues which stated:

> The United States desires to substitute ex-German U-Boats now located in the Western Hemisphere for those now allocated to the United States now located in the United Kingdom with the one exception of *U-1105*. Unless the Soviet Union or the United Kingdom have objection, it is requested that [the TNC's] Official Statement No 1 containing [details of] U-Boats assigned to the United States be corrected as follows:
>
> Release for assignment, now in United Kingdom: *U-1023*, *U-2351*, *U-2356*, *U-3041*, *U-3515*.
>
> To be assigned to the United States, now in ports of Western Hemisphere: *U-530*, *U-858*, *U-977*, *U-2513*, *U-3008*.[1]

Whilst the Soviet Navy was thus frustrated in its attempt to be allocated *U-1105*, Admirals Ghormley and Miles readily agreed that *U-2502* should be exchanged for *U-3041*. This was an advantage for the Soviet Navy as *U-2502* had been damaged by fire in August prior to its proposed RN trials, the result of which was its swift return to its moorings at Lisahally.

The Minutes of the 20th TNC Meeting on 5 November are notable for recording agreement about the treatment of Category C vessels which, in the case of U-boats, was that they were to be sunk in a depth of water of not less than 100m. The Admirals nevertheless turned a blind eye to the fact that at their 13th Meeting on 10 October they had already agreed the allocation of the two Category C 'Walter' U-boats, *U-1406* and *U-1407*, to the USA and UK respectively.

The remaining TNC meetings (up to 6 December) concentrated on disagreements concerning a variety of surface vessels as well as the details to be included in the Commission's final report, the drafting of which had been delegated to the Technical Sub-Committee, and scant attention was accorded to matters relating to the U-boats. Also, the Minutes of the 25th Meeting on 28 November illustrated the limits of the TNC's powers by recording a recommendation that the Allies should request the Governments of other countries to destroy or sink any Category C vessels located in their territorial waters, thereby – by implication – acknowledging that they had no power to direct France and Norway to dispose of the unserviceable U-boats located in their ports.

During this time there was one further (unsuccessful) change proposed to the UK allocation, this time by Admiral Miles, who wrote to his TNC colleagues on 16 November stating that: 'The British Admiralty are ... desirous of exchanging two of their [allocation of] submarines for two [*U-190* and *U-889*] now in Canada.'[1] In response, Admiral Ghormley wrote on 29 November that:

> *U-889* and *U-190*, former German submarines, are located in Canada. I have been advised that the United States Navy Department desires to retain former German submarine *U-889* in the United States allocation, but [has] no objection to the exchange of the former German submarine *U-190*.[1]

The UK therefore dropped its proposal concerning *U-889*, which remained in the US allocation.

There was yet another late exchange effected before the issue of the TNC's final report on 6 December. This was brought about because, on 23 November, when *U-3514* was being prepared to leave Lisahally for delivery to the Soviet Union, it collided with another U-boat, damaging its steering gear and aft hydroplanes. The stern was distorted, and the U-boat could not be transferred, even under tow. Thus, after a certain amount of ritual procrastination, Admiral Levchenko agreed that *U-3515* should be transferred instead of *U-3514*.

The final resolution of Molotov's letter of complaint dated 28 September occurred on 4 December, just before the TNC signed-off its final report, when Gousev replied to Bevin, concentrating solely on the U-boat situation, and saying:

> In connection with the memorandum of the British Government dated 16 October, I am instructed to inform you that the Soviet Government is unable to agree with a number of the statements contained in that memorandum.
>
> Thus for example, it is stated in the memorandum that when the work of the Tripartite Commission began, the British representatives knew nothing of the existence of the eleven submarines seized by the

Soviet Forces in Danzig. These uncompleted submarines were, however, shown in the list of German naval vessels seized by the Soviet Forces, which was handed to his British and American colleagues by the Soviet representative on the Tripartite Commission.

True, the Soviet Representative on the Tripartite Commission was unable, for technical reasons, to notify at the time the British and American representatives on the Tripartite Commission that the hulls of these eleven submarines had been transferred from Danzig to Soviet ports.

It is pertinent here to point out that in the preliminary lists of German vessels the British representatives gave no information at all about the uncompleted submarines under the control of the British authorities. In addition, the British representatives on the Tripartite Commission supplied no information at the time about the new type of German submarine, Series XVII, with turbine, which, as it proved, was under the control of the British authorities.[6]

Gousev then concluded on an unexpectedly conciliatory note, by saying: 'As, however, the Tripartite Commission's work, which in general has proceeded satisfactorily, is now completed, the Soviet Government feel there is no need to continue discussing the unsatisfactory features of the Commission's work.'[6]

The Foreign Office similarly concluded that it was time to close the debate, although the Admiralty nevertheless produced a defensive internal response to the Foreign Office on 19 December, perchance it might be required at some future date, which concluded that: 'In spite of the fact that we can give solid answers to Mr Gousev's assertions, we would on the whole prefer to let the correspondence drop, unless you have strong views to the contrary.'[6]

In the end, the situation cooled, and the social relationships between the admirals reflected well on each of them. However, there were obviously some sticky moments during the TNC debates. The different national attitudes towards the difficult task confronting them, the very different personalities of the admirals themselves as well as their views about each other and their respective nations clearly had a direct impact on both the conduct of business and the decisions of the Commission.

The 27th Meeting of the TNC took place on 6 December when the Report of the Commission was presented for signature. As recorded in the Minutes: 'The Report was signed by the six representatives of the Commission [and] after mutual expressions of esteem, the Commission adjourned.'[3] The TNC's Final Report dealt with all the 2,000 or so

German naval vessels, and comprised five parts, of which three specifically related to the U-boats. These were Section A: 'Report of Proceedings of the Tripartite Naval Commission', Section B: 'Recommendations of the Tripartite Naval Commission', and Section E, which contained three Appendices listing the allocated U-boats (Appendix 1), the unallocated U-boats (Appendix 2) and the scuttled U-boats (Appendix 3).

The key U-boat-related recommendations in the TNC Report's Section B were:

1. Specified ships and craft of the German surface navy and submarine fleet be allocated in accordance with Appendix 1.
2. German naval ships and craft not allocated be destroyed in accordance with Appendix 2.[7]

The U-boat allocations, which were set out in Appendix 1, and which reflected the exchanges already agreed from the original (10 October) list, were:

UK: *U-712, U-953, U-975, U-1108, U-1171, U-1407, U-2326, U-2348, U-2518* and *U-3017*

USA: *U-234, U-530, U-858, U-873, U-889, U-977, U-1105, U-1406, U-2513* and *U-3008*

USSR: *U-1057, U-1058, U-1064, U-1231, U-1305, U-2353, U-2529, U-3035, U-3041* and *U-3515*

Appendix 2 was much more comprehensive, and began with a series of recommendations, including:

Submarines under construction on slips shall be destroyed or scrapped for metal. This destruction or scrapping shall be completed by 15 May 1946.

All unallocated submarines which are afloat shall be sunk in the open sea in a depth of not less than one hundred meters by 15 February 1946.

Ships and craft [including submarines] sunk in shallow water, not in obstruction of normal shipping, shall be destroyed in such a manner that the possibility of salvage and partial or full use for naval purposes is precluded. This destruction, shall be completed by 15 May 1946.[7]

The Appendix then listed the U-boats which fell under each of the headings and, predictably, it was very different to the TNC's original Agreed List, the 25 August version of which had comprised just 176 U-boats. In contrast, even without the 30 U-boats which had been allocated to the Allies, the Final Report's Appendix 2 now listed a total of 452 U-boats, comprising:

Unallocated Submarines Afloat	173
Submarines Under Construction in British Zone	54
Submarines Scuttled in Shallow Water	225[7]

As far as the 'submarines under construction' were concerned, no details were provided in relation to any in the Soviet-controlled ports in the Baltic. However, a later statement from the USN's CNO to the US Joint Chiefs of Staff on 12 December 1945 said: 'It has been ascertained that there are located within the Bremen Enclave approximately 135 submarine sections, 16 uncompleted submarines on launching ways and two submarines afloat.'[8]

The large number of submarines defined as 'scuttled in shallow water' is primarily a reflection of the mass scuttling of U-boats that had taken place under the auspices of Operation 'Regenbogen' in early May 1945. Their discovery, plus additional intelligence information concerning the U-boats remaining in France, Portugal and Romania was the cause of the TNC's interest in their ultimate disposal. Indeed, so many U-boats had been discovered during the TNC inspections as well as during the British and American harbour clearance activities that the TNC's decision to extend its ToRs to include recommendations for the disposal of such U-boats was fully justified. The locations of the scuttled U-boats were said to be:

US Zone:	15	USSR Zone:	2	UK Zone:	199
France:	4	Portugal:	2	Romania:	2
Denmark:	1[7]				

Even after the TNC's final report was signed and issued, there was still one change to the TNC's proposed allocations, with the formerly unallocated *U-190* which had surrendered in Canada being allocated to the UK, and *U-975* which had been allocated to the UK, being added to the list of the unallocated U-boats. The basis for this change was a follow-up to the request made in November by Admiral Miles in relation to *U-190* and *U-889*. At that time, both Admiral Ghormley and Admiral Levchenko had said that they would have no objection to the UK retaining *U-190*, but the formal change was not implemented until the end of January 1946. Thus, after this last-minute amendment, the final list of the ten U-boats which were allocated to the UK comprised: *U-190, U-712, U-953, U-1108, U-1171, U-1407, U-2326, U-2348, U-2518* and *U-3017*

After the production of the TNC's final report, the Allies (or at least the British and Americans) took steps to implement the recommendations.

Ten U-boats were handed over to each of the RN, the USN and the Soviet Navy, the RN sunk 116 afloat but unallocated U-boats in Operation 'Deadlight', and the USN sank two off the east coast of the USA as well as two decommissioned U-boats in the north of the River Elbe estuary in Germany. Out of its allocation of ten U-boats, the UK then transferred two on long-term loan to France and one to Canada, giving rise to the false rumours that France and Canada had been allocated these U-boats by the TNC.

Of the seven U-boats which were listed in the TNC report after their surrender in the Far East in August 1945 whilst flying the Japanese flag, four were sunk on time by the RN, whilst the other three which were located in Japan were sunk by the USN in April 1946 after the USA had successfully persuaded the TNC that they were outside the TNC's responsibility and thus its recommendations.

It had always been clear that the TNC had no formal rights of direction over any countries other than the Allies, so there was some concern as to the possible fates of those U-boats which remained in French and Norwegian ports, and which were either damaged beyond repair or which had been afloat but unfit to be moved to the UK together with the bulk of the seaworthy U-boats in May, June and July 1945.

In the event, France scrapped the four U-boats which were listed in the TNC Report as scuttled in shallow water, but retained the one that was afloat but unseaworthy. Similarly, the Norwegians scrapped thirteen of the U-boats recorded by the TNC as being in Norwegian ports in various states of repair, whilst retaining and repairing four of the seven afloat but unseaworthy U-boats that had surrendered in Norway. This, again, gave rise to the subsequent false rumours that France and Norway had been allocated these U-boats by the TNC.

For practical reasons, as well as adhering to the TNC recommendations, there was a great deal of harbour clearance activity in and around the German ports and shipyards in the second half of 1945 and early 1946. This had been initiated by the British Naval Commander-in-Chief Germany on 31 October 1945 in a message to Flag Officer Schleswig-Holstein and Flag Officer West Germany saying:

The following disposal policy for all U-Boats remaining in the British Zone is to be adopted:

1. Hulls which are afloat are to be sunk and demolished by explosives as early as convenient and in any case before 1 February 1946
2. Hulls on building slips are to be reduced to scrap. In cases where reduction to scrap cannot be undertaken before 1 February these

hulls are to be wrecked by explosives or any other convenient method as a preliminary to scrapping at a later date

3. All hull sections should be reduced to scrap as convenient
4. No attempt should be made to remove machinery or other equipment from hulls prior to destruction as no requirement other than scrap exists for this material
5. Disposal of Type XVII U-Boats should be delayed.[1]

Similarly, the USN authorities made it clear that the former German U-boats, U-boat sections and uncompleted U-boats in the US Bremen Enclave were to be destroyed in accordance with the recommendations of the TNC.

There was also a considerable amount of confusion as the UK and US salvage crews sunk and demolished the U-boats which they found. Many could neither be identified individually nor aligned to the U-boat numbers listed in the TNC's Final Report. Nevertheless, a report from the British Army of the Rhine (BAOR) in February 1946 recorded that 204 U-boats, including those in the Bremen Enclave, had been destroyed:

Kiel	62 demolished
Wilhelmshaven	26 demolished, 1 not located
Travemünde	35 demolished, 1 sunk
Flensburger Fjord	63 demolished, 7 not located
Eckernförde	5 demolished, 1 not located
Bremen (US)	12 demolished or sunk.[9]

The TNC's previously secret recommendations in relation to the U-boats which had surrendered were approved by the Allies in January 1946 when they announced as recorded in the London *Times* on 23 January 1946 that:

The following Anglo-Soviet-American statement was issued last night [22 January] in London:

It was decided at the Berlin conference that operable service units of the German fleet, including units which could be made operable within a specified time, together with 30 U-Boats should be divided equally between the three Powers, and that the remainder of the German fleet should be destroyed.

A tripartite naval commission was accordingly appointed to make recommendations to implement this decision, and it has recently reported to the Governments of the three Powers. Its report is now under consideration by these Governments, and its recommendations on the allocation of the main units have been accepted, and their division between the three Powers is now being made.

Surplus U-Boats in United Kingdom ports have been sunk in accordance with this agreement.[5]

This was followed by an internal Admiralty memo on 5 March 1946 saying:

Moscow and Washington have been informed through diplomatic channels that all unallocated U-Boats afloat in British controlled ports were sunk by 15 February. No report of sinkings by [the] Russians [in respect of the 11 U-boats captured in Danzig which had been listed in the TNC report] has yet been received.[9]

In similar vein, the Americans had advised the Senior Russian Representative on the TNC in February and March 1946 that they too had sunk the remaining unallocated U-boats in US custody.[1]

There was, however, no similar Russian response, and the British and Americans were not prepared to allow this omission to remain unresolved. As a result diplomatic pressure continued throughout 1946 and 1947 with the aim of encouraging the Russians to confirm that they had completed the actions recommended by the TNC. Eventually, in answer to a question in the UK House of Commons on 5 November 1947, the Parliamentary Secretary to the Admiralty was able to report that: 'An intimation has been received from the Soviet Government that they have fulfilled their obligations to destroy units of the German Fleet.'[10] Thus, 21 months after the Russians, in accordance with their agreement in Berlin, should have destroyed the eleven unfinished U-boats which they had captured in Danzig in March 1945, they finally confirmed that the necessary action had taken place. The British and Americans had completed their actions by the February 1946 target date, but the Russians clearly wished to milk every advantage, especially from the eight Type XXI U-boats, and they were not prepared to discard them until they had gained the maximum possible knowledge about their construction and technical features.

It is therefore fair to record that, as far as the U-boats were concerned, with the exception of those that remained in Norwegian and French ports and which had been unilaterally taken over by the Norwegian and French Navies, all the TNC's recommendations about their allocation and destruction were finally met.

As for the TNC itself, whilst the Commission as originally constituted had adjourned at the end of its 27th Meeting on 6 December 1945 and whilst the three Senior National Representatives had moved on to other naval duties, it continued to exist for three more years in skeleton form. Its business during this time was primarily concerned with tying up the loose ends concerning the many surface vessels which were allocated to each of the Allies. This was achieved by the TNC adopting a process of producing agreed Supplements to the Final Report (called 'The Red Book') which, though not suggesting that the Red Book itself should be formally amended, were sufficient for all three delegations to agree and register the necessary amendments.

The TNC's First Supplement was issued on 23 March 1946 and contained a list of 366 amendments, the Second Supplement was issued on 31 May 1946 and contained 102 amendments, and the Third Supplement was issued on 28 June 1947 and also contained 102 amendments. One of the recommendations of the Summary Report attached to the Third Supplement was that the TNC should finally be dissolved, but although this was supported by the Americans, the Russians remained determined to squeeze every last drop of advantage from the decisions of 1945. Thus the TNC continued to exist in skeleton form until after the issue of the Fourth Supplement on 20 April 1948. The December 1945 version of the TNC's Final Report was itself never formally amended and re-issued, so to obtain a complete picture of the activities of the TNC between 1945 and 1948, the Final Report's recommendations need to be taken together with its four formal Supplements, albeit that none of the latter concerned the U-boats.

Finally, having worked together on the TNC between August and December 1945, it is interesting to note the views of Admirals Miles and Ghormley about their Russian colleague Admiral Levchenko whilst dealing with the task of dividing-up the remaining vessels of the German Navy, including the U-boats. Miles' views are taken from his Final Report of 8 November 1945, and Ghormley's views were recorded in a series of personal letters that he wrote to a variety of USN colleagues between August and October 1945.

Ghormley's assessment comprises a series of short statements which succinctly convey his thoughts about the Russians (and also the British):

17 Aug 45:   It is a tough job working with the Russians on account of differences in language and perspective.

22 Aug 45:   We are making progress on the Tripartite Naval Commission. At first the Russians were suspicious, iron-bound by directives from their government, and I think a little ignorant too. We have succeeded in thawing them out, so we are making progress.

4 Sep 45: It is a difficult job as we are dealing with both the British and the Russians, and I feel it may take longer than one would expect at first glance.

14 Sep 45: We are making headway, but that is not as fast as we would like as we are dealing not only with the British, but the Russians and language difficulties enter into the problem as well as differences in points of view.

19 Sep 45: The Russians, of course, want everything they can get their hands on. The Russian Admiral, Levchenko, wants everything classified in the Navy so that when he gets it, the Russian merchant marine cannot take it away from him. The Russians do not trust the English nor the English trust the Russians, so we are sitting in an advantageous spot for I think we have the confidence of both sides.

7 Oct 45: The Russians want everything they can get. The British are not going to let them have any floating equipment if they can help it. We will probably reach a deadlock on that question.[11]

In contrast, Miles' comments about his Russian colleague were rather more comprehensive. They included the statements that:

Admiral Levchenko is a typical product of the Soviet Regime. Disguised as an Admiral, he waves the Party Flag. He has all the shrewd cunning of the Russian and the poker-face of the Oriental. But he is not as bad as he has been painted, provided one is prepared to pay him back in his own coin. We crossed swords on many occasions, and it required great patience to withstand his persistence in pursuing his point far past any logical argument. But when he lost, he did so with a wry smile and his enjoyment of the wrangle was little less than if he had won. His guile was delightful. He enjoys a joke, and has a good sense of humour. It is difficult to say whether his feelings lean more towards the Americans or us, but I am quite sure he likes us and respects us for our honesty and fair-dealing, however crooked a deal he may try himself to put over.

Although both the Russian and American Senior Representatives paid nice complements regarding the work of the British Navy in the war, I might as well have talked to a brick wall. Sentiment has no appeal to the Russian mind when it comes to realities, which in this case was to lay their hands on as much as possible of the more valuable part of the swag.

When I was battling to get the division of the Fleet done my way, the letter from Mr Molotov, accusing me of being an obstructionist, was received. I feel sure now that this was merely part of a Russian offensive caused by the breakdown of the Foreign Ministers' Conference in London and was not a personal attack on me by Levchenko. Although we had argued and quarrelled a good deal ... I am sure that Levchenko enjoyed these sparring matches and, if anything, respected me more for standing up to him. Anyhow, after my return from my short visit to London, he showed more signs of friendship and of enjoying our arguments than he did before the letter was sent.[12]

CHAPTER 11

U-Boats in the UK

THE LOCATION IN THE UK of almost all the U-boats that had surrendered in the Eastern Atlantic area (including the North Sea and the Baltic) at sea and in ports meant that the RN was able to initiate inspections and trials of several of the U-boats well before anyone else had any opportunity to do so. Much of this activity even took place before the TNC had allocated the ten U-boats which were to be retained by the UK for technical assessment and experimental purposes despite the RN already possessing intelligence about the various U-boat types operated by and being developed for the Kriegsmarine.

There were two separate strands of action. One primarily involving publicity tours as well as the unloading of cargo from several U-boats that had been transporting strategic materials to and from Japan, and the other involving the study of the technical aspects of the various U-boat types.

In respect of the former, three of the U-boats which had surrendered at sea in the South-West Approaches had been escorted into Portland, near Weymouth in Dorset. They were *U-249*, *U-776* and *U-1023*, but instead of being immediately transferred to either Loch Ryan or Lisahally to await decisions about their future all three were first used by the RN. *U-249* was temporarily retained to undertake some urgent unplanned signals trials whilst *U-776* and *U-1023* were despatched on extended publicity tours of UK ports.

On 18 May the Admiralty instructed Flag Officer Portland to retain *U-249* to carry out special GSR (German Search Receiver) trials in conjunction with the Admiralty Signals Establishment. The reason for this was that the U-boat was fitted with an experimental radar warning receiver, the 'FuMB 35 – Athos', which had been installed for front-line testing and *U-249* was the only operational U-boat equipped with the device. Its electronics were much more sophisticated than earlier versions with the output being displayed on a cathode ray tube.

As a result, *U-249* (Pennant Number N.86) remained at Portland for three weeks. It was taken to sea for handling trials on 24 May but whilst these were completed satisfactorily except for some engine defects, it was considered inadvisable to attempt to dive the U-boat. Three GSR trials were then conducted whilst the U-boat, manned by a mixed British and German crew, was on the surface off Weymouth Bay. The first took place on 24 May in conjunction with the corvette HMS *Dianthus*, the second on 25 May in conjunction with the motor torpedo boat *MTB 795* and the third on 27 May in conjunction with an RAF Wellington bomber.

The trials with *U-249* were described in a report written by the Admiralty Signal Establishment in July 1945 the conclusions of which stated:

> The 'Athos' is capable of picking 3cm and 9cm radar signals at distances at least twice the radar range and this gives the U-boat a very valuable warning.
>
> The 'Athos' is not an accurate D/F instrument, yet it gives in most cases a fair indication of the sector of signal incidence within an arc of 60 and 120 degrees at 9 and cm respectively for average conditions.
>
> A valuable feature of the instrument is its ability of keeping an all-round watch on both bands simultaneously.
>
> The apparatus is small in size, light in weight, and suitable for use in submarines.[1]

After the completion of these trials on 29 May the RN's Admiral (Submarines) confirmed that *U-249* was no longer required for further investigations and proposed that it should proceed to Loch Ryan for laying-up. The U-boat, escorted by HMS *Loch Shin*, sailed from Portland on 3 June for Loch Ryan where it arrived on 5 June.

Whilst the trials with *U-249* were underway, the other two U-boats which had arrived at Portland after surrendering at sea had departed in the latter half of May, crewed by RN sailors, on two long public exhibition tours, one of the east coast UK ports and the other of the west coast UK ports to raise money for the King George V's Fund for Sailors.

U-776 (Pennant Number N.65) left Portland on 21 May for a 10-day visit to London and then visited numerous ports in the south and east of the UK during a tour that lasted 60 days. Towns visited included Southampton, Yarmouth, Hull and Newcastle on the south and east coasts of England, Edinburgh and Aberdeen in Scotland, and Lerwick in the Shetland Islands before arriving in Loch Ryan on 22 August.

There was a somewhat embarrassing incident shortly after *U-776*'s arrival on 22 May at London's Westminster Pier near the Houses of

Parliament when as recorded in Admiral (Submarines)'s War Diary it 'fell over' in the Thames' mud at an angle of 45 degrees at low tide. However, this is not quite how the incident was recorded in the Report of Proceedings (ROP) submitted by *U-776*'s RN CO on 20 August who carefully described it using slightly different words, viz:

> At 1925 the same evening conditions at Westminster Pier were found to be not wholly suitable for *U-776*, and the vessel was therefore moved to a buoy near London Bridge as soon as such an operation became practicable.
>
> On the following day *U-776* returned to Westminster pier for a prudent period and a number of distinguished visitors came on board, including Admiral of the Fleet Sir Andrew Cunningham, Field Marshal Sir Alan Brooke and Mr A V Alexander, the First Lord of the Admiralty. On completion of these visits, *U-776* returned to her buoy.[2]

U-776 was then moved to a berth in the London Docks where it was open for inspection between 1000 and 1900 daily until it departed London on 6 June for the reminder of its tour.

Similarly another RN crew took *U-1023* (Pennant Number N.83) on an 80-day tour of sixteen ports in the south-west and west of the UK. The officers and ratings who were to form the crew of *U-1023* had arrived in Portland on 18 May and at once set to work to clean the U-boat and to learn how to operate it and as recorded in the CO's ROP dated 13 August discovered that:

> The interior of the submarine was in a filthy condition, and all machinery showed evidence of extreme lack of attention and maintenance. The port engine was in a bad state with one burnt exhaust box, and much work had to be undertaken to put it in reasonable order.
>
> The submarine was taken to sea for engine trials in Weymouth Bay on 24 May, with a few of her German crew on board. These passed off satisfactorily except for the engine defects.
>
> It was considered inadvisable to attempt to dive the submarine.[3]

U-1023's tour started with its departure from Portland on 25 May, and after arriving at Plymouth on the same day, included visits to Bristol, Cardiff, Liverpool, Manchester, Belfast, Glasgow, and Oban on the west coast of Scotland, before ending in Loch Ryan on 14 August. After the tours had been completed and the two U-boats were safely moored in Loch Ryan the Admiralty issued a Press Release on 25 September under the heading 'King George V Fund for Sailors Collects £9,379 from National Tour of U-Boats' saying:

The Royal Navy arranged for the captured U-boats *U-776* and *U-1023* to visit 35 ports and cities in Great Britain. This tour commenced on 23 May and finished on 23 August. During this time over 700,000 people saw the U-boats, whilst nearly 40,000 passed through them. Subscriptions to the King George V Fund for sailors amounted to over £9,000.

Naturally enough London headed the list of visitors and subscriptions, but there was generally an enthusiastic response in all the provincial cities and in the ports all over the country.[3]

This was complemented by a letter from the Chairman of the General Council of the King George's Fund to the Secretary to the Admiralty in which he said:

The General Council of King George's Fund for Sailors would be grateful if the Commanding Officers of *U-1023* and *U-776* could be informed how very much the Council appreciate all the hard work and discomfort which their cruise round the ports have entailed.

They would be glad if their thanks could be conveyed to the officers and ratings who took part in the cruises and who helped so considerably in the most successful collection of £9,309 for the Fund.

The Council wish you to convey their sincere thanks to the Board of Admiralty for organising the cruises and allowing collections to be taken for the Fund.[3]

Amongst the U-boats which had surrendered and were then being held in the UK there were four blockade runners, two of which had just returned from Japan (*U-532* and *U-861*) and two of which had been scheduled to transport freight from Germany to Japan (*U-874* and *U-875*) but their original missions had been cancelled before they were able to depart. Whilst their internal freight had been unloaded before the latter two U-boats departed on their final operational patrols, their keels were still loaded with materials that had been destined for delivery to Japan.

The first such U-boat was *U-532* which had surrendered at sea on 10 May and arrived at Loch Eriboll on 13 May at the end of its return trip from the Far East. It was then taken via Loch Alsh, where its torpedoes and many of the crew were removed, to Liverpool on 17 May for its cargo to be unloaded. This was reported in an article in *The Times* on 18 May under the heading 'Cargo U-Boat: 110 Tons of Pure Tin as False Keel' which said:

The cargo-carrying U-boat *U-532* arrived at Liverpool yesterday and was taken into the Gladstone Dock. The German crew remained on board and handled the hawsers during the process of docking. The 110 tons of pure tin, it is understood, is carried in the keel. The remainder of the cargo, rubber, wolfram, molybdenum and quinine is carried inboard. The arrival of *U-532* was watched, among others, by Rear Admiral J W Dorling and Mr Hodge, Secretary of the Mersey Docks and Harbour Board.[4]

Whilst in Liverpool the U-boat was inspected by Admiral Sir Max Horton amid considerable publicity, giving rise to the erroneous story that it had surrendered there. It did not prove possible to remove all the U-boat's cargo in Liverpool, especially the tin that was stored in the keel, so *U-532* was transferred to Barrow-in-Furness on 25 May for completion of the unloading. The transit to Barrow was made with its mixed German and Royal Navy crew, with its arrival being recorded on 26 May in an article in *The Barrow News* under the headline 'Nazi Submarine Comes to Barrow' viz:

> In the Graving Dock at Barrow lies the *U-532*. There was no demonstration, just a little anxiety as the big submarine came up Walney Channel on Friday. She had come from Liverpool with a German crew aboard guarded by a British naval party. Opposite the docks she was taken in tow by a tug while another steamed ahead.
>
> At the entrance to the Graving Dock the tugs left the U-boat and she moved in under her own power. A gangway was slung aboard, and dockers went onto the U-boat and squared her into position preparatory to the dock being emptied of water. It is stated that the submarine has been brought to Barrow to have 'certain work' carried out. Rusted and pitted with all distinguishing marks removed, the submarine looks as if she was in need of several coats of paint.[5]

The unloading of the remaining cargo took place in the dry dock in the Vickers Shipyard but that too created its own story when one of the bureaucrats from HM Customs and Excise attempted to invoke the Admiralty's 'Prize Regulations' and issued a Seizure Notice in respect of *U-532*'s cargo together with the complaint that: 'There were no Bills of Lading or other shipping documents in respect of these goods.'[6] What did he expect when there was a war on? Whilst in Barrow, *U-532* was open for public inspection on 2 and 3 June when some 7,500 local people paid a token admission fee for the opportunity to visit the U-boat before it was moved to Loch Ryan.

The second such U-boat was *U-861* which had surrendered in Trondheim on 9 May having returned from the Far East with war materials for Germany. It was moved to Lisahally, arriving there on 2 June, but it was still carrying its cargo which included wolfram, iodine crystals, tin and rubber, much of which was stored in its keel. This cargo needed to be removed and on 10 June *U-861* was transferred to Milford Haven in south-west Wales by a mainly British crew but also with twenty Germans on board where it was put into the dry dock at the RN's Pembroke Dockyard on 11 June. Fifty-five tons of tin and 52 tons of wolfram were removed from its keel and 36 tons of rubber was removed from the main ballast tanks together with 140lbs of iodine crystals all of which were handed over to the Ministry of Supply. The U-boat was then made available for public viewing after a RN Press Release was published in *The Western Telegraph* saying: 'The public will be admitted to the Dockyard from Friday 15 June to Wednesday 20 June inclusive. Visiting hours will extend from 2 pm to 7 pm. Identity cards will be inspected at the gate.'[7] After a VIP visit from local dignitaries on 21 June organised by the Flag Officer Milford Haven the de-stored *U-861* returned to Lisahally.

The other two cargo-carrying U-boats were *U-874* and *U-875* which were scheduled to transport war materials to Japan before being withdrawn from their blockade-running role late in the war. *U-874* had surrendered in Horten on 9 May and been moved to Lisahally where it arrived on 30 May, and *U-875* had surrendered in Bergen on 9 May and been moved to Lisahally where it arrived on 6 June. Although their planned voyages to Japan had been cancelled it was soon realised that both these U-boats were still carrying cargo in their keels and they were therefore transferred to Birkenhead, near Liverpool for this to be removed.

U-875 was the first to move, leaving Lisahally on 25 August with a joint RN and German crew and then spending three weeks in a dry dock in Birkenhead where its keel cargo of optical lenses, mercury and iron was unloaded before it returned to Lisahally on 12 September. This visit was recorded in the *Birkenhead News* on 8 September under the headline 'Failed to Deliver the Goods – U-Boat's Interrupted Voyage – Jap Cargo Comes to Birkenhead' saying:

> The *U-875*, grey-painted and rusty, is today lying in a dry-dock in Birkenhead. Two weeks ago the *U-875* at the dock of Messers Grayson, Rollo and Clover in Birkenhead. Only sixteen of her original crew remain on board, together with a number of technical personnel of the Royal Navy, and work has proceeded in discharging the valuable cargo from the submarine's holds.[8]

It was followed by *U-874* on 19 September, again with a mixed RN and German crew, which was also docked in Birkenhead and from which optical lenses, mercury and zinc were unloaded. This time a delayed *Birkenhead News* report, published on 29 September under the headline 'Another Sea-Wolf at Birkenhead – Second U-Boat with Valuable Cargo', recorded that:

> The *U-874*, a sister ship to the *U-875*, which came to Birkenhead some weeks ago, has arrived at Messers Grayson, Rollo and Clover's shipyard. A 750-ton sea-going vessel, she was captured with a valuable cargo of optical lenses, mercury and zinc. She carried the cargo in three false keels, one centre and two wing. The optical lenses were packed in metal-bound wooden boxes, and the mercury in iron bottles. A notable point of the keel cargo space is that it is not waterproof and when the cargo was unloaded at the shipyard the iron bottles were rusted and the wooden boxes were covered in slime.
>
> The German crew now aboard number 18, and are under the command of Ober Leutnant Engineer Ulmer. They are under the supervision of officers and men of the Royal Navy, but they still wear Nazi decorations and Iron Crosses. The *U-874* will remain in the shipyard for about nine days.[9]

U-874 returned to Lisahally on 22 October.

The second strand of action concerning the RN's involvement with the U-boats held in the UK related to the plans to use of some of them in early formal technical trials. These began with a meeting held in London on 25 June chaired by Flag Officer Submarines, Admiral Creasy, to discuss 'Trials to be carried out in, and with, U-Boats' and the Minutes of the meeting record that:

> Rear Admiral Creasy emphasised that, in considering what trials could be carried out with the U-Boats, two things must be taken into consideration:
>
> 1. That the Admiralty was acting as caretaker on behalf of the United Nations and that, therefore, the greatest care would have to be taken during trials that no damage was caused to the U-Boats.
> 2. That owing to the manpower situation only a very limited number could be manned for trials … He had been able to earmark four complete British submarine crews to man U-Boats for trials, one Type XXI, one Type XXIII and two Type VIICs (one rubber covered).[10]

To illustrate the scale of the RN involvement in the U-boat activities in Loch Ryan and Lisahally, the minutes of the meeting also recorded that: 'At the moment there were between 400 and 500 officers and men employed in looking after and maintaining the U-Boats.'[10]

Following his meeting on 25 June Admiral Creasy wasted no time in making the preparatory arrangements for the proposed trials with two Type VIIC, one Type XXI and one Type XXIII U-boats. Whilst none of these U-boats were formally commissioned into the RN even though they had RN COs and crews, they were with one exception (*U-2502*) each allocated an N-series Pennant Number for administrative purposes. The Type VIICs, the rubber-covered *U-1105* (N.16) and the standard *U-1107* (N.19), arrived in Holy Loch from Lisahally on 29 June and the Type XXI *U-2502* and the Type XXIII *U-2326* (N.35) joined them on 6 July.

Admiral (Submarines) in a letter dated 12 July then formally proposed to the Admiralty that the RN should conduct First of Class trials on *U-2502* and *U-2326*. It was expected that the trials with *U-2326* could start quickly but *U-2502* needed to be docked and inspected before its trials could commence. The Navy Board approved the proposed programme of trials and as time was limited it agreed that they should take place in and around the south-west of Scotland – hence the transfer to Holy Loch. Unfortunately the trials with both the Type XXI and the Type XXIII U-boats proved to be very disappointing.

The trials with the Type XXIII *U-2326* showed that the U-boat suffered from engine and schnorkel defects. It did not complete its first dive until late July and the First of Class trials which took place between 27 and 31 August revealed that its speed was less than anticipated. Also, there was a lack of on-board accommodation, and it suffered from poor sea-keeping qualities. Thus, once this and other trials had been completed Admiral Creasy returned *U-2326* to care and maintenance status at Lisahally where it arrived on 15 October.

The Royal Navy's experience with the Type XXI *U-2502* turned out to be even worse. The U-boat suffered from a whole series of defects which required it to be docked in the Cammell Laird Shipyard in Birkenhead before the trials could begin. *U-2502* arrived there on 22 July prior to docking and inspection but on 23 July its starboard main motor's insulation caught fire, and the starboard auxiliary motor overheated. The result was that *U-2502* would have needed 4 to 6 weeks in dry dock to repair the defects as well as it being a complicated and expensive process which would have involved cutting out a section of the hull. The proposed trials with *U-2502* were therefore cancelled on 28 July and the U-boat was returned to Lisahally on 2 August. *U-3017* (N.41) was selected for the Type XXI's First of Class trial instead.

U-3017 was in little better state than *U-2502* and after leaving Lisahally on 8 August for docking and inspection in the Vickers Shipyard at Barrow there was a battery explosion during hydrogen content trials on 29 August. This incident injured eight members of the crew and caused considerable damage, including severe fuel leaks and numerous other defects, all of which combined to put the U-boat out of commission, as well as causing Admiral Creasy, in his report to the Admiralty on 7 September, to say: 'It is therefore submitted for very early consideration that all trials with the Type XXI U-Boats be cancelled.'[11]

In the same report and although the UK was about to be allocated ten U-boats by the TNC the Admiral clarified the RN's longer-term interest in the U-boats saying:

If the above proposals [to complete outstanding trials on *U-2326* and then pay it off, and to cancel all trials with the Type XXI U-boats] are approved, Admiral (Submarines) will only require five U-Boats for trials, viz:

Type XVIIB	Type VIIC	Type XXIII
U-1407	*U-1105*	*U-2326*
	U-1171	1 spare[11]

Following the formal RN Board of Inquiry (BoI) into the battery explosion on *U-3017* and the discovery of what he considered to be fundamental design faults Admiral Creasy stated on 4 October that:

It is now apparent that, before *U-3017* or any other Type XXI U-Boat could be considered suitable for trials of a prolonged nature such as First of Type trials, a complete and extensive refit and survey would be necessary. This is not so in the case of *U-2326*, the Type XXIII U-Boat which has completed First of Class trials, preceded by hydrogen content trials, nor in the case of the two Type VIIC U-Boats [*U-1105* and *U-1171*] now nearing completion of their trials. The necessity for this refit would, I consider, have been apparent early on in the proposed First of Class trials, even if the battery explosion had not taken place, in view of the number of defects which kept arising.[12]

Although it took some time for the Admiralty to approve Admiral Creasy's proposals, *U-3017* arrived back at Lisahally on 21 October. The Type XXI trials were therefore suspended as it seemed questionable whether these U-boats would be any faster than the Royal Navy's existing modified 'S' class submarines. The problem was exacerbated because the capacity of British shipyards to refit any Type XXI U-boats was limited and there was a higher priority requirement to work on British submarines which needed urgent refits.

It was nevertheless clear that the USN was intending to refit and carry out trials on at least one of the two Type XXI U-boats that had been transferred to the USA in August and it was therefore decided that the RN would rely on the USN's experience concerning their performance. Thus, the Admiralty accepted Admiral Creasy's recommendation that there should be no further trials with any Type XXI U-boats. Also, by that time, the TNC had made its initial decisions and of the ten remaining Type XXIs at Lisahally *U-2518* and *U-3017* had been allocated to the UK.

U-2518 and *U-3017* remained moored at Lisahally on a care and maintenance basis although it was acknowledged that both would require a substantial amount of work before they could be made ready for any future trials. There was however little prospect that this would occur nor was there any enthusiasm to do so.

As far as *U-2502* was concerned it had been returned to the moorings at Lisahally in a very poor condition after its breakdown and somewhat surprisingly in mid-October it was initially allocated to Russia despite its numerous defects and the fact that it had been cannibalised for spares. This quickly became obvious and on 1 November the Russians requested that it be exchanged for *U-3041* (another of the Type XXIs at Lisahally) a request that was agreed by the TNC on 14 November.

One of the consequences of the UK's decision to abandon trials with any of the Type XXIs and the US decision not to bid for a TNC allocation of any of the small Type XXIII U-boats was an informal agreement between the USN and the RN to exchange copies of any trial reports. Whilst the UK's trial report on the Type XXIII U-boat (*U-2326*) was provided to the US naval authorities in London in late 1945 the reciprocal arrangement in respect of the Type XXIs was not so easily achieved. This was because the USN needed to refit *U-2513* before any trials could begin in February 1946 and because *U-3008* did not become available to the USN until August 1946. Even the USN's formal Type XXI U-boat Design Study Report did not become available until July 1946.

In respect of *U-1105* there had been a certain amount of competition between the Allies, each of which wanted it for testing. This was because the U-boat's hull was covered with rubber sheeting. The Admiralty had known about this development since 1944 but was unsure as to its purpose although it was thought that it was to help avoid detection by either radar or sonar. There was very considerable interest in *U-1105* which had eventually been allocated to the USA. However, both the RN and RAF Coastal Command were keen to check the implications of the rubber coating and so *U-1105* was included in the RN's early testing programme together with the standard Type VIIC U-boat *U-1171*.

There was nothing special about *U-1171* other than that it was one of the newer of the Type VIIC U-boats in British hands and though it had been commissioned in March 1944 it had been used only for training rather than operational purposes. However, a standard Type VIIC was required to take part in the important comparison tests with *U-1105* before the latter departed for the USA.

The trials with these Type VIICs were conducted in several phases. The first phase was conducted in the sea area to the south-west and west of Scotland with the U-boats operating out of Holy Loch. After that trials were carried out with Coastal Command at Tobermory and Londonderry before the U-boats were returned to Holy Loch on 18 and 19 August for further trials. Thereafter both U-boats were moved to Gosport in the south of England on 2 October prior to a further set of tests. After all the noise and detection tests were complete and after spending Christmas in Holy Loch *U-1171* was returned to Lisahally on 3 February 1946 for decommissioning and storage pending its final disposal, whilst *U-1105* returned to the RN Submarine Base at Gosport where it was handed over to a USN crew in early December.

In late October after all the early U-boat-related activities had been completed by the RN the final TNC list of the ten U-boats allocated to the UK was formally published. It comprised *U-190, U-712, U-953, U-1108, U-1171, U-1407, U-2326, U-2348, U-2518* and *U-3017*. Eight of these U-boats were moored at Lisahally, one (*U-190*) was in Canada, and the remaining one (*U-1407*) was in the Vickers Shipyard at Barrow in the UK.

During the debates which led to the Potsdam Agreement, France had been keen to be allocated a share of the surrendered German submarines, but this was vetoed by the Russians. Thus, the TNC allocated no U-boats to France. Nevertheless the UK decided that it did not need all the

U-boats that it had been allocated and so the RN agreed that one of its Type XXIs and one of its Type XXIIIs could be loaned to France. The Type XXI was *U-2518*, and it was originally intended that the Type XXIII should be *U-2348*. However, on 11 January 1946 whilst it was being prepared for transfer at Lisahally there was a battery explosion on *U-2348* and the remaining Type XXIII *U-2326* was earmarked for the French instead. Notification that *U-2348* was no longer a candidate for the loan to France was made by the Admiralty on 23 January and the executive instruction for the transfer of the two U-boats was issued on 3 February, an action which took place between 5 and 13 February under the codename Operation 'Thankful'.

The remaining seven U-boats which had been allocated to the UK comprised four Type VIICs (*U-712*, *U-953*, *U-1108* and *U-1171*), one Type XVIIB (*U-1407*), one Type XXIII (*U-2348*) and one Type XXI (*U-3017*), six of which – the exception being the Type XVIIB 'Walter' U-boat – had been in the UK since late May and early June, and examples of each type had been subjected to the early trials all of which had been completed by the end of 1945. Thus, by Spring 1946 the status of the five U-boats which Admiral (Submarines) had specifically requested in September 1945 was as follows:

U-1407 had been commissioned into the RN (eventually to become HMS *Meteorite*)

U-1105 had been transferred to the USA after its RN trials

U-1171 had been returned to Lisahally on 3 February 1946 after its RN trials

U-2326 had been loaned to the French Navy in February 1946 after its RN trials

U-2348 (the 'spare' Type XXIII) remained moored at Lisahally

So, other than *U-1407* which had been allocated Pennant Number N.25 on 25 September 1945 and once *U-1171* had returned to Lisahally on 3 February 1946, none of the six U-boats that remained in the UK (*U-716*, *U-953*, *U-1108*, *U-1171*, *U-2348* and *U-3017*) were required by the RN. This was confirmed on 2 January 1946 in a Foreign Office file minute which when discussing the possibility of the provision of U-boats to France had said: 'We have apparently finished our trials with nine of the U-Boats allotted to us and intend shortly to sink most of them.'[13]

After the final three U-boats which remained at Loch Ryan on the completion of Operation 'Deadlight' (*U-712*, *U-953* and *U-2348*)

were transferred to Lisahally on 30 December 1945 Loch Ryan's role in relation to the U-boats came to an end. However, the same was not true of Lisahally. After the transfer of the ten U-boats to Russia, the completion of 'Deadlight' and the transfer of the two U-boats to France, six U-boats remained there.

Of these, *U-3017* had been earmarked for trials but had been returned to Lisahally after the on-board explosion in August 1945, *U-1171* had been used for trials between June 1945 and January 1946 before being returned to Lisahally, and *U-712*, *U-953*, *U-1108* and *U-2348* had neither been used by the RN nor was there any further interest in them for trial purposes. Thus, in February 1946 four of the six had been 'hulked' and only two were being maintained to keep the remainder afloat. Also, by then the reason for which the base at Lisahally had been set up in May 1945 had ended and it was paid off to care and maintenance on 19 July 1946.

In September 1946 the Admiralty announced that the six remaining U-boats had been allocated to the Ship Target Trials Committee for use as targets. However, even then they remained unused and tied up to the jetties at Lisahally until 1947 when the Admiralty decided to re-commission the base as a school for anti-submarine warfare training. There was therefore a need to remove the six U-boats from Lisahally and they were towed up the River Foyle for berthing at Londonderry. Despite this, no action was taken with them and they were never used for the planned ship target trials before being authorised for sale as scrap in early 1949.

In the case of *U-1407* the RN was very attracted by the possibility of HTP being an air-independent propulsion option. Thus, after arriving at the Vickers Yard in Barrow in a very poor condition in early September 1945, being allocated Pennant Number N.25 and being formally commissioned as HMS *Meteorite* on 26 August 1947, it was eventually refitted with a new HTP turbine engine constructed from parts which had been transferred from the 'Walterwerke' in late 1945. The HTP turbine needed further repairs and development, and this work was undertaken by Professor Hellmuth Walter and a small team of German engineers who were moved from Germany to Barrow to continue the work that they had started in Kiel.

The Admiralty's intention was that *U-1407* was to be used purely experimentally and that if the trials were successful a decision would be taken as to its future use as a possible high-speed anti-submarine target for training purposes. The refitting of the submarine was however a lengthy business which involved a complete overhaul, its re-equipment with new components brought from Germany, and other major changes to the original U-boat. These included the fitting of a new escape system, a complete change of the ventilation system, the replacement of all electrical equipment and the removal of the torpedo tubes.

The RN's trials of the much-modified *U-1407* (by now HMS *Meteorite*) did not begin until March 1948. Despite the lack of its HPT turbine plant at that stage the trials successfully tested both surface and submerged speeds, surface and submerged turning circles, and diving and change of depth performance, after which HMS *Meteorite* returned to Barrow to have its HPT turbine plant fitted, an action that was not completed until July 1948. Further surface trials then began the results of which were very promising. A speed of over 14 knots was achieved and the 'Walter' engine worked very well despite rough handling. The report on these trials concluded that:

> It is realised that the disadvantage of expense of an HTP submarine is undoubtedly large. But while it remains the only proven method of very high speed propulsion, it is considered that the disadvantage is outweighed by the speed/time factor. This speed would probably be used mainly for escaping after an attack. With its help big changes of direction and depth could rapidly be made whilst at the same time, large distances are being covered, thus increasing by enormous proportions the difficulties of an escort vessel.[14]

The main operational trials, surfaced and submerged, with HMS *Meteorite* took place in March and April 1949 and were summarised in a report from the CO to Captain (S/M), Third Submarine Flotilla dated 1 June 1949, viz:

> It was during these runs that the staggering manoeuvrability of HMS *Meteorite* at high speeds was discovered.
>
> It is considered that a small and fast submarine, even with the very high manoeuvrability of HMS *Meteorite* at 14 knots, would be a very hard target for an A/S ship to sink.
>
> It would have been extremely interesting to have been able to observe the manoeuvrability of HMS *Meteorite* if she had been refitted with the two [HPT] turbines as designed, thereby giving her a designed speed of 25 knots.[14]

Despite the changes to the submarine as well as the optimism concerning its propulsion system and the successful high-speed trials, HMS *Meteorite* was not popular with the RN crews who regarded it as a risky piece of machinery. Nevertheless, the trial results were sufficiently encouraging for the Admiralty to place an order for two larger British-built experimental HTP-powered submarines with the original intention – which was not pursued because of the advent of nuclear propulsion – of eventually ordering an operational fleet of up to twelve. In mid-1949, HMS *Meteorite* was taken out of service with the RN and an Admiralty notice dated 16 July 1949 recorded that: 'HMS *Meteorite* was paid-off on 8 July 1949.'[15]

The seven surplus U-boats which remained in British custody were then handed over to the British Iron and Steel Corporation for breaking up as scrap. Thus, in early 1949 the six U-boats moored at Londonderry as well as HMS *Meteorite* at Barrow were transferred to various UK shipbreaking yards for scrapping later that year or in early 1950:

U-712   Towed from Londonderry on 30 May 1949 by the tug *Guardsman*. Arrived at the Clayton and Davie yard at Dunston-on-Tyne, Newcastle on 4 June 1949 and broken up during 1949/1950

U-953   Arrived at the Thomas Ward yard at Hayle, Cornwall on 26 June 1949 and broken up during 1949/1950

U-1108   Arrived at the Thomas Ward yard at Briton Ferry, Glamorgan, S Wales on 12 May 1949 and broken up during 1949

U-1171   Towed from Londonderry on 9 June 1949 by the tug *Guardsman*. Arrived at the Thomas Young yard in Sunderland on 13 June 1949 and broken up during 1949/1950

U-1407   As HMS *Meteorite*, it was moved from the Vickers yard at Barrow to the Thomas Ward Ltd ship-breaking yard at Barrow on 7 September 1949 to be broken up.

U-2348   Allocated for scrapping to the John Lee and Co shipyard at Belfast (Larne) in April 1949

U-3017   Arrived at the J Cashmore and Co yard in Newport, S Wales on 25 October 1949 and broken up during 1949/1950

In relation to the scrapping of the Type VIICs *U-712* and *U-953*, most sources say that the U-boat scrapped at the Clayton and Davie Yard on the River Tyne was *U-953* and that the U-boat scrapped at Hayle in Cornwall by Thomas Ward Ltd was *U-712*. But new evidence shows that this was incorrect, viz:

The British Iron and Steel Corporation (BISCO) allocated *U-953* to Clayton and Davie at Dunston (as per the BISCO records), and the United Towing Co (UT) was contracted to tow *U-953* from Londonderry to the Tyne (as per the UT records).

The UT tug *Guardsman* left Londonderry with a U-boat in tow on 30 May 1949. The pair arrived in the River Tyne on 4 June 1949. However, it had no identification marks nor does any of the surviving Clayton and Davie paperwork indicate the U-boat's number.

The Tyne Improvement Commission's (TIC) archives for 1949 record the U-boat which arrived there on 4 June 1949 as being *U-192*. However, this was not possible as *U-192* had been sunk in the Atlantic in May 1943.

The U-boat contained several artifacts from the Type VIIC *U-1052*. But it could not have been *U-1052* as this U-boat was sunk in Operation 'Deadlight' in December 1945.

A slightly blurred photograph shows that the U-boat in the River Tyne had a modern schnorkel and a 'normal bow line'. *U-953* had neither of these features, having an old-style schnorkel installation with the outside fresh air tube along the conning tower, and an 'Atlantic bow'. Both the U-boat in the photograph and *U-712* had a 'normal bow line' and a modern schnorkel.

Between June and December 1945 all three U-boats (*U-712*, *U-953* and *U-1052*) had been moored in Loch Ryan. The U-boats at Loch Ryan were moored in groups – called Trots. Trot K.5 comprised *U-712*, *U-1052*, *U-1104*, *U-1163* and *U-1271*. Of these U-boats only *U-712* was retained and the other four were sunk in Operation 'Deadlight'.

U-1052 had been used as the K.5 Trot accommodation boat. This establishes that there was a direct link between *U-712* and *U-1052* in Loch Ryan and thus various artifacts could have been transferred to *U-712* (for possible later recovery). *U-953* was on a different Trot in Loch Ryan. So, whilst there is a link between *U-1052* and *U-712* there is no such link between *U-1052* and *U-953*.

As the U-boat in the River Tyne could not have been *U-953* because of its bow shape and schnorkel installation, because of the confusion in the TIC records, because of the lack of any identification details in the Clayton and Davie paperwork, and because of the previous association between *U-712* and *U-1052* in Loch Ryan, the U-boat in the Tyne in 1949 must have been *U-712*. The unmarked U-boat was obviously picked up in error from Londonderry by the United Towing Co's tug and delivered to the wrong ship-breaking yard. The corollary is that the U-boat scrapped at Hayle in Cornwall was *U-953*, not *U-712*.

The very last part of the story of the U-boats in the UK post-May 1945 was formally recorded (albeit well after the event) by an Admiralty announcement dated 15 December 1949: 'The following ships have been handed over to the British Iron and Steel Corporation for breaking up: *U-712*, *U-953*, *U-1108*, *U-1171*, *U-2348*, *U-3017* and [HMS] *Meteorite*.'[16]

Finally, some 50 years later another U-boat arrived in the UK. This was *U-534* which had been sunk in an air attack by an RAF Coastal Command Liberator in the Kattegat on 5 May 1945 whilst in transit from Denmark to Norway. It had been located by divers in 1986 and it was raised on 23 August 1993. It was first taken to Hirtshals in northern Denmark and then transported to Liverpool where it arrived on 30 May 1996. The original intention was to renovate *U-534* and display it in the Maritime Museum at Birkenhead. But this was not possible and instead the U-boat was cut into four separate sections and is now on public display at the Woodside Ferry Terminal at Birkenhead, near Liverpool.

CHAPTER 12

The Sinking of U-Boats in Operation 'Deadlight'

AFTER THE TNC HAD RECOMMENDED on 10 October 1945 which of the U-boats were to be allocated to the UK, the USA and the USSR, it was agreed at its meeting on 29 October that all the unallocated submarines still afloat were to be sunk in the open sea in a depth of not less than one hundred metres by no later than 15 February 1946 the intention being that they: 'Shall be destroyed in such a manner that the possibility of salvage and partial or full use for naval purposes is precluded.'[1]

Of the 156 U-boats that had surrendered at the end of the European war the Allies had each been allocated ten, one had been returned to Holland (*UD-5*), eight remained in Continental ports after they were found to be unseaworthy (one in France and seven in Norway), and two which had surrendered to the USN (*U-805* and *U-1228*) were due to be sunk off the west coast of the USA in early February 1946, leaving the remainder to be sunk in UK waters.

In October 1945 135 of these U-boats were moored in Loch Ryan and at Lisahally, all under the control of the RN but eight had been allocated to the UK, one to the USA and ten to the USSR, and they included *U-760* which had been interned in Spain since September 1943. This left 116 U-boats awaiting disposal and this led to the RN's Operation 'Deadlight' which covered their destruction between 27 November 1945 and 12 February 1946. It was the culmination of the UK's determination to ensure the elimination of the German Navy's submarine fleet after the end of the Second World War as agreed by the political decisions taken at Potsdam.

As these 116 remaining U-boats were to be sunk at sea it was decided that the disposal action should be initiated without delay. This was not only to meet the 15 February deadline but because the imminent onset of winter and its associated rough seas in the area to the west of Loch Ryan and to the north-west of Lisahally would make it a hazardous task.

Preparations for Operation 'Deadlight' were formally initiated immediately after the TNC meeting on 29 October. However, prior to that the RN's Flag Officer (Submarines) (FOS/M) sought advice from the Admiralty as to exactly where the sinkings would take place as well as producing an early outline of the arrangements that would be required.

On 18 October FOS/M had suggested that the U-boats should be sunk either to the north of Rathlin Island or to the west of Galloway. Both these areas were close to Loch Ryan and Lisahally and this would minimise the towing task. However, the Admiralty's response on 23 October had indicated that neither of these areas was suitable because of the presence of undersea telegraph cables and because both areas had been earmarked for fishing. It would therefore be necessary to sink the U-boats to the north-west of Ireland west of 10 degrees West.

FOS/M then submitted his preliminary proposals for the sinkings in a message to the Admiralty on 25 October. The latter included the statements that:

> The number of U-Boats to be scuttled will be 110 [sic], of which 24 are at Lisahally and 86 at Loch Ryan.
>
> The British crews are only sufficient for steaming a very small number of U-Boats to the scuttling area, and the majority will have to be towed unless German crews are employed.
>
> The towing gear in all U-Boats is at present either non-existent or very poor, and the cables, where fitted, are of poor quality ... Good weather for towing is therefore essential.
>
> As the U-Boats have been specially lightened to enable them to berth in their present shallow water berths, they will probably have to be sunk with demolition charges or by gunfire instead of opening the vents and hatches.
>
> A round trip for each tow would be three days from Loch Ryan and two days from Lisahally.
>
> As all the U-Boats are to be sunk by 15 February 1946 it is requested that an early start be made. Towing and scuttling will have to take place in the now infrequent good weather, and it is considered that unless a large number of tugs and scuttling parties are made available it will take at least two months to sink them all.
>
> Bad weather has already caused the stranding of four U-Boats at Loch Ryan.[2]

Time and the weather were major problems, as were the poor towing gear and the lack of sufficient submarine crews. Equally, it was obvious that this was likely to be a major exercise which would require the support of considerable numbers of RN warships and tugs.

The next step in the process came on 31 October when the Admiralty instructed the C-in-C Rosyth to begin making the detailed arrangements for the disposal of these unallocated U-boats. The Admiralty message stated that:

> It is intended to scuttle 86 U-Boats from Loch Ryan and 24 from Lisahally in position 56 degrees North, 10 degrees, 05 mins West.
>
> A large proportion of these will require towing and therefore as many destroyers, escort vessels and tugs as can be spared from other commands will be sent to assist.[2]

A further message from the Admiralty on the same day emphasised that: 'It is essential that scuttling should be completed in shortest possible time taking every advantage of favourable weather.'[2]

With the aim of completing the operation as quickly as possible an initial planning meeting to discuss the necessary arrangements was held on 5 November under the chairmanship of the Chief of Staff to the C-in-C Rosyth. The principal business of the meeting was concerned with the arrangements for towing the U-boats, for scuttling most of them and for using some as targets for air attacks as well as torpedo attacks from submarines. The main points decided were:

> All U-Boats will have to be towed to the scuttling area.
>
> It was decided to clear Loch Ryan first.
>
> All U-Boats shall be towed by double bridles.
>
> Should an escort part her tow whilst on passage to the scuttling area and conditions did not permit the recovery of the tow, the escort vessel is to sink the U-Boat where she is, provided that she is not in a position to become a danger to navigation.
>
> The method of scuttling if weather is suitable for boarding is by Safety Fuse Method.
>
> The method of scuttling if weather is unsuitable for boarding is by Electric Method.
>
> It was decided to allocate 3 U-Boats each day for air practices as mutually arranged between Coastal Command and Admiral (Air), and that the aircraft carrier HMS *Nairana*, with No.816 Sqn FAA embarked, would be made available to co-ordinate and supervise the practices.
>
> A number of U-Boats would be made available as torpedo targets for the Third Submarine Flotilla.[3]

The formal order for Operation 'Deadlight' was issued by the C-in-C Rosyth on 14 November; it being defined as the plan for scuttling 110 U-boats from Loch Ryan (86) and Lisahally (24) in deep water off the north-west coast of Ireland starting on 25 November.

The omission of six U-boats from the list in the 'Deadlight' Operation Order has caused considerable confusion ever since despite the UK's 1946 Naval Estimates (Cmd 7054) subsequently publishing the correct figure of 116. The six U-boats missing from the Operation Order, all of which were moored at Lisahally, were *U-975, U-1023, U-2351, U-2356, U-2502* and *U-3514* and in each case there had been or were ongoing discussions about their possible inclusion in the lists of the U-boats to be allocated to one or other of the Allies. Because these six U-boats were therefore included in the initial TNC allocation lists they were omitted from the Operation Order. However, as they did not feature in the final allocations they were added to the original list of 110 unallocated U-boats after the 'Deadlight' Operation Order was published. The total requirement was therefore to scuttle eighty-six U-boats from Loch Ryan and thirty from Lisahally.

The datum point for the disposal of the U-boats designated as 'Point XX' was at 56.00N, 10.05W, the air target position 'Point ZZ' was at 55.50N, 10.05W and the main scuttling position 'Point YY' was at 56.10N, 10.05W.

The aim of 'Deadlight' as set out in the Operation Order was that the U-boats should be towed unmanned to the designated area which was 130 miles to the north west of Lough Foyle and 180 miles west of Loch Ryan where they would be scuttled or sunk in the vicinity of positions YY or ZZ, completing the operation in the shortest possible time and taking every advantage of any favourable weather.

The prime disposal method was to be by demolition charges but if the weather conditions allowed thirty-six of the U-boats from Loch Ryan were to be sunk by aircraft from the RAF (eighteen) and the RN Fleet Air Arm (eighteen) and a small but undefined number were to be made available as targets for trials of non-contact torpedoes fired by RN submarines. If any of these planned methods of disposal failed the U-boats were to be sunk either by gunfire or by use of the then still secret anti-submarine weapon 'Squid'. The most important points contained in the Operation Order many of which had been taken from FOS/M's earlier advice were:

> Loch Ryan is to be cleared of U-Boats first and escort vessels and tugs will be sailed to Loch Ryan on commencing the operation. When Loch

Ryan has been cleared of U-Boats, escort vessels and tugs are to be sailed to Moville [at the mouth of Lough Foyle].

Tows are to be sailed to the scuttling area in groups, as convenient, to suit conditions of light and tide. Tug tows are always to be accompanied by an escort vessel tow.

U-Boats are to be towed with double bridles. During passage, conning tower hatches are to be closed in Type 23 U-Boats and are to be left open in all other U-Boats.

If the weather is suitable for boarding, the method of scuttling will be by safety fuse, charges being placed so as to collapse the bow and stern torpedo tubes and also to blow certain hatches. If the weather is unsuitable for boarding, the scuttling charges will be fired electrically. Should both these methods fail the towing vessel is to sink the U-Boat.

From each group of U-Boats sailing, three U-Boats are to be detailed as targets for air practices. If the aircraft taking part in the practice fail to sink a U-Boat, the accompanying vessels are to sink her by gunfire and/or by 'Squid'.

On certain days, U-Boats will be allocated to the Flag Officer (Submarines) for non-contact pistol trials using submarines of the Third Submarine Flotilla for this purpose.[4]

An appreciation of the scale of this RN operation can be gained from the fact that it involved one aircraft carrier, fourteen destroyers, five frigates, two submarines and at least half a dozen tugs.

Of the 116 U-boats, eighty-six were moored in small groups (trots) in Loch Ryan and thirty were tied up to pontoons at Lisahally and they comprised four Type IIDs, seventy-three Type VIICs, one Type VIID, one Type VIIF, 11 Type IXCs, four Type IXDs, four Type XXIs and eighteen Type XXIIIs.

The individual U-boats which were to be sunk during 'Deadlight' were:

Ex-Loch Ryan (86)
U-143, U-145, U-149, U-150, U-155, U-170, U-218, U-245, U-249, U-255, U-281, U-291, U-293, U-295, U-298, U-299, U-312, U-313, U-318, U-328, U-368, U-369, U-427, U-481, U-483, U-485, U-532, U-539, U-637, U-680, U-716, U-720, U-739, U-760, U-773, U-775, U-776, U-778, U-779, U-806, U-826, U-868, U-907, U-928, U-956, U-968, U-978, U-991, U-992, U-994, U-997, U-1002, U-1004, U-1005, U-1009, U-1019, U-1052, U-1061, U-1102, U-1103, U-1104, U-1110, U-1163, U-1194, U-1198, U-1203, U-1230, U-1233, U-1271, U-1272, U-1301, U-1307, U-2321, U-2322, U-2324, U-2325, U-2328, U-2329, U-2334, U-2335, U-2337, U-2345, U-2350, U-2354, U-2361 and U-2363.

Ex-Lisahally (30)
*U-244, U-278, U-294, U-363, U-516, U-541, U-668, U-764, U-802,
U-825, U-861, U-874, U-875, U-883, U-901, U-930, U-975,
U-1010, U-1022, U-1023, U-1109, U-1165, U-2336, U-2341,
U-2351, U-2356, U-2502, U-2506, U-2511* and *U-3514.*

The U-boats from Loch Ryan were to be sunk first and it would take two days for the towed U-boats to reach the designated scuttling area. So, although the first sailing from Loch Ryan took place on 25 November, the sinking of the first five U-boats (*U-2322, U-2324, U-2328, U-2345* and *U-2361*) did not occur until 27 November 1945.

The decision to scuttle most of the U-boats was supposed to be kept secret until after the allocated U-boats and the German Navy's remaining surface ships had been moved to either the USA, the UK or the USSR. However, whilst the final decisions about the U-boats which were to be transferred to the USSR and those which were to be sunk were not formally made by the TNC until November 1945, UK press and public interest in the U-boats and their fate had been building-up ever since the first of them had arrived at Loch Eriboll and Weymouth on 10 May. Newspapers in Scotland and Northern Ireland had carried details of the surrenders throughout May and interest had heightened in June and July as more U-boats were transferred to the UK from Norway and Germany.

By that time wartime press censorship no longer applied and there were several 'leaks' to the Press with – on 10 October – the very day that the TNC decided (in secret) the initial allocations to each of the Allies, *The Times* and *The Manchester Guardian* each publishing stories under the headline 'Disposal of U-Boats'. The report in *The Times* on 10 October which had been filed in Hamburg on 9 October by its 'Special Correspondent' said:

> Provisional agreement, subject to the ratification of the Powers concerned, has been reached on the disposal of the former German U-boat fleet, it is understood here. Under the terms of the decisions taken by the naval representatives of Great Britain, Russia and the United States, each one of these three Powers will receive six [it should have said ten] boats for experimental purposes. The remainder of the fleet, totaling approximately 150 submarines, will be scrapped.[5]

A similar story was published in *The Daily Express* a week later. So much for security, even though the Minutes of the TNC Meetings were classified as top secret. At the same time the TNC was aware of the planned British operation and on behalf of the Admiralty the UK representative requested his colleagues on 16 November to agree that as the destruction of the unallocated U-boats in Operation 'Deadlight' obviously could not be kept secret the TNC should issue a joint communiqué on 20 November which would include the words: 'It has been agreed between the Three Powers that U-boats not required for Allied purposes should now be sunk or destroyed.'[6]

In his reply on the same day the US TNC representative did not support such action as the original decision had been taken by the Allied leaders at Potsdam and he believed that any announcement should be made jointly by the three Governments in their respective national capitals. This US line was strongly supported by the Soviet representative who stated unequivocally on 17 November:

> In connection with the release of the announcement, the TNC is not authorised to do so.
>   Independent of the official announcement, the transfer of submarines to the USSR should not be delayed.
>   The sinking of submarines should be considered independently and has no relation to the transfer of submarines to the USSR.[6]

The Admiralty therefore had a problem. Ten U-boats were due to be transferred to Russia starting on 24 November in Operation 'Cabal' and 116 U-boats were due to be sunk off Northern Ireland in Operation 'Deadlight' starting on 25 November. However, there was no Allied authorisation to announce either of these two security classified activities. The Press already knew all about Operation 'Deadlight' and the expected arrival of Russian naval officers at Lisahally prior to the transfer of the 10 U-boats to Russia would be difficult to keep secret. Thus, the ongoing reports in the papers were not well received by an embarrassed UK Government which was precluded from making any comments.

Of the two operations, the one that really concerned the Admiralty was 'Cabal' and it was therefore proposed on 16 November that the joint Admiralty, War Office, Air Ministry and Press Committee should issue a 'D Notice' which would prevent any mention in the papers of the proposed transfer to Russia. However, despite the Admiralty saying that any disclosure would render the UK liable to a charge of bad faith, the Press members of the Committee refused the request on the basis that defence security was not involved. This was despite genuine fears that disclosure could possibly initiate sabotage by the German naval crews, especially those manning the remaining surface vessels in Wilhelmshaven.

As a result, the Admiralty sought a compromise with the Press whilst still pursuing the official line that it was unable to make any detailed comments due to the restrictions of the Potsdam Agreement. The First Lord himself held a meeting with newspaper editors, news agencies and representatives of the BBC on 19 November under the heading 'Transfer of U-Boats to Russia'. At this meeting the Admiralty put its cards on the table and discussed both 'Cabal' and 'Deadlight' with a strong point being made about the very real danger of any publicity concerning 'Cabal'.

The Admiralty's briefing note for the meeting included the information that:

> The Admiralty are nevertheless anxious that the Press should have full opportunities of witnessing and publishing the operations for sinking surplus U-boats. Invitations are therefore being issued to the Press to witness the operations, though the agreement of our Allies to publicity has not yet been obtained.[7]

The meeting ended with two requests from the Admiralty. First, an unequivocal one: 'To meet our request for the preservation of complete secrecy concerning the allocation of U-boats to any of the Three Powers.'[7] Second, a more equivocal one: 'To refrain from publicity concerning the sinking of surplus U-boats until the permission of our two Allies has been obtained to publication.'[7]

Whilst the implicit but unwritten agreement concerning Operation 'Cabal' held firm the requested restraint about 'Deadlight' did not last long. On 25 November *The Daily Express* and *The Evening Standard* published full details. However, even then, because of the lack of Allied agreement the Admiralty was forced to hide behind a cloak of sham secrecy issuing a message on 29 November to the naval forces involved which said: 'In spite of breach of faith by *Daily Express* and *Evening Standard*, Operation Deadlight is still to be treated as secret.'[8]

Also, several Members of Parliament including the MP for the Loch Ryan area as well as businessmen and individuals raised questions concerning the perceived advantages of scrapping rather than sinking the U-boats, some of them directly with the First Lord of the Admiralty and some of them in Parliament. They were all met with the same bland UK Government response saying: 'The arrangements for the use and disposal of the surrendered German fleet had been agreed in principle at the Potsdam Conference, and a joint statement by the three Governments setting out the details would be issued in due course.'[9] Despite considerable diplomatic pressure throughout November and December, the Soviet Government declined to accede to the UK appeal for an early announcement and 'due course' eventually turned out to be 22 January 1946 by which time almost all of the unallocated U-boats had been sunk.

In the meantime, there had been a great deal of publicity about Operation 'Deadlight' in a whole variety of publications written by reporters who by invitation were aboard some of the RN naval vessels and RAF aircraft involved in the operation. For instance, on 12 December 1945 the Aeronautical Correspondent of *The Times* reported that he had flown as a passenger in an RAF Mosquito aircraft of No. 248 Sqn which had attacked three of the U-boats in rocket attacks.[10] In similar vein the magazine *The War Illustrated* published an account on 4 January 1946 describing the scuttling of several U-boats from Loch Ryan as seen from on board the Polish Navy's destroyer *Blyskawica* which was one of the towing/escort vessels.[11]

As expected, the weather to the north of Ireland was particularly bad in November and December and most of the planned disposal arrangements failed to work especially as far as sinking the U-boats with demolition charges were concerned. There were also major problems with the towing of the unmanned, unmaintained and in many cases almost unseaworthy U-boats.

There were three distinct phases to Operation 'Deadlight'. First, the eighty-six U-boats from Loch Ryan were sunk between 27 November and 30 December 1945. Second, twenty-eight of the thirty U-boats from Lisahally were sunk between 29 December 1945 and 8 January 1946. Third, the remaining two U-boats from Lisahally were sunk on 10 and 12 February 1946 respectively.

Before Phase 1 of 'Deadlight' could commence a considerable number of towing and escort vessels were needed at Loch Ryan, and these began arriving on 24 November. The plan was that the U-boats should leave their moorings under power and move north to link-up with their towing vessels towards the mouth of Loch Ryan, where the crews would be disembarked. The U-boats were then to be towed unmanned to 'Position XX' which was some 180 miles to the north-west of Ireland, two days towing distance from Loch Ryan.

In the event things did not go according to plan. Many of the towing vessels were not properly equipped or designed for the task, many of the U-boats flooded due to either unserviceability or because their conning tower hatches were deliberately left open (except for the small Type XXIII U-boats), and the increasingly bad weather made the task doubly difficult. Thus, many of the scuttling plans were not feasible.

Of the eighty-six U-boats from Loch Ryan, only fifty reached the designated scuttling area. Of these, one was sunk by demolition charges, nine were sunk by torpedoes fired by HMS/M *Tantivy*, twelve were sunk by aircraft (five by the Fleet Air Arm, and seven by the RAF), and twenty-eight were sunk by gunfire. The remaining thirty-six were lost en-route. Of these, one was sunk by demolition charges, eighteen were sunk by gunfire (including two after their tows were deliberately slipped when crew members from the towing vessels needed to be taken ashore for urgent medical treatment), and seventeen foundered and sank of their own accord.

Despite the bad weather and the various operational challenges, the Loch Ryan contribution to 'Deadlight' was completed in 33 days, which was less than the two months that had been anticipated. Also, whilst all the hard work to fit demolition charges was largely wasted the charges themselves contributed to the process in several cases when they were hit by gunfire and exploded, aiding the rapid disintegration of the U-boat.

Details of Phase I were summed up by Captain (Submarines) Loch Ryan in his Monthly General Letters to FOS/M for November and December 1945 viz:

> Nov 45: Operation Deadlight (scuttling of U-Boats) started on 25 November in favourable weather. Details of the operation will be rendered when it has been completed.
> Dec 45: A full report on Operation Deadlight is being rendered separately. It has fully occupied all the Submarine Personnel at Loch Ryan for the whole month, except for five days over Christmas. It was very disappointing that all sailings could not be completed by Christmas; only three U-Boats remained out of the eighty six with which we started.[12]

The Report of Proceedings submitted by Captain (Submarines) Loch Ryan on 3 January 1946 contained, as promised, the complete details of every tow and sinking, and he summed up the activities as well as the difficulties encountered in a few succinct sentences:

> Sinking by gunfire proved in many cases a difficult and lengthy procedure, except when the demolition charges were exploded by hitting the initiating charges, in which case the result was sudden and spectacular.
> Of the seventeen U-boats which foundered, practically all went down during exceptionally bad spells of weather.

The causes of parting tows are not clear, since recovery of the tow was seldom practicable and evidence was not forthcoming. But here again practically every parting can be attributed to a great extent to heavy weather.

It was disappointing that only two U-boats were deliberately scuttled by demolition charges as a great deal of work was put in by the Vernon party. The scuttling of *U-2345* by demolition charges was a most impressive explosion, fragments falling on and around the firing ship at a range of a thousand feet.

In no case was boarding the U-boat to initiate the time fuses the primary method of firing considered practical. Weather in the North Atlantic in mid-winter not being conducive to boat work.

The decision reached at Rosyth on 5 November that it was essential for U-boats to be towed to the scuttling area as it would not be possible to remove the crews on arrival was clearly justified.

To begin with, the U-boats sailed with their bow and stern caps and their conning tower hatches open in order to ensure certain sinking, when the demolition charges were exploded, but this state of affairs was soon altered and all bow and stern caps were shut, as a considerable number of U-boats sank prematurely and it was thought that flooding might have somehow occurred through the firing gear and tube fittings

As the U-boats had been at Loch Ryan for some six months and had been jumping about in all sorts of weather there is no doubt that the main ballast tanks had been punctured, which with the working of the submarine in a seaway, would have opened up again causing external flooding and possibly flooding elsewhere.

A large number of the U-boats which sank went to their watery graves between Innisthrahull and the meridian of 8 degrees W. Here they began to experience the force of the open Atlantic and any faults, either in themselves or the towing gear, became apparent. This area might well be called 'Natures Graveyard' i.e. Nature versus the Admiralty.

The Operation from Loch Ryan was completed in 33 days, a considerably shorter time than had been anticipated here. If the weather had been suitable for connecting up the tows on 8 December, it would have been over by Christmas.

If this Operation was to be repeated again, there are no suggestions which can be put forward to make it work better except that as found out early in the proceedings, it was necessary to make the U-boats as watertight as possible.[13]

The first tranche of the Lisahally phase of 'Deadlight', which began on 29 December, involved twenty-eight of the thirty U-boats which were moored there. However, despite the relatively small number of U-boats at Lisahally it was still a major exercise involving almost as many RN and other vessels as the number of U-boats themselves. The surface fleet, which included nineteen destroyers and frigates, of which three belonged to the Polish Navy was moored at Moville near the mouth of Lough Foyle.

The formal objective was very simple: 'To tow six U-boats from Moville each day and sink them on the following day in the Scuttling Area, providing submarine targets as necessary.'[14] The plan was that each day during the operation, and after the demolition charges had been installed at Lisahally, the small groups of U-boats would be sailed down the river to Moville by skeleton German crews who would hand over each U-boat to one of the surface vessels, disembark, and then be ferried back to Lisahally. The U-boats would then be towed to the designated position 130 miles to the north-west of Lough Foyle where they would be sunk.

Despite the earlier disappointing experience with the U-boats from Loch Ryan, the prime disposal method for the U-boats from Lisahally was still expected to be by demolition charges. On arrival in the scuttling area the groups were to heave-to with the towing vessels keeping the U-boats' head-to-wind. A demolition officer from the RN Mine and Torpedo School was then to board each U-boat and set the fuses. If that was not possible the charges were to be fired electrically. Also, if weather conditions allowed two U-boats were to be sunk by torpedoes from the submarine HMS/M *Templar*. If either of these methods of disposal failed then the U-boats were to be sunk 'as ordered by the Senior Officer present' – which was normally by gunfire.

The weather was particularly bad in late December 1945 and early January 1946, and there were major problems with the towing of the unmanned U-boats by vessels which were not suited to such activity. The disposal arrangements therefore failed on most occasions especially as far as the plan for sinking the U-boats with demolition charges was concerned with not one of the twenty-eight U-boats from Lisahally being sunk by this method.

A similar deviation from the plan occurred with the two U-boats selected for destruction by torpedo. *U-764* and *U-2502* departed Moville on 2 January 1946 as designated targets for HMS/M *Templar* but the sea was so rough on 3 January that they both had to be sunk by gunfire. Then on 5 January *U-2506* was designated as the target for the submarine. However, the U-boat's tow parted en route to the sinking area and it too had to be sunk by gunfire. Instead, one of the other U-boats that had departed Moville on 5 January, *U-1109*, was allocated as a target for HMS/M *Templar* and it was successfully torpedoed on the morning of 6 January. As recorded in the Lisahally ROP: '*Templar* fired a salvo of three torpedoes, one of which detonated under the stern of the target. The U-boat sank stern first in two minutes.'[14]

Once again, the poor weather had made it far too dangerous to follow the pre-planned demolition procedure. Of the twenty-eight U-boats, twenty-two never even reached the designated scuttling area. Of these, nineteen had to be sunk by gunfire whilst en-route whilst the other three foundered under tow. Of the six U-boats which reached the scuttling area five had to be sunk by gunfire leaving just the one to be sunk by HMS/M *Templar*. Thus, although all the U-boats were sent to the bottom in one way or another, the plan was defeated by a combination of bad weather and the unsatisfactory towing arrangements.

The ROP submitted by Captain (Submarines) Lisahally was much more succinct than that of his opposite number in Loch Ryan albeit that it neatly summed up the main difficulties encountered:

> The method of towing proved satisfactory except that in the case of the Types VIIC, IXC and IXD2 the single bridle had to be replaced by a double bridle, owing to the weakness of the German cable.
>
> There was a succession of gales throughout the operation, which made conditions both at Moville and at sea extremely difficult and this is considered to be one of the reasons why so many of the tows parted before the scuttling area was reached.[14]

An equally succinct comment was included in Captain (Submarines) Lisahally January 1946 Monthly General Letter to Admiral (Submarines), which recorded that:

> The first week of the month was a very busy one, and saw the completion of 'Operation Deadlight'. On 7 January the last lift of three submarines *U-2511*, *U-1023* and *U-1010* was sailed to Moville, towed away and sunk. In all 114 U-boats went to the bottom, accompanied by few tears, even from the German prisoners. *U-3514* was the only unallocated submarine not scuttled [as also was *U-975*], but at the time of writing it seems that her days are numbered.[15]

The final phase of Lisahally's contribution to Operation 'Deadlight' occurred in February 1946 with the sinking of two of the U-boats (*U-975* and *U-3514*) which had been involved in the last-minute changes to the TNC allocations.

U-3514 had been part of the initial Russian allocation until 23 November, but it had been damaged on the day before it was due to be towed to Libau in Latvia in Operation 'Cabal'. *U-3515* was substituted for it and the RN therefore held the damaged *U-3514* in reserve until *U-3515* successfully arrived in Libau, which did not occur until 2 February 1946.

U-975 had originally been part of the TNC's UK allocation, but the latter was keen to ensure that one of the unallocated U-boats that had surrendered from sea in Canada should be made available for use by the RCN. However, after a debate between the Senior TNC Representatives in November 1945 it was not until 23 January 1946 that the formal UK request was made to the TNC and this was not finally agreed until 31 January, hence the delay in scuttling *U-975* in the earlier phases of Operation 'Deadlight'.

The Lisahally Operation Order dated 7 February covering the scuttling of these two U-boats was code-named 'Deadlight 2' and involved towing the two U-boats to the scuttling position and then sinking them by either gunfire or anti-submarine (a/s) weapons. It involved two frigates, HMS *Loch Arkaig* and HMS *Loch Shin*, the ocean-going tug *Prosperous* and two harbour tugs. The operation was planned to begin on 9 February with HMS *Loch Shin* towing *U-975* and *Prosperous* towing *U-3514*. HMS *Loch Arkaig* was to undertake the sinkings.[14]

Both U-boats were moored at Lisahally, and *U-975* was to sail down river to Moville under its own power whilst *U-3514* was to be towed down river by the three tugs. Whilst the plan worked for *U-975* difficulties were encountered with *U-3514*. On 9 February the tug *Prosperous* went aground during the transit from Lisahally to Moville and by the time she was re-floated it was too late to proceed further. *U-3514* was therefore towed back to Lisahally by the two harbour tugs. The process was repeated the following day but this time *U-3514* went aground and it was not until 1800 that *Prosperous* was able to tow it out to sea.

In the meantime, *U-975* had left Moville on the afternoon of 9 February and by 1500 on 10 February was at the scuttling position. First, it was unsuccessfully attacked by gunfire from HMS *Loch Arkaig*, but a second attack using the 'Squid' a/s weapon was successful and *U-975* sank at 1610.

The tug *Prosperous* and *U-3514* which had eventually left Moville at 1800 on 10 February were only able to proceed to the scuttling area slowly and so did not arrive there until 0900 on 12 February. This time HMS *Loch Arkaig* attacked with both gunfire and the 'Shark' a/s weapon. The gunfire began at 0936 and at 0958 'Shark' was fired. Two hits were registered, and at 1004 *U-3514* sank, thus bringing 'Deadlight' to an end.

In typical RN style, which included some artistic license, this episode was summed-up in Captain (Submarines) Lisahally's Monthly General Letter to Admiral (Submarines) in February 1946 in just a few perceptive words:

> On 9 February the last two German U-boats to be scuttled were sailed for Operation Deadlight. *U-975* got clear away without any trouble but the Type XXI (*U-3514*) lived up to the revolting reputation this class of submarine has achieved in ten months at Lisahally, by running aground when towed by three tugs, and had to be brought back to Lisahally. On the following day she was sailed again with the same three tugs and, after nearly seven hours of billiards, cannoning from mudbank to mudbank and side to side of the Channel, she finally cleared Lough Foyle Buoy and Operation Deadlight was completed. It is interesting to note that both these U-boats joined the very select few which were sunk in approximately the right position. This was unquestionably due to the fact that the towing ships were in no hurry and did not try to force the pace.[15]

C-in-C Rosyth reported the completion of Operation 'Deadlight' in two messages to the Admiralty. The sinking of 114 U-boats was confirmed in his message on 8 January 1946 and the sinking of the final two U-boats was confirmed in his message on 12 February 1946.[3]

As expected, the weather had been particularly bad in November and December 1945 as well as in January 1946 and the planned disposal arrangements did not work on most occasions. There were also major problems with towing the unmanned, unmaintained and in many cases almost unseaworthy U-boats. Comparison of the planned disposal arrangements with what happened in practice shows the scale of disruption.

Only two U-boats were sunk by demolition charges, only ten by submarines and only twelve by aircraft. Of the remainder, almost 50 per cent sank before they ever reached the designated target area. These either foundered under tow and sank directly or had to be sunk by gunfire, some of them in positions close to the entrances to Loch Ryan and Lough Foyle. The remaining U-boats were sunk by gunfire in the target area when it became obvious that it was far too dangerous to follow the pre-planned demolition procedure. A summary of the actual disposal methods illustrates the situation:

a. U-boat sunk by demolition charges en-route to the target area – 1
b. U-boats foundered under tow en-route to the target area – 20
c. U-boats sunk by gunfire en-route to the target area – 37
d. U-boat sunk by demolition charges in the target area – 1
e. U-boats sunk by submarines in the target area – 10
f. U-boats sunk by RAF aircraft in the target area – 7
g. U-boats sunk by RN Fleet Air Arm aircraft in the target area – 5
h. U-boats sunk by gunfire in the target area – 33
i. U-boats sunk by anti-submarine weapons in the target area – 2

CHAPTER 13

U-Boats in the USA

TWELVE OF THE U-BOATS which surrendered at the end of the war in Europe in 1945 saw service with the US Navy. Five had surrendered in the USA and one had surrendered in Canada. Two others had surrendered in Argentina, and four had been transferred to the USA after their surrender in Europe. Additionally, *U-505* had been captured in June 1944 (see Chapter 14) but it was exempt from consideration by the TNC.

As a result of the TNC review *U-234*, *U-530*, *U-858*, *U-873*, *U-889*, *U-977*, *U-1105*, *U-1406*, *U-2513* and *U-3008* were formally allocated to the USA. By then eight were already in the possession of the USN, *U-889* was to be transferred from Canada and *U-1105* was to be transferred from the UK. In the meantime, *U-889* had been the subject of trials by the RCN and *U-1105* had been the subject of trials by both the RN and the RAF in the UK. Two of the five U-boats which had surrendered in the USA, *U-805* and *U-1228*, were not allocated to any of the Allies and therefore needed to be sunk by no later than 15 February 1946.

Even before any U-boats had arrived in a US port the USN took early action to outline its approach to their use, starting with a message from the Commander-in-Chief (Cominch) to the Commander of the Eastern Sea Frontier (ESF) on 11 May 1945 which said: 'As convenient deliver 1 each type surrendered U-Boat to Navy Yard Portsmouth. Remainder to CINCLANT [Commander-in-Chief US Atlantic Fleet] for Sub Base New London'.[1]

In the event, only five U-boats surrendered at sea to the USN in May 1945:

U-234   Surrendered on 12 May. Arrived at Portsmouth, NH on 19 May

U-805   Surrendered on 9 May. Arrived at Portsmouth, NH on
        15 May
U-858   Surrendered on 9 May. Arrived at Fort Miles, DE on 14 May
U-873   Surrendered on 11 May. Arrived at Portsmouth, NH on
        16 May
U-1228 Surrendered on 9 May. Arrived at Portsmouth, NH on
        17 May

The first of these to signal its intention to surrender was *U-805* which reported its position in the central North Atlantic at 0310 on 9 May. The destroyer escorts USS *Otter* and USS *Varian* were ordered to intercept and escort *U-805* to Casco Bay where it arrived at 0800 on 15 May. There it was handed over to US Coast Guard cutter USCGC *Argo* for delivery to Portsmouth Navy Yard (PNY).

The next to report its position in the mid-Atlantic was *U-1228* which it did at 1022 on 9 May. The destroyer escorts USS *Sutton* and USS *Neal A Scott* were ordered to intercept the U-boat on 11 May and escort it to the Casco Bay. The intercept was made at about midday on 11 May but, after encountering bad weather during the transit, and after the departure of USS *Sutton* on other duties the U-boat and its remaining escort were ordered to proceed directly to Portsmouth Lower Harbour, arriving there at 0600 on 17 May.

The third to report its position south-east of Newfoundland on 9 May was *U-858* which it did at 1610. On 10 May the U-boat was intercepted by the destroyer escorts USS *Sutton* and USS *Neal A Scott* whilst on their way to find *U-1228*. The latter soon left the scene to continue their search and *U-858* was joined by the destroyer escorts USS *Carter* and USS *Muir*. The escort duties were then taken over by the destroyer escorts USS *Pillsbury* and USS *Pope* and they were ordered to escort *U-858* to the Delaware Capes where they arrived at 0700 on 14 May. Subsequently the U-boat was moved to Fort Miles and after the removal of its torpedoes it was transferred up the Delaware River to the Philadelphia Navy Yard on 19 May.

The fourth to surrender in US waters was *U-873* which reported its position in the vicinity of the Azores at 0144 on 11 May. It was initially ordered to set course for Bermuda and was met by the destroyer escort USS *Vance* in the early hours of 12 May. The destination was then changed, first to the Delaware Capes, and then to Casco Bay. However, the latter order was changed yet again, and the pair was directed to Portsmouth Lower Harbour where they arrived at 1400 on 16 May.

The final U-boat to surrender to US naval forces at sea was *U-234* which reported its position in the mid-North Atlantic early on 12 May. Several USN and RCN warships were ordered to intercept it with, eventually, the destroyer escort USS *Sutton* arriving on the scene in the late evening of 14 May. The initial instruction was to head for Casco Bay, but this was later changed to Portsmouth Lower Harbour. In the meantime, USS *Sutton* had been joined by the destroyer escorts USS *Carter* and USS *Muir* with all four vessels arriving in Portsmouth Lower Harbour early on 19 May.

These surrenders were followed on 19 May by a message from the USN's CNO containing initial instructions about the inspection and testing of the U-boats which were now located in the USA. Dockyard inspections were to be supervised by the Commandant of the PNY and operational tests were to be co-ordinated by Commander Submarines Atlantic (ComSubLant), the objective being to determine which of the five U-boats might be of any future use to the USN.

On 28 May 1945 a more comprehensive policy letter titled 'Inspections and Tests of Surrendered German Submarines' was distributed to a wide USN audience, in which the Vice Chief of Naval Operations stated:

> There are five surrendered German U-Boats of various types in East Coast Ports. At a later date additional U-Boats will be received, and it is expected that there will be two U-Boats of each major type in the custody of the United States. They will be available for inspections and tests.
>
> Tests will be scheduled in two distinct categories, namely underway operational tests and dockside research tests.
>
> Upon completion of the trials, tests and inspections, it is desired that the Navy Yard, Portsmouth compile reports for each design type so that the data may be readily available for reference in connection with future design work.[2]

In response to this policy letter the USN's Bureau of Ships (BuShips), in a letter dated 23 June 1945 titled 'Surrendered German Submarines – Recommendations for Trials and Tests', focused on the five U-boats: *U-234* (Type XB), *U-805* (Type IXC/40), *U-873* (Type IXD2) and *U-1228* (Type IXC/40) at PNY, and *U-858* (Type IXC) which was located in the Navy's base at New London, CT and said:

> It is desired to conduct underway operational tests and trials on one vessel of each major design type available. Of the [five U-Boats] listed above, it is considered that the priority of underway trials, based upon

the expected value of the results, should be in the order Type IXD2 (*U-873*), Type XB (*U-234*), and Type IXC (*U-858*). Type XB is a mine laying and 'milch cow' design, but has a number of operational features not found in other submarines. In view of the fact that *U-858* will apparently be ready for underway operations before *U-873*, it will be satisfactory to the Bureau to conduct trials on this vessel first, to be followed by trials on *U-873* and *U-234* in the order named.

When *U-858*, *U-873* and *U-234* are cleaned, inspected and tested as necessary for underway operations, minimum preservative measures should be taken for preservation of tanks, hull interior and exterior, and operating equipment for a period of one year. *U-805* and *U-1228* should be used for spare parts required to maintain the three U-Boats mentioned above in an operating condition.

In the case of any additional German submarines received, it is recommended that those selected for operation be treated similar to *U-858*, *U-873* and *U-234*, and others similar to *U-805* and *U-1228*.[2]

So, within less than two months of the end of the war in Europe the USN had set out a clear policy for dealing with the surrendered German U-boats in its custody. PNY was to prepare formal design studies, perform tests and compile reports on one each of the three U-boat types then in American custody (Type IXC, Type IXD and Type XB), and ComSubLant was to conduct any necessary underway trials, a process which would be replicated if any other major design types became available. The remaining U-boats were to be used as sources of spare parts.

Thus, without waiting for Allied authority or the TNC allocations, the USN had wasted no time in initiating the action necessary to make use of three of the U-boats which they had earmarked for retention. *U-234*, *U-858* and *U-873* were to be cleaned, inspected and tested as necessary for underway operations, but only minimum preservative measures were to be taken, the implication being that they were unlikely to be used for more than a year. The first essential action was to make them seaworthy and fit for use in the planned trials. Originally it was thought that they could be made available for the initial trials quite quickly, but this proved to be optimistic, and the planned availability dates kept slipping to the right, particularly because of problems with the availability of spares.

In the meantime, controversy was beginning to build up in relation to *U-234*, which was a Type XB ex-minelayer that had been modified to become a transport U-boat, and which had been en-route to Japan prior to its surrender loaded with some 200 tons of cargo and carrying nearly a dozen important passengers. Amongst the cargo, and in addition to the mercury and optical glass stored in *U-234*'s keel, the pre-sealed cargo containers included arms, ammunition, medical supplies, instruments and various raw materials, as well as a very large number of plans and production drawings, many relating to the Me 262 jet aircraft. Also, it included 560kg of uranium oxide which was packed in ten separate 56kg cases stowed in the sealed amidships cargo containers. Almost inevitably conspiracy theories began to arise, and they included the false allegations (which persist to this day) that not only was *U-234* carrying three complete Me 262s, but that the uranium oxide was actually radioactive weapons-grade uranium which was then used in the atomic bombs dropped on Japan in August 1945.

The lead U-boat for the trials was *U-858* and the work to make it serviceable was undertaken at the New London submarine base where it had arrived from Fort Miles on 5 June, via Philadelphia Navy Yard. A great deal of work needed to be undertaken by both the base and the dockyard staff and this included a 21-day spell in dry dock from the end of July until 18 August. Whilst *U-858* was being renovated at New London, similar action was being undertaken at PNY on the other two U-boats. *U-858* joined the other two U-boats at PNY on 23 October and the dockyard concentrated on improving the serviceability of all three in whatever order they became available. *U-858* eventually left PNY for New London in December 1945 with *U-234* and *U-873* following in January 1946.

The two U-boats that had surrendered from sea in Argentina and which were subsequently allocated to the USA were *U-530* and *U-977*. The COs of these U-boats had deliberately chosen to escape to Argentina rather than obey the surrender instructions but very soon after their long transits and arrival in Mar del Plata they and their U-boats were handed over to the local US authorities.

U-530 had been on patrol to the east of New York in early May but did not receive Dönitz' recall message. Nor did it receive any surrender messages until 15 or 16 May. The CO nevertheless decided that the latter might not be genuine and therefore opted to head for Argentina rather than to surrender in an American port. In the meantime the USN believed that *U-530* had probably been sunk on 30 April and was therefore no longer searching for the U-boat. Thus *U-530* began its long covert transit south, arriving off the Argentinian port of Mar del Plata on the evening of 9 July. Before entering the base the CO ordered battery acid to be added to the lubrication system and the diesel engines were run at high speed without full lubrication in order to sabotage them. At the same time various components were removed or damaged and electric wires were severed. The next morning it became clear to the Argentine Navy that *U-530* wished to surrender and it was allowed to enter the Naval Base at Mar del Plata. On 12 July *U-530* was officially taken over by the Argentine Navy but on 17 July the Argentine Foreign Office decided to transfer it to the USN. Thus on 28 July *U-530* was towed to the Naval Base at Rio Santiago in Buenos Aires arriving there on 29 July prior to its hand-over.

U-977 had left Kristiansand in Norway on 2 May and whilst it did not receive the recall order on 4 May, it was still in the Bergen area when the surrender order was received. The CO nevertheless decided to disobey the order and to proceed to Argentina but not before sixteen married members of the crew had been put ashore on an island north of Bergen on 10 May. The Allies were unsure of the fate of *U-977* for the remainder of May but at the end of the month the sixteen ex-crew members arrived in Bergen stating that they were the only survivors from *U-977* which, they said, had been wrecked near Bremanger on 9 May whilst returning from its patrol with a damaged periscope. This story was accepted by the Admiralty and on 1 June it advised the USN that *U-977* had sunk after running aground in Norway. In the meantime the undamaged U-boat headed south and after 107 days at sea it was sighted on the surface off the port of Mar del Plata on the morning of 17 August by vessels of the Argentinian Navy. It was boarded and surrendered, being the last U-boat to do so, and was then towed into the Naval Base. The US authorities were immediately notified of the surrender and in late August *U-977* was moved under its own power to the Rio Santiago Naval Base where it was formally handed over to the USN on 6 September.

Almost immediately after *U-530*'s arrival in Buenos Aires it was handed over to the USN and urgent arrangements were made for it to be scraped, tested and painted, and for the engines to be repaired. In contrast there was no time for *U-977* to be docked or even painted prior to its departure for the USA. In the meantime two USN crews had arrived to sail the U-boats to the USA, and the tug USS *Cherokee* had been ordered to Buenos Aires to escort them to the USA, the three vessels comprising Task Group CTG 21.4. The two U-boats with their US crews left Buenos Aires in company on 11 September with *U-530* initially under tow by USS *Cherokee* and with *U-977* under power. On their journey north *U-530* and *U-977* made a civic visit to Rio de Janeiro in Brazil from 16 to 20 September and after having to repair the engines of both U-boats whilst at sea the Task Group stopped at Trinidad in the British West Indies from 2 to 5 October where they were reviewed by the TNC's Western Hemisphere Inspection Party on 3 October. The Group left Trinidad on 5 October and after an uneventful transit arrived at the USN's Submarine Base at New London on 12 October.

As already described, none of the latest high-tech U-boats, including any Type XXIs and XVIIBs, had surrendered in the Western Atlantic. Nevertheless, in anticipation of this the USN was determined to acquire examples of these two new types, and it had created the US Submarine Mission in Europe (SubMisEu) the key task of which was to locate two examples of each of the Type XXI and XVIIB U-boat and to move them to the USA irrespective of any Allied agreement concerning their disposal.

Twelve Type XXIs had surrendered in northern European ports, eleven in Norway and one in Germany, and they were all moved to Lisahally in June 1945 without prior agreement by the Russians. Thus, if the USN was to obtain two Type XXIs they would have to be selected from either the many damaged examples in the German shipyards or those that had been scuttled by the Kriegsmarine just before the end of the war or the twelve which were in RN custody. It was clear that any Allied decisions about their future were unlikely to be taken before the end of 1945 and the USN, with the active support of the RN but without informing the Russians, decided to initiate unilateral action to transfer two of the Type XXIs at Lisahally across the Atlantic just as soon as possible.

After the Type XXIs began to arrive at Lisahally *U-2513* was quickly transferred to USN control. This U-boat had surrendered in Norway on 9 May and been transferred to Lisahally on 3 June arriving on 9 June. During June further Type XXIs arrived from Norway as did *U-3008* which had surrendered at sea on 11 May and arrived in Kiel on 21 May. It was then transferred to Wilhelmshaven from where it sailed to Lisahally on 21 June, arriving on 27 June. As well as *U-3008*, the USN also took over *U-2506* which had arrived at Lisahally from Norway on 21 June, but it was eventually decided that *U-3008* and *U-2513* would be the Type XXIs to be moved to the USA.

One of the reasons for the selection of *U-2513* and *U-3008* was that the USN wished to obtain an example from each of the two German shipyards which had assembled the prefabricated sections of the Type XXIs. *U-2513* had been built at the Blohm and Voss Yard in Hamburg and *U-3008* had been built at the Deschimag Yard in Bremen. However, they both needed a considerable amount of work to clean, paint and restore them to full serviceability before their planned Atlantic crossing.

The two U-boats were ready to sail to the USA by mid-July 1945 but there was a short delay because the Potsdam Conference was still in session and because it had not yet been formally decided that only ten U-boats would be allocated to each of the Allies. An interesting diversion from the normal USN routine occurred on 19 July when there was a Royal Visit to Lisahally by HM King George VI and HM Queen Elizabeth. The King had asked to see the surrendered U-boats and at the time *U-2513* and *U-3008* were the only ones that were operational as well as being freshly painted. Thus, His Majesty was invited to inspect an American Honor Guard, after which he and the Queen viewed the two U-boats and talked to the USN COs and the crews – although they did not go on board.

The completion of the Potsdam Conference on 2 August gave an unofficial green light for *U-2513* and *U-3008* to be moved to the USA escorted by the salvage tug USS *Brant*. The Atlantic crossing was made in poor weather and on the surface, a trip that was not at all easy because of the poor surface manoeuvring quality of the Type XXIs as well as a variety of defects in their steering systems. Very shortly after first departing from Lisahally on 6 August *U-3008* had problems with its steering gear and it had to be towed back to Lisahally for repairs. The Atlantic crossing resumed on 8 August but by the 10th *U-2513* had problems with its reduction gear and this was followed by more problems with *U-3008*'s rudder as well as flooding in the stern, requiring it to be towed by USS *Brant*.

The problems were still not over and on 18 August *U-2513* encountered engine problems which caused the rescue ship USS *Restorer* to rendezvous with the Task Group with orders to escort the U-boat into the USN's Operating Base at Argentia in Newfoundland. On 20 August *U-3008* was also taken into Argentia where both U-boats were repaired. The three vessels departed Argentia on 21 August and with no further mechanical problems arrived at New London on 25 August. After that, the U-boats were moved to the PNY with *U-2513* arriving at Portsmouth on 5 September and *U-3008* on 13 September.

Following the arrival in the USA of these two U-boats, PNY wrote to the CNO on 18 September requesting authority: 'To consider *U-2513* in the same category as *U-234*, *U-858* and *U-873* (for trials), and *U-3008* on the same basis as *U-805* and *U-1228* (for spares).'[2] The decision concerning *U-3008* was later reversed and it too was subsequently taken into long-term use by the USN albeit after first being cannibalised for spares for six months.

In a similar manner to the USN's covert acquisition of two Type XXIs, the acquisition of the Type XVIIB *U-1406* was the result of SubMisEU's detective work. Having been located in Cuxhaven where it had been illegally scuttled on 7 May after surrendering on 5 May, *U-1406* was raised with great haste and moved to a shipyard in Kiel at the beginning of July though not before a fire had started in the U-boat requiring its immediate re-immersion in Cuxhaven harbour.

Despite this, the SubMisEu advised Cominch that just one of the two Type XVIIBs which had been recovered would be sufficient for USN research purposes and by early August, despite any possible Russian aspirations, *U-1406* was earmarked for the USN. All that remained to be done was to ensure that a decision was taken about where and how it was to be made serviceable. Thus *U-1406* was moved directly to the USA without waiting for TNC agreement, without seeking prior permission from the Russians and before the publication of the formal TNC allocations. *U-1406* was towed from Kiel to Bremerhaven in mid-August and on 14 September it was loaded as deck cargo onto the US freighter SS *Shoemaker* before being transported to PNY arriving there on 11 October 1945.

The result of the TNC's review was published in December 1945 and ten U-boats – *U-234, U-530, U-858, U-873, U-889, U-977, U-1105, U-1406, U-2513* and *U-3008* – were formally allocated to the USA. Of these, eight were already located in the USA, *U-889* was to be transferred from Canada and *U-1105* was to be moved across the Atlantic from the UK. In the meantime, *U-889* had been the subject of trials by the RCN and *U-1105* had been the subject of trials by both the RN and the RAF in the UK. Thus, the USA was formally authorised to retain only ten U-boats and the TNC decision meant that two of the U-boats that had surrendered from sea in the USA, *U-805* and *U-1228*, were surplus to requirements and needed to be destroyed.

The Type VIIC *U-1105* was one of the first U-boats to surrender at sea. It had surfaced and broadcast its position on 9 May and was instructed to head for Loch Eriboll before being moved to Lisahally on 14 May. All three of the Allies wanted *U-1105* for testing after the war. This was because the U-boat's schnorkel and hull were covered with rubber sheeting known as 'Alberich'. The British and American intelligence staffs had known about this development since 1944, but there was uncertainty as to its purpose although it was thought that it was designed to help avoid detection by either radar or sonar, most probably the latter.

Both the RN and the RAF were keen to check the implications of *U-1105*'s rubber coating and its location in the UK meant that the British had a unique opportunity to initiate early trials with *U-1105*. However, after these trials had been completed there was very nearly a major hiatus concerning *U-1105*'s future, as in its first response to the initial TNC allocations the USN had incorrectly indicated that it did not require *U-1105*. This caused an urgent exchange of messages between the TNC's British, American and Russian Admirals and it was not until 1 November that the USN made it clear that it wished *U-1105* to be allocated the USA.

When the initial TNC allocation of *U-1105* to the US was proposed on 10 October it was still undertaking its UK trials and as a result on 16 October the Royal Navy's First Sea Lord personally wrote to Admiral H Kent Hewitt, USN, who was the London-based Commander of the US Naval Forces in Europe (ComNavEu), asking if the U-boat could be retained by the RN until December. Whilst Admiral Hewitt quickly agreed to this request, *U-1105* was by then suffering from several serious defects and was not fit to sail across the North Atlantic. Thus, a somewhat embarrassed First Sea Lord wrote again to Admiral Hewitt on 30 October stating that the U-boat would first need a four-week refit before it could be handed over to the USN.

This delay allowed the USN crew for *U-1105* to be moved to England in mid-November to await the completion of the refit and agreement of a date for its handover. The warning order to move *U-1105* to the US was issued on 12 December and this was followed by an executive instruction on 15 December saying that it was intended to sail the U-boat on 17 December by 'unrestricted surface navigation'. Eventually *U-1105* left Gosport on 19 December on its surface crossing of the Atlantic because despite it having been used for both surface and submerged trials during the previous six months its CO had specific orders that he was not to dive the U-boat because of the fear of a German booby trap.

As the Atlantic storms which had caused the postponement of the transit were still raging, this was not a good omen. After two days *U-1105* encountered very heavy seas and by the fourth day it was in the middle of a hurricane which was not the best situation for an unescorted U-boat on the surface. At one stage the U-boat nearly rolled over, the radio failed and *U-1105* was out of contact for 10 days, causing the USN to fear the worst. Also, one of its engines failed and although this was temporarily repaired once *U-1105* was off Newfoundland, a tug was despatched to help bring the U-boat into PNY where it arrived on 2 January 1946. By then *U-1105* was not in a good state. The storm had bent the schnorkel, ripped the gun mounts off the deck, severely bent and rolled the decking and, most importantly, much of the remaining rubber coating had been torn loose and lost.

U-889, which was one of the two U-boats which had surrendered from sea in Canada, was a new example of the Type IXC U-boat and had been on only its first operational patrol when it surrendered. It was fitted with special hydrophone gear, modified to use acoustic torpedoes and the schnorkel head had a radar-absorbing rubber coating, and the USN was thus very keen to acquire it. There was no question of Canada being formally allocated either of the U-boats in its temporary possession and *U-889* which had been inspected by the TNC on 12 September and assessed to be the only one of the seven U-boats that surrendered in North America to be in an operational condition was allocated to the USA. Thus, after its trials in the RCN had been completed at the end of 1945 *U-889* could no longer remain in Canada, and it was therefore delivered to the USA, arriving at PNY on 12 January 1946. However, whereas when *U-889* had been inspected by the TNC in September 1945 and found to be in a good condition, it was in a non-operational state when transferred to the USN. The RCN trials had taken their toll.

In the latter part of 1945, it was decided that *U-530* and *U-977* were to undertake War Bond tours of the US East Coast and Caribbean ports. The two U-boats had arrived from Buenos Aires in October and were moored at the New London submarine base. Neither of them was in a good condition but on 18 October the CNO nevertheless authorised their preparation for the tours.

When ready, *U-977* took part in a five-week tour of seven East Coast ports starting in New London on 5 November and arriving back at New London on 13 December. The U-boat visited Albany, Poughkeepsie, Newburgh, Wilmington, Lewes, Richmond and Washington, and this gave the American public in those places an opportunity to see a German U-boat, the objective being to stimulate interest in the American Victory Loan fund-raising drive.

Simultaneously, *U-530* took part in a seven-week tour to seven ports in Texas. It travelled on the surface throughout leaving New London on 5 November and after calling at the Key West naval base, it visited Port

Arthur, Houston, Galveston, Corpus Christi, Brownsville, Beaumont and Orange. On the return journey north *U-530* had overnight stops at the Key West and Norfolk naval bases before it arrived back in New London on 22 December 1945.

After these War Bond tours had been completed, the USN decided that it had no further operational requirement for *U-530* and *U-977*, and the CNO issued the following instruction on 9 January 1946: 'Sail *U-530* and *U-977* to Naval Base Boston for care and preservation, place out of service and retain for explosive tests'.[2]

In the same week the general US Navy policy in relation to these two U-boats was set out by BuShips in a memo to PNY stating:

> The *U-530* and *U-977* that were formerly on War Bond Tours have completed that duty and are now berthed at the Boston Shipyard.
>
> No further operations are expected from these submarines other than as possible targets for explosives tests.
>
> Permission is granted to take such material and equipment as is needed for spare parts for the operating U-Boats from these submarines.
>
> Removal of material should not be such that the submarines could not be towed to a target area and submerged in a static dive.[2]

Despite having surrendered from sea in the USA *U-805* and *U-1228* were both in poor condition and it was estimated that it would take at least three months to make them serviceable for use in trials and experiments. Also, another Type IXC/40 (*U-858*) had already been selected for USN trials. There was therefore no need to put either of these Type IXCs into any sort of use and so even before the TNC had made its initial allocations in October 1945 PNY wrote to BuShips on 19 September saying: 'The surrendered German submarines *U-805* and *U-1228* are in ship keeper status to be utilised, by cannibalisation, for the operation of other surrendered German submarines'.[2]

Predictably, because of their poor condition *U-805* and *U-1228* were neither bid for nor allocated to the US by the TNC and they were therefore formally earmarked for early disposal. The USN was meticulous in following the TNC's recommendations and on 11 December the CNO sent a message to CincLant directing him to: 'Destroy by sinking in open sea depth not less than 100 meters prior to 15 February 1946 ex-German submarines *U-805* and *U-1228*. Report destruction date and geographical location.'[2]

In view of the shortage of time this was then followed on 8 January 1946 by an urgent instruction to PNY from BuShips which stated that:

'Removal of equipment from *U-805* and *U-1228* may be accomplished without restriction, other than not destroying the watertight integrity of the ships. Removal of any material from the two submarines should be expedited in view of early disposal.'[2]

On 4 February *U-1228* was towed out of Portsmouth by the tug USS *Penguin* and sunk on 5 February by a torpedo fired from the submarine USS *Sirago*. The first torpedo missed (passing under the U-boat), the second torpedo hit *U-1228* near the stern and caused it to list to starboard, the third torpedo missed (passing under the target) and finally the fourth torpedo struck *U-1228* amidships causing the U-boat to sink immediately to the north-east of Cape Cod.

Two days later on 7 February *U-805* was towed out of Portsmouth to the same position by USS *Penguin* where on 8 February it too was sunk by a torpedo fired from USS *Sirago*. On this occasion the first torpedo missed (passing under the target) as did the second torpedo. The third torpedo hit and caused *U-805* to break into two pieces and the fourth torpedo missed (passing over the target as the U-boat had already sunk).

By this action the US Navy had carried out the requirements of the Potsdam Agreement and the American Representative on the TNC formally advised his British and Russian colleagues on 14 February 1946:

> I desire to inform you that, in conformity with paragraph 7 of Appendix 2 of the Report of the Tripartite Naval Commission, submarines *U-805* and *U-1228* were sunk in open sea at an approximate depth of 130 fathoms on 8 and 5 February respectively. Submarines *U-805* and *U-1228* were the only unallocated submarines in the territorial waters of the United States.[3]

After their mini-refits *U-858*, *U-234* and *U-873* undertook a series of tests. Operational control of these U-boats was exercised by the Special Submarine Group (SSG) which was located at New London. After the initial standardisation tests in late 1945 (with *U-858*) and early 1946 (with *U-234* and *U-873*) the SSG published a schedule of proposed trials for each starting on 25 February 1946 from which it was clear that they were expected to have only very short-term futures in the US Navy, viz:

U-234

25 Feb	Sound survey in New London area
4 Mar	Diving trials in New London area
11 Mar	Tests for Underwater Sound Lab in New London area

18 Mar	Uncompleted sound survey tests in New London area
25 Mar	Magnetic ranging
1 Apr	Further trials or disposition as directed[2]

U-858

25 Feb–15 Apr	Torpedo firing tests at Key West
22 Apr–29 Apr	Upkeep in New London area
6 May	Sound survey in New London area
13–20 May	Tests for Underwater Sound Lab in New London area
27 May	Schnorkel operations in New London area
3 Jun	Diving trials in New London area
10 Jun	Possible periscope and fire control equipment tests if not completed earlier at Key West
17 Jun	Further trials or disposition as directed[2]

U-873

25 Feb	Diving trials in New London area
4 Mar	Uncompleted Oceanographic Institute tests in New London area
11 Mar	Uncompleted sound survey tests in New London area
18 Mar	Magnetic survey
25 Mar	Further trials or disposition as directed[2]

By 27 March 1946 the trials with *U-234* and *U-873* were complete and the CNO directed CincLant to: 'Sail *U-234* and *U-873* to Portsmouth. Upon arrival report to Com 1. About 1 April place subject vessels out of service. Both shall be retained. *U-234* for cannibalisation of spare parts. *U-873* for preservation and use in explosive program.'[3]

As a result, *U-234* was transferred from New London to PNY on 2 April and it was followed by *U-873* on 3 April. Finally, the trials with *U-858* were completed and on 14 June it too was transferred from New London to PNY. Thus, by the middle of June 1946 the USN had completed its planned trials with these three U-boats, and they had been returned to and were moored at PNY pending decisions about their final disposal. In respect of *U-234* it was planned to be disposed of after the cannibalisation of its equipment and spare parts, an action which was completed in the summer of 1946 with BuShips advising the CNO on 27 September that *U-234* was ready for disposal. The original disposal plan for the other two U-boats was that *U-858* and *U-873* would be retained as targets for the USN's conventional depth charging programme. However, this was cancelled on 21 April 1947 as the result of a joint BuShips/BuOrd review and *U-858* and *U-873* then became available either for use in torpedo tests or for sale as scrap.

The next indication of USN policy in respect of the U-boats then in its possession was revealed in the Minutes of the USN's Submarine Officers Conference held in Washington on 26 March 1946 which recorded that:

> Nine [this should be eight] U-Boats are being retained for explosive programs.
> The *U-2513* (Type 21) has been made available for OPDEVFOR.
> The *U-3008* (Type 21) is being placed in service at Portsmouth with high priority.
> The *U-1406* (Type 17-B) will not be placed in service, but the hull will be retained for the present.[1]

This policy confirmed that by the spring of 1946 the USN's long-term interests were concentrated on just the single Type XVIIB (*U-1406*) and the two Type XXIs (*U-2513* and *U-3008*) and that the remainder had been earmarked for early disposal. Thus it was no surprise when on 28 May the CNO made the USN's position quite clear saying:

> In regard to German submarines, it is desired to retain the following:
>
> | | |
> |---|---|
> | *U-858* | for conventional depth charging |
> | *U-873* | for conventional depth charging |
> | *U-2513* | for operations |
> | *U-3008* | for operations |
> | *U-1406* | for indefinite retention |
>
> All other German submarines will be disposed of upon completion of exploitation of equipment, and cannibalisation of equipment and spare parts. The Chief of the Bureau of Ships and the Chief of the Bureau of Ordnance are requested to advise this office when *U-234*, [*U-505*], *U-530*, *U-889*, *U-977* and *U-1105* are ready for disposal.[3]

This policy was subsequently modified on 6 August 1947 when BuShips set out the latest status of the remaining U-boats. First, it confirmed that the two U-boats previously retained as target vessels for the depth charge programme *U-858* and *U-873* had been released for disposal by the CNO. Second, it confirmed that *U-977* had already been disposed of by sinking in November 1946. Third, it confirmed that *U-1105* would be utilised for depth charge tests and then disposed of by sinking on completion of those tests. Finally, it confirmed that the stripping of material from *U-234*, (*U-505*), *U-530* and *U-889* had been completed and that these U-boats were ready for disposal.

The BuShips letter summarised the situation:

> The following ex-German submarines are now located in Portsmouth Naval Shipyard awaiting disposal by the Chief of Naval Operations: *U-234*, [*U-505*], *U-530*, *U-858*, *U-873* and *U-889*.
>
> Originally, BuShips had recommended that the vessels be sold as a hulk or be scrapped. Since then, the Bureau has determined it is in the best interests of the Government to sell surplus combatant vessels rather than to demolish in Naval Shipyards or by private contract. Accordingly, it is recommended that the above vessels by declared to the US Navy Vessel Disposal Office (NVDO*)* [located in the Naval Shipyard in Brooklyn, New York] for sale.[3]

As far as the 'Walter' U-boat *U-1406* was concerned it had been informally accepted by the TNC, even before the latter's initial recommendations were produced and despite its very poor condition, that it would be allocated to the USA. However, after its arrival at PNY on 11 October 1945 the USN neither repaired nor operated the U-boat. After a preliminary inspection PNY estimated that it would cost $1 million and take 15 months to put it into service. Also, whilst the USN's initial intention had been to use *U-1406* as a fast target its hydrogen peroxide fuel presented a serious fire risk and was very costly and in any case it seemed probable that the U-boat's performance was unlikely to achieve the enhanced speeds and depths required. Thus, the plans to use it were rejected.

Instead, the US Navy concentrated on a study of the Mk 17B HTP-powered 'Walter' gas-turbine engine which had been fitted to *U-1406* of which the USN had two examples, one from *U-1406* itself and one which had been found in the' Walterwerke' at Kiel and then shipped to the USA. Both of these Mk 17B engines were taken for study to the USN's Experimental Engineering Establishment at Annapolis but whilst at the time the 'Walter' turbine was seen as a most effective means of achieving air-independent, high-speed underwater propulsion it was quickly overtaken by the advent of nuclear propulsion, and the USN's interest waned. In the meantime *U-1406* remained moored at PNY without any plans for its future use.

Whereas when *U-889* was inspected by the TNC in Canada in September 1945 and found to be fully operable and in the best condition of all the U-boats that had surrendered from sea in the Western Hemisphere, it was in a non-operational condition when transferred to the US in January 1946. The CNO therefore quickly granted PNY permission to 'kill' the battery on *U-889* particularly as by that time the USN was already conducting trials on the Type IXC/40 U-boat *U-858* and had no need for yet another example to be included in its short trials programme. Thus *U-889* remained moored at PNY for use as a potential source of spares until BuShips advised the CNO on 27 September 1946 that the planned cannibalisation action was complete and that *U-889* was ready for disposal.

After *U-1105*'s very difficult solo trans-Atlantic surface crossing in the latter half of December 1945 and arrival at PNY in early January 1946, there was initially some indecision concerning the future of the rubber-covered submarine especially as the USN had no requirement for a Type VIIC U-boat. The USN was nevertheless keen to learn the secrets of *U-1105*'s Alberich coating and on 1 February 1946 BuShips ordered two sections of the remaining rubber coating to be removed. One was for the Naval Research Laboratory (NRL) in Washington and the other was for the Massachusetts Institute of Technology's (MIT) Acoustic Laboratory in Cambridge, Mass both of which were keen to conduct research on the U-boat's unique sonar-reflecting skin.

Once the sections of anti-sonar rubber tiles had been removed from *U-1105* at the beginning of February and passed to the NRL and the MIT for research the USN had no further use for *U-1105* other than in explosives tests. However the projected way ahead for *U-1105* was amended. First, after the Bureau of Ordnance (BuOrd) had proposed on 25 July that only one of the surplus U-boats awaiting disposal should be used specifically for testing both live and dummy demolition equipment and, second, after BuShips had requested a U-boat on which it could evaluate new salvage equipment and methods.

The CNO approved these proposals and allocated *U-1105* to the joint BuShips/BuOrd project on 29 November 1946. He also directed that *U-1105* should be towed from Boston Navy Yard to the Mine Warfare Test Station at Solomons Island, Maryland. However, rather than being held at Solomons Island *U-1105* was moved instead to the Naval Gun Factory in Washington to await the commencement of the planned tests, progress on which was exceedingly slow. Indeed, they did not take place for another 18 months during which time *U-1105* remained moored at the Naval Gun Factory.

After *U-2513* and *U-3008* had arrived in New London in August 1945 and before they were moved to PNY in September it was decided that in accordance with USN policy only one of these two Type XXIs (*U-2513*) would be subject to trials – which were planned to last for up to a year. At the same time *U-3008* became an authorised source of spares both for *U-2513* and the other U-boats allocated to the trials programmes.

A short time later, because of the USN's increasing interest in the design and technology of the Type XXI, it became clear that it might be necessary to make an exception to the general policy and instead for the USN to conduct extensive trials for more than a year with the two Type XXIs. The prospect was first discussed in October 1945 and was formally implemented when on 7 March 1946 the CNO sent a message to PNY saying: 'Overhaul and place in service *U-3008*. Report to CINCLANT for duty.'[3]

These two large, high-speed, ocean-going Type XXIs were of particular interest to the USN which was very keen to learn whatever it could about the German designs and associated technology, and it was therefore decided that they would both be subject to testing for as long as the spares situation and their battery lives allowed. This decision was supported by the results of PNY's formal 'Type XXI Design Study Report 2G-21' of July 1946, mostly carried out on *U-3008*, which stated:

> This type of vessel is a radical departure in hull form and in certain mechanical and electrical respects from earlier types of German submarines, for the purpose of increasing submerged speed, and permissible submergence depth.
>
> The changes have been made at the expense of surface speed and other surface characteristics. Further, the design was not completely thought out before the beginning of construction, and has a number of shortcomings as a result.
>
> Nevertheless, the results obtained indicate the need to exploit the possibilities of the type to the maximum.[4]

Whilst, as described in the Design Study report, there were a number of drawbacks evident in *U-2513* and *U-3008* the USN nevertheless embarked on a series of extended operational trials with these two U-boats and satisfied itself that the German advances in design, propulsion and performance justified their replication in its own submarines. The first step was to incorporate the best features of the Type XXI into two of the USN's wartime *Tench* class fleet submarines in 1946/47, essentially converting them into look-alike Type XXIs and calling them 'Guppies' in view of their **G**reater **U**nderwater **P**ropulsion **P**ower. The improvements included increasing the submarines' battery capacity, streamlining the boats' structures, adding snorkels and improving their fire-control systems. Thereafter, whilst the Guppy programme was itself extended the best aspects of the German developments were designed into the USN's new *Tang* class of fleet submarines which delivered the diesel-electric powered higher speeds and improved performance that had been envisaged by the German engineers when they designed the Type XXI U-boat.

Once *U-2513* had arrived at PNY in September 1945 and been selected as the (then) single trial Type XXI, the USN wasted no time in initiating the actions necessary to make use of it. The first essential action was to make *U-2513* seaworthy and fit for use in the planned trials. However, whilst it was originally thought that it could be made available for the initial standardisation trials quite quickly this proved to be optimistic particularly because of problems with the availability of spares. The delays were also caused partly because of the need for a considerable number of domestic modifications and improvements to the U-boat.

After its extensive overhaul in Portsmouth *U-2513* was ready for sea, leaving PNY for New London on 17 January 1946 where it was involved in trials in the New London area before heading south to Key West on 10 March for a long series of evaluation tests in conjunction with the development of submarine and anti-submarine tactics. On 5 November 1946 it was visited by the CNO (Admiral Chester Nimitz) and on 21 November President Truman became the first American President to travel on a submarine when he visited *U-2513*.

On 15 March 1947 *U-2513* headed north from Key West to PNY for a major overhaul which lasted until September. In October it returned to Key West where it remained until the summer of 1949. On 5 December 1947 *U-2513* was visited again by President Truman but this time without going to sea. In mid-June 1949 *U-2513* again moved north from Key West to PNY where it was decommissioned and declared out of service on 8 July because there was no life remaining in its batteries. On 7 November 1950, the CNO certified that *U-2513* was no longer needed but it remained at Portsmouth until 23 August 1951 when it was returned to Key West this time under tow for final disposal as a target in surface warship weapons trials.

After the receipt of the CNO's message in March 1946 instructing PNY to overhaul and place *U-3008* in service despite its considerable cannibalisation the overhaul was completed by mid-summer and *U-3008* was commissioned into the USN on 24 July. It initially operated out of New London and Portsmouth but in March 1947 it departed for Key West where like *U-2513* it was involved with the development of submarine and anti-submarine tactics. That deployment lasted until October 1947 when *U-3008* returned to Portsmouth. *U-3008* then conducted more operations out of New London and Portsmouth until February 1948 when it left New London to return once again to Florida to resume duty with the Operational Development Force until early June. On 7 June 1948 it headed north once more and on 18 June, with its battery life finally expended, *U-3008* was placed out of service at PNY to be used as a source of spares for *U-2513*. It was formally declared as surplus to requirements on 7 November 1950 but with the proviso that it should be preserved for explosive tests, a decision that was formally approved on 29 June 1951.

After the TNC-directed sinkings of *U-805* and *U-1228* in February 1946 the USN disposed of its ten allocated U-boats during the course of the following 10 years with all of them either being sunk in explosive tests or sold for scrap.

The first of the U-boats for disposal was *U-977* which had been berthed in an out-of-service condition in Boston since January 1946 where it was used as a source of spares for the other in-use U-boats. It had been declared as ready for disposal on 1 August and on 13 November, after *U-977*'s transit under tow from the Boston Navy Yard via the Cape Cod Canal, the submarine USS *Atule* effected a rendezvous with *U-977* and the yard tug *ATR 64* off Cape Cod and fired a Mk 23 torpedo which destroyed the U-boat.

The next four U-boats for disposal were *U-234*, *U-530*, *U-858* and *U-889*. Of these, *U-234* and *U-858* had been returned to PNY after their trials to await disposal: *U-234* on 2 April 1946 and *U-858* on 14 June 1946. Of the other two, *U-889* had been at PNY since 13 January 1946 and *U-530* since 2 May 1946 after which both had been used as sources of spares. In November 1947 the four U-boats were towed to Provincetown Harbour at Cape Cod and then to a torpedo firing area 40 miles northeast of the Cape. They were sunk by torpedoes fired from four separate USN Atlantic Fleet submarines on 20 and 21 November 1947:

U-234   Sunk by US S/M *Greenfish* on 20 Nov 1947
U-530   Sunk by US S/M *Toro* on 21 Nov 1947
U-858   Sunk by US S/M *Sirago* on 21 Nov 1947
U-889   Sunk by US S/M *Flying Fish* on 20 Nov 1947

It was then the turn of *U-873* which after the completion of its trials in the New London area had been returned to PNY on 3 April 1946 to await a decision about its disposal and to be used in the meantime as a source of spares for the other U-boats in USN service. It had initially been retained as a target vessel for BuOrd's planned depth charge programme, but after this was reviewed in April 1947 *U-873* was added to the list of U-boats at PNY awaiting disposal. The formal disposal decision was taken in late 1947 but rather than being sunk in torpedo tests off Cape Cod *U-873* was sold for scrap to the Interstate Metals Corporation of New York. Finally *U-873* was towed out of PNY on 10 March 1948 en-route for the ship-breakers and it was broken-up later in the year.

The disposal of *U-1105* was a very long drawn-out process. After it had been moved to the Naval Gun Factory in Washington at the beginning of 1947 the planned salvage and depth charge tests did not commence for another 18 months. Then, between August 1948 and September 1949 *U-1105* was sunk five times and raised four times. The process began in 1948 when *U-1105* was scuttled in shallow water off Piney Point in the Potomac River on 17/18 August. The initial salvage and lifting tests on the sunken hulk were conducted from 24 to 26 August but a hurricane was due to pass through the area and for safety reasons *U-1105* was flooded and returned to the seabed on 30 August. The tests then resumed when *U-1105* was raised on 2 September and continued until 21 September when the emphasis changed to towing exercises.

With the completion of the salvage and rescue tests together with the towing exercises the demolition test programme took priority. Thus, after being towed across Chesapeake Bay on 28 September *U-1105* was sunk on 29 September off Point No Point on the east side of the bay in the first of two explosive tests designed to determine the effective range of depth charges. In the event, even though it had been sunk *U-1105* was not fatally damaged by this first depth charge trial. Thus, after 29 September the salvage and rescue tests continued off Point No Point. However, *U-1105* was not raised to the surface and on 13 November with the onset of the winter weather the flooded hulk was temporarily abandoned on the seabed off Point No Point remaining there for the following nine months.

On 11 July 1949 another set of salvage operations began but it was not until 18 August that the waterlogged *U-1105* was once more on the surface. On 19 August the U-boat was towed back to the area off Piney Point before being sunk yet again. The final events marking *U-1105*'s time in the USN took place in September. First, it was raised from the seabed on 2 September. It was then moored on the surface whilst an

Explosive Ordnance Disposal Team from the Naval Powder Factory suspended a newly-developed 250lb depth charge 30ft below the keel. Then, on 19 September, *U-1105* was towed to a position a mile offshore from Piney Point where the depth charge was detonated. This caused *U-1105* to sink in less than a minute in about 90ft of water where it remains today as a registered underwater monument and official dive-site.

U-1406 remained at PNY throughout 1946 and 1947 until BuShips recommended on 2 January 1948 that *U-1406*'s hull should be declared surplus to requirements and made available for disposal. The USN authorised the U-boat's disposal in February 1948 and it was sold to the Interstate Metals Corporation of New York. Finally *U-1406* left Portsmouth under tow on 18 May 1948 en-route to the ship-breakers prior to being broken up.

On 2 September 1951 the USN ordered that *U-2513* should be sunk by gunfire. Thus on 4 October it was towed to the Dry Tortugas project area to the west of Key West by USS *Petrel* and the tug *YTB-543*. The following day the three vessels were joined by the destroyer USS *Robert A. Owens*, and on 6 October both USS *Petrel* and USS *Robert B. Owens* attacked the U-boat with gunfire and rockets. The rockets were fired by the destroyer as part of the US Navy's test programme for what was initially called 'Weapon Able' but later known as 'Weapon Alfa'. However, *U-2513* was not allowed to sink on 6 October and instead was kept afloat with its decks awash by the frequent blowing of its ballast tanks using a salvage hose from USS *Petrel*. *U-2513* was finally sunk on 7 October 1951 after being hit by 'Weapon Able' rockets from USS *Robert B. Owens*. Subsequently the underwater wreck of *U-2513* was used by the USN for sonar, diving and demolition exercises as well as being used as a weapons test target.

On 31 July 1951, *U-3008* was towed from PNY to Puerto Rico for full-scale tests of a new underwater explosive. A series of five demolition tests took place in Brewers' Bay in St Thomas in the US Virgin Islands, with the first being on 22 May 1952, the second on 19 September 1953 and the last in June 1954. The final test left *U-3008* so badly damaged that the CNO authorised it to be sold for scrap. *U-3008* was therefore raised in the summer of 1954 and towed to the USN base in Puerto Rico where it was put up for sale. It was sold to Loudes Iron & Metal Company on 15 September 1955 and Loudes took possession of it on 17 January 1956 prior to scrapping.

In summary the twelve U-boats which had surrendered in 1945, ten of which had been allocated to the USA by the TNC and which saw service with the USN post-May 1945 were disposed of as follows:

U-234   Sunk on 20 Nov 1947 by US S/M *Greenfish* off Cape Cod.
U-530   Sunk on 21 Nov 1947 by US S/M *Toro* off Cape Cod.
U-805   Sunk of 8 Feb 1946 by US S/M *Sirago* off Cape Cod.
U-858   Sunk on 21 Nov 1947 by a US S/M *Sirago* off Cape Cod.
U-873   Sold for scrap in New York in Mar 1948.
U-889   Sunk on 20 Nov 1947 by US S/M *Flying Fish* off Cape Cod.
U-977   Sunk on 13 Nov 1946 by US S/M *Atule* off Cape Cod.
U-1105 Sunk on 19 Sep 1949 by a depth charge in the Potomac River.
U-1228 Sunk on 5 Feb 1946 by US S/M *Sirago* off Cape Cod.
U-1406 Sold for scrap in New York in May 1948.
U-2513 Sunk on 7 Oct 1951 off Key West by USS *Robert A Owens*.
U-3008 Sold for scrap in Puerto Rico in Sep 1955.

CHAPTER 14

The Capture and Use of *U-505* by the US Navy

ON 16 MARCH 1944 *U-505*, a 740-ton Type IXC long-range ocean-going German U-boat, had begun its seventh war patrol when it departed from France for operations off the west coast of Africa. But on 23 May whilst in the Gulf of Guinea south of Liberia, having failed to sink any Allied shipping and with *U-505* beginning to run low on fuel, its CO (Lieutenant Harald Lange) decided to head for home.

At the same time USN Task Group (TG) 22.3 led by the aircraft carrier USS *Guadalcanal* was in the vicinity of West Africa and its CO (Captain Dan Gallery) was determined to see if he could capture a U-boat. A previous action had convinced him that when a submarine surfaced during an attack it was highly probable that the main objective of its CO would be to save his crew. Captain Gallery decided that if the opportunity arose he would encourage the evacuation of the U-boat by concentrating anti-personnel weapons on it, by not using any weapons that could sink it and by attempting to board it as quickly as possible.

On 3 June *U-505* was on its way north about 150 miles off the coast of Africa midway between the Canary Islands and the Cape Verde Islands and to the west of Cape Blanco when TG 22.3 received an ULTRA-based intelligence message which said: 'U-Boat estimated homebound off Cape Blanco.'[1]

That same day a U-boat had been detected by aircraft from TG 22.3 and in the early morning of 4 June USS *Guadalcanal* and the destroyer escort USS *Pope* picked up radio bearings and USS *Guadalcanal* picked up a U-boat signal, although nothing came from any of these contacts. Despite this a U-boat was detected again in the late morning by the destroyer escort USS *Chatelain*. The latter attacked the U-boat, the results of which were so serious that what turned out to be *U-505* was forced to surface very close to the middle of the TG when, after being subjected to intense small-arms fire, Lange ordered his crew to abandon ship. He believed that *U-505* was about to sink but although the sea valves were opened he failed to order the activation of the scuttling charges and the destruction of the U-boat's papers and secret equipment.

Contrary to both German and American expectations *U-505* failed to sink and though it was flooding and lying very low in the water Captain Galley decided to activate his capture plan. *U-505* was therefore boarded by sailors from the destroyer escort USS *Pillsbury* who closed the sea valves, and the U-boat was prevented from sinking. As a result, the United States flag was hoisted from *U-505*'s conning tower and the U-boat was captured. The first action by the boarding party was to remove the ship's papers and then with a skeleton crew on board *U-505* was taken in tow by USS *Guadalcanal*.

The details of the detection, attack and capture of *U-505* on 4 June are described in the Deck Log of USS *Guadalcanal*, viz:

1109   USS *Chatelain* reported underwater contact on starboard bow and proceeded to investigate

1118   USS *Chatelain* opened attack with hedgehogs. Immediately after the USS *Chatelain*'s attack, pilot of VF#1 reported sighting submarine below the surface and made strafing runs on submarine, which was commencing to surface

1119   USS *Chatelain* aided by VF#1 and VF#7 continued further attacks on submarine

1121   Submarine surfaced off starboard quarter, and Commander Task Force broadcast following message: 'I want to capture this bastard if possible'. Escorts opened fire with deck guns. VF#1 and VF#7 made strafing runs on surfaced submarine

1125   Escorts reported submarine appeared to be surrendering

1138   Escorts commenced picking up survivors

1146   Boarding party from USS *Pillsbury* boarded submarine

1215   Boarding party from USS *Pillsbury* reported that submarine was shipping water aft rapidly. The condition of the submarine was as follows:

> Afloat but with stern down
> Approximately 12 feet of the bow raised above level of water
> Deck tilted at about 15 degree angle which left the upper part of conning tower above the surface
> The deck from the bow to about 20 feet forward of the conning tower was above the level of the water
> Deck between this point and aft of conning tower was completely submerged
> All attempts to pump water from submarine failed

1248   Cdr Trosino left the ship in charge of a salvage party
1315   USS *Jenks* reported the number of the submarine as *U-505*
1419   Maneuvered in position to put over a line to U-Boat
1450   Proceeded ahead with submarine in tow astern
1545   Raised the Ensign of the United States of America on the
       submarine in tow
1800   Laying-to with *U-505* in tow
1802   Prisoners were brought aboard[2]

At first there was confusion about what Captain Gallery should do with
U-505. His initial action was to send a message to the USN's Commander
Morocco Sea Frontier in Casablanca, with copies to CincLant and the
Commander-in-Chief of the US Navy (Cominch), at 1445 on 4 June,
saying: 'Request immediate assistance to tow captured submarine.'[1] An
hour later he sent a similar message directly to CincLant with a copy
to Cominch, saying: 'Have *U-505* in tow. Kaptan Lieutenant Lange.
80 days out. 49 [*sic*] Prisoners. Don't have fuel for Casablanca. Request
permission proceed Dakar.'[1]

The information about the capture had been immediately passed by
Washington to the Admiralty in London, and later that evening Gallery
received a message from the RN's Flag Officer West Africa (FOCWAF)
in Freetown congratulating him on the capture and authorising him
to tow *U-505* to Dakar. Such action would, however, have destroyed
any security benefits arising from the capture and though the RN was
just attempting to be helpful the suggestion was not well received in
Washington, especially as more and more people were now becoming
aware of the capture of the U-boat.

A flurry of messages followed starting with one at 2042 on 4 June from
the RN's First Sea Lord in London, Admiral Sir Andrew Cunningham, to
the USN's Cominch, Admiral Ernest King, saying:

Personal for Admiral King from First Sea Lord. In view of the importance
at this time of preventing the Germans suspecting a compromise of
their ciphers I am sure you will agree that all concerned should be
ordered to maintain complete secrecy regarding the capture of *U-505*.
I am instructing Flag Officer Commanding West African Forces and
Flag Officer Gibraltar Mediterranean Approaches in this sense.[1]

Admiral King was not amused by this deteriorating security situation and
replied sharply at 1409 on 5 June, saying:

Personal for First Sea Lord. Before receipt of your 042042 I had taken
initial action to preserve security and expect to take further action today.

In this connection I consider it most unfortunate that FOCWAF in his 042022 should have taken it upon himself to inform COMAR Dakar of the incident because if there is a leak it is most likely to come from such a source.[1]

Two minutes later at 1411 King sent a message to Captain Gallery directing him:

To ensure enemy does not learn of *U-505* capture

(A) If *U-505*'s condition warrants tow her to Bermuda under escort of Task Group 22.

(B) Emphasise to all concerned need for absolute secrecy regarding capture.[1]

In similar vein CincLant sent a message at 1343 on 5 June to the RN's FOCWAF making it clear – between the lines – that this was a USN operation and saying: '*Guadalcanal* Group will not proceed to Dakar.'[1]

U-505 was then towed to the USN's Operating Base in Bermuda, first by USS *Guadalcanal* and from 7 June by the ocean-going tug USS *Abnaki* which had been directed to the capture scene to offer assistance. Details of the 2,000-mile towing operation are set out in the Deck Logs of USS *Guadalcanal* and USS *Abnaki*.[2]

As early as 6 June the USN concluded that it needed to create the illusion that *U-505* had been sunk rather than captured and so, under the assumption that it could be successfully towed to Bermuda, it was suggested by the Chief of Staff of the USN's 10th Fleet that it should be given an appropriate cover (code) name with two being suggested – USS *Ark* or USS *Nemo*. Whilst the 10th Fleet had no ships, it was charged with directing anti-submarine warfare in the Atlantic Ocean. Admiral Ernest King (the CNO and Cominch) was its nominal commander but day-to-day operations were directed by the Chief of Staff, Admiral Frances Low. Thus, with Cominch's personal approval the code name USS *Nemo* was chosen by HQ 10th Fleet and retained while *U-505* was kept in Bermuda for the remainder of the war. The executive instruction was sent out from Washington on 12 June, saying:

Cover name quote *Nemo* unquote assigned *U-505*. Retain her and prisoners in US Naval custody at Bermuda making such arrangements as necessary to ensure maximum security. Cominch will provide for inspection by representatives of Navy Department and Tenth Fleet and for interrogation of prisoners.[1]

All the USN personnel who had taken part in or witnessed the U-boat's capture and subsequent tow to Bermuda were sworn to secrecy, an action that was amazingly successful considering the number of personnel involved in all the various aspects of the U-boat's time with the USN between 4 June 1944 and 8 May 1945. This security imperative was emphasised in no uncertain terms both by Captain Gallery personally and by the USN's threat of courts martial and possible death sentences should anyone break the required silence. On 14 June Gallery published a memo to everyone in TG 22.3 saying:

> The operations which we have conducted since 4 June have been classified as top secret.
>
> The capture of the *U-505* can be one of the major turning points in World War 2 provided repeat provided we keep our mouths shut about it.
>
> The enemy must not learn of this capture.
>
> I fully appreciate how nice it would be to be able to tell our friends about it when we get in, but you can depend on it that they will read about it eventually in the history books that are printed from now on.
>
> If you obey the following orders it will safeguard your own health as well as information which is vital to the national defence: 'Keep your bowels open and your mouths shut.'[3]

On a more formal level all concerned were required to sign a statement which read:

> I, ..., having had the necessity explained to me for maintaining absolute secrecy regarding the capture of the German submarine *U-505*, do hereby swear that I will reveal this information to no one until the end of the war unless sooner released to the public by the Navy Department. ('No one' includes my nearest relatives, friends, military or naval personnel – even an Admiral unless I am directed by my Commanding Officer to tell him).
>
> I fully realise that should Germany learn from any source of the capture of *U-505* that the tremendous advantage which we have gained by her capture would be immediately nullified, resulting in a great loss to the United States.
>
> I am also aware that should I break this oath, I will be committing a grave military offence, thereby subjecting myself to a General Court Martial, which court has the authority in time of war to award as punishment the death sentence.[3]

The seriousness of this situation and the importance accorded to it by the USN in Washington was re-emphasised on 17 June in a message from

CincLant to the Commander of TG 22.3 saying: 'This is Top Secret. Prior to detachment or arrival, again warn all personnel [and] ships your command including tug as to necessity for maintaining absolute secrecy concerning recent operations.'[1]

Additionally, evidence of Washington's special interest in *U-505* was apparent from the urgent arrangements made on 15 June to fly a party of eighteen intelligence, engineering and other specialists to Bermuda on 20 June to allow for the immediate inspection of the U-boat and the interrogation of prisoners which again emphasised that: 'Attention is invited to necessity for maintaining absolute secrecy concerning *Nemo* and associated matters.'[1]

After its initial enthusiasm to become involved in *U-505*'s post-capture activities, the RN was equally circumspect about the release of details of the USN's acquisition of the U-boat and only minimal information was provided even for the intelligence community. For instance, the Admiralty's 'U-Boat Situation Report' for the week ending 5 June simply recorded that: 'Of the three boats now returning from West Africa after unsuccessful patrols, one was captured by USS *Guadalcanal* on 4 June near Cape Blanco and is being towed to Dakar.'[4] Similarly, the Admiralty's 'U-Boat Trend Report' for the period 29 May to 7 June recorded that: 'On 4 June USS *Guadalcanal* captured a U-Boat off Cape Blanco and is towing it to Dakar. The U-Boat is a 740-tonner and was probably returning from a patrol in the Takoradi area.'[4]

The RN of course benefitted from the treasure-trove of intelligence and technical material that the USN had acquired but whilst only a very limited number of people knew its source there was never any mention that the U-boat that had been captured was *U-505*. The secret remained as safe in the UK as in the USA.

U-505's arrival in Bermuda is recorded in the War Diary of the USN Operating Base Bermuda with the entry for 19 June 1944 saying: 'USS *Guadalcanal* and escorts arrived in Bermuda bringing in a captured submarine and prisoners of war. The prisoners of war and the submarine will remain in Bermuda until further orders from Commander-in-Chief.'[5]

As far as the members of *U-505*'s crew of fifty-nine officers and men were concerned, one died during the capture on 4 June and the remaining fifty-eight were taken on board ships of TG 22.3 before most of them were transferred to USS *Guadalcanal*. They were then transported to Bermuda with TG 22.3 where after their arrival on 19 June 56 of them were handed over into the custody of the US Marine Corps. The two exceptions were the CO, Lieutenant Lange, who had been shot in the legs during the capture and a young engine-room mechanic, Ewald Felix, who had assisted the USN salvage parties which prevented *U-505* from sinking during its long tow.

By the middle of July the authorities in Washington had decided what to do about *U-505*'s crew in view of the need to maintain complete secrecy concerning the capture of the U-boat and on 24 July Cominch sent a message to CincLant and NOB Bermuda saying: 'Transfer *Nemo* POWs to Norfolk with Captain Huston USMC in charge. Advise me ETA at least 3 days in advance in order that necessary arrangements may be made to receive POWs at Norfolk. Continue highest security.'[1]

Thus, on 30 July after the POWs had been held for some six weeks in Bermuda, the Commandant of NOB Bermuda sent a message to Cominch confirming that: '*Nemo* POWs – 4 officers and 52 men, plus Marine detachment. ETA Norfolk 2000Z Thursday 3rd [August] via *PCE(R) 851* and *852*.'[1]

This was followed a day later by Naval Operating Order No. 390-44 which instructed two patrol craft escort (rescue) vessels, USS *PCE(R) 851* and USS *PCE(R) 852* which were already in Bermuda to transport the fifty-six POWs to Norfolk, VA. The latter were then embarked at the NOB at 0830 on 1 August with thirty of them travelling in USS *PCE(R) 851* and twenty-six of them travelling in USS *PCE(R) 852*. Two days later, on the afternoon of 3 August, they were disembarked at Newport News (to the north of the Norfolk NOB) presumably to keep them out of sight of prying eyes.[2]

Thereafter responsibility for *U-505*'s crew was handed over to the US Army's Provost Department and the POWs were moved by train from Newport News to the large Army-run POW Camp Ruston at Grambling in northern Louisiana. However, before they arrived there on 5/6 August the USN's Commander-in-Chief had asked the US Army to ensure that for security reasons they be held incommunicado rather than being treated as normal POWs.

To achieve this, on 3 August the Provost Marshal General in Washington instructed the CO of the 8th Service Command in Dallas, Texas who was responsible for Camp Ruston to make it clear to the camp authorities that the fifty-six German Naval POWs from *U-505* (four officers and fifty-two enlisted men) were not to be allowed to mingle or communicate at any time with any of the other 4,000 POWs in the camp. Also, provision was to be made to ensure that no communications of any nature should reach Germany from this group of prisoners. To achieve this, and contrary to the Geneva Convention, *U-505*'s crew were kept in a special isolated area at Camp Ruston and no reports of their capture were submitted to either the protecting power, Switzerland, or to the International Red Cross (IRC) for the remainder of the war. To reinforce the point an officer from the Office of Naval Intelligence was sent to Ruston to brief the Camp Commandant about the background of the prisoners as well as to ensure that arrangements were made for all mail written by *U-505*'s POWs to be sent to the Chief Postal Censor in New York and for such mail to be kept separately from all other mail.[6]

Despite all these precautions there was nevertheless a security scare in January 1945 when several letters from a German Army POW at Camp Ruston were intercepted in which he referred to one of *U-505*'s crew who was a cousin of his wife.[6] Thus, information as well as mail was probably being smuggled out of the isolation compound and, whilst the US Army authorities could not guarantee that this had not happened before, the incident served to emphasise the need to continue to keep the information about *U-505*'s capture secret.

As far as the IRC was concerned it was aware that Camp Ruston held POWs who it was not permitted to visit, recording in a visit report in autumn 1944 that: 'The commander did not permit us to visit one of the sections containing 50 prisoners, and our efforts to visit this section failed. Admission to this section was forbidden to civilians by superior authorities, even to representatives of the Committee of the International Red Cross.'[7]

This report did not, however, persuade the US military authorities to relax their security precautions and in his visit report in March 1945 the Red Cross Inspector observed in a similar vein that: 'The last one [compound] is occupied by naval officers which we are not allowed to visit as was the case at the time of the preceding visit in spite of representations made before the War Department.'[7]

To reinforce the point about the need for continued secrecy, on 26 April 1945, just two weeks before the end of the war in Europe, the War Department sent a message saying: 'Inform the 8th Service Command that under no circumstances should the Swiss representatives be permitted to ascertain that these Navy prisoners are at Ruston. In other words, move the boys out of Ruston before the Swiss arrive and then return them to Ruston as soon as the Swiss depart.'[7]

It is unclear what happened to the POWs from *U-505* in Camp Ruston after VE Day on 8 May 1945 and once the security restrictions surrounding their captivity were no longer necessary. Some of them worked on local cotton farms whilst others seem to have been transferred to other POW camps in the USA. After that they were transferred to the UK, arriving there in December 1945 and early 1946 where they were held in a variety of POW camps in England and Scotland until the latter half of 1946 and in some cases even until late 1947 before being finally released back to Germany.

Quite how long the capture of *U-505* was kept from the Germans naval authorities is uncertain. The only evidence concerning this is offered by Gunter Hessler who was Dönitz' son-in-law as well as being Staff Officer (Operations) to Flag Officer (U-Boats) from 1942 until May 1945 and who, when describing events in the second half of 1944 to the British and American Intelligence staff after the end of the war, wrote:

> Neither did we know of the capture of *U-505*, owing to the excellence of Allied security and to the strict isolation of her crew by the Americans. It was not until the end of 1944, or the beginning of 1945, that a U-Boat officer held in a Canadian prisoner-of-war camp managed to pass us a message warning of the probable capture of a U-Boat, intact and complete with signal publications. We were thus provided with a possible explanation of many curious incidents which had occurred in the Atlantic since the summer of 1944, when enemy forces had contrived to turn up at our re-arranged rendezvous with the same punctuality as the U-Boats themselves.[8]

In the case of Lange, *U-505*'s CO, after being disembarked in Bermuda on 19 June he was taken to the USN Hospital in Bermuda where he spent much of the remainder of the war on the Officers' Ward after his left leg was amputated at the knee shortly after he arrived.[9]

It was not until early February 1945 that he was fit enough to be able to leave Bermuda and be taken to Camp Ruston. His name was then added to the list of prisoners who were to be segregated and kept incommunicado with specific instructions being issued by the Director of the US Army's Prisoner of War Operations Division to the Chief Postal Censor on 8 February saying:

> The name of an additional prisoner is hereby added to that original list of fifty six prisoners that was transmitted to your office with our letter of 18 October 1944. This fifty-seventh prisoner is Oberleutnant Harold Lange. It is requested that Prisoner of War Lange be accorded the same precautions by your office as the other fifty six [members of *U-505*'s crew] previously mentioned, and that steps be taken to ensure

that he remains incommunicado and not be reported for a period of 270 days from 6 August 1944.[6]

What happened to Lange between 10 May and his return to Germany is unknown but he was back in Hamburg in May 1946.[10]

There was one other prisoner who was treated differently from all the other POWs. He was Ewald Felix, a German of Polish origin who was a junior member of *U-505*'s crew and who after being taken on board USS *Guadalcanal* had helped to keep the U-boat afloat. Quite how much assistance was given by Felix is unclear although USS *Guadalcanal*'s Deck Log records that 'a prisoner of war' was amongst the fifteen-man salvage party transferred to the U-boat on 9 June. After that, Felix was kept separate from the remainder of *U-505*'s crew whilst on board the aircraft carrier with the latter being told that he had died suddenly and been buried at sea. Despite this USS *Guadalcanal*'s Deck Log records that 'Ewald Felix prisoner of war' was transferred to *U-505* on 18 June.[2]

When *U-505*'s crew was off-loaded in Bermuda Felix was not listed as one of the fifty-seven men handed into the custody of the US Marines and it is therefore probable that he remained on board either USS *Guadalcanal* or one of the destroyer escorts when TG 22.3 returned to Norfolk, VA after leaving Bermuda on 20 June. Felix was then interned separately from the rest of the U-boat's crew, possibly at Fort Hunt in Washington, DC and under the direct control of the USN's Office of Naval Intelligence (ONI) before he returned to Germany after the war. Certainly he must have been kept separate from his colleagues who might well have punished him harshly for facilitating the capture of *U-505*.

After the end of the war in Europe the USN recorded its gratitude to Ewald Felix when the Head of the Special Activities Branch of the Division of Naval Intelligence wrote on 25 June 1945 that:

> During his time as a prisoner of war in the United States subject prisoner, of his own free will and because of anti-Nazi beliefs, gave invaluable assistance to the United States in the prosecution of the war effort and was of material assistance. It is strongly recommended that, should subject prisoner of war ever enter an application for an entry permit to the United States or apply for a quota or other visa for entry into the United States, the facts set forth herein should be given due and favorable consideration. Subject prisoner of war is, from all knowledge available, considered to be desirable and suitable material for citizenship.[11]

Some three years later, on 4 March 1948, the (then) Admiral Gallery – who was well known for exaggeration in his speech and writing – wrote a 'Memo to Whom it May Concern' saying: 'While the *U-505* was being towed to Bermuda, Ewald [Felix] went aboard the submarine about a dozen times with salvage parties in their efforts to keep the submarine afloat. Without this expert advice and direction from Ewald, I am convinced that the submarine would have sunk.'[12]

In 1956 the Hamburg-based magazine *Kristall* (Issue No 20) contained an article headed 'U-505 Geheimnis un Felix' ('The Secret around Felix') in which it was alleged quite wrongly that during the war Felix had been killed in a prison camp by his fellow POWs after being accused of being an informer. The truth is that at the time Felix was living in Poland with his parents. He subsequently moved to Germany where he lived with his son until his death in the 1990s.[12]

After *U-505*'s arrival in Bermuda one of the first actions of the USN was to remove its torpedoes (which included two T-5 acoustic homing versions) and to transfer them urgently to the US for inspection and testing. The other action was to exploit the 1,200 or so documents that had been found on board *U-505* as well as its electronic equipment. Of particular interest and immense value were of course the Enigma machines and the German top secret code books, the contents of which were immediately given to the Intelligence staffs in Washington and London. A USN assessment written on 13 July 1944 set out the details, saying:

> In addition to all the technical material and operational instructions, the following are the most important communications documents obtained from *U-505*:
>
> (a) Atlantic and Indian Ocean U-Boat cipher keys for the month of June 1944
> (b) Effective grid-chart cipher
> (c) Reserve Short Signal cipher (to be effective 15 July 1944)
> (d) Reserve Bigram Tables (expected to be made effective about 1 August 1944)
> (e) Effective Short Weather cipher used by U-Boats[1]

Of these, the USN assessed that from a long-range viewpoint the most important by far were the Reserve Bigram Tables but from an operational viewpoint during the second half of June 1944 the Atlantic and Indian Ocean U-boat cipher keys were the most important.

Initially *U-505* remained moored alongside USS *Abnaki* in Bermuda but after the tug was recalled to New York on 29 June the U-boat was moored to a buoy in Port Royal Bay. That same day Cominch released a message to CincLant setting out his views concerning *U-505*'s future use, viz:

> Present intention [is to] retain *Nemo* at Bermuda until we have information that Germany knows of capture. At which time VCNO [Vice Chief of Naval Operations] will arrange that *Nemo* be rehabilitated, subjected to trials, and then placed in commission for employment as an anti-submarine training ship. Arrangements will be made in near future for POWs to proceed to US.[1]

On 3 July, in support of either this intention or to assist the USN with the removal of equipment from *U-505*, the ONI in Washington ordered a co-operative German POW, Lieutenant Maximilian Coreth, who had been the First Officer on *U-172* and who been rescued when it was sunk in December 1943, to Bermuda: 'You are instructed to proceed by such transportation as may be furnished you on or about 6 July 1944 to the Naval Operating Base [NOB], Bermuda, for temporary duty as a Naval Technician. Upon completion of this duty you will return to Washington.'[11]

Events then moved quickly and on 11 August the Commander of NOB Bermuda advised Cominch that: 'Will dry-dock *Nemo* Sunday 13th estimated time 10 to 14 days. Will replace missing port bow plane [which had been torn off in a collision with USS *Pillsbury* during the capture]. Suggest Naval Constructor experienced in submarine construction examine hull.'[1]

Three days later, on 14 August, NOB Bermuda advised that: 'Inspection *Nemo* underwater body shows one 20mm shell hole in outer hull, starboard side, Number 7 ballast tank. Port bow plane missing and shaft broken. Can be manufactured here. No apparent depth charge damage. Hull in good condition. Inspection by Naval Constructors not now considered necessary.'[1]

The repair of *U-505* turned out to be a relatively simple task and on 29 August NOB Bermuda reported again to Cominch saying: 'Undocked *Nemo* Monday 28th. Conditions most satisfactory. Request authority to operate on surface and submerged. Desire make stationary dive in harbour max depth 60 feet. Will then report readiness for other tests as desired.'[1]

This was followed two days later by yet another message, this time saying: '*Nemo* ready for surface operations [and] can make US port under own power. One Ensign, two Warrants and 30 men in crew. Ensign qualified in submarines, but not for command but capable. Commander Christensen ComSubDiv 72 is supervising.'[1]

So, by the end of August 1944 the US Navy was able return *U-505* to the water with an American crew. This was subsequently confirmed by the Engineering Officer (and Second-in-Command) of *U-505* when it arrived in Philadelphia after the war who was reported in the *New York Times* on 30 May 1945 as saying that the U-boat had: 'Been restored to full efficiency except for the holes in the superstructure, and is allowed to do everything but submerge.'[13]

Exactly what happened to *U-505* (under its code-name USS *Nemo*) whilst it was in Bermuda between August 1944 and May 1945 is difficult to discover. The most likely scenario is that under control of the US Navy's ONI a series of sea trials took place under the close supervision of the Navy's intelligence and engineering staffs because of the need to learn as much as possible about the Type IXC U-boat's technology and operational capability. After this it seems probable that in accordance with Cominch's original intention the USN used the fully-manned *U-505* as a training boat in Submarine Squadron 7 (which was based in Bermuda) for the rest of the war.

The evidence in support of these suppositions is that *U-505* was obviously in an immediately seaworthy condition on 18 May 1945 when it was ordered to proceed to Philadelphia after NOB Bermuda had sent a message to Cominch on 17 May saying: 'Recommend restrictions on *Nemo* be removed and vessel sailed under escort to States with present crew.'[1]

Additionally, when it arrived in New York on 29 May 1945 it was being operated by a crew of three officers and thirty-three enlisted men who were reported to have taken it over in Bermuda.[13] The final piece of firm evidence is that when *U-505* arrived in Savannah on 7 November 1945 on its War Bond Tour it was reported that the crew included a native of Savannah who had served on the U-boat for the previous 12 months.[14] Also, Admiral Samuel Morison in his official *History of United States Naval Operations in World War II* stated that after its capture *U-505* served as a 'tame' submarine for the rest of the war.[15]

Thus, contrary to other versions of the story, it seems most likely that *U-505* was not tied up to a buoy in Port Royal Harbour or hidden out of sight and under tarpaulins in Bermuda between June 1944 and May 1945. Rather, with a full crew on board from 31 August 1944 it was operated by the USN under the control of the ONI, contributing to the

Navy's technical knowledge of the U-boat as well as helping to train ASW crews in the techniques for detecting and destroying them.

On 16 May 1945, just a week after VE Day, a USN Press Release told the American people the story of the capture of *U-505* for the very first time and two days later the US Treasury Department announced that with the co-operation of the USN the U-boat was to be exhibited in six north-eastern seaboard cities in order to boost the sales of War Bonds.

The itinerary for the War Bond Tour had been agreed by Cominch on 17 May although the dates were changed on 18 May to allow for the initial movement of *U-505* from Bermuda to Philadelphia. Then on 20 May ComSubLant advised that: 'Upon arrival *U-505* at Philadelphia about 22 May, ComSubRon 7 [will] assume operational and administrative control of *U-505* until further notice.'[16]

Thus *U-505* was released by the ONI and sailed on 20 May from Bermuda to Philadelphia arriving at the latter on 23 May for the start of its first exhibition tour. After that and because of the great success of the first tour and the interest that *U-505*'s capture had evoked, the U-boat later took part in a second much longer War and Victory Bond tour of the US East Coast and Caribbean ports in order to raise funds for the war against Japan.

Indeed, the interest in *U-505* and the story of its secret capture in June 1944 was so great across the whole of the USA that there is an amusingly cryptic hand-written note attached to the USN's message of 18 May which set out the details of the first War Bond Tour written by from someone on Cominch's staff saying: 'The only city left to request a visit from *Nemo* is Denver.'[1]

For the first short tour to the north-east coast ports as well as the transit from Bermuda the patrol craft *PCE-846* was the escort vessel until it arrived in New York. The destroyer escort USS *Otter* (DE-210) then took over as the escort vessel for the remainder of the tour from New York until its return to New London in early July. As to the tour itself, with a US Navy crew, *U-505* visited Philadelphia, New York, Boston, Baltimore, Washington and Norfolk spending about five days in each. It was open to the public in Philadelphia from 23 to 27 May, in New York from 28 May until 5 June, in Boston from 7 to 12 June, in Baltimore from 15 to 21 June, in Washington from 23 to 28 June and in Norfolk from 30 June to 5 July before returning to the US Navy Submarine Base at New London, Connecticut on 7 July.

On 1 August 1945 the destroyer escort USS *Neunzer* (DE-150) sailed to New London to escort *U-505* on its second (and longer) War Bond tour this time both to the East Coast ports and to some of those in the Gulf of Mexico. The first part of the tour started in New York for a month (2 August to 3 September) and then included New Haven (3 to 10 September) and New London (10 and 11 September) in Connecticut, Portland in Maine (12 to 18 September), Portsmouth in New Hampshire (18 to 24 September) and New Bedford in Massachusetts (24 September to 1 October).

U-505 was back in New London on 1 October and from there it headed south on the second part of the tour which started on 8 October. The U-boat was on display at the Centenary Celebrations of the US Naval Academy at Annapolis, Maryland from 9 to 14 October, and then visited Wilmington in Delaware (14 to 18 October), Portsmouth in Virginia (19 to 30 October), Charleston in South Carolina (31 October to 7 November) and Savannah in Georgia (7 to 13 November).

Thereafter, *U-505* together with USS *Neunzer* visited five ports in Florida: Jacksonville (13 to 21 November), Miami (22 to 30 November), Key West (30 November to 5 December), Tampa (6 to 12 December) and Pensacola (13 to 18 December). It also visited New Orleans in Louisiana (19 to 27 December) and Mobile in Alabama (28 December to 1 January 1946). After its visit to Mobile and after the need for the sale of more War Bonds had ceased, *U-505* was ordered back to New London to await a decision about its final disposal. During the transit north it called at the USN Base at Key West (3 to 8 January) but on 9 January and whilst *U-505* was still at sea the CNO sent a message to C-in-C Atlantic Fleet (CincLant) that he was to: 'Sail *U-505* ... to Naval Base Boston ... for care and preservation. Place out of service and retain for explosive tests.'[17]

After the Potsdam Conference ended on 2 August 1945 it was thought that the TNC might have jurisdiction over the fate of *U-505* and as a result, the USN had some early doubts about the arrangements for its disposal once the War Bond tours were over. However, the TNC accepted that as the U-boat had been captured during the war rather than surrendering at the end of the war it was not bound by the constraints of the Potsdam Agreement and did not therefore need to be considered for early disposal by sinking.

After the two War Bond tours and its arrival back at the Boston Naval Base on 12 January 1946 the USN decided that as the investigations during *U-505*'s time in Bermuda had made it fully familiar with the design of the Type IXC U-boats and that as a further Type IXC/40 U-boat (*U-858*) was already being refitted prior to testing there was no further operational requirement for *U-505*.

The detailed USN policy in relation to *U-505* as well as to two of the other U-boats that had surrendered (*U-530* and *U-977*) and which had also undertaken War Bond tours in late-1945 was set out in a memo from the USN's Bureau of Ships (BuShips) to ComSubLant and the Commander of the Portsmouth Navy Yard (PNY) on 8 January 1946, which stated that:

> The *U-505*, *U-530* and *U-977* that were formerly on War Bond Tours have completed that duty and are now [*sic!*] berthed at the Boston Shipyard.
>
> No further operations are expected from these submarines other than as possible targets for explosives tests.
>
> Permission is granted to take such material and equipment as is needed for spare parts for the operating U-Boats from these submarines.
>
> Removal of material should not be such that the submarines could not be towed to a target area and submerged in a static dive.[17]

After *U-505* arrived at the Boston Naval Base on 12 January and had formally reported to Commander Submarine Squadron 1 on 14 January the latter sent a message to the CNO on 15 January saying:

> *U-505* ... directed [to] report [to] Commandant Navy Base Boston for placing out of service at Boston Navy Shipyard. In view probable future operations required [for *U-505*] and prospect additional U-Boats reporting for similar disposition recommend retention all or part present experienced qualified U-Boat personnel on board.[17]

This proposal was agreed by the CNO on 18 January and action on *U-505* was put on temporary hold. However, on 10 April the CNO directed Com Subron 1 to:

> Place *U-505* out of service. As soon as practicable tow *U-505* ... to Naval Shipyard Portsmouth NH for removal main storage batteries. Upon completion removal and when advised by ComNavShipyard Portsmouth, tow *U-505* ... to Boston for continued retention for explosive tests. Personnel allocated *U-505* by CNO on 18 January hereby assigned to U-977.[17]

Thus, pending its disposal, *U-505* was decommissioned and retained in its role as a source of spares for the other U-boats in USN service whilst awaiting disposal as either a gunnery or torpedo target. To allow it to be stripped of equipment and spares whilst awaiting a formal disposal decision, an action that had been completed by the end of September, *U-505* remained at PNY after its transfer there on 3 May.

Right: The 'Instrument of Surrender' to 21st Army Group on 4 May, showing Field Marshal Montgomery's handwritten addition which resulted in twenty-one U-boats surrendering prior to the German capitulation on 8 May.

Below: *U-249* alongside at Weymouth on 10 May with Royal Navy ratings onboard after its surrender in the English Channel on 9 May.

Instrument of Surrender

of

All German armed forces in HOLLAND, in

northwest Germany including all islands,

and in DENMARK.

1. The German Command agrees to the surrender of all German armed forces in HOLLAND, in northwest GERMANY including the FRISIAN ISLANDS and HELIGOLAND and all other islands, in SCHLESWIG-HOLSTEIN, and in DENMARK, to the C.-in-C. 21 Army Group. This to include all naval ships in these areas. These forces to lay down their arms and to surrender unconditionally.

2. All hostilities on land, on sea, or in the air by German forces in the above areas to cease at 0800 hrs. British Double Summer Time on Saturday 5 May 1945.

3. The German command to carry out at once, and without argument or comment, all further orders that will be issued by the Allied Powers on any subject.

4. Disobedience of orders, or failure to comply with them, will be regarded as a breach of these surrender terms and will be dealt with by the Allied Powers in accordance with the accepted laws and usages of war.

5. This instrument of surrender is independent of, without prejudice to, and will be superseded by any general instrument of surrender imposed by or on behalf of the Allied Powers and applicable to Germany and the German armed forces as a whole.

6. This instrument of surrender is written in English and in German.

The English version is the authentic text.

7. The decision of the Allied Powers will be final if any doubt or dispute arises as to the meaning or interpretation of the surrender terms.

B. L. Montgomery
Field-Marshal

4 May 1945
1830 hrs

Above: *U-1305* arrives in Loch Eriboll on 10 May after surrendering at sea earlier in the day.

Right: *U-278* en-route to Loch Eriboll on 19 May together with fourteen other U-boats which had surrendered in Narvik, Norway on 9 May.

Below: *U-1231* in Loch Eriboll on 13 May after surrendering at sea on 11 May.

Above: *U-541* arriving in Gibraltar on 12 May after surrendering at sea on 10 May, with the White Ensign flying above the Swastika.

Below: *U-532* in Liverpool in late May where its cargo was partly unloaded. It had surrendered at sea on 10 May whilst en-route from Japan, and had arrived at Loch Eriboll on 13 May.

Above: *U-776* visiting London in late May 1945 whilst on a publicity tour of UK east coast ports. It had surrendered at sea on 14 May and been escorted into Weymouth on 16 May. The tour ended with *U-776*'s arrival in Loch Ryan on 22 August.

Below: *U-1009* entering Lough Foyle on 14 May. It had surrendered at sea on 9 May and arrived at Loch Eriboll on 10 May. It was transferred to Loch Alsh on the same day, and left there for Lisahally on 13 May with seven other U-boats as part of 'Operation 'Commonwealth'.

Above: U-boats rafted together in open water in Loch Ryan in southwest Scotland in Autumn 1945 whilst awaiting disposal.

Left: U-boats tied up to the jetties at Lisahally in Lough Foyle in Autumn 1945 whilst awaiting decisions about their disposal.

Below: U-530 and U-977 in Rio de Janiero in September 1945 whilst en-route from Argentina to the USA.

Above: Two scuttled U-boats in a German harbour. The result of Operation 'Regenbogen'.

Above: *U-1105* undertaking Royal Navy trials prior to its formal allocation and transfer to the USA in December 1945. Today the wreck lies off Piney Point in the Potomac River in Maryland where it was sunk in a demolition test on 19 September 1949.

Below: *U-1171* undertaking Royal Navy trials in Autumn 1945 prior to its formal allocation to the UK. After the trials it was returned to Lisahally, but was of no further use and was scrapped in 1949.

Above: *U-1407* (HMS *Meteorite*) during Royal Navy trials in 1948/49 after being recovered from Cuxhaven where it had surrendered on 5 May 1945 and then allocated to the UK. Despite a long and expensive refit, it was scrapped in 1949 soon after the trials were completed.

Above: *U-2513* in service with the US Navy. It had surrendered in Norway on 9 May and transferred to Lisahally before being secretly moved to the USA. It was allocated to the US Navy, commissioned as USS *U-2513*, and finally scrapped in 1951.

Right: *U-234* is destroyed by the US Navy off Cape Cod on 20 November 1947. It surrendered at sea on 12 May 1945 and was escorted into Portsmouth, New Hampshire, on 19 May. After early USN trials it was declared surplus to requirements and sunk by a torpedo fired by USS/M *Greenfish*.

Above: *U-2529* in Russia in 1973 prior to scrapping after use with the Baltic Fleet. It had surrendered in Norway on 9 May and been transferred to Lisahally. It was allocated to the USSR and moved to Libau in late 1945/early 1946 as part of Operation 'Cabal'.

Below: *U-995* on public display near Kiel. It surrendered in an unseaworthy state in Norway on 9 May and should have been scrapped. Instead, it was repaired and commissioned into the Royal Norwegian Navy in 1952 as the submarine *Kaura*. In 1965 it was sold to the German Navy Association who installed it at Laboe in 1971.

The U-boat's proposed fate then came to the attention of Admiral Gallery who came from Chicago and who was by then one of the Assistant Chiefs of Naval Operations, and he wrote to Frank Hecht, the President of the Illinois State Council of the Navy League of the United States, on 13 January 1947 asking if the Council would be interested in sponsoring a proposal to have U-505 transferred permanently to the City of Chicago. Hecht replied to Admiral Gallery on 10 February 1947 thanking him for his 'most interesting communication' and saying that:

> I quite agree with you on the desirability of going ahead with your idea. I am passing it on to one of our Directors asking him to explore the question and present it at the [next] Directors' Meeting.[18]

The proposal was then explored with various organisations in Chicago specifically the American Society of Mechanical Engineers and the Museum of Science and Industry (MSI). The Museum had for a long time had an ambition to display a submarine and so the possible acquisition of U-505 was an attractive idea. However, it was not until late September 1947 that the project began to move forward, which was fortuitous as the USN was then making specific plans to dispose of several surplus U-boats in torpedo tests.

Admiral Gallery knew of the proposed disposal plans and thus he used his brother, John Gallery, who was a priest in Chicago, as a go-between to determine if there had been any progress in relation to his proposal. By that time Major Lenox R Lohr, US Army (Rtd) the MSI Director had become involved and had met with E R Henning who was a New York-based member of the Mechanical Engineers Society as well as being a retired US Navy Captain. John Gallery thus met Major Lohr on 26 September to discuss whether or not the MSI was interested in the U-505 project.

The answer was affirmative, and the next key event was a visit to the USN in Washington on 6 October 1947 by Henning, the purpose of which was to: 'Make inquiries regarding the possibility of bringing the ex-German U-505 to the lagoon of the Museum.'[18] The same day, Henning had lunch with Lohr and the former's follow-up letter makes the subject of their debate very clear:

> From the policy angle there appears to be no objection. Indeed, it was indicated by the officers concerned in this field that they thought the idea had much to commend it, particularly from the standpoint of naval publicity. The submarine was scheduled for sinking but recently

this was countermanded for further study of its disposition. Some tentative consideration has been given to placing it at Annapolis.[18]

Henning advised Lohr that there did not appear to be any insurmountable obstacles from a technical point of view though he did say that:

Cost will be a big obstacle.

The boat has been cannibalised to some degree for parts for other German submarines.

With this preliminary inquiry indicating no substantial policy or technical objections, a formal request to the Secretary of the Navy would appear in order promptly [and] the Navy League in Chicago might be a help.[18]

As a result of this meeting the afternoon of 6 October saw a telegram being sent jointly by Lenox Lohr and the Chicago Navy League's President (Frank Hecht) to the Secretary of the Navy (John L Sullivan) and the Chief of Naval Operations (Admiral Chester W Nimitz), saying:

We understand German submarine *U-505* captured June 4, 1944 ... is to be destroyed. We feel this craft should be preserved as a monument to the spirit of the USN and [an] inspiration to youth of our nation. The Navy League joins with the Museum of Science and Industry in requesting the USN to install this submarine at the Museum for public display.[18]

Encouragingly, Nimitz responded with a message on 7 October saying:

Your message to the Chief of Naval Operations quoting your telegram to SECNAV regarding preservation of the captured German submarine *U-505* as an historic relic has been received. Your interest in this matter which is now under study is appreciated and it is hoped that it may be found practicable to carry out your suggestions.[18]

Similarly, John Sullivan, the Secretary of the Navy, wrote to both to both Lohr and Hecht on 23 October saying that *U-505* had been removed from the list of U-boats to be destroyed in November. However, he also stressed that any financial implications of the transfer of *U-505* to the MSI would have to be met by organisations and groups in the Chicago area.

Following this, Lohr wrote to Admiral Gallery on 21 November concerning the costings and possible funding arrangements as well as asking if the Admiral could find anyone who might be interested in sponsoring the project and backing it financially. He also asked: 'To be assured that the Navy will keep open their offer during the period necessary to investigate the possibility of securing a sponsor.'[18]

The Admiral's reply on 24 November written on official CNO-headed paper stated that:

> A move is being started here which I believe will result in the Navy reconditioning and delivering the *U-505* to Chicago. It is too early to say definitely to say that this will be done, but so far it looks promising. In the meantime, you can be assured that the Navy will hold the offer of the *U-505* open for you.[18]

Although the USN was now aware of the MSI's interest in acquiring *U-505* as an exhibit there were serious problems concerning the financing of the project. The MSI and all the interested groups in Chicago were keen that the USN should pay the costs but despite Admiral Gallery's informal optimism the USN was equally determined not to do so. In essence, therefore, the project became stalled and in the meantime *U-505* remained in the Navy Yard at Portsmouth tied up to a jetty, rusting and neglected.

Thus began the second major delay in the *U-505*/MSI project, a characteristic that was to be repeated over the next six years. Chicago was unwilling to take the project forward without a clear view of the funding sources but was loath to begin arranging the latter until formal transfer arrangements had been made by the USN. On the other hand despite Admiral Gallery's suggestions to the contrary the USN had no intention of funding the project and therefore awaited Chicago's proposals. Stalemate ensued.

By the end of 1949 it was clear that the USN was losing patience and *U-505* was once more formally included in a list of ships to be struck from the inventory and used either for target practice or sold for scrap. Fortuitously, John F Floberg, who took up his new appointment as Assistant Secretary of the Navy (Air) on 5 December 1949, was also the USN's Controller and was responsible for signing-off the orders for the scrapping of obsolete equipment and vessels. He noted that *U-505* was due for disposal and in view of the U-boat's history decided to advise Admiral Gallery of its pending demise.

Thus Admiral Gallery, who was still a serving officer but who was nevertheless doing a great deal of lobbying behind the scenes for which he was later informally admonished, once again decided to take action. This time he brought the situation to the attention of Alderman Clarence Wagner who was a powerful and influential member of Chicago City Council.

As a result Alderman Wagner initiated a motion on 20 January 1950 which asked the City Council to make a formal request to the Secretary of the Navy: 'To present *U-505* to the City of Chicago for the purpose of installing this vessel as a permanent exhibit [at the MSI].'[19] However, no formal action flowed from this initiative though the *Chicago Daily Tribune* published an article about the project on 8 March 1950 concluding that *U-505* would make a worthy trophy for the City.

In retrospect it seems that Alderman Wagner's action in early 1950 was designed to indicate to the USN in general and to John Floberg in particular that there was still local public interest in the project. Thus, whilst as a result of John Floberg's personal involvement and no doubt Admiral Gallery's behind the scenes lobbying the USN kept the disposal of *U-505* on hold, there was still no resolution of the funding problems. Indeed, it was to be another three years (March 1953) before any further serious action was initiated in Chicago to bring the project to fruition.

By early 1953 *U-505* was the sole remaining U-boat at the Portsmouth Navy Yard and it was in a very poor state. There was therefore pressure in the USN to dispose of the vessel and the public debate was re-opened by a dramatic headline in the *Chicago Daily Tribune* which on 8 March 1953 declared: 'City Told: Act or Lose U-Boat as War Trophy.'[20]

This was based on advice from Admiral Gallery on the previous day that Portsmouth Navy Yard needed the space that was being occupied by *U-505* and that although the USN had promised to make the U-boat available to Chicago its patience was wearing thin. Unless something positive was done it was likely that *U-505* would be sold for scrap.

As a result, a whole variety of actions were initiated. The City Council debated and approved Alderman Wagner's original 1950 resolution on 11 March, the Mayor of Chicago, Martin Kennelly became involved and after a meeting between him and John Floberg on 1 April 1953, Floberg wrote to the Mayor on 7 April 1953 saying:

> The Navy will cooperate in every practical way to help bring the *U-505* to Chicago. Please tell your Committee that it can count on my official and personal cooperation. I earnestly hope that Chicago will be able under your leadership and that of your Committee to preserve this combat trophy in the Naval District which furnished the Navy one third of its personnel in World War Two.[18]

Though there were still hopes and aspirations to the contrary, it was at last beginning to be understood that the USN was not prepared to fund the transfer of *U-505* from Portsmouth to Chicago and that a major fund-raising drive was necessary. The latter was therefore initiated on 3 April 1953 but even then there were dissenting voices.

For instance, an article in the *Chicago American* on 22 April 1953 offered the pessimistic view that:

> [*U-505*], a museum piece, lies at an East Coast dock but to get it Chicagoans will have to act fast. It's nearing the time for it to be sold for scrap or sunk at sea.
>
> Had the city taken action when the boat was first offered to Chicago as a war memorial in 1948, the cost would have been much less. In fairly good condition then and with all its original equipment aboard, the vessel is now a stripped and neglected rusted hulk. Navy officials fear to move *U-505* too far or to experiment with her diving tanks because of the possibility of it sinking or capsizing.
>
> The Navy Department has thus far refused to allot any money for the upkeep of the vessel. There are no plans at present to dry-dock her and Navy men fear such an operation might result in her destruction.[21]

The question of funding was also raised in a letter in late April 1953 from the Secretary of the Navy, Francis Matthews, to the City Council which provided details of the estimated costs that would be involved in preparing *U-505* for towing from Portsmouth Navy Yard to Chicago.

There then followed a high-level exchange of letters as well as discussions between the USN and the City of Chicago in which the Senator for Illinois, Everett M Dirksen as well as two Chiefs of Naval Operations, Admirals William Fechteler and Robert Carney, as well as Vice Admiral Roscoe Good, the Deputy Chief of Naval Operations (Logistics), became personally involved in the proposal to transfer *U-505* from the USN to the MSI. Perhaps the most important of these was the letter from the Under Secretary of the Navy, Charles S Thomas, to Senator Dirksen on 1 June 1953 which said that:

> Transfers of this nature [concerning captured vessels] are covered by Public Law. The law stipulates in part that no expense shall result to the United States as a consequence of such transfer. The Mayor of the City of Chicago has been informed that the Department of the Navy is willing to transfer the *U-505* to the City of Chicago in accordance with the law.
>
> The most difficult obstacle in the way of transferring the *U-505* to the City of Chicago is funding. Funds are not currently available to the Navy for the specific purpose of repairing the *U-505* for tow.[18]

This was followed on 12 June 1953 by a formal application by the President of the MSI to Admiral Carney, the Chief of Naval Operations stating:

> The Museum of Science and Industry hereby applies for the ex-German submarine *U-505* under the terms of Public Law 649 of the 79th Congress.
>
> The proposed use [is to] establish [*U-505*] as a permanent memorial in Chicago to the Americans who lost their lives at sea in World War II.
>
> The Museum agrees that the U-505 will be maintained at no expense to the United States in accordance with the terms of Public Law.
>
> A committee has been formed ... to raise the money to prepare the *U-505* for towing, to tow it to Chicago, and to prepare it as an exhibit.[18]

The sparring was over at last; the USN fully intended to transfer title to *U-505* to Chicago as long as all preparations had been duly performed and as long as Chicago accepted that the funding of the project was its responsibility. The fund raising and the planning for *U-505*'s move were now put on a serious basis, interest in the project rose, money and offers of help were received from a whole variety of sources and although there were still a number of delays for legal, sponsorship and financial reasons, the Secretary of the Navy, Robert B Anderson, personally signed the transfer of title of *U-505* from the USN to the MSI on 9 March 1954.

U-505's last day in USN custody was 14 May 1954 when two USN tugs towed the U-boat down the Piscatauqua River from the Portsmouth Navy Yard to a buoy in the harbour at Kittery, Maine. The following day *U-505* started its journey to Chicago under tow by the civilian tug *Pauline L Moran*.

Though it had taken eight long years of hard if intermittent lobbying, planning, work and fund raising to bring the aspirations to fruition, the movement of *U-505* to Chicago proved to be a monumental and expensive undertaking. The tug began towing the U-boat from Kittery on 15 May 1954 on its journey which covered 3,000 miles through twenty-eight locks on the St. Lawrence River and through four of the five Great Lakes.

U-505 arrived in Chicago on 26 June, and on 25 September 1954 it was dedicated as a war memorial and a permanent exhibit at the Museum of Science and Industry. However when *U-505* was donated to the Museum it had been thoroughly stripped of parts during the early years that it had lain neglected alongside the dock in PNY and still more hard work was necessary to restore and replace the missing components.

In 1989, *U-505*, the only Type IXC U-boat still in existence, was designated a US National Historic Landmark. However, by 2004 the U-boat's exterior had suffered significant damage from the weather and in April 2004 the Museum moved *U-505* into a new underground location which was opened to the public on 5 June 2005.

CHAPTER 15

U-Boats in Russia

IN THE LATE 1930s STALIN had an ambition to create a blue-water navy which would enhance the Soviet Union's worldwide influence. However, the war prevented the achievement of that ambition and from 1941 to 1945 the Soviet Navy was essentially limited to operations in coastal waters, especially in the Baltic and the Black Sea. When the war in Europe ended in May 1945, Stalin was keen to resurrect his pre-war plans for the Soviet Navy but was thwarted by the lack of suitable surface ships and ocean-going submarines. No U-boats had surrendered in any ports controlled by the USSR, all serviceable U-boats having been transferred to the western end of the Baltic in the face of the Red Army's advance. As a result, Stalin was determined to obtain at least a one-third share of the surviving German fleet, including U-boats.

The Russians therefore pushed very hard at the Potsdam Conference for the maximum possible allocation of U-boats but eventually they settled for the allocation of ten to each of the Allies and it was the job of the TNC to recommend which U-boats should be allocated to each nation. The ten finally allocated to the USSR in late-1945 were *U-1057*, *U-1058*, *U-1064*, *U-1231*, *U-1305*, *U-2353*, *U-2529*, *U-3035*, *U-3041* and *U-3515*. Originally the list had included *U-3514* but at the end of November, during the final preparations for the delivery of the ten U-boats to the USSR, the steering gear on *U-3514* was damaged so seriously that it would have required the U-boat to be docked for repairs before the transfer could take place. The TNC therefore agreed that *U-3515* should be substituted for *U-3514*.

The ten U-boats allocated to the USSR comprised four large ocean-going Type XXIs, four smaller ocean-going Type VIICs, one large ocean-going Type IXC and just one small coastal Type XXIII. They were all moored in the UK, either at Lisahally or in Loch Ryan, and as the transfer to Russia had to be completed by not later than 15 February 1946 urgent action was required especially in view of the onset of winter, the prospects of stormy seas around the west and north coasts of Scotland and the annual freeze-up of the Baltic.

During the TNC Inspection Team's routine visit to Danzig in August to assess the condition of the German surface warships that had surrendered there it was discovered that the Russians had failed to declare that they had captured some uncompleted U-boats in the local shipyard when the Red Army entered Danzig on 30 March. The Inspection Team leader's report dated 31 August showed that the Russians were not averse to conducting such deception if it would assist their attempts to gain access to and advantage from advanced German submarine technology and it included the information that:

> During inspection of the vessels at Schichau AG, Danzig on 28 August it was obvious that most of the submarine production had been removed.
>
> Approximately 16 Type 21 submarines, completed or nearly completed, were removed by the Germans shortly before the fall of Danzig.
>
> There were at that time somewhere between nine and twelve submarines either still on the ways or having been so recently launched as to be incapable of movement under their own power. After capture of the city by the Russians, those vessels still on the ways were completed sufficiently for launching and launched. The Russian Navy then removed these vessels to unknown destinations. Whether these vessels were towed or moved under their own power is not clear.
>
> The implications of the above seem to contradict the statement of the Russian Delegation of the Tripartite Naval Commission to the effect that no German naval vessels are in Russian ports. It is to be assumed that these submarines went to Russian ports since there is no indication that they were delivered elsewhere. It is recommended that the matter be investigated at the next meeting of the Tripartite Naval Commission, since it appears possible from this evidence that there may after all be German naval vessels in Russian ports.[1]

The Inspection Team had been accompanied by Admiral Miles, the Head of the UK Delegation to the TNC, and his personal commentary amplified the Team Leader's report saying that:

> At Danzig it transpired that there was now a Polish Director of Works. I got him to send for some German workmen and as a result the cat was let out of the bag. They confirmed that at the time of the Soviet occupation there were eleven completed submarine hulls, some with

and some without engines, and that they had all subsequently been towed away. My Soviet colleague became more and more confused and uncomfortable, and he eventually admitted that he thought there had been eleven submarines here originally.

He asked if I really wanted Admiral Levchenko to be told about this, to which I of course insisted that as the Senior Soviet Representative he would have to offer an explanation and give the details of these submarines to his British and American colleagues.[2]

This information was contrary to an earlier Russian statement which had said that there were no U-boats in Soviet ports and the matter was therefore raised at the 7th Meeting of the TNC on 12 September. In his response, Admiral Levchenko the Head of the USSR's Delegation admitted that:

In March of 1945 the naval bases of Danzig and Gydnia were liberated by the Soviet troops and there on the docks unfinished submarine hulks were found. They were not equipped with any machinery. These submarine hulks were towed to bases in the Soviet Union. Since there are no plans for completing their construction nor any machinery they are going to be scrapped for the metal.[1]

Admiral Miles was not prepared to let the matter rest and he replied to Admiral Levchenko, saying:

The information given to the Tripartite Naval Commission at Danzig was that of the 11 submarines towed away from there some had their main engines on board.

In accordance with paragraph 5 of part A of the Potsdam Protocol I consider that all these submarines should be inspected by the Tripartite Naval Commission.[1]

The Russian response on 19 September was that:

As to the series of the hulls of the eleven submarines, they are as follows: three of series 7 [Type VIIC], eight of series 21 [Type XXI]. These hulls are located in Libau and several of them are being fitted with machinery (equipment). If your curiosity is sufficient to warrant looking them over, such opportunity will be presented.[1]

This also failed to impress Admiral Miles and he responded to his Russian colleague on 24 September saying:

The Tripartite Naval Commission have not yet been told of the number, types and location of the German submarines removed from Gydnia in addition to the eleven which were taken from Danzig and are now

in Libau. On receipt of this further information, it will be necessary
to arrange a Tripartite inspection team to see all of these submarines.[1]

The TNC inspection team's follow-up visit to Libau in Soviet-occupied
Latvia took place on 8 October and the team's report gave comprehensive
information about the eleven partially-completed U-boats that had
been launched and removed from Danzig. There were three Type VIIC
U-boats at Libau, *U-1174*, *U-1176* and *U-1177*. Each was fitted with
most of its main propulsion machinery, and it was estimated that each
could be completed within four months if moved to a first-class shipyard.

There were also six Type XXI U-boats at Libau, *U-3535*, *U-3536*,
U-3537, *U-3538*, *U-3540* and *U-3542*, each of which was also fitted with
most of its main propulsion machinery. It was estimated that *U-3535* and
U-3536 could be completed within two months, *U-3537* and *U-3540*
within three months, *U-3542* within five months and *U-3538* within
six months. The other two Type XXI U-boats, *U-3539* and *U-3541*, had
already been towed from Libau to Tallinn in Soviet-occupied Estonia and
were therefore not inspected by the TNC team. The Russians had also
taken steps to incorporate these eight Type XXI U-boats into the Soviet
Navy and had allocated them alphanumeric designations – first *TS-5* to
TS-12, and then *R-1* to *R-8*.

It was clear that despite their earlier statements that these eleven
U-boats were not fitted with any machinery and that they were simply
going to be scrapped the Russians intended to make the best possible
use of these valuable trophies. Nevertheless, the American and British
Representatives on the TNC decided that there was no point in continuing
the debate about the future use of these eleven or any other U-boats
captured by the Russians, preferring instead to believe that they would be
treated as unallocated, uncompleted or damaged U-boats which would
be destroyed in accordance with the Potsdam Agreement. The eleven
uncompleted U-boats were therefore listed in the TNC's Final Report as
being 'unallocated submarines afloat' and it was assumed that they would
be sunk no later than 15 February 1946.

The net result of these actions was that by the end of 1945 the Russians
had acquired twenty-one German U-boats, eleven from Danzig and ten
from the UK, seven of which were good-quality Type VIICs and twelve
of which were ocean-going Type XXIs. The other two were the single
Type IXC and the single Type XXIII.

Also, although the British and Americans did not become aware of the
full details until early 1946, after removing the eight partially-complete

Type XXI U-boats (*U-3535* to *U-3542*) from Danzig the Russians had completely dismantled the Schichau shipyard and moved everything to the Soviet Union as war reparations. During the course of this process they gained access to a large number of prefabricated Type XXI U-boat sections which though earmarked for specific U-boats had not yet reached the keel laying/assembly stage. As a result, it was estimated that the Russians had sufficient prefabricated sections and other parts as well as the assembly jigs and facilities to complete additional Type XXI U-boats, plans for the final keel-laying and building of which had been underway before Danzig was captured at the end of March 1945.

It was assessed by Western Intelligence that these U-boat sections would if assembled have comprised the twelve Type XXI U-boats *U-3543* to *U-3554*. However, although they were all formally allocated Russian TS (War Prize) alphanumeric designations and although they were most probably located in the Russian shipyard at Kronstadt near Leningrad it is highly unlikely that any of them were ever either launched, completed or commissioned into the Soviet Navy. Nevertheless, their presence in Russia posed a potential threat.

The transfer of the U-boats which had been allocated to the USSR by the TNC took place in late 1945 and early 1946 and was code-named Operation 'Cabal', the aim of which was the safe delivery by the RN of the ten U-boats from Lisahally to Libau in Latvia. Prior to the transfer seven of these U-boats were moored at Lisahally but the other three (*U-1057*, *U-1064* and *U-2353*) which had been moored in Loch Ryan were moved to Lisahally on 31 October 1945.

The original intention of the Russians was that the ten U-boats should be fully serviceable, should have Russian crews and should be transferred to Russian ports under their own power. However, this was strongly opposed by the RN's Flag Officer (Submarines) who made his views clear on 17 October when he advised the Admiralty that:

> All except the Type XXIs, although having minor defects, are capable of proceeding under their own power. The Type XXIs are however most unreliable and would undoubtedly have to be towed. The Americans had to tow their Type XXIs to the USA, and we have been unable to get any running satisfactorily.[3]

There was also a Russian proposal that four of the U-boats should go to Murmansk in North Russia and six to the Baltic but this too fell on very stony ground with the Admiralty on 26 October saying: 'Our offer is to sail all – repeat – all U-Boats to a Russian-controlled German port.

It is out of the question that British crews should take any U-Boats to North Russia.'[3]

Eventually a compromise was reached and the Russians agreed that all ten U-boats should be transferred to Libau. They were to have RN crews but there was to be one Russian naval officer on each as an observer. In the event only five of the U-boats were deemed to be capable of proceeding the whole way under their own power and it was decided to tow the remaining five. As each U-boat had an RN CO and crew, for administrative purposes each was allocated an RN Pennant Number in the series N.22 to N.31.

The start of 'Cabal' was not without its problems and Captain P Q Roberts, who was Captain (Submarines) Lisahally and who was responsible for the transfer arrangements, sent a cryptic message to the Admiralty on 23 November, saying:

> At Conference this evening Russians raised a catalogue of defects and deficiencies which they require making good.
>
> Major items of these were pointed out to previous mission [the TNC Inspection Board who visited Lisahally and Loch Ryan in September] who nevertheless were not deterred in their selection [of the U-boats to be transferred to Russia].
>
> Remaining defects are in my opinion minor.
>
> Russians asked me to delay sailing and on my refusal have telephoned their London Mission to apply to Admiralty.
>
> Have informed Russians that my instructions are that they are observers for the passage and not an Inspection Commission and in any case I do not consider things complained about justify delay. It was never pretended that they were taking delivery of 10 new submarines.[4]

The transfer began on 24 November when nine of the U-boats, less *U-3515*, sailed from Moville at the mouth of Lough Foyle downstream from Lisahally. The planned route was around the north of Scotland then through the Pentland Firth between Scotland and the Orkney Islands. After that it was across the North Sea to south Norway then through the Skagerrak and Kattegat to Copenhagen and finally across the Baltic to Libau. The five under power were *U-1057*, *U-1058*, *U-1064*, *U-1231* and *U-1305* and they were escorted by HMS *Garth*, HMS *Eglinton* and HMS *Zetland*. The four under tow were *U-2353* (HMS *Riou*), *U-2529* (HMS *Zephyr*), *U-3035* (HMS *Tremadoc Bay*) and *U-3041* (HMS *Narborough*).

The five U-boats which sailed under their own power had a relatively trouble-free journey to Libau. But it was a very different matter for those that were under tow. The four which set out on 24 November experienced considerable bad weather en route, including Force 10 gales, and all had problems with their towing gear. Thus, only seven of the U-boats (*U-1057*, *U-1058*, *U-1064*, *U-1231*, *U-1305*, *U-2353* and *U-2529*) arrived at Libau on 4 December. The three remaining U-boats (*U-3035*, *U-3041* and *U-3515*) all suffered extended delays due to a combination of poor weather, technical defects and towing problems.

U-3041, which was being towed by HMS *Narborough*, encountered problems with the towing gear which necessitated a diversion into Rosyth on 26 November. It then developed steering and other defects in the North Sea off Norway. This necessitated a diversion into Kristiansand (S) on 29 November for repairs which took five days. After repairs, the transfer resumed on 5 December and it arrived in Libau on 10 December. Similarly, *U-3035*, which was being towed by HMS *Tremadoc Bay*, developed steering defects off the north of Scotland. This resulted in a jammed rudder which necessitated a diversion into Rosyth on 28 November. After repairs, the transfer resumed on 7 December and it arrived in Libau on 14 December.

The transfer of *U-3515* which had started late because of the last-minute exchange with *U-3514* was itself beset with problems. After leaving Lough Foyle on 6 December under tow by HMS *Icarus* and after poor weather caused it to take shelter in the Orkney Islands, ongoing towing problems together with numerous defects caused a diversion into Rosyth where it arrived on 11 December. The pair sailed again on 12 December but returned yet again on 14 December after the tow parted in more poor weather. After that and as described by the CO of HMS *Icarus* in his voyage report: '*Icarus* and *U-3515* then remained in Rosyth Dockyard waiting for a serious defect in the submarine to be made good, and subsequently for the weather to moderate until Saturday the 26th January.'[5]

The exact nature and cause of *U-3515*'s defects are unclear but on 20 December the starboard main electric motor was found to be damaged. The Soviet Embassy in London believed that this might have been caused by sabotage and there was a protracted argument between the Embassy and the Admiralty about the problem, starting with a message from the Soviet Naval Attache on 24 December saying that: 'The damage was caused by strange objects in the form of a spanner and metal filings being found after damage in the working part of the motor. It is not known by whom and when they were inserted.'[4]

Even though it was probably true, the Admiralty had no intention of confirming this allegation and after a final trial of the repaired motor had taken place on 23 January 1946 the departure of *U-3515* from Rosyth, again under tow by HMS *Icarus*, was restarted on 26 January. Thereafter the remainder of the journey was uneventful, and *U-3515* finally arrived in Libau on 2 February, thereby completing Operation 'Cabal'.

Perhaps the last word on 'Cabal' should be those used by Captain Roberts who in his formal report dated 10 January 1946 said:

> On the whole the turn over of these submarines to the Russians went more easily than I had expected.
>
> The 10 observers arrived in Lisahally five days before we sailed and made a fairly comprehensive examination of each boat. Some of their complaints were of a ridiculously minor nature and others were defects and deficiencies which had already been pointed out to the visiting Tripartite Mission [in early September].
>
> As usual we started right at the beginning again and had to go over much of the ground which had been covered by the Mission. They expressed surprise, for instance, that the allocated boats had any defects at all and said that they had been given to understand that all defects would have been made good including defects requiring docking. This, of course, was absolutely false.
>
> As reported by signal the Russians at Lisahally twice applied to me for the sailing to be delayed. Both these applications were refused.
>
> Spare gear, drawings and instruction books were, as expected, rather a bugbear, and deficiencies in them were continually being complained about. The whole argument was re-opened when we arrived at Libau and it was proposed that the boats should not be taken over until all spare gear, etc, had been checked and all defects examined. As I estimated that this would take anything up to three months I said that this was quite unacceptable to me.
>
> The whole attitude of the observers inspection at Lisahally would have been perfectly correct for a final acceptance committee taking over 10 brand new boats from Vickers, but was quite impossibly meticulous under the circumstances. They were eventually persuaded to see my point of view.[4]

The ten U-boats delivered to Russia in 'Cabal' were commissioned into and used by the South Baltic Fleet under a variety of alphanumeric designations until the Russians' own submarine designs made the German ones obsolete. In respect of the Type VIIC, Type IXC and Type XXIII U-boats allocated to the USSR, *U-2353* remained with the Baltic Fleet until December 1950, *U-1231* remained with the Baltic Fleet until

August 1953 and *U-1057*, *U-1058*, *U-1064* and *U-1305* remained with the Baltic Fleet until December 1955. Though there is evidence that some of them were used for training purposes, there is no evidence of any operational use before they were placed in reserve and employed in a variety of support roles before eventually being scrapped in the 1950s and 1960s. Two of them, *U-1057* and *U-1305*, were used as targets in Russian atomic bomb tests in the Arctic in 1955 and 1957.

In respect of the Type XXIs, *U-2529*, *U-3035*, *U-3041* and *U-3515*, it seems that after they too were incorporated into the Soviet Navy in 1946, they as well as the other six U-boats, were allocated alphanumeric designations relating directly to their 'N' series RN Pennant Numbers. The four Type XXIs were later allocated the Soviet Navy designations *B-27*, *B-28*, *B-29* and *B-30* in June 1949. There is however some uncertainty concerning exactly which of the 'N' series and then the subsequent 'B' series designations were allocated to which of the four Type XXI U-boats. Some sources say that *U-2529* became *N.28/B-28*, *U-3035* became *N.29/B-29*, *U-3041* became *N.30/B-30* and *U-3515* became *N.27/B-27*, whilst others say that *U-2529* was *N.27/B-27*, *U-3035* was *N.28/B-28*, *U-3041* was *N.29/B-29* and *U-3515* was *N.30/B-30*. Without direct access to the original Soviet Navy records uncertainty remains.

It is equally difficult to determine exactly what use the Russians made of the Type XXIs after they were incorporated into the Soviet Navy. They were certainly all commissioned, they all had Russian COs and crews, and they were all used for testing and training purposes in the Baltic before they were decommissioned and transferred to the reserve in 1955. After this they, like the other six allocated U-boats, were used in a variety of static support roles before eventually being scrapped.

It seems unlikely that any of them were given ocean-going operational roles, but instead were under the control of the Central Research Institute for Warships in Libau which was primarily interested in details of their construction and capabilities, with the only known 'excitement' occurring when in 1949 (or more probably on 30 April 1950) *U-3035* (*N.29*) sank in the Gulf of Finland when an open diesel exhaust valve in the schnorkel allowed water to flood the engine compartment. Fortunately, the problem was not fatal; the valve was closed, the water was pumped out and *U-3035* was saved.

In view of this, it seems that the American concerns about the possible warlike use of the Type XXIs based on intelligence information which may not have been entirely accurate, was not the threat that was assumed. The ten U-boats which were allocated to the USSR by the TNC for 'experimental and technical purposes' seem to have been used by the Russians for just that, their aim being to establish a baseline for its future blue-water navy rather than using them in any sort of warlike roles.

As far as the eleven U-boats captured in Danzig and then transferred to Libau are concerned, no information is known about the fate of the Type VIIC/41 U-boats *U-1174*, *U-1176* and *U-1177*. It seems probable that they were not completed and thus neither commissioned nor used by the Soviet Navy before being scrapped in 1947. But the same did not apply to the eight Type XXI U-boats at least three of which were completed, commissioned and not sunk or otherwise destroyed until late 1947 or early 1948, but there is no evidence that they were ever used operationally. In respect of the twelve unassembled Type XXI U-boats (*U-3543* to *U-3554*), whilst there is a very remote possibility that they too were launched, completed and commissioned, this is highly unlikely.

Whilst the British and Americans were meticulous in informing each other (and the Russians) that, as recommended by the TNC, that they had sunk their unallocated U-boats on time, the Russians were particularly tardy in providing the response to which they too were committed:

> Former German submarines not allocated to [the] Three Powers shall be sunk by 15 Feb 1946. Similarly former German submarines on ways or building shall be destroyed by that date. On 15 Feb 1946 [the] Three Powers will exchange notes verifying completion [of the] submarine sinking or destruction.[6]

The information about the Russian capture of the Type XXI U-boat sections in Danzig did not become clear until after the publication of the TNC's Final Report in December 1945, which therefore made no specific mention of them. Nevertheless, their disposal was covered by the general TNC recommendation that surface ships and submarines under construction on slips shall be destroyed or scrapped.

The TNC's previously secret recommendations in relation to the U-boats which had surrendered were approved by the Allies in January 1946 and this was followed by a statement from the Admiralty on 5 March 1946 saying:

> Moscow and Washington have been informed through diplomatic channels that all unallocated U-Boats afloat in British controlled ports were sunk by 15 February. No report of sinkings by [the] Russians [in

respect of the 11 U-boats captured in Danzig and which were listed in the TNC Report] has yet been received.[7]

In similar vein the Americans advised the Senior Russian Representative on the TNC in February and March 1946 that they too had sunk the two unallocated U-boats in US custody. The British and Americans were therefore not prepared to allow the lack of a Russian response concerning the Danzig U-boats to continue unresolved and diplomatic pressure continued throughout 1946. The result of this joint pressure was the receipt of separate notes from the Russians to the American and British Embassies in Moscow on 6 and 9 December 1946 respectively with the one to the British Government saying:

> As regards the vessels [including the unallocated U-Boats] referred to under Category 'C', in view of the large scale of the work involved in lifting and destroying these vessels, the Soviet military authorities have been unable to fulfil the recommendations of the Commission completely in the period laid down. At the present time the Soviet Naval authorities are taking steps to fulfil those recommendations.[8]

Despite these messages, the UK continued to press the Russians for a clear answer but it was not until 27 March 1947 that the Russians issued a short formal statement saying:

> In its notes of 6 December 1946 to the Government of the United States of America and of 9 December 1946 to the Government of Great Britain the Soviet Government communicated that the Soviet military authorities were taking measures for the removal and destruction of the ships of the German Navy assigned to Category 'C' by the Tripartite Commission for the Division of the German Navy.
>
> The Soviet Government communicates herewith that the complete destruction of the ships of Category 'C' of the German Navy will be fully accomplished in August 1947.[9]

The subject had also been raised in the British House of Commons on 19 March 1947 when during an obviously orchestrated question and answer exchange about the RN's disposal of the unallocated U-boats under British control in late 1945 and early 1946 Lieutenant Colonel Sir Ronald Ross, the MP for Londonderry in Northern Ireland, asked: 'Have all the submarines been sunk within the two months, including those allotted to other Powers?'[10] To which the answer from the Parliamentary Secretary to the Admiralty was that: 'That is quite another question.'[10]

Eventually the Russians succumbed to the British pressure and closed the matter with a letter from the Ministry of Foreign Affairs to the British Embassy in Moscow on 1 October 1947 saying:

> The Ministry of Foreign Affairs of the USSR presents its complements to the Embassy of Great Britain and has the honour to inform them [that] the Naval authorities of the Soviet Union have carried out by the date fixed their obligations resulting from the declaration of the Soviet Delegation at the Moscow Session of the Council of Foreign Ministers, concerning the destruction of German Naval ships in Category 'C', which were in waters controlled by Soviet Naval forces.[10]

To complete the story, this was followed-up again in the House of Commons towards the end of the year when in answer to two more obviously 'planted' written questions on 5 November 1947 about 'German Submarines (Destruction)' the Parliamentary Secretary to the Admiralty reported that: 'An intimation has been received from the Soviet Government that they have fulfilled their obligations to destroy units of the German Fleet.'[11]

The desired result had been achieved. Of the semi-complete U-boats and U-boat sections captured in Danzig, the three Type VIICs had already been scrapped as had all the Type XXI U-boat sections. The final action by the Russians had been to destroy the remaining eight Type XXIs. Of these three, *U-3535* (*R-1*), *U-3536* (*R-2*) and *U-3537* (*R-3*), were sunk off Cape Ristna in Estonia on 7/8 August 1947 and the remainder *U-3538* to *U-3542* (*R-4 to R-8*) had been broken up for scrap being formally struck from the Soviet Navy list in February 1948.

Thus, some 21 months after the Russians should have destroyed the eleven unfinished U-boats and the additional Type XXI U-boat sections which they had captured in Danzig in March 1945, it was finally confirmed that the necessary action had taken place. The British and Americans had completed their U-boat-related actions by the TNC's February 1946 target date but the Russians clearly wished to milk every last advantage especially from the eight Type XXI U-boats as well as from the Type XXI U-boat sections which they had captured, and they were not prepared to discard them until they had gained the maximum possible knowledge about their construction and technical features. The British in particular were keen to encourage the Russians to cease their procrastination and to honour their post-Potsdam commitments. They therefore refused to drop the topic and eventually the diplomatic pressure was rewarded and the files could be closed albeit much later than originally agreed.

The TNC's Final Report had also highlighted a number of other U-boats that had been scuttled in Russian-controlled waters before the end of the war, and had directed that they too should be destroyed. They included *U-18* and *U-24*, both of which had been scuttled by the Germans off Constanza in the Black Sea. Despite this, although *U-18* and *U-24* were raised they were not put into service, and they were both sunk off Sevastopol by the Russian submarine *M-120* on 26 May 1947.

Additionally, the Russians found several sunk, scuttled and damaged U-boats in and around various eastern Baltic ports (including *U-4*, *U-6*, *U-10*, *U-21*, *U-108*, *U-902*, *U-929* and *U-1308*) but none of these (as well as *U-9* in the Black Sea) were taken into use before they were broken up, mostly in-situ. Also, the Russians salvaged the heavily damaged Type VIIC U-boat, *U-250*, which had been sunk in the Gulf of Finland in July 1944. On 25 September 1944 it was taken to Kronstadt near Leningrad, but it was found to be non-repairable, and it was eventually broken up.

Finally, it is worth considering the impact of the U-boats in the Soviet Navy particularly as the Russians clearly wished to obtain as many surrendered and captured U-boats as possible, especially the Type XXIs.

Whilst the U-boats that were captured at Danzig were formally designated as Soviet 'War Prizes' in the *TS* series, only the ten U-boats comprising the TNC allocation to the USSR were given formal Soviet Navy alpha-numeric 'names' in the *B* (large), *S* (medium) and *M* (small) series, although the latter ten U-boats were allocated to the Soviet Baltic Fleet. But even then this did not mean that they were ever used operationally. Rather, it seems that, like the RN to a very limited extent and the USN to a much greater extent in respect of their two Type XXIs, *U-2513* and *U-3008*, the ten U-boats allowed the Soviet Navy to gain experience of operating such submarines as well as to obtain knowledge of their advanced technical features as the basis for the planned expansion of the Soviet Navy's submarine fleet.

In respect of the latter ambition, the Type XXIs were of much greater interest to the Soviet Navy than the earlier Type VIICs and they made a major contribution to the development of the 'Whiskey' class which became the early backbone of the Soviet Navy's non-nuclear ocean-going submarine fleet. It is probable that the Soviet Navy was primarily interested in the design features of the Type XXIs and their production techniques. Thus, it seems at least in part, the Soviet Union probably adhered to the principles behind the decisions taken at the Potsdam Conference and the recommendations of the TNC that the allocated U-boats were to be used for technical assessment and experimental purposes. However, the captures in Danzig caused the Soviet Union to contravene that part of the Potsdam Agreement which fixed the number of U-boats at just ten to each of the Allies, and which specifically stated that all other unallocated U-boats were to be sunk not later than 15 February 1946.

Initially none of this was clear in 1946 and 1947 and there was a great deal of concern, particularly in the USA, about the number of Type XXI U-boats that seemed to have fallen into Russian hands. The USN itself was investing a great deal of time, effort and interest in its own Type XXIs and was even replicating many of their design characteristics into the 'Guppy' and *Tang* class of submarines. The US was therefore fearful that the Soviet Navy likely to commission twenty or more Type XXI U-boats into operational service. As a result on 23 July 1946 the USN's CNO advised the Secretary of the Navy that the Soviet Navy could have at least 300 submarines of advanced design based on the German Type XXI U-boat by 1950.

The Soviet Navy's intentions regarding the exploitation and use of the U-boats in its inventory were understandably difficult to discern and on 9 May 1947 the CNO produced a (then) top-secret paper based on the latest intelligence information, giving an 'Estimate of Russian Exploitation of German Submarine Types'. Most of the USN's attention was focussed on the Type XXIs but the paper also included assessments concerning the Type VIIC, the Type IXC, the Type XXIII and the 'Walter' U-boats. The paper's conclusions were:

Type VIIC and IXC U-Boats: It is believed that the Russian interest is more in material and design features rather than operational use.

Type XXIII U-Boat: It is believed that their interest in the Type XXIII is merely examination of design and construction for future use.

Type XVII and XXVI ('Walter') U-Boats: It seems probable that the Russians will construct some type of 'Walter' propelled submarine for test purposes. There is no indication as yet that they will adopt a Type XXVI construction programme, and it seems unlikely that they will do so. All of their activity to date points to investigation and evaluation with a view to use in their own design.[12]

However, the paper was equivocal about the Type XXIs. Firstly, it said that:

No large Russian Type XXI program is apparent at this time. The Russians are interested in the Type XXI submarine. They have secured all

·the material, equipment and personnel concerned with its construction that became available to them, and are now engaged in tests and studies with a view to improving their submarine knowledge and design.

The Russians are not embarking on a Type XXI building program, but are conducting tests and investigations for future construction.[12]

But, secondly, it said that:

The Type XXI constitutes a potential threat in Russian hands because:

(a) 7 vessels are operational [this wrongly included 3 U-boats (*U-3531*, *U-3533* and *U-3534*) which had been moved to Kiel before Danzig was captured]
(b) 8 vessels are probably operational
(c) 6 vessels can be made operational in 2 months [from captured sections]
(d) 39 vessels can be assembled from sections within 18 months

Within the very near future the Russians will have a flotilla of about 15 Type XXI submarines. There are an additional six vessels which could be made operational within two months. Present intelligence of Russian policy indicates intention to employ all captured or allocated German submarines. A school has been organised to implement this program.[12]

Despite its obvious errors, together with some dubious calculations about the prospects of assembling additional Type XXIs from the sections that had been captured in Danzig, this important paper was nevertheless accepted as the baseline for future USN briefings. As a result, in January 1948 the US Joint Intelligence Committee advised the US Joint Chiefs of Staff of their estimate that the Soviet Navy had fifteen operational Type XXI submarines, could complete another six within two months and that thirty-nine more could be assembled from prefabricated parts within 18 months.

Furthermore, on 19 November 1948 the US Office of Naval Intelligence stated that it had 'confirmed' information that there were 229 submarines in the Soviet Fleet, plus another 52 probably in service. Of those, between 130 to 160 were considered to be 'modern ocean patrol submarines', a category which included the ex-German Type VIIC, Type IXC and Type XXI U-boats. In particular, the November 1948 report stated that there were certainly four Type XXIs and probably an additional twenty in service with the Soviet Navy and that these were the only truly modern submarines being operated by the latter.

The result of all this intelligence information, which in retrospect seems to have been somewhat exaggerated in terms of immediate operational capability, was that the USN became convinced that the Soviet Navy had sufficient examples of the Type XXI U-boats to provide a sound basis for the design of the ocean-going submarine fleet that the Soviet Union was determined to build. The other result was that it convinced the US Government that the Type XXIs already in the Soviet Navy represented a serious threat to the USN's domination of the world's oceans and it was therefore possibly one of the sparks that initiated the huge submarine building programme on which the USN itself then embarked.

The four Type XXI U-boats which had been allocated to the USSR by the TNC (*U- 2529, U-3035, U-3041* and *U-3515*) together with the other twenty that were removed from Danzig, some incomplete and some simply as sets of unassembled prefabricated sections therefore seem to have created a threat many times greater than their own inherent power.

CHAPTER 16

U-Boats in France

DESPITE A GREAT DEAL of diplomatic pressure during 1944 and 1945, France was not invited to join the 'Big Three', to participate in the Potsdam Conference nor to join the TNC. This did not please the French Government which was very keen to be allocated some of the U-boats that had surrendered, and throughout 1945 the French applied diplomatic and military pressure on both the USA and the UK to facilitate their ambition.

The UK's attitude towards the future of any U-boats that might surrender at the end of the war was quite clear; with just a few exceptions they should all be sunk. Despite this, the British Government was favourably inclined to support the French, and a pre-Potsdam Foreign Office Briefing Note dated 6 July 1945 recommended that consideration should be given to the French case:

> The French claim to a share in the German fleet, which has already been put forward semi-officially to the Admiralty, is weak in equity. But the French are an equal partner in the Allied supreme authority and control over Germany, and it is in our interest to preserve the good relations between the Royal Navy and the French Navy and to encourage the latter to work with us in the future. Accordingly, it is submitted that we should allow the French a few ships, on the grounds that the destruction of their ship-building and dockyards during the war will preclude France from replacing losses by her own construction for some time.[1]

This Briefing Note was followed by a UK Cabinet Paper 'Disposal of the German Fleet' on the next day in which the First Lord of the Admiralty suggested that France should be allocated six U-boats from those that had surrendered.[2]

The US military authorities were also initially sympathetic to the case for France to be allocated a share of the surviving German naval vessels. Thus, even before the Potsdam Conference began in mid-July, they were party to moves (albeit unsuccessful) by the French Navy to obtain examples of the latest high-tech German U-boats, with a USN Department of Naval Intelligence paper dated 7 July 1945 recording that:

> The French Navy is very anxious to obtain the 16 [Type XXI] submarines found in a partially completed condition in the important Weser Shipyard of the Deschimag Company, Bremen. At the request of the French Naval Mission, the US [Naval Authorities in Germany have] authorised a survey of the Weser Yard, with the understanding that no commitments whatsoever could be made to the French Mission with respect to future disposition of the submarines.[3]

However, the official US position concerning the allocation of German naval vessels remained. Except for a small number of ships to be retained for experimental purposes the entire German naval fleet including the U-boats should be destroyed by sinking or scrapping.

Despite this, the UK continued to be sympathetic to the French desire to share the spoils of war and on 30 July 1945, just as the Potsdam Conference was coming to an end, the UK Delegation tabled a formal memorandum which said:

> It was agreed on 19 July that the German surface ships should be shared equally between the Three Powers. The British Delegation suggest that consideration should now be given to allocating a share to France which is an equal party to the terms of surrender for Germany.[4]

The British proposal was considered on 31 July 1945 by the 'Technical Sub-Committee on the Disposition of the German Navy and Merchant Marine',[5] the decision sheet of which whilst recording that the British representatives had expressed the view that a portion of the German surface warships, as well as two U-boats, should be allocated to France went on to recommend that the remaining German naval vessels should only be divided between the UK, the USA and the USSR.

The minutes of the Technical Sub-Committee's meeting also recorded that the British proposal was now that only two U-boats should be allocated to France. But even this proposal caused protracted discussion and it fell on very stony ground as far as the Russians were concerned. Their view was that the German surface fleet should be divided equally between the Allies and that most of the U-boats were to be sunk. This had already been agreed in principle and as was pointed out by Mr Gromyko:

He had been present at the Plenary Meeting, and he was in no doubt that full agreement had been reached for transfer to the Soviet Union of one third of the German Navy ... and that Generalissimo Stalin had attached great importance to the maintenance of this matter. He stated that at no time had it been suggested that any share should go to France.[5]

Similarly, Admiral Kuznetsov who was both the Head of the Soviet Navy and the Chairman of the Sub-Committee emphasised that: 'As France had not been discussed in connection with the German Navy, he suggested that there was no reason to discuss it here and proposed that the discussion of this point could now be closed.'[5] Whilst the British proposal in support of the French request was included in the Sub-Committee's report it was not taken forward.

Unsurprisingly, the French remained unhappy about this situation and so after the Potsdam Conference the French Government made yet more attempts to raise the matter. However, its military pressure on the USA once more fell on stony ground. Similar pressure was applied in the UK with the French Ambassador in London writing to the British Foreign Secretary on 28 August asking for the allocation of specific types of ex-German warships to the French Navy. In respect of U-boats the French requirement was for at least eleven for two different purposes:

For Operational Use:	Six Type XXI U-Boats
	All U-Boats found in occupied French ports
For Technical Research:	One Type XXIII U-Boat
	One Type IXD2 U-Boat
	One Type XB U-Boat
	One Type XXI U-Boat
	One Type XVIIB 'Walter' U-Boat[6]

The French raised the matter again at a meeting of the Council of Foreign Ministers held in London on 11 September 1945. But in response Molotov said that he had no authority to review decisions reached by Heads of Government at the Berlin Conference. The French delegation had probably realised by this time that their formal approaches had failed and that their best chance of rescuing anything from the situation was to concentrate on their informal links with the RN staff in London.

In the meantime, the TNC had started work in mid-August 1945 and it had no mandate to allocate any U-boats to France. Nevertheless, in addition to the single U-boat that remained afloat in St Nazaire in western France it recognised that some other U-boats remained in French harbours, all of which were unseaworthy and most of which had been wrecked by bomb damage. There was, however, no formal inspection of the ports in France, with the TNC relying instead on information provided by the American and British Naval Attachés. Thus, as became obvious when the TNC issued its final report, the 'Agreed List' of the U-boats that remained in France was not as comprehensive as it was in respect of the U-boats in German and Norwegian ports. Nevertheless, British interest in the provision of a small number of German warships to France remained as had been made clear in the Admiralty's Directive to the British TNC Representatives dated 13 August 1945, which said:

> His Majesty's Government proposed at Potsdam that a small share of the German Fleet should be allocated to France, but received no support whatever from either the USSR or USA. The Protocol, in consequence, makes no provision for France. Nevertheless, it is His Majesty's Government's desire that the French Navy should receive such ships as can be spared from the British share after satisfying essential British requirements. You should bear this consideration in mind particularly with reference to the allocation of destroyers and torpedo boats. It is not known what is the intention of the US Government in this respect.[7]

The French Navy took a close interest in the actions of the TNC, as recorded by Admiral Miles in his Final Report dated 8 November:

> Although the French should officially be unaware of the existence of the Tripartite Naval Commission, as they were not represented at the Potsdam Conference, they did in fact know that we had started our work. I have been approached by Admiral Still, and Captains Benesch and Peltier, to ask if I can do anything for them. I have always replied that officially I can do nothing, as officially they do not know of my existence. Off the record I have told them that their wishes are known and will be borne in mind as far as possible, and with that they have all been profuse in their thanks.[8]

Once the TNC's initial U-boat allocations to the three Allies had been made on 10 October, the debate was immediately reignited when in a blatant breach of security *The Times* published a story on the very same day which stated:

> Provisional agreement, subject to ratification of the Powers concerned, has been reached on the disposal of the former German U-Boat fleet, it is understood here. Under the terms of the decisions taken by the naval representatives of Great Britain, Russia and the United States, each

one of these three Powers will receive six [*sic*] boats for experimental purposes. The remainder of the fleet, totalling approximately 150 submarines, will be scrapped.[9]

This caused a diplomatic storm in Paris. *The Times* reported on 26 October:

> The British, American and Russian plan for the disposal of German submarines has caused grave misgivings in French Government circles. The French Government at once raised objections to this decision.
>
> In the view of the French Government this agreement violates the principle by which, since the establishment of the Allied Control Commission, all decisions affecting Germany should be taken jointly by the four Powers represented on that Commission. It violates still more, in the French view, the canons of equity and fair play which should govern the disposal of German assets.
>
> The French demand is for six German submarines.[10]

Predictably, this spat did nothing to influence the decisions of the TNC, which was quite clear that no U-boats were to be allocated to France. Nevertheless the diplomatic debate was re-started by a memorandum from the US State Department to the French Embassy in Washington on 5 November which whilst indicating the former's willingness in principle to transfer a share of the US allocation of surface vessels to France said:

> At the Potsdam Conference vigorous efforts were made by the United States to ensure that the largest possible proportion of the German submarine fleet would be sunk or otherwise destroyed. In accordance with this position the United States will not transfer to any other Government any of the submarines included in the United States share of the German Naval Fleet.[6]

This strong stance by the Americans led to a review by the Admiralty of their previous inclination to support the transfer of some U-boats to France with a minute dated 8 November recording that:

> The Foreign Office is being bombarded by the French in London and in Paris and at all levels, upon the subject. The Americans have said that they do not intend to let the French have any U-Boats, and the Board are likely to want to conform to the American policy in this respect.[6]

The Admiralty's Director of Plans supported the latter view and he observed that the French had inflated ideas both as to what was available and to what they were morally entitled. Also, in view of the unequivocal US position and the probability that it would be supported by the Admiralty

Board he suggested that it was unlikely that the French would receive any U-boats from Great Britain. Thus on 13 November the Admiralty sent a message to the British Naval Attache in Paris saying: 'For your personal information we shall probably follow US policy concerning U-Boats.'[6]

It was, however, a very fast-moving situation and the British attitudes all changed within a day as a result of a new two-pronged French approach. Firstly, as the result of a short message from the Private Secretary to the First Lord of the Admiralty on 13 November which said: 'Admiral Nomy [of the French Navy] mentioned to the First Lord at dinner last night that the French were anxious to obtain some German U-Boats. The First Lord would be glad to know what the position is.'[6]

Secondly, as the result of a letter from the Foreign Office on 14 November which advised the Admiralty that the French had changed their stance in relation to their earlier requirement for up to eleven U-boats including six for operational purposes, and that they were now saying: 'The French Navy was very anxious to have [just] one or two German submarines to experiment with.'[6] The letter also explained that there was a wider diplomatic dimension to the debate which had now: 'Assumed quite exaggerated importance in the minds of the French Admiralty, and that failure to meet their wishes would have a painful effect in French Naval circles and also on general political relations between Great Britain and France.'[6]

Thus, the Foreign Office stressed to the Admiralty the hope that:

> It might be possible to find some way of meeting French wishes while maintaining our own position of principle, eg. By the loan of a couple of German submarines to the French after we have finished with them on the understanding that they would be returned to us in due course for destruction.[6]

As a result of this new situation, a comprehensive re-assessment was undertaken by the Admiralty on 15 November and, despite the support just days earlier for the US-led hard line in respect of the provision of any U-boats to France, it recorded that:

> HMG [had] proposed to the Americans that each should allot to France an appropriate part of their share. Our object was to satisfy the increasingly insistent French demands for German warships and to compensate them for having been left out of the discussions concerning the German Fleet, in which they could legitimately claim to participate as one of the Powers enforcing the surrender of Germany. The Americans have replied to the French refusing absolutely to

transfer U-Boats on the grounds of their advocacy at Potsdam of the destruction of the largest possible part of the German submarine fleet.

We know that the French have taken the US reply about the question of U-Boats hardly, and it appears that in Paris the whole question of the disposal of the German Fleet has obtained an exaggerated importance in French eyes for reasons of prestige. Admiral Nomy mentioned the question of U-Boats to the First Lord earlier this week. A senior member of the French Embassy has also raised the question semi-officially with the Foreign Office. The Foreign Office recognise that the Admiralty, particularly in view of the American attitude, may be loath to transfer U-Boats outright to the French Navy. They ask, however, whether we might not make available two U-Boats on loan.[6]

Additionally, the conciliatory Admiralty report went on to say:

The French Naval Representative on the Council of Foreign Ministers, Capitaine de Vaisseau Rebuffel came to see me yesterday and he too mentioned the question of U-Boats. He mentioned that the French possess five U-Boats found in French bases [and] asked whether the French title to these U-boats could be confirmed. The U-Boats in French bases were discussed at Potsdam at the Technical Sub-Committee, when we pointed out the awkwardness of trying to extract shipping in French hands. The Russians, according to my clear recollection, intimated that they were content to leave the French boats out of account. There is, however, no official record of Russian acquiescence in the French title. I have consulted the Foreign Office who are strongly of the view that the French will be wise to let sleeping dogs lie and simply assume the recognition of their title to these U-Boats. I entirely agree.[6]

This softer line was reflected in the Admiralty's response to the Foreign Office on 19 November which, when referring to the French request for an allocation of U-boats, stated that it could now:

See no objection to the French having opportunities for technical examination of the U-Boats allocated to us. We are prepared to offer one Type XXI and one Type XXIII U-Boat to France on loan for six months for technical purposes. These are the two latest types which the French Navy particularly desired to examine.[6]

The same letter also confirmed that Capitaine Rebuffel had asked about the French title to the unserviceable U-boats already in France most of which had previously been classified as war losses and had been captured at the end of the war rather than surrendering. The Admiralty had therefore re-iterated the earlier advice that had been given to Rebuffel reminding him that it would be best if events were allowed to proceed on the assumption that the French Navy had a title to the U-boats remaining in the French ports.

A day later, on 20 November, the Foreign Office wrote to the British Embassy in Paris summarising the situation and saying:

> I am replying to your letter of 6 November about French restiveness over the German fleet and the other demands which they have upon us in respect of German war material.
>
> Both we and the Admiralty have repeatedly explained to the French that we put in a claim for them at the Potsdam Conference to have their own share of the German fleet, but could not get the agreement of our Allies. The Russians were dead against and the Americans, whose line at Potsdam was to appease the Russians on the German ships in the vain hope that it would make them more reasonable in major matters, gave us no support. However, I think there is a good chance that, so far as we are concerned, we may succeed in reaching a friendly settlement with the French under this head.
>
> The Admiralty are prepared to be quite generous in transferring German surface ships assigned to us and (for your own information at the present stage) we hope that the Admiralty will agree to let the French have one or two German submarines for experimental purposes, after we have looked at them ourselves, provided that they are eventually destroyed together with the rest of our share of ten.
>
> According to what the French have told both us and the Admiralty here in London, their main interest is to play about with one or two of the later types, and they have already picked up two in the Atlantic ports. There is no question of giving the French more than experimental rights, as the conclusion of the Potsdam Conference, which represented a victory for the Anglo-American thesis of destruction against the Russian desire to acquire a large U-Boat fleet, was in favour of destruction apart from the allocation of ten to each party for (ostensibly) experimental purposes.
>
> Incidentally, the French tactics over their claims on German ships and war material have been unfortunate. Their demands have been absurdly exaggerated and peremptory in tone. They have followed them up by nagging at all the British authorities concerned concurrently and through as many different channels as possible. The irritation which this has provoked in the Service Departments has made it difficult to persuade them to bear with French methods and to be as generous as possible in the general interest of good relations and high policy.[11]

As a result, the French Embassy in London was informed that the UK proposed to offer the French Navy two U-boats from the UK's TNC allocation on loan for technical purposes. This proposal was followed by protracted discussions about the loan period which was eventually agreed as two years and at Admiral (Submarines)'s suggestion the two U-boats to be transferred to France were the Type XXI *U-2518* and the Type XXIII *U-2348*.

Predictably, the French continued to be impatient and January 1946 was marked by a further flurry of minutes and meetings about the U-boats already in France and the two to be transferred on loan from the UK. It was complicated by the fact that the TNC's Final Report on 6 December 1945 had specifically listed five of the U-boats that were located in France, one of them being described as afloat and the other four as being scuttled in shallow water, all of which were recommended to be sunk or otherwise destroyed. In accordance with the Potsdam decisions and the TNC recommendations the Allies were duty bound to request the French to destroy these five U-boats but a file minute from the Foreign Office to the Admiralty on 2 January 1946 suggested as a compromise that:

> I imagine that it would be possible for us simply to notify the French of the action required under the Report of the Tripartite Naval Commission and to leave it to them to decide for themselves what steps they will take. We obviously cannot force them to destroy the submarines in question.[12]

The UK position was then amplified on 14 January in a Foreign Office file minute by Sir Anthony Rumbold, when he said:

> Unless I am mistaken, the [TNC] report only binds the Potsdam powers and only covers the German ships in the actual control of these powers. If this is so, is there any reason why we should either ask the French to destroy the submarines or, in accepting the report, make any reservation in regard to these submarines? They are surely not our concern and we have no responsibility in relation to them. We have told the French what the report provides for, and if they like to ignore its recommendations, that is nothing to do with us.[12]

This eventually led to an authoritative statement in the UK Cabinet Paper CP (46) 49, dated 6 February 1946, which was presented to the Cabinet by The First Lord of the Admiralty on 14 February and which dealt with the UK's reaction to the TNC's Final Report, viz:

The Commission has recommended that the three Governments simultaneously request that inoperable German warships at present in the territorial waters of other countries be sunk or destroyed by the Governments in whose waters they lie within the time limits proposed by the Commission.

Before accepting this recommendation, we must consider its effect on France. We are aware that a small number of German submarines were left in an inoperable state in French ports by the enemy, and that the French Navy is anxious to retain them for training and research. It is our policy to assist France in rebuilding her Navy and we are going so far as to transfer to her certain German warships from our own allocation, including two operable U-Boats. But the latter will be on loan and returned to us for destruction. While, therefore, we should, I think, formally associate ourselves with the joint request recommended by the Commission, we need feel under no obligation to press it in the face of a reasonable French objection.[13]

This position was slightly different from the one previously suggested by the Admiralty and the Foreign Office, but the result was the same. Also, at the Cabinet Meeting itself the First Lord of the Admiralty reported that the matter had been informally resolved because: 'He had since learned that the Governments of both the United States and the Soviet Union had already decided to act independently in this matter and that the United States Government were unlikely to make the request to France.'[14]

In the meantime, the Assistant Chief of Naval Staff (Weapons) had also had a meeting on 3 January with the Head of the French Naval Mission in London (Admiral Sala) to discuss the transfer of German warships to the French Navy which included the two U-boats on loan which was the maximum and final offer that could be made by the RN. At the meeting the Chief of Staff to Admiral (Submarines) said: 'The two offered were of the latest types: with regard to their condition he strongly advised that *U-2518* must have a major refit before being dived, while *U-2348* was in good running order.'[12]

In response Admiral Sala: 'Expressed his personal appreciation of the offer which he realised was made at the initiative of Great Britain and said it would be understood that he must submit it to his Government. It was his personal opinion that the offer should be accepted in its entirety.'[12]

There was, however, a complication because on 11 January 1946 whilst it was at Lisahally being prepared for transfer to France there was a battery explosion on *U-2348*. Thus, the remaining Type XXIII, *U-2326*, which was in a very poor state after the earlier RN trials, had to be substituted instead. The detailed arrangements for the transfers were then agreed in anticipation of French acceptance with the Admiralty's executive instruction saying:

> The two U-Boats [*U-2326* and *U-2518*] would be towed over by the Royal Navy to a French port and would be ready to leave Londonderry about 1 February 1946. They would have British crews only who would remain to hand over to the French. The period of turn-over would probably take two weeks, and they [the British crews] would then be returned to England by the French authorities.[12]

The high-level staff work associated with the transfer then ended with a letter from Admiral Sala to the Admiralty later in the month confirming that the French Minister of Defence had agreed the proposals and saying that the latter had instructed him to thank the Admiralty for its gesture which he greatly appreciated.

The transfer of *U-2326* and *U-2518*, both of which were located at Lisahally, from the RN to the French Navy took place in February 1946 and was code-named Operation 'Thankful'.[15] HMS *Tremadoc Bay* was to tow *U-2326*, and HM Tug *Bustler* was to tow *U-2518*, and the move began on 5 February when HMS *Tremadoc Bay* and the tug *Bustler* sailed from Lisahally to Moville at the mouth of Lough Foyle. The following morning the two U-boats arrived, the tows were connected, and the four vessels left Lough Foyle at 1400. Both U-boats were crewed by RN personnel to allow them to move independently in case of emergency.

On 7 February heavy weather in the Irish Sea, towing problems and a number of defects caused a diversion into Dublin Bay. Before that the group had reached the vicinity of the Tuskar Rocks in the southern Irish Sea but *U-2326*'s periscope had failed and *U-2518*'s tow had parted. As bad weather was then forecast, the group headed north first to the sheltered anchorage of Dublin Bay in the Irish Republic and then into Dublin's Kingstown Harbour. The decision to move the two escorts and their accompanying U-boats into the harbour at Dublin was made with some trepidation for fear of causing a diplomatic incident but permission was granted – apparently by the Irish Prime Minister himself.

The transfer resumed on 10 February again with both U-boats under tow and the remainder of the passage to Cherbourg was made in calm weather albeit with two minor incidents. On 11 February a detour was made into Lyme Bay in order to transfer a sick rating from *U-2518* to HMS *Tremadoc Bay* as well as to lose some time to avoid arriving at Cherbourg during darkness and for the last 36 hours of the transit *U-2518* was unable to steer owing to a leaking rudder gland. The group finally arrived off Cherbourg at 0930 on 13 February and the two U-boats were handed over to the French Navy.

The only commissioned U-boat that formally surrendered afloat in France on 9 May 1945 was *U-510* but as it was in dock prior to having a schnorkel fitted it was unseaworthy and therefore remained in St Nazaire rather than being moved to the UK to await a decision on its fate. Nevertheless, *U-510* was unallocated by the TNC and it was therefore earmarked in the TNC's Final Report to be sunk by 15 February 1946. The four decommissioned/sunk (war loss) U-boats in French harbours which the TNC report specifically recorded as being scuttled in shallow water and which like *U-510* were recommended for early destruction by the French were:

> *U-178*, a Type IX D2 which had been decommissioned in Bordeaux on 20 August 1944. It was unable to move and had been scuttled in the U-boat pen in Bordeaux on 25 August 1944.
>
> *U-188*, a Type IXC/40 which had been decommissioned in Bordeaux on 20 August 1944. It was unable to move and had been scuttled in the U-boat pen in Bordeaux on 25 August 1944.
>
> *U-466*, a Type VIIC which had been damaged in an air attack on Toulon on 5 July 1944. It had been scuttled at Toulon off St Mandrier-sur-Mer on 19 August 1944.
>
> *U-967*, a Type VIIC which had been damaged in air attacks on Toulon on 5 and 11 July 1944. It had been scuttled at Toulon off St Mandrier-sur-Mer on 19 August 1944.

As the TNC had no jurisdiction over France the French Navy could not be compelled to comply with any of its recommendations. Instead, with unofficial support from the UK the French decided not only to ignore the TNC's recommendations concerning the five specified U-boats but also to see if any of the other wrecked U-boats in French ports could be returned to an operational status. As it happened, none of the four scuttled (war loss) U-boats highlighted in the TNC report was capable of retrieval. Despite all the earlier debates they were therefore scrapped in situ.

Instead, French attention was focused on the other decommissioned and/or wrecked (war loss) U-boats in French harbours which had not been reported to the TNC and which were not therefore highlighted in the TNC's Final Report. Whilst most were incapable of any further use it was estimated that three of them in addition to *U-510* could be restored to an operational status. The French Navy therefore raised, repaired and commissioned these four U-boats, all of which were initially recovered with the help of German Navy POWs captured in western France at the end of the war:

U-123, a Type IXB which had been decommissioned in Lorient on 17 June 1944, laid-up in the U-boat pen and used as an electricity generator.

U-471, a Type VIIC which had been damaged in an air raid on Toulon on 5 July 1944 and was sunk in a further air raid on Toulon on 6 August 1944.

U-510, a Type IXC which had surrendered in St Nazaire on 9 May 1945 but which was insufficiently seaworthy to be transferred to the UK for disposal.

U-766, a Type VIIC which had been decommissioned at La Pallice (La Rochelle) on 21 August 1944 and laid-up in the U-boat pen.

So, together with the two U-boats on loan from the UK, the French Navy acquired and operated six U-boats, none of which had been formally allocated to France by the TNC under the terms of the Potsdam Agreement.

U-510, which had surrendered in St Nazaire in May 1945, was taken over by the French Navy and remained there for its initial repair and recovery. Thereafter it was transferred to Brest in mid-1946 where it was modified by removing the deck guns and fitting a streamlined conning tower and a schnorkel. It was commissioned as *Commandant Bouan* (*S 612*) on 24 June 1947 and transferred to Toulon for use as an operational submarine. Later *U-510* was used for training and as a target in French ASW exercises. *Bouan* was decommissioned and placed in reserve on 1 April 1959 before being declared surplus to requirements on 23 November 1959. It was sold and scrapped in Toulon in 1960.

U-123 was taken over by the French Navy in October 1945 and was repaired and refitted in the ex-German Keroman submarine base at Lorient between then and September 1946. However, preliminary tests at sea revealed a number of residual problems and it returned to Lorient for further work before being commissioned as *Commandant Blaison* (*S 611*) on 23 June 1947. It was used for a variety of training duties before returning to Lorient on 17 February 1949 for a major overhaul which lasted until 14 March 1950. Thereafter it was employed on various operational and training duties and had a further major and two minor refits. *Blaison* was decommissioned and placed in reserve on 1 August 1957 before being declared surplus to requirements on 18 August 1959. It was then sold and scrapped at La Seyne (near Toulon) by the shipbreakers Les Abeilles.

U-471 was raised by the French Navy in 1946 and the initial repair and restoration work commenced at Toulon in February, with its first sea trials taking place on 23 October 1946. It was commissioned as *Mille* (*S 609*) in early 1947 and transferred to Lorient for the fitting of a schnorkel before becoming operational in July 1947. Thereafter *Mille* remained in the French Navy mostly in the Mediterranean until it was decommissioned and placed in reserve on 16 December 1962 before being declared surplus to requirements on 9 July 1963 and then scrapped in Toulon.

U-766 was taken over in the La Pallice dockyard in August 1945 and repaired there with the assistance of German Navy POWs before being moved to Lorient on 15 July 1946 for updating including the fitting of a schnorkel. It was commissioned as *Laubie* (*S 610*) on 24 June 1947 after a dockyard shake-down cruise to Casablanca in October 1946. It was subsequently transferred to the Mediterranean during which time it took part in the Suez operations in 1956 as well as being involved in three collisions (the first with a frigate, the second with a steamer, and the third with a submarine), the last in September 1961. The severely damaged *Laubie* was decommissioned and placed in reserve in October 1961 before being declared surplus to requirements on 11 March 1963. It was broken up for scrap in Toulon later in 1963.

Of the two ex-Royal Navy U-boats, the Type XXIII, *U-2326*, was used by the French Navy for schnorkel trials but was lost with all its crew on 5 December 1946 when it failed to surface after a deep diving test off Toulon. The Type XXI, *U-2518*, remained at Cherbourg for repairs until August 1946 and was then used by the French Navy for tests, trials and experiments at Lorient, Brest and Toulon until October 1948 when it was transferred to the ex-German Keroman submarine base at Lorient for further repairs, modifications and updating; work which lasted until May 1949. Thereafter its busy test programme continued until February 1951 when the UK loan was extended until February 1954.

Despite their advanced technical aspects, the build quality of the Type XXI U-boats was suspect and it was not surprising that the French Navy was very cautious before deciding to take *U-2518* into use as an operational submarine. However, after the extension of the UK loan

U-2518 was formally commissioned into the French Navy at Toulon as *Roland Morillot* (*S 613*) on 9 April 1951. It was then used operationally until 15 April 1967 (22 years after it had surrendered on 9 May 1945) when it was decommissioned and placed in reserve at Toulon. It was declared surplus to requirements on 17 October 1967 and was sold on 21 May 1969 to the Italian ship breakers SPA Loti before being scrapped in August 1969.

Finally (for completeness), two incomplete French submarines, *L'Africaine* and *L'Astree*, had been taken over by the Germans in June 1940 but although they were given the designations *UF-1* and *UF-3* respectively on 5 May 1941 they were neither completed nor commissioned into the Kriegsmarine. After the war the French resumed the construction of these two submarines and they were commissioned into the French Navy. *L'Africaine* was launched on 7 December 1946 and *L'Astree* was commissioned in October 1949. Eventually *L'Africaine* (ex-*UF-1*) was withdrawn from service on 1 July 1961 and scrapped on 28 February 1963, and *L'Astree* (ex-*UF-3*) was withdrawn from service in 1962 and scrapped on 27 November 1965.

CHAPTER 17

U-Boats in Canada

AFTER THE GERMAN CAPITULATION on 8 May 1945 two U-boats (*U-190* and *U-889*) surrendered at sea to units of the Royal Canadian Navy (RCN), the latter on 10 May and the former on 11 May. However, the RCN had made no separate arrangements for the surrender of any U-boats in the western North Atlantic in May 1945, preferring instead to follow the procedures set out by the Admiralty and the RN's Commander-in-Chief Western Approaches. The RCN had nevertheless specified two surrender points in the waters controlled by the Commander-in-Chief of the Canadian Northwest Atlantic (C-in-C, CNA), one to the east of St John's, Newfoundland and one to the south of Halifax, Nova Scotia, as it was expected that several of the U-boats still at sea might head for Canada rather than either the USA or UK, a sentiment that was reflected in a report in the *Ottawa Journal* on 7 May, which said: 'U-Boats in the area are likely to give themselves up at eastern ports rather than make the long trip back to Europe.'[1]

In the event neither of the two U-boats sailed directly to either of the designated surrender points or to any Canadian ports but instead they surrendered and were intercepted at sea by RCN warships.

The first to surrender was *U-889* which was sighted by a Royal Canadian Air Force (RCAF) Liberator aircraft on 10 May whilst the U-boat was on the surface and flying the black flag of surrender some 250 miles south-east the Flemish Cap, an area of shallow water in the North Atlantic which is about 350 miles east of Newfoundland.

The nearly new *U-889* had sailed from Kristiansand in Norway on 5 April on its first patrol with orders to undertake weather reporting duties in the mid-North Atlantic and with instructions not to make any attacks. However, these instructions were subsequently changed and the

U-boat was instead ordered to attack Allied shipping between New York and Cape Hatteras in North Carolina.

Because of difficulties with wireless transmissions in early May it is unclear if *U-889*'s CO ever sent an initial 'position, course and speed' (PCS) surrender message especially as according to the crew in their initial interrogation it was not until 10 May that *U-889* received the Allied orders which required it to surface and fly a black flag indicating its surrender.

At 1920 on 10 May and after its initial sighting by the Liberator, *U-889* was intercepted by four RCN warships, the minesweepers HMCS *Oshawa* and HMCS *Rockcliffe* and the corvettes HMCS *Dunvegan* and HMCS *Saskatoon*, whilst still some 175 miles south-east of Newfoundland. Poor weather made it impossible to board the U-boat so *Oshawa* closed to loudhailer distance and passed instructions to the U-boat in German, ordering it to head for Bay Bulls in Newfoundland escorted by the four RCN warships.

However, at 2300 these orders were changed. *Oshawa* and *Saskatoon* were detached for return to St John's, and *Rockcliffe* and *Dunvegan* were instructed to escort *U-889* to Shelburne in south-west Nova Scotia. Later the next day the escort duties were taken over by the frigates HMCS *Buckingham* and HMCS *Inch Arran* after the C-in-C, CNA had sent a message at 0310 saying:

Relieve HMC ships *Dunvegan* and *Rockcliffe* and escort *U-889* to Shelburne, NS. Boarding party is to be put on board *U-889* if weather conditions permit and all possible precautions are to be taken to prevent scuttling. Report PCS.[2]

To which the CO of *Buckingham* responded: 'My PCS at 2200Z [is] 43.53N, 57.07 W, 261 degrees, 11 knots. Escorting U-889. Not boarded. Weather unsuitable.'[2]

After a two-day transit to Nova Scotia *U-889* was boarded on 13 May and a formal surrender ceremony took place whilst the U-boat was some seven miles south of the entrance to Shelburne harbour, details of which were reported in the *Halifax Herald* on 14 May:

Under an overcast threatening sky a twelve-man boarding party of the Royal Canadian Navy, accompanied by Captain G R Miles, Chief of Staff to the Commander-in-Chief of the Canadian Northwest Atlantic, and a squad of RN submarine technicians, climbed onto the defeated enemy vessel and a few seconds later the White Ensign was hoisted at the undersea raider's flagstaff to officially mark the taking over of the craft.[3]

Similarly, on 14 May the *Ottawa Journal* reported in the highly charged and emotive language of the day that: 'One of Germany's underseas [*sic*] demons of destruction lay harmless in Shelburne Harbour today.'[4]

The much older *U-190* had left Kristiansand on 21 February en route to its operational area off Nova Scotia and the east coast of the USA. On 16 April, whilst operating close to the approaches to Halifax harbour, it fired a torpedo at the minesweeper HMCS *Esquimalt*, which was the last Canadian warship to be sunk in the war.

On 29 April, with all its torpedoes expended, *U-190* began its way home to Norway but because of wireless reception difficulties it was almost in mid-Atlantic some 500 miles east of Newfoundland's Cape Race before the first clear surrender orders were received. The U-boat's CO responded by sending the required PCS messages in the early hours of the morning on 11 May to the USN in New York and Boston as well as to the RCN wireless station at Cape Race.

An RCAF Liberator was sent to investigate and at 1205 the C-in-C, CNA sent a message to the RCN escort vessels saying: 'Detach two units forthwith to proceed [at] best speed to intercept U-190 reported in 42.35N, 43.06W about 1000Z/11th. Report names [of] units detached.'[2]

As a result, the frigate HMCS *Victoriaville* and the corvette HMCS *Thorlock* were ordered to the scene of *U-190*'s surrender and at 1805 the C-in-C CNA sent a further message saying: '*U-190* PCS 1500Z/11 43.30N, 41.35W, 300 degrees, 8.5 knots. Join and escort to Bay Bulls. Boarding party to be put on board *U-190* if weather permits, and all possible precautions are to be taken to prevent scuttling.'[2]

In response, *Victoriaville* reported at 2320 that *U-190* had been contacted and that the Admiral's instructions had been carried out. *Thorlock*'s boarding party went aboard *U-190* at 2340 on 11 May and *Victoriaville*'s boarding party went aboard the U-boat an hour later at 0040 on 12 May. All except thirteen members of the German crew were transferred to the two RCN warships and a short time later whilst on board *Victoriaville* the U-boat's CO signed a formal surrender document.

At that stage, the three vessels were still well to the east of Cape Race so at 0200, with *U-190* flying the White Ensign, they set course for Bay Bulls with armed sentries on board *U-190*. It was not until two days later at 0630 on 14 May that they arrived at Bay Bulls just south of St John's on the east coast of Newfoundland where, as recorded in the report of the Senior Naval Officer Bay Bulls:

> Lieutenant M Wood, RNVR with Boarding Party boarded the submarine outside the entrance and escorted by MLs [motor launches] 085 and 098 secured at the Eastern Entrance trot buoy.
>
> Prisoners of War on HMCS *Victoriaville* and HMCS *Thorlock* and on U-190 were transferred to HMCS *Prestonian*, which sailed for Canada [at] 1200Z on 14th.
>
> When prisoners were removed the *U-190* was moved and secured to two buoys off Boom Defence Jetty and Lieutenant Wood with his party commenced examination and overhaul. A guard was supplied from St John's with Lieutenant Sweeney in charge. De-storing was carried on during the time *U-190* was at the buoys. On the 23rd *U-190* was removed and secured to the Naval Jetty.[5]

Almost immediately after *U-190*'s arrival at Bay Bulls the inevitable post-war bureaucrats began to exercise their craft. First, on 17 May the National Secretary for Customs wrote to the CO of the Central Victualling Depot at HM Dockyard St John's wanting to know what had become of the liquor removed from *U-190*:

> The Collector of Customs at Bay Bulls informs us that certain liquors were transferred from the German U-Boat recently brought into Bay Bulls by the Royal Canadian Navy. Permission was granted for this to be done but the goods were transferred to St John's before a list could be taken and I would be very grateful, therefore, if you could supply me with a detailed list of the liquors obtained from the U-Boat and transferred to your Headquarters.[5]

Second, on 18 May the Base Naval Health Officer at St John's who had inspected *U-190* on 16 May complained that contrary to International Quarantine Regulations he had not been able to examine the POWs as a precautionary measure against the possible introduction of diseases such as typhus fever and smallpox. His report said:

> In so far as could be ascertained from this survey there was no visible evidence of infestation. The ship, however, was found to be in a definitely unsanitary state, presumably due in some measure to an exceptionally long period at sea, of which time she probably remained submerged for many days before her capture.[5]

What did the man expect? Perhaps he had forgotten that only 10 days previously his country had been at war with Germany.

The Surgeon Lieutenant Cdr's report went on to say:

In order to prevent the spread of any possible infection, the following precautionary measures are now being carried out:

(a) Bacteriological analysis of the submarine's fresh water supply.
(b) Disinfestation of the ship's galley and all living quarters.
(c) Precautionary delousing treatment of clothing stores by the use of DDT insecticide.[5]

The third element of hassle related to the loss of kit and personal items from the U-boat and its crew which caused the crew of *Victoriaville* to be searched by shore patrol officers on three separate occasions, all with negative results. This was the cause of considerable concern to the frigate's CO and after *Victoriaville* arrived in St John's he sent a memo to the Naval Officer in Charge on 23 May in which he suggested that the latter should perhaps search the crews of the other vessels involved, *Thorlock* and *Prestonian*, as well as the various shore authorities involved in the surrender of *U-190* stating that:

It is requested that Naval Service Headquarters be informed of the circumstances surrounding [the] loss of articles from *U-190*. The feeling in this ship is that unnecessary reflection has been put on us due to the fact that:

(1) Our boarding party was mustered on the quarterdeck of HMCS *Prestonian* and searched by shore authorities before returning on board from *U-190*.
(2) They were subjected to a second search after arrival in St John's Newfoundland at the request of Captain (D): both with negative results.
(3) On arrival at Saint John's, NB, we were boarded by shore patrol officers and ratings with orders from Naval Service Headquarters to search the entire ship and ship's company. This third search was carried out with negative results.

In view of the fact that considerable gear is missing from *U-190* and our ship has been subjected to three searches with negative results it is suggested that the shore Authorities connected with *U-190* be similarly subjected to an intensive search.[5]

The two U-boats were in very different states of maintenance when they arrived in their surrender ports. *U-190* had been commissioned in September 1942 and was very war-weary whilst *U-889* had been commissioned in August 1944 and was just over a month into its first patrol. Also, the latter was equipped with the most up-to-date German

U-boat technology including the latest acoustic torpedo system and a 'Zwiebel' experimental hydrophone array as well as carrying six intact T-5 GNAT (German Navy Acoustic Torpedo) torpedoes which were designed to home-in onto a target's noise signature.

The RCN was naturally keen to take early advantage of its unexpected possession of the two U-boats. *U-190* was commissioned (back-dated to 14 May) at the end of May as HMC S/M *U-190* and *U-889* was commissioned (again back-dated to 14 May) at the end of June as HMC S/M *U-889*, initially with joint Canadian and British crews as the RCN did not have its own Submarine Branch.

U-889 was transferred from Shelburne to the RCN's major naval base at Halifax on 23 May where it was handed over to the Naval Research Establishment (NRE) for detailed inspection, testing and trials. In contrast, *U-190* was deemed to be too unseaworthy for early transfer to Halifax and instead it was moved the short distance from Bay Bulls to the RCN naval base at St John's on 3 June. The transfer was no covert affair, with the U-boat under its own power being escorted by the minesweeper HMCS *Red Deer*, six motor launches and the RN rescue tug HMS *Tenacity*.

The purpose of the move was to facilitate essential repairs as well as the cleaning and repainting of *U-190*. The U-boat was quickly taken in hand by the staff at St John's and it was ready for surface sea trials on 12 June. It was then made available for visits by US Army, RCAF and Canadian Army personnel. But there was no time to allow the public or even any RCN personnel to go onboard so, as a compromise *U-190* was moved to a wharf in St John's harbour and the public were allowed onto the wharf on 17 June to view the U-boat. After these visits were complete the (by then) HMC S/M *U-190* was transferred to Halifax on 21 June where it arrived on 23 June.

Despite their transfer to the main RCN naval base at Halifax, the futures of both U-boats were in doubt because the wartime Allies were determined to ensure that all elements of the German Navy were eliminated just as soon as possible and especially that all the surviving U-boats should be sunk. Nevertheless, whilst awaiting the formal decision about the future of the U-boats that had surrendered the RCN was determined to take advantage of its temporary ownership of *U-190* and *U-889*.

As *U-889* was in the best condition and was equipped with the latest German technology, it was the focus of most Canadian interest and an early series of trials was undertaken in the Halifax area from 1 June to

27 July 1945. The RCN lost no time in making the necessary arrangements for these trials, with a request from the C-in-C, CNA to the Air Officer Commanding- in-Chief, Eastern Air Command on 23 May saying:

> Ex German submarine *U-889* is being brought to Halifax on 23 May in order that certain trials may be carried out by the Naval Research Establishment. Your co-operation is requested in these trials which will require the use of aircraft.[6]

However, even then there was a recognition that the use of *U-889* was likely to be temporary as, when the RCN Headquarters formally agreed on 26 June that it should be commissioned, it was with the caveat that it would be for the period of the trials only. The purposes of the trials were set out in NRE Report PHx-59 dated 7 November 1945, being to determine the following points:

a. The diving qualities of the U-Boat
b. The operation of the schnorkel
c. Speed and turning trials
d. The anti-radar qualities of the coating on the schnorkel
e. The performance of the GSR [German Search Radar] and the Tunis Radar Detection gear
f. The performance of the German Hohentweil Radar
g. The H.E. of the submarine when schnorkeling
h. The performance of the Balkon and the Zweibel listening gear[7]

The hydrophone (listening gear) trials were conducted in conjunction with *U-190* in mid-July as both U-boats were fitted with the standard but older 'Balkon' listening apparatus with its forty-eight hydrophones, whereas *U-889* was also fitted with a 'Zwiebel' array, with fifteen hydrophones. This was a trial fit designed for use in the more modern U-boats whilst they were underway when either using their schnorkel or when just submerged.[8]

The NRE trials did not take place without a certain amount of excitement, as is described in the informal history of the Research Establishment, viz:

> The new Captain and crew of *U-889* were eager to dive her so that trials of her unusual equipment could be carried out. After learning the handling of the controls, they did a series of practice dives in the shallow waters of Eastern Passage, where they felt they could not get into too much trouble. First attempts demonstrated great difficulty in maintaining a horizontal position, and the wide, flat deck of the U-Boat made her much harder to handle than her rounded British

counterparts. First the screws and then the bow appeared above water as the crew struggled for control, which they finally achieved.

In order to test the directional qualities of the [Zwiebel] array it was necessary that the bow be submerged, while in order to maintain communication we wanted the control tower above the water surface and open. This arrangement required a delicate balancing operation in the ship's trim. On the first attempt, something went wrong and she settled to the bottom of Bedford Basin. Immediate attempts to return to the surface, blowing the tanks and even using the engines, were fruitless – we were stuck in the mud. We relaxed for half an hour and tried again. This time the ship came loose and we popped to the surface. On the next attempt, the ship was provided with the required trim, and we carried on with our measurements.

Shortly after this, a message was received from the Flag Officer Submarines [stating] that under no circumstances were these submarines to be dived.[9]

The latter instruction was perhaps not unexpected, as on 18 June the NRE had been asked to explain in writing by Halifax Dockyard's clearly very wary Captain (D) just why any diving trials were thought to be necessary. The response from NRE on 19 June was that:

With reference to your [query] re diving trials of *U-889*, it is submitted that the following submerged trials are necessary to complete the information required relative to this ship.

1. Practice diving on schnorkel in preparation for anti-radar trials and general report on schnorkeling.
2. Listening trials with hydrophone in bow of submarine, requiring submarine to do a static bottom dive.
3. Anti-radar trials on periscope and schnorkel.
4. Trials of submarine's own radar equipment on schnorkel.
5. Turning trials when submerged to determine turning radius of submarine.[6]

There was also a plan for *U-889* to undertake trials with its GNAT acoustic torpedoes but these were postponed until later in the year albeit that they were expected to be complete by the end of November.

Almost immediately after the war there was a groundswell of public interest in the two U-boats amongst the population in the maritime cities and ports in eastern Canada which had obviously been heightened by the sensational newspaper headlines at the time of their surrender. Pressure to exhibit them began as early as 14 May with the receipt of a letter by the RCN's Chief of Naval Staff from the Co-Coordinator of Sea Cadet Activities for the Naval Services, saying that:

> In confirmation of our conversation, I would like to suggest that a captured German submarine be brought up the St Lawrence River, through to the Great Lakes, being put on exhibition at various ports, starting with Quebec, Three Rivers and Montreal, and carrying on to other suitable ports. I understand from newspaper reports that a precedent has been set in England by the exhibition of a German submarine.
>
> I would further suggest that the submarine be accompanied by an escort of one or two corvettes, preferably those ships and crews who have been responsible for the sinking of submarines.[10]

Unfortunately, the suggestion initially drew a pessimistic response from the RCN on 24 May, which said:

> I should like to explain to you just what the present position is regarding captured German submarines for exhibition purposes.
>
> Both in the United Kingdom and the United States, the circumstances making possible the immediate availability of such vessels for public inspection are much more favourable by reason of the fact that many more of them are held in their ports than is the case in Canada. They are in a position to withhold a requisite number for experimental purposes and release others for exhibition, while in this country the opposite is the case.
>
> The one or two U-Boats in the custody of the Canadian authorities are required for study and trials by the Royal Canadian Navy and arrangements in this respect are rapidly being carried out. How long it will take to complete this most necessary programme, it is impossible at this moment to say.[10]

Nevertheless, whilst the need for trials was paramount for operational reasons, the RCN relented in late June and it was decided that both *U-190* and *U-889* would undertake exhibition cruises after the completion of the initial technical inspections and any urgent trials, with the Minutes of the 297th Naval Staff Meeting on 3 July recording that:

> In a submission dated 25 June, C-in-C CNA requests consideration of a proposed tour schedule for *U-190* and *U-889*. The object of the proposed tour is to permit the general public to see an enemy submarine and a typical anti-submarine ship of the Royal Canadian Navy.
>
> It was pointed out that the RN has established a precedent for such a tour by putting captured German U-Boats on display in England.[10]

The object of the tours was to permit the public to see a U-boat together with a typical anti-submarine ship of the RCN. It was envisaged that at each port the two warships would to be secured separately alongside a convenient jetty where the public could view them but if only one berth was available the U-boat would be berthed on the inside to make access easier.

Thus, after Ministerial approval and with the proviso that approximately 10 days would be required for the torpedo trials at Halifax after its exhibition tour was complete *U-889* was selected to visit cities and towns on the north, west and south coasts of western Nova Scotia in the second half of August. The tour began in Halifax on 10 August and after four days there, where it was visited by over 10,000 people, *U-889* visited Saint John and St Andrews in New Brunswick as well as Digby, Cornwallis, Yarmouth, Shelburne, Liverpool and Lunenburg in Nova Scotia before returning to Halifax on 5 September.[11]

Similarly, after spending time in the naval dockyard at Halifax on a mini-refit between 23 June and 18 July and then conducting some limited trials, *U-190* undertook an exhibition tour of the ports and communities along the St Lawrence River and in the Gulf of St Lawrence, arriving at Montréal on 27 July for an extended visit which attracted some 30,000 visitors, and then making short visits to Three Rivers, Québec City, Gaspé, Campbellton, Chatham and Charlottetown (on Prince Edward Island) as well as Pictou and Sydney in Nova Scotia before arriving back in Halifax on 7 September.[12]

Even before the two tours had been completed and any decisions had been taken by the Allies concerning the future of all the U-boats that had surrendered, the RCN's thoughts about the future location and possible use of *U-190* and *U-889* began to develop, with the CO of the NRE advising the C-in-C, CNA on 1 September that:

> *U-889* will be required here for acoustic torpedo running until about the end of October, dependent considerably on weather conditions, as these trials will have to be carried out at night in Halifax Approaches.
>
> Recommended that *U-889* be allocated to Canada for experimental purposes with a view to eventual scrapping. When all running trials are completed, we would like to take out all her special equipment such as listening gear, radar, etc, before she is disposed of.
>
> *U-190* is an older boat, built in 1942, and would not be much good as an operational boat. Recommended that she be made available for transfer to any other Navy, or alternatively that she be scrapped in Canada after removal of any special fittings that we wish to keep for experimental or reference purposes.[13]

Once the tours had been completed it had become obvious that *U-190* was in such a poor state that it was unlikely to be of much further use to the RCN. The CO of HMCS *Stadacona*, the shore base at Halifax, therefore spelt out his instructions for the future administration of the two U-boats on 20 September:

> The following arrangements for the administration of HMC ex-German submarines *U-889* and *U-190* are to go into effect as from 21 September 1945, consequent upon the reduction of *U-190* to Care and Maintenance status.
>
> Lieutenant E A D Holmes, RNVR, Commanding Officer HMC S/M *U-889* will assume the duties of Senior Submarine Officer [S S/M O] of the flotilla, and be in general charge.
>
> A Duty Submarine Officer of the Day will be detailed by the S S/M O in rotation from flotilla officers, and will be responsible to him for both boats during non-working hours. Rounds are to be carried out by the Duty Submarine Officer during silent hours at sufficiently frequent times to ensure the safety of the boats.
>
> Duty watches are to be detailed by individual boats, *U-889* making up any deficiencies for *U-190*. These will be detailed for 24 hour periods, and are to sleep on board at night.
>
> During working hours, each crew will normally work in their own boats, but for special work beyond *U-190*'s capacity, *U-889* is to provide the necessary additional hands, subject to her own requirements.
>
> The Senior Submarine Officer is to issue such additional orders as may be required to put these orders into effect, and as may be required for administration of the flotilla, forwarding copies to the Captain, Stadacona, and the Officer in Charge, Naval Research Establishment for information.[6]

The RCN then conducted a comprehensive engineering study of the two U-boats and on 20 October the Commanding Officer Atlantic Coast (COAC) submitted a report to the Naval Board in the Department of National Defence in Ottawa setting out his views about the status and future disposition of *U-190* and *U-889*, viz:

> The present status of these submarines is as follows:
>
> (a) *U-889*. In good operational condition except for the auxiliary diesel air compressor. The main electric air compressor still being in good shape. Manned with three RCNVR s/m-trained officers, 7 RCN ratings, 16 RCNVR ratings and 7 RN ratings. The RCN and RCNVR ratings are now sufficiently trained to operate the boat on the surface for Torpedo Trials purposes.

(b) *U-190*. Due to a bad earth on her starboard main motor, this
boat is not in operational condition, as it cannot be used. She is
an old boat (1942) and, with other defects present, would take
considerable work to bring into operational state. Manned with
one RNVR s/m-trained officer, 2 RCN and 8 RCNVR ratings on
a maintenance basis.[14]

Not only were the futures of the two U-boats dependent on their
serviceability but they were also dependent on the forthcoming Allied
decisions about their future and on the availability of trained crews,
as well as the RCN's desire to undertake the planned trials with the
acoustic torpedoes which had been captured on board *U-889*. As far as
the crews were concerned, there was a great deal of pressure not only
to demobilise the RCN wartime volunteers, who were keen to return
to their civilian occupations and carers, but also the RN officers and
ratings on secondment to the RCN wanted to return to the UK as soon
as possible.

Despite the on-going uncertainty about the long-term future of the
two U-boats, especially doubts about the retention of *U-889* as well as
U-190's serviceability, the RCN, having acquired the former's acoustic
torpedoes, was loath to forgo the opportunity to conduct evaluation
work likely to assist with the RCN's ongoing development of appropriate
countermeasures, called Canadian Anti-Acoustic Torpedo (CAT) gear
which had started in 1943. This was a noise maker towed behind warships
to act as a decoy for acoustic torpedoes and which might be needed for
use in any future expansion of the RCN's submarine fleet.

Unfortunately, two of *U-889*'s six GNAT torpedoes had been lost in a
huge ammunition explosion in the naval magazine at the Bedford Basin
in Halifax Harbour on 18/19 July 1945. The explosion was caused by
a fire which started on the South Jetty on the evening of 18 July which
quickly spread to the North Jetty both of which were overloaded with
badly stored surplus ammunition and other explosives which had been
hastily off-loaded from naval vessels which were being decommissioned.
The two U-boats were moored in Bedford Basin at the time and though
they were unaffected by the explosion itself the incident was recorded in
U-190's Deck Log for 18 July:

1842: Violent explosion in Bedford Basin
2000: All ships ordered to slip and proceed to Outer Harbour
2115: Slipped and proceeding to anchorage
2322: Anchored Georges Island[15]

Fortunately, the four remaining GNAT torpedoes were undamaged and thus were available for the planned NRE trials after the explosive had been steamed out and the warheads had been instrumented for running and other investigations. However, whilst the torpedo trials had been expected to take place during the second half of September and that *U-889* would not therefore be required after they had been completed, the Bedford magazine explosion caused a two-month delay in getting the warheads steamed out and fitted for the running trials. This was therefore the cause of considerable concern as to whether the necessary engineering work would be complete before the onset of poor winter weather possibly meaning that the trials would have to be postponed until May 1946.

In the light of this new situation the CO of the NRE wrote a comprehensive review on 18 October which revealed that either *U-889* needed to be retained by the RCN for an extended period or that the planned CAT trials would need to be completed by the USN. His opinion was that in view of the work already completed the full-scale trials should still go ahead but that they should be postponed until the spring of 1946 when all four of the re-worked torpedo warheads would be available and when maximum use could be made of nights suitable for the running trials. His report recommended that:

> Bearing in mind that at present the RCN is in the lead of both the RN and the USN in respect to knowledge of the acoustic torpedo and possible counter-measures:
>
> a. *U-889* be retained in commission as at present in order to complete the acoustic torpedo trials.
> b. The USN be informed of the latest developments in acoustic torpedo investigation, and if possible the trials be done at a suitable USN port, east coast ports' winter weather being unsuitable.
> c. Alternatively postpone trials until next spring at Halifax.[16]

In view of the state of the two U-boats the almost simultaneous engineering report to the Naval Board on 20 October which had been written before it became clear that *U-889* was unlikely to remain in RCN custody much after the end of 1945 had also included several detailed recommendations about their future use, saying:

> It is recommended that *U-190*, being unfit for further service, be disposed of at an early date, after removal of certain equipment required by [the] Naval Research Establishment.
>
> Disposal of *U-889* is contingent upon policy considerations whether the RCN should carry out the complete trials to establish

acoustic torpedo performance against a CAT, or turn the preliminary information over to [the] RN and USN for the final running trials. In any case, on completion of the confirming Bedford Basin trials [the] RN and USN should be informed of this new development.

It is considered improbable that the running trials can be completed at Halifax before unfavourable weather conditions set in and, to complete them before [the] demobilisation of the RCNVR ratings will require that they be carried out at a US base, say New London or Bermuda.

It is therefore recommended that, unless prestige considerations require [the] RCN to complete these trials, that *U-889* be reduced to C&M at Halifax. The RCNVR officers and ratings can then be demobilised and RN ratings returned to UK. In the event that it is found necessary to carry out running trials next spring, she could then be re-commissioned.[14]

Meanwhile talks were underway at Potsdam concerning the future of the surviving German naval vessels, including the U-boats which had surrendered. The result of which was that the TNC was deciding which of the surviving U-boats should be allocated to the Allies. Thus, at face value, the chances of the RCN being allowed to retain either of the two U-boats which had surrendered in Canada were very slim.

One of the TNC's first actions had been to inspect each of the U-boats which had surrendered, and of those which had surrendered in the USA and Canada the only one to be assessed as operational (both on the surface and submerged) was *U-889*. In comparison the TNC assessed that *U-190* would need at least one month's repair work to bring it to an operational condition.[17]

Once all the assessments had been made the TNC then turned its attention to deciding which U-boats should be retained and of these which should be allocated to each of the Allies. At that stage the RCN was relaxed about the future of the two U-boats in its temporary custody. It was expected that the CAT trials with *U-889* would be complete by the end of September and it was already clear from the state of *U-190* that there was no need for its retention. The initial allocation lists were announced by the TNC on 10 October and of the two U-boats located in Canada *U-889* was allocated to the USA and *U-190* was scheduled for sinking no later than mid-February 1946.

The situation changed dramatically in the latter half of October when it became apparent to the RCN that the CAT trials were bound to be delayed and because of this in November the Canadian Government sought British support for the retention of both U-boats in Canada. To this end the Admiralty in London was keen to do all it could to ensure that *U-190* and *U-889* were retained and on 16 November Admiral Sir Geoffrey Miles, the senior UK member of the TNC wrote to his US and Russian colleagues stating that: 'The British Admiralty are desirous of exchanging two of their submarines for two now in Canada.'[17] In response, Admiral Robert Ghormley, the senior US member of the TNC wrote on 29 November saying:

> *U-889* and *U-190*, former German submarines, are located in Canada. I have been advised that the United States Navy Department desires to retain former German submarine *U-889* in the United States allocation, but [has] no objection to the exchange of the former German submarine *U-190*.[17]

The UK therefore dropped its proposal concerning *U-889*, which remained in the US allocation, meaning that sometime prior to mid-February 1946 it would have to be transferred to the USN which was keen to acquire it especially because of its apparently excellent condition. Thus, the decision relating to *U-889* meant that despite its poor condition the RCN needed to retain *U-190* after all.

Unfortunately, when the TNC's Final Report was issued *U-190* was still not included in the UK's allocation. Thus, a formal change was required so that the previously unallocated *U-190* could be allocated to the UK with one of the U-boats which had already been allocated to the UK being added to the list of those to be sunk. This change was a follow-up to the request made in November by Admiral Miles in relation to *U-190* and *U-889* when both Admiral Ghormley and Admiral Levchenko had said they would have no objection to the UK retaining *U-190*.

The need for *U-190* to remain in Canadian custody was reinforced in a message on 22 December from the Secretary of State for External Affairs in Ottawa to the Foreign Office in London saying:

> We are advised that submarine *U-889* has been allocated to the United States Government. The Canadian Government therefore wishes to retain submarine *U-190* in order to complete experiments originally undertaken on *U-889*.
>
> Request that Tripartite Commission be asked to leave Canadian Government in possession of *U-190* for a period not exceeding one year with the understanding that on completion of experiments *U-190* is to be sunk.[18]

The TNC had no authority to allocate any of the U-boats to Canada, the only authorised recipients being the UK, USA and USSR. So, to overcome this hurdle it was necessary for the TNC to agree that *U-190* should be allocated to the UK and then for the UK to make its own arrangements with Canada. As a result, the Foreign Office in London advised on 5 February that:

> It has been arranged with the Tripartite Naval Commission that *U-190* should be substituted for a submarine of the original British allocation. The latter will be sunk at once in accordance with the Potsdam Agreement and the trials planned for her by the Admiralty will be transferred to *U-190* and postponed for a year.
>
> His Majesty's Government in the United Kingdom are, therefore, agreeable to *U-190* remaining in the possession of His Majesty's Government in Canada for one year on the understanding that she is available to the Admiralty at the end of that period.[18]

The formal change to the TNC paperwork was implemented at the end of January 1946 and *U-190* was then loaned to Canada for a year. As a result, as one of the thirty U-boats authorised for retention by the Allies it was allowed to remain in Canada in the temporary custody of the RCN.

Whilst these discussions were taking place the RCN remained keen to take every possible advantage of their temporary charges particularly as they wished to initiate the CAT trials with the four remaining GNAT torpedoes. It was therefore decided to continue with the NRE torpedo trials with *U-889* for as long as possible, and a number of such trials took place between 23 September and 30 October in and around Halifax harbour before it too was reduced to care and maintenance status on 12 November before the trials programme had been completed.

Whilst *U-889* was being put to good use by the RCN in the latter part of 1945, the same could not be said of *U-190*. It was based at Halifax but despite all the high-level staff work to ensure that it could be retained in Canada, *U-190* was by that time deemed to be of little further use to the RCN. It was generally moored alongside *U-889* and it was deteriorating fast. Nevertheless, winter was approaching and the situation was complicated by the need to transfer *U-889* to the USN despite the fact that the RCN's CAT trials remained unfinished. Thus there was a very real probability that despite its poor state *U-190* might now be needed to take over the torpedo trials work in the spring of 1946 rather than being subject to early disposal.

At the end of 1945, and in accordance with the TNC recommendations, *U-889* could no longer remain in Canada. The U-boat was therefore delivered to the USA by its RCN crew, arriving at Portsmouth Navy Yard on 12 January 1946. However, whereas when *U-889* had been inspected by the TNC in Canada in September 1945 and found to be in the best condition of all the U-boats that had surrendered from sea in the Western Hemisphere, it was now thoroughly worn out and in a non-operational condition.

The result of the transfer of *U-889* to the USN left the RCN with just *U-190* which was in care and maintenance status. Despite this and despite the fact that in October 1945 COAC's report to the Naval Board had recommended that *U-190*, being unfit for further service, should be disposed of at an early date, by mid-March 1946 the situation had been reviewed and it had been decided that the U-boat should be retained as the firing platform in support of the NRE's remaining CAT trials. However, other than taking part in these torpedo trials at various times between May and the autumn of 1946 *U-190* was involved in no other RCN-related activities.

This was not surprising, as on 2 August 1946 *U-190*'s CO had advised in a report headed 'Steaming Capabilities and General Conditions of U-190' that:

> At present *U-190* is in such a condition as to warrant a major refit before she could be considered in a satisfactory sea-going condition.
>
> The submarine is not capable of diving, due to lack of personnel for maintenance of main vents, hydroplanes, underwater valves, Diesel Air Compressor, Diesel engine exhaust blowing system and the overall watertightness of the ship.
>
> There are a number of defects that have arisen in the last few months which indicate the state of deterioration of the ship. The port main motor has developed a full earth, making independent manoeuvring impossible. The galley electric range is unserviceable and is lacking spare parts. The forward bilge pump has defective wiring circuits. No. 8 main ballast tank has developed a leak into number 3 torpedo tube.
>
> Many of the navigational aids on board are unserviceable. The Echo Sounder and the Radar Set are defective, and were found unreliable at their best. The low frequency transmitter and receiver are not working.
>
> In my opinion *U-190* is not capable of leaving Halifax harbour, and it appears that more defects will arise unless she is soon docked for a well deserved refit.[19]

Thus, other than the intermittent torpedo trials, the same pattern of general inactivity continued into autumn 1946. The approaching completion of these trials thus marked the end of *U-190*'s already limited usefulness to the RCN and this meant that a decision could be sought about the disposal of the shortly to be surplus-to-requirements *U-190*, the loan period for which was due to expire in February 1947. This process started in mid-September and on 26 September the RCN's Director of Naval Plans and Intelligence wrote to the Assistant Chief of Naval Staff saying:

> After the surrender of the German submarine fleet the RCN acquired *U-889* and *U-190*, and the former was subsequently used for experiments with her acoustic torpedo gear and special hydrophone system.
>
> The Tripartite Naval Commission sitting in Berlin in November 1945 agreed that 30 German submarines only should be retained and divided equally between the USSR, the USA and the UK. The 10 allocated to the United States included *U-889*.
>
> Following this decision the RCN requested that the Tripartite Commission might authorise the retention by Canada of *U-190* until acoustic torpedo trials were completed after which she would be sunk.
>
> In January 1946 however it was arranged that *U-190* should be substituted for one of the 10 submarines allotted to Britain. The latter was then sunk and it was agreed [with the UK, not the TNC] that *U-190* should be retained by Canada for one year after which she should be made available to the Admiralty.
>
> It is anticipated that the acoustic experiments will be completed early in October and there will then be no further requirement for *U-190*. Should the Admiralty require her return to the United Kingdom however the boat is not at present in a sufficiently seaworthy condition to make an Atlantic passage and a refit will be necessary.
>
> It is therefore recommended that the Admiralty should now be informed of the condition of *U-190* and a decision on her disposal requested.[18]

In January 1947, the CO of the NRE formally confirmed that the weather conditions in Halifax had become so bad as to make it impossible to carry out any further GNAT trials with *U-190* and he recommended that they should cease. As a result, on 24 January the C-in-C, CNA advised that: 'Further acoustic torpedo trials are to be abandoned. Torpedoes [are] to be landed and stored. *U-190* is to be reduced to Care and Maintenance status.'[12] This was followed by advice from the Canadian Naval Mission in London on 21 March saying that:

> The Admiralty has no further requirement for this U-Boat and are enquiring whether the RCN would wish to retain her as a war relic.

If not, the Admiralty would be grateful if the RCN would dispose of her by scrapping or sinking in deep water. It is suggested that the disposal of the submarine might provide valuable data on the damaging power of weapons, or the resisting power of the ship's structure, and the Admiralty Ship Target Trials Committee would be glad to advice the RCN on experiments that might be arranged.

The Admiralty point out that the circumstances under which this submarine was acquired make it inadvisable to transfer her to a third party before she is reduced to scrap.[18]

This debate was finally completed on 16 April when the Chief of Naval Staff wrote to the Minister of Defence saying that the Admiralty had no requirement for *U-190* and had requested that the U-boat should be disposed of by one of the following three methods:

a. Retention as a war relic. This would be of little value to the RCN and would involve the expense of care and maintenance.
b. Scrap. As the Admiralty specify that U-190 is not to be transferred to a third party for scrapping, this would entail the expense of the work being done by the RCN.
c. Sinking in deep water.[18]

The CNS went on to say that neither of the first two alternatives was desirable and that as there was no further requirement for *U-190* and to derive the greatest benefit, *U-190* should be sunk as a target for ship and aircraft practice and asked the Minister to agree this course of action. The result was that on 23 April 1947 the formal decision was taken to sink *U-190* after the removal of any equipment that might be of further interest. In June it was forecast that the de-storing activity would be completed by 5 July and that the submarine would then be ready for disposal. This was followed by a recommendation on 19 July that *U-190* should be paid-off at an early date and be placed in reserve pending disposal. Approval for the latter was granted on 21 July and the U-boat was formally paid-off on 24 July 1947.[12]

On the same day, COAC issued instructions concerning the care of *U-190* until such time as it was sunk, saying:

When *U-190* is berthed at a jetty where electrical power is not available, the power is to be obtained from the ship's main batteries which will last approximately 10 more days, at which time the ship will be in darkness and the bilge pump and ventilation fans, being electrical, will be unserviceable. It will be noted that the batteries when dead will no longer give off oxygen gas and there will be no danger of explosion.

However, in order to ensure that all danger is avoided, the ventilation fans are to be run for one-half hour twice daily for one week after the batteries are dead.

A 50 ton portable pump is to be made available for pumping the bilges.

It will be noted that No. 3 torpedo tube is flooded by a leak from No. 8 main ballast tank and there is reason to believe that a similar leak might develop into No. 4 torpedo tube from No. 8 tank: care is to be taken accordingly.

All underwater connections to the sea are shut off and the ship is taking a negligible amount of water into the engine room and motor room bilges. As the ship has not been on the dry dock since being taken over by the RCN the condition of these underwater valves and sea connections is highly questionable.

Every possible care is to be taken to ensure that HMC S/M *U-190* is kept in an adequate condition in order to prevent sinking.[14]

The only remaining question was how to dispose of the unwanted U-boat and as was the case with most matters relating to *U-190* that too took several months to answer. The initial proposals for sinking the U-boat were discussed at a meeting on 27 May and these were formalised in a memorandum to the RCN's Assistant Chief of Naval Staff on 6 June which recommended that:

a. Date of sinking to be about 22 October 1947 in order that as many RCN ships as possible be available to take part in the exercise, and to allow air squadrons to participate.
b. Position of sinking to be about 50 miles SE off Halifax (over 100 fathoms).
c. Ships and aircraft to carry out rocket firings, gunnery, A/S weapon firings and bombings during the exercise.[18]

This proposal to sink *U-190* in some style was agreed on 21 July and during a visit to Halifax later in the month the Minister of National Defence confirmed that *U-190* would be destroyed by the RCN 'with explosives'. To this end it had already been announced by the Director of Naval Information in a Press Release on 15 July that:

Naval authorities have indicated that this [the sinking of *U-190*] will probably take place in the early fall, and that it is possible that both surface craft and aircraft will play a part in sending the one time sea raider to its last account in a realistic anti-submarine exercise.[20]

This announcement nevertheless caused a complication in that it motivated the Managing Director of Halifax Shipyards Ltd to write to the Head of the RCN's Naval Administration and Supply Department on 21 July, saying:

> I notice by a press report recently that the German submarine *U-190* is to be taken out to sea and sunk. This seems to me to be a pity. Here are the steel mills in our country crying for scrap. There is a definite shortage and this submarine could well be used for that purpose.[18]

Unfortunately the RCN's response on 24 July was somewhat equivocal. It did not make clear that the Admiralty in London had specifically ruled out scrapping by a third party and it left the door open for a further review. Thus the inevitable happened and the Managing Director of Halifax Shipyards Ltd wrote yet again this time to the Deputy Minister of Defence on 30 September when final arrangements for *U-190*'s sinking were well advanced. As a result the matter had to be taken to the Defence Minister himself who then accepted that there was a need to follow the Admiralty's request.

Additionally, in July the Chief of Naval Staff had personally invited the Chief of the Canadian Air Staff (CAS) to consider whether or not he would like the RCAF to participate in the arrangements for sinking *U-190* but somewhat surprisingly the CAS declined the invitation saying:

> Your invitation to participate in this exercise would have been speedily accepted were it not for the fact that the aircraft and personnel which would normally participate are fully engaged on prior commitments, My staff have endeavoured to arrange for the fitting out of other aircraft for this exercise, but I feel that any makeshift arrangements would be unwise.[18]

Reading between the lines, the RCAF were not interested in participating what seemed very likely to turn into a publicity stunt so, as forecast in his earlier Press Release and after a dummy run on 14 October, the Director of Naval Information gave further information of the RCN's intentions on 18 October, saying:

> Preliminary arrangements have been completed for the destruction by ships and aircraft of the Royal Canadian Navy of the former German submarine *U-190* off Halifax on Trafalgar Day, October 21.
>
> The U-Boat, which surrendered to ships of the RCN in May 1945, will be sent to the bottom not far from where she torpedoed and sank the minesweeper HMCS *Esquimalt* on 16 April 1945.[21]

The scenario that was invented for the exercise and thus the purpose of the RCN's joint air and sea attacks was that: '*U-190* is assumed to have been damaged during an attack carried out by a ship on patrol in the Halifax approaches. The patrol vessel having been sunk by GNAT, *U-190* is attempting to escape on the surface.'[19]

The formal RCN orders for this highly publicised event, which went by the very un-original code name of 'Exercise Scuppered', indicted that it was due to take place on 21 October, that it was expected to take approximately 90 minutes to complete, that it would be located approximately 50 miles south-east of Halifax and that the redundant U-boat would be towed into position by the dockyard tug *Riverton*.

A considerable amount of trouble was taken to ensure that *U-190* would be ready for the event and would not simply sink under its own devices when towed out of Halifax prior to its planned demise. The forces involved were the destroyers HMCS *Nootka* and HMCS *Haida*, and the minesweeper HMCS New *Liskeard*, as well as aircraft of the 18th Canadian Carrier Air Group (comprising eight Seafires, eight Fireflys, two Ansons and two Swordfish). The event was given maximum publicity and it was covered by press, radio and newsreel, with twenty-four reporters, commentators and photographers on-board the RCN ships, and one reporter was even able to view the exercise from the air in one of the Anson aircraft.

However, despite all the careful planning the whole event eventually went off like a damp squib because after the initial rocket attacks by the Fireflys *U-190* started to settle slowly by its stern. *Nootka* then opened fire with her guns but was able to fire only two salvoes, both of which missed the target, before the U-boat suddenly up-ended and sank from sight less than 19 minutes after the start of the exercise. Nevertheless the Director of Naval Information sought to give the affair the best possible positive gloss stressing that it was solely an exercise designed to give ships' crews and the RCN aircraft crews training in combined air-sea operations and saying in a somewhat emotive Press Release on 29 October that:

> The former German submarine *U-190* made its last descent to the cold depths of the Atlantic on Trafalgar Day, October 21. The once deadly sea raider came to a swift and ignominious end when, as a target for ships and aircraft of the Royal Canadian Navy, it was sunk in less than 19 minutes in the same waters in which it torpedoed HMCS *Esquimalt* in April 1945.[22]

Details of the event were forwarded to Naval Service Headquarters by COAC and his Exercise Report dated 22 December 1947 concluded with the somewhat low-key words:

> The fact that *U-190* was eventually sunk in the required position and without accident is considered to be the most important factor.
>
> Although all phases of the proposed exercise were not carried out as a result of the effectiveness of the rockets, it is still considered that the sequence of attack was the best from the point of view of training to be obtained and the cooperation required between Air and surface ships.
>
> It is also felt that 'Exercise Scuppered' provided very good publicity for the Royal Canadian Navy and gave the press an opportunity to understand more fully the duties of Naval officers and men.
>
> In general I consider that great benefit was derived from the sinking of the *U-190* by the Royal Canadian Navy.[19]

The last words about the demise of *U-190* after its two and a half years in the RCN were written by the Naval Secretary, whose equally low-key and belated comments on 23 January 1948 said:

> The administration for the exercise and the detail of the orders were admirably prepared, and reflect great credit on those who took part in the planning. The air attacks speak for themselves, but it was a disappointment that sufficient of *U-190* was not left for Captain (D) to dispose of.[19]

CHAPTER 18

U-Boats in Norway

AT THE END OF the war there were almost 100 U-boats in Norway. This was because of the German abandonment of the U-boat bases in France in mid-1944 and the transfer of most of the operational U-boats to Norway in the second half of 1944 and early 1945. Also, in the first few days of May, as the inevitability of Germany's defeat became obvious, there was a last-minute rush to abandon the Baltic U-boat bases in favour of those in Norway.

On 3 May Captain (U/B) West advised the BdU (Befehlshaber der Unterseeboote – HQ of Commander Submarines) that: 'Ref ... proposal for transfer of all operationally not-effective boats to Norway. All boats to go to Christiansand South. From here to be ... distributed among Stavanger and Bergen Skerries area which is more suitable than cramped and exposed Skagerrak.'[1] Then, on the morning of 4 May BdU advised that: 'Norway is the Headquarters of U-Boat operational control. The U-Boat war goes on.'[1]

The number of U-boats in Norway was also increased by the Kriegsmarine's decision on 4 May 1945 that all U-boats at sea were to return to Norway, as well as by the order on 5 May to the U-boats remaining in the Danish and German ports that if possible they were to go to Norway.

Thus, at the time of the German capitulation on 9 May most of the remaining serviceable U-boats were located in Norwegian ports for reasons that were succinctly summed up in a US Navy U-Boat Intelligence Summary issued on 19 May which said:

Despite the loss of almost all U-Boat construction centres, operational ports and training areas in northern Germany, Dönitz clearly intended to make a last ditch fight from Norwegian bases. Several messages to U-Boats and U-Boat bases early on 4 May reiterated the fact that the U-Boat war was to be carried on with headquarters in Norway.[2]

On 4 May Admiral Dönitz ordered that all U-boats at sea were to cease warlike activities and return to Norway. This was followed by the various surrender agreements but, despite there being no RN forces present in Norway when the main German capitulation came into effect, the surrender of the U-boats in ports in Norway was a relatively straightforward affair. The terms of surrender had been notified to the German C-in-C Norway by Field Marshal Keitel on 7 May and this was followed by a message from the German Naval War Staff in Flensburg on the morning of 8 May. The latter made it clear to the head of the Kriegsmarine in Norway that he was responsible for the notification of the conditions of surrender to all relevant naval organisations in Norway including the Admiral Commanding U-Boats. This reinforced an earlier message sent late on 7 May from BdU (Ops) at U-Boat Headquarters to Captain (U/B) West saying:

> U-Boats which are at present lying in Norwegian harbours or are still arriving there are to hand over heavy diesel oil, provisions and ammunition.
>   Crews are to remain on board or in the bases
>   It is expedient that boats quietly lose their 'Eels' [torpedoes]
>   Inform Captain (U/B) Northern Waters, flotillas and bases from your end.[1]

To avoid the confusion that had overtaken the surrender events in Denmark and the northern German ports on 5 May, especially the 'Regenbogen'-related scuttlings, Captain (U/B) West issued an order to all U-boat bases in Norway at 0125 on 8 May saying:

> Do not allow any U-Boats to sail, nor permit transfers of any kind between the bases. The Admiral of the Fleet has ordered: U-Boats in Norway are neither to be scuttled nor destroyed.[1]

The surrender process itself began in Oslo on 8 May with a meeting between Commodore Per Askim of the Royal Norwegian Navy (RNoN), representing the Royal Navy's Flag Officer Norway, Rear Admiral James Ritchie, and the Kriegsmarine's Admiral Theodor Krancke who was clear about the need to cooperate fully with the Allied naval representatives. The local German naval authorities in Norway therefore followed the Allies' surrender and disarmament orders passed via the Kriegsmarine HQ in Oslo to organise the prompt surrender of all the U-boats in Norwegian ports on 9 May and by this means the surrender was successfully accomplished.

A total of eighty-seven U-boats surrendered in Norwegian ports on 9 May and a further nine surrendered from sea – five on 9 May, one on 10 May, one on 12 May, one on 14 May and one on 15 May – making a total of ninety-six:

In port:	Bergen	28
	Kristiansand (S)	17
	Trondheim	13
	Narvik	12
	Horten (Holmstrand)	10
	Stavanger	7
From sea:	Bergen	4
	Narvik	3
	Stavanger	2

Eighty-nine of these U-boats were moved to the UK in May and June 1945 as part of the RN's Operation 'Pledge' transfers, but seven remained in Norway because they were found to be unseaworthy. They were:

U-310, *U-315* and *U-995* in Trondheim
U-324, *U-926* and *U-1202* in Bergen
U-4706 in Kristiansand (S)

This was confirmed by an entry in the Admiralty War Diary on 7 June 1945 which stated that: 'All serviceable U-Boats have been sailed to the UK from Norway except *U-2511* and *U-2506* which leave Bergen on 14 June. Seven unserviceable U-Boats remain.'[3]

There is a view that the British and Norwegian naval authorities might have conspired to ensure that these seven remaining U-boats were all in good condition and therefore suitable for use by the RNoN in due course. However, this is not borne out by the facts. Rather, the reports of the local Royal Navy Port Officers as revealed by their Admiralty War Diary entries record that:

Trondheim:	*U-310*, *U-315* and *U-995* – all unfit for sea.
Kristiansand (S):	*U-4706* – defective main engine and requires new piston.
Bergen:	*U-324* and *U-1202* – major defects requiring 3 months to repair. U-*926* – completely u/s, hull and frame badly strained by blowing tank with excessive air pressure.[3]

Additionally, in respect of *U-926* a message from Admiral U-Boats to Captain U-Boats (West) on 23 April 1945 had stated: '*U-926* (Rehren), only limitedly able to dive owing to pressure hull damage, is to pay off in the Norwegian area and to be released for breaking up'.[4]

There were also, according to the TNC's Final Report and as confirmed in earlier Admiralty War Diary entries, seven other decommissioned and/or damaged (war loss) U-boats remaining in Norwegian harbours in May 1945:

> *U-228*, *U-256*, *U-437* and *U-993* in Bergen
> *U-92* and *U-622* in Trondheim
> *U-985* in Kristiansand (S)

U-92 had been decommissioned in Trondheim on 12 October 1944 and accidentally sunk in March 1945. *U-228* had been sunk in an air raid on Bergen on 4 October 1944 and whilst it had been raised on 26 January 1945 it had been cannibalised for spares. *U-256* had been damaged by air attacks in France and after being transferred to Bergen it was decommissioned on 23 October 1944. *U-437* had been decommissioned in Bergen on 5 October 1944 after which it had been cannibalised for spares. *U-622* had been sunk in Trondheim harbour in an air raid on 24 July 1943. *U-985* had been decommissioned following damage after hitting a mine on 23 October 1944 and then being beached in Kristiansand (S) and cannibalised for spares. *U-993* had been sunk in Bergen harbour in an air raid on 4 October 1944 after which it was raised and decommissioned.

There was one other U-boat hulk in a Norwegian port which by omission was not highlighted by the TNC. This was *U-673* which had sunk near Felsafiord on 24 October 1944 following a collision. It had been raised on 9 November 1944 and towed to Stavanger where it was decommissioned.

The TNC's Final Report included Recommendation No 4 which said:

> Upon approval of the Report of the Tripartite Naval Commission, but not later than 15 February 1946, the three Governments [will] request simultaneously that German naval ships and craft in Category 'C' at present in the territorial waters of other countries, be sunk or destroyed, by the Governments of the countries concerned in accordance with Appendix 2.[5]

This recommendation was made to ensure that the seven afloat but unserviceable U-boats as well as the additional seven U-boat hulks, all of which were highlighted in Appendix 2 of the TNC Report as remaining in Norwegian ports, should be made unavailable for warlike purposes in the future. Nevertheless, as the TNC had no direct jurisdiction over Norway and therefore the fate of these U-boats, it was only able to request that the US, Britain and the Soviet Union should ask that the U-boats be scrapped or sunk by the due date. Similarly, the Allies had no direct jurisdiction over Norway and thus nothing could be done to guarantee that the Norwegian authorities would take the necessary action.

However, even before the TNC had made its recommendations, the American authorities had been taking a close interest in the future of the German equipment that had remained in Norway after the end of the war. This was illustrated in a letter to the British Foreign Office from the US Embassy in London on 11 September 1945 saying: 'The Department of State trusts that any German arms released to the Norwegian Government will be only for temporary use pending the arrival of British and American equipment.'[6]

The response from the Foreign Office dated 8 October, which was primarily concerned with German Army equipment, stated:

> We have agreed to hand over to the Norwegian Government a limited amount of German equipment, in cases where ammunition, spare parts, etc, were held in Norway in sufficient quantity to outlast the probable life of the main equipment ... The understanding is that this equipment shall be for temporary use pending the arrival of Allied equipment.[6]

A consequence of this debate was the initiation of a review of British policy concerning the German naval equipment that had remained in Norway, the results of which were set out in a memorandum by the First Sea Lord (COS (45) 252) dated 11 October 1945 titled 'Disposal of German Naval Equipment in Norway' and which was discussed at the UK Chiefs of Staff Committee Meeting on 12 October. This indicated that the Admiralty was generally sympathetic with the Norwegian desire to retain certain naval equipment especially as its disposal would take an extended time and need considerable effort. There were, however, conditions relating to this agreement, with the COS paper stressing:

> If we are satisfied that the Norwegian requirements are reasonable and retention is consistent with the policy of the Combined Chiefs of Staff, we shall agree to the material being retained upon an express undertaking that ... equipment retained is subject to any later decisions on its final disposal.[7]

The TNC's Recommendation No 4 was clearly a 'later decision' and the US authorities therefore lost no time in their desire to ensure that it was implemented by Norway without delay. To this end, in November 1945, even before the TNC's final report had been issued, the US Navy's C-in-C Germany asked the US Naval Attache in Oslo to bring the requirement to the attention of his host nation. This was followed by yet more unilateral action in December 1945 when the US State Department instructed the US Ambassador in Oslo to ask the Norwegian Government to carry out the TNC's recommendation concerning the destruction of the inoperable German warships in Norway. The American note to the Norwegian Minister of Foreign Affairs dated 24 December 1945 said:

> The Tripartite Naval Commission in Germany unanimously agreed that the destruction of German inoperable warships be recommended by the United States, British and Soviet Governments. This recommendation was to be extended to the Governments of Poland, Denmark and Norway, and the mentioned German warships are either [to be] sunk or otherwise destroyed in their areas.
>
> The American Embassy has been instructed to bring this decision to the attention of the Norwegian Ministry of Foreign Affairs. [It is therefore requested] that the Norwegian Government take such steps as recommended by the above-mentioned Tripartite Naval Commission.[8]

At the time the US State Department was apparently under the incorrect impression that the TNC Report had already been approved by the British and Soviet Governments and it was on this basis that the instructions were issued. It did not, however, explain why the American action had been taken without any reference to either the British Foreign Office or the Admiralty. As a result, the US action caused a flurry of diplomatic exchanges between London and Washington especially as the American action was not supported by the British Government. First, because it had not at that stage approved the TNC's Final Report. Second, because it was loath to agree with Recommendation No 4 which if implemented would compromise the UK's desire to allow France to retain the single U-boat which had surrendered in a French port as well as others which had been war losses, but which remained in French ports.

In Norway the result of this action was that the RNoN was advised about the American request and took steps to review the status of the German warships (including submarines) that remained there. However, it appears that the Norwegian Government was never officially informed either of the provisions of the TNC's Final Report or the details of the German warships listed in it.

Eventually, on 16 July 1946 the American Naval Attache in Oslo provided a list of the warships to the RNoN together with details of the TNC's recommendations concerning the cannibalisation and destruction of the unallocated U-boats in Norwegian ports. He also gave the RNoN for the first time details of the deadline for destruction which then encouraged them to consider what needed to be done: an action that was reviewed in detail in November 1946, the result of which was that the Norwegian Government advised the Americans that: 'The Norwegian Navy has taken over four German submarines, which it wants to incorporate into the Norwegian submarine fleet [and] the Ministry believes that these [four] should be deleted from the [TNC] list without further discussion.'[8] There were, however, some anomalies in the list prepared by the RNoN in November 1946 as the four U-boats listed as being located in Trondheim and temporarily in the Norwegian Navy were *U-324*, *U-926*, *U-1202* and *U-4706* which was at odds with the eventual list of U-boats taken into the RNoN.

The topic was re-visited by the Americans in early 1947 when the State Department indicated that it was considering raising it at the Conference of Foreign Ministers in Moscow in March. However, the topic was quietly dropped from the US delegation's internal agenda and was not tabled during the wider debate about the failure of the Russians to implement the TNC's recommendations. Evidence of the State Department's original intention to raise the matter of the U-boats which remained in Norway was included in the response to a query from Washington on 24 March by the US delegate to the TNC who belatedly advised the USN 's CNO on 24 July 1947 that: '[The State Department] indicates that the United States may transmit to the UK and USSR information that Norway has temporarily included in her Navy four unallocated ex-German submarines.'[9] The US TNC delegate's message of 24 July then went on to say:

> However, it [the State Department] may prefer to defer any further action until the UK or the USSR take steps, at least equal to those already taken by the United States, to implement paragraph 11, Section A of the TNC Report, and by such deferment, avoid possible embarrassment to France.[9]

The UK also let the matter drop and the Russians took no specific action on Recommendation No 4. So, despite the unilateral action by the United States which had been keen to encourage their destruction in early 1946, no more pressure was put on the Norwegian Government in relation to its actions concerning the four U-boats highlighted by the US State Department in March 1947. Thus, there is no truth in the many post-war rumours that these U-boats were formally allocated by the TNC to either Norway or the UK, or that the UK either donated or transferred ownership of any of them to Norway. Rather, they were simply 'afloat and unallocated' but unserviceable U-boats which remained in Norwegian ports at the end of the war and the ultimate responsibility for their futures lay entirely with Norway.

There were some suggestions, despite the lack of evidence, that the eventual retention, renovation and use of three of the U-boats by the RNoN might have received the formal approval of the UK Government. There was however no question of Britain being able to grant the Norwegians unilateral permission especially as the U-boats were not under any sort of British control. It seems most likely that the process leading to the take-over of these U-boats by the RNoN was similar to that which had applied to the U-boats in France as described in an assessment of the French situation by the Admiralty on 15 November 1945, which said: 'I have consulted the Foreign Office who are strongly of the view that the French will be wise to let sleeping dogs lie and simply assume the recognition of their title to these U-Boats.'[10]

This informal sentiment was also formally carried over into a UK Cabinet Paper dated 6 February 1946 which sought approval of the recommendations of the TNC's Final Report. As it happened, the Russian position was severely compromised because they too held the eleven ex-Danzig U-boats which had been listed in the TNC Report as due to be sunk or scrapped not later than 15 February 1946 and which in the end were not destroyed until late 1947. The Russians therefore had no incentive to put any overt diplomatic pressure on Norway in respect of the remaining U-boats located there.

Meanwhile in Norway itself *U-926*, despite being unable to dive, had been restored to a basic seaworthy condition in Bergen by the RNoN in September 1945, assisted by the transfer of batteries from the Norwegian submarine *B-1* which had returned to Bergen from wartime service in the UK prior to decommissioning and scrapping. *U-926* was then sailed from Bergen to Trondheim where on 1 October it was able to join the escort for three of the ex-British 'V' class submarines that had arrived in Trondheim Fjord for service in the RNoN. However, public knowledge of this event could have been embarrassing for the RNoN and so *U-926* was ordered to return to the ex-German U-boat bunker DORA 1 in Trondheim to be hidden out of sight before it was seen by the Press and the public.

Shortly after this, on 12 October 1945 the Commander-in-Chief of the RNoN set up a commission under the leadership of Lieutenant Commander Sigurd Valvatne to conduct a brief investigation to determine whether any of the U-boats that remained in Norway could be repaired and made operational at a reasonable cost. The commission's report was issued on 31 October 1945 and it recommended that subject to a decision about how Norway could acquire them the four Type VIIC U-boats, *U-310*, *U-926*, *U-995* and *U-1202*, should be chosen for retention.

The Valvatne Report was limited to just the German Type VIIC U-boats though it also included comments about the German Navy's spare parts stores in Bergen and Trondheim. Of the U-boats in Bergen, Valvatne reported that *U-228*, *U-256*, *U-437* and *U-993* were total wrecks but that material could be recovered from two of them for use as spares. Of the other three in Bergen, *U-926* and *U-1202* were recommended for repair and overhaul prior to operational use but *U-324* was assessed as only being suitable for cannibalisation of its equipment and spare parts. In Trondheim, of the three U-boats which had surrendered, *U-310* and *U-995* were assessed as being suitable for service after major overhauls but *U-315* was recommended for cannibalisation.

Valvatne and his colleagues therefore concluded that just four of the Type VIIC U-boats in Bergen and Trondheim should be considered for operational use after being overhauled including the replacement of defective parts. However, his report included a note of caution about the uncertainty surrounding any Norwegian acquisition of both the U-boats themselves and the stocks of spare parts.[11]

The RNoN was also interested in the possible recovery of the Type XXIII U-boat *U-4706* which though in a very poor condition was thought to be suitable for trials and other experiments. When it surrendered in Kristiansand (S) it had a defective main engine and required a new piston. It could not therefore be repaired locally prior to its planned move to the UK under Operation 'Pledge' and as a result the schnorkel was removed to enable another Type XXIII to be transferred to the UK instead.

U-324, *U-926* and *U-1202* were therefore restored to a basic seaworthy condition and moved from Bergen to Trondheim as was *U-4706* which was moved from Kristiansand (S) to Trondheim. However, at that stage there were no funds allocated for the repair of the five U-boats that the

RNoN wished to retain, so four of the Type VIICs and the one Type XXIII were initially serviced and maintained by the crews of the ex-British 'V' class submarines. Also, the fact that the RNoN intended to repair these U-boats and was already working on them was kept secret and the U-boats themselves were hidden from the public gaze in either the DORA 1 bunker in Trondheim or moored in inlets in Trondheim Fjord.

The seven decommissioned and damaged (war loss) U-boats (as well as U-637) were sold by the Norwegian Government's Directorate of Enemy Property to the salvage company A/S Friis & Tandberg of Drammen, near Oslo and were scrapped in situ. So too were U-315 (in Trondheim) and U-324 (ex-Bergen, but now in Trondheim) but only after they had been stripped of spares and equipment in support of the other Type VIIC U-boats which the RNoN wished to recover for operational use. In the case of U-310, despite it being one of the Type VIICs that the Valvatne Report had recommended for repair and retention, it was assessed in late 1946 that it would be too costly to renovate and it was therefore cannibalised before being scrapped.

Thus Norway chose to ignore the TNC's recommendation as well as the diplomatic pressure from the United States in the case of the (by then) four U-Boats: U-926, U-995, U-1202 and U-4706. However, it was not until 14 May 1948 that funds became available for the project and when the RNoN HQ in Oslo authorised the CO of the Trondheim Naval Base to use 300,000 Norwegian kroner: 'For the repair of the 3 ex-German [Type VIIC] submarines.'[12]

As a result, in 1948 U-926, U-995 and U-1202 (as well as U-4706) were formally taken over by the RNoN at Trondheim where they were repaired and renovated with a view to their future use. Despite this decision an RNoN note dated 27 September 1948, proposing the Norwegian names Kya, Kaura and Kinn for the Type VIIC U-boats, made it clear that: 'The ownership of these boats has not yet been determined.'[11]

Nevertheless, in October 1948 Norway unilaterally assumed ownership of these U-boats. The lead U-boat in the repair process was U-926 and the first test dive on this newly renovated RNoN submarine took place on 24 April 1949. Unfortunately, U-4706, which had been named Knerten, was damaged by a battery explosion and an engine-room fire before its renovation was complete and because of this together with the general shortage of funds and spares for the Type XXIII U-boat it was decided that U-4706 was unsuitable even for experimental use. It was therefore never formally commissioned into the RNoN. Instead on 14 April 1950 it was sold to the Royal Norwegian Yacht Club which then used it as a storeroom in Trondheim before it was scrapped in 1954.[13]

In contrast, once repaired and overhauled the other three Type VIIC U-boats were commissioned into the RNoN as operational 'K' class submarines: *U-926* as *Kya* on 10 January 1949, *U-1202* as *Kinn* on 1 July 1951 and *U-995* as *Kaura* on 6 December 1952.[13]

Between their commissioning in 1949/1952 and their decommissioning in 1961/1964, these three ex-U-boats served as an integral part of the RNoN's submarine force being used for both operational and training purposes. In the late 1950s *Kya* underwent extensive renovations in the RNoN dockyard in Horten including the fitting of advanced sonar equipment and a streamlined sail aimed at extending its service life until new modern German-manufactured submarines became available to the RNoN in the 1960s.

After their operational use for 10 or more years these three ex-U-boats were disposed of as follows:

U-926 (Kya)   Decommissioned on 4 April 1964. In May 1965 it was sold for scrap in Oslo to the firm Andreas Stoltenberg. It was subsequently scrapped in West Germany.

U-995 (Kaura)   Decommissioned on 15 December 1962 and sold to the German Navy Association on 14 October 1965 for the symbolic price of one Deutsche Mark. It was then overhauled and restored and on 2 October 1971 it became a museum ship at the Laboe Naval Memorial near Kiel where it remains on display.

U-1202 (Kinn)   Decommissioned on 1 June 1961 and sold for scrap in 1962. It was subsequently scrapped in Hamburg in 1963.

In summary, of the fifteen U-boats that remained in Norway after May 1945, eleven were scrapped as being of no further use and one other, the Type XXIII – *U-4706* – which had been earmarked by the RNoN for possible experimental use was never commissioned before being sold for scrap. This then left three Type VIICs which had surrendered but which had been too unseaworthy for transfer to the UK: *U-926*, *U-995* and *U-1202*. These should have been sunk or scrapped in accordance with the TNC's recommendations but instead, they were taken over by the RNoN in 1948 and after lengthy overhauls were commissioned into the RNoN between 1949 and 1952. Subsequently they served in the

RNoN as operational 'K' class submarines until they were taken out of service between 1961 and 1964. They were all intended for scrap but one of them – *U-995* (HNoMS *Kaura*) – was sold to the German Navy Association in 1965 and is on display today at the Laboe Naval Memorial near Kiel.

CHAPTER 19

U-Boats in Other Nations

SEVERAL U-BOATS SURRENDERED IN countries other than those specifically described in earlier chapters and there were others that had been classified as war losses, but which were nevertheless specifically recommended for destruction in the TNC's Final Report.

Japan

As the end of the war in Europe approached there were six U-boats in the Far East engaged in blockade-running and operations against Allied shipping, all of which were undergoing maintenance/repair. They included two ex-Italian U-boats in dockyards in Japan. There was therefore concern about what should become of these U-boats after the German Naval Attache in Tokyo advised Admiral Dönitz on 5 May 1945 that: 'Combat action of East Asia U/Bs has ceased. Return of U/Bs impossible since they are not ready for travelling.'[1]

As a result, it was decided on 7 May to disembark the German crews and to hand over the six U-boats to Japan. Two were in Singapore (*U-181* and *U-862*), one was in Batavia (*U-219*) and one was in Surabaya (*U-195*). With the addition of the two ex-Italian U-boats (*U-IT-24* and *U-IT-25*) which were in Kobe, Japan, this meant that all six U-boats were made available to the Imperial Japanese Navy (IJN) though none of them was fully serviceable.

U-181 had arrived in Singapore on 15 January for repairs after an abortive start to its planned return journey to Germany and it was still there awaiting the installation of a schnorkel in early May. *U-195* had arrived in Batavia on 4 March but had been moved to Surabaya on 7 March where it was undergoing repairs in early May. *U-219* had arrived in Batavia in December 1944 but was damaged when a Japanese ammunition ship was torpedoed and blew up in the harbour, and *U-862* was being overhauled in Singapore. *U-IT-24* had left Singapore en-route for Kobe on 1 February to deliver cargo. However, on 3 February it suffered a battery explosion. It arrived at Kobe in mid-February and it was under repair in the shipyard in May after delays caused by bomb damage. *U-IT-25* had been under repair at Kobe since the beginning of 1945 and its departure was also delayed by bomb damage.

These six U-boats therefore entered service with the IJN in July 1945 and were given the IJN designations *U-181* (*I-501*), *U-195* (*I-506*), *U-219* (*I-505*), *U-862* (*I-502*), *U-IT-24* (*I-503*) and *U-IT-25* (*I-504*). There was also one other ex-U-boat in the IJN. This was *U-511* which had been gifted to Japan and handed over in Penang in July 1943 and had served in the IJN as *RO-500*.

As far as the future of the surviving warships in the IJN at the end of the war was concerned, this was covered in outline in the Potsdam Proclamation. However, the negotiations at Potsdam did not attempt to specify the precise fate of the ex-U-boats which had surrendered as IJN submarines. Nevertheless, the US was quite clear as to the meaning of the Potsdam Proclamation. Thus, just before the Japanese surrender on 15 August 1945 the US Government issued a document 'United States Initial Post-Defeat Policy Relating to Japan' which stated: 'Japan's naval forces are to be totally disarmed and disbanded. Naval materiel, vessels and installations are to be surrendered or destroyed.'[2]

Whilst it was clearly the American intention that all Japanese submarines which had surrendered were to be demolished, scuttled or otherwise destroyed, there had at that time been no specific Allied discussions about the detailed arrangements. However, even before the necessary diplomatic exchanges began there had been a meeting of minds between the USN and the RN about the way ahead with the latter, confirming that the Admiralty was ready to support the US policy of scrapping the whole of the Japanese fleet.

On 17 October, the US Secretary of State wrote to the American Ambassador in Moscow asking him to:

> Please deliver following message to Mr Molotov: While in London I advised you that the United States Government desired to sink the units of the Japanese fleet which were surrendered to the United States Navy and that I requested that this action be delayed until I could inform you and Mr Bevin of our plan. You did not then present any views.[3]

Two days later on 19 October Molotov replied saying:

Having considered the proposal of the Government of the United States regarding the scuttling of the vessels of the Japanese fleet, the Soviet Government is ready to agree that the large vessels of the Japanese navy such as battleships and cruisers as well as Japanese submarines be scuttled.[3]

Similarly, in late-September the US Secretary of State had sought British views about the disposal of the Japanese fleet and the UK Chiefs of Staff considered the matter in view of a memorandum by the First Sea Lord (COS (45) 239) dated 2 October 1945. Action was delegated to the Admiralty whose response included the statement: 'We strongly support the scrapping of submarines.'[4]

These views were passed to Washington in early October and on 22 October Admiral King, the USN's CNO wrote to Admiral of the Fleet Sir James Somerville, the Head of the British Admiralty Delegation in Washington, saying: 'I appreciate the receipt of the information contained in your aide memoire of 13 October and was particularly gratified to learn that the Admiralty are ready to support the policy of scrapping the Japanese fleet.'[5]

The final decision that the surviving IJN submarines found in Japan were to be sunk or scrapped was taken in Moscow on 24 December at a meeting of the Allied Foreign Secretaries. Subsequently, the USN implemented this decision and on 26 March 1946 at a Submarine Officers' Conference in Washington DC it was reported that: 'Orders are being issued to dispose of all Japanese submarines by sinking. Those in Japan will be sunk at once.'[6]

This statement included, by definition, the three ex-U-boats *U-511*, *U-IT-24* and *U-IT-25* that were still in Japan but which had not already been destroyed in accordance with the Potsdam Agreement. This was because the USN's CNO had successfully argued that they were Japanese submarines at the time of their surrender and therefore not subject to either the Potsdam Agreement or within the TNC's jurisdiction.

In the meantime, the TNC had chosen unilaterally to assume that as the war with Japan had by then ended it had the authority to recommend the fate of the U-boats which had surrendered under the IJN flag. All seven of the ex-U-boats, four of which were under British control in Singapore and Indonesia and three of which were under American control in Japan, were therefore listed in the TNC's Final Report as unallocated submarines to be sunk in the open sea no later than 15 February 1946. The result of which was that there were then two separate strands of policy setting out Allied intentions about the fate of the U-boats that had surrendered under the Japanese flag.

After the TNC's Final Report was issued the British and American Representatives initiated action to ensure that their respective navies were aware of the need to effect the necessary sinkings but encountered very different reactions from London and Washington. The RN accepted the authority of the TNC and began action to dispose of their four IJN U-boats by mid-February 1946 but the USN disputed the TNC's authority and insisted that any such disposal action was the responsibility of the naval authorities in Japan and that the USA was not therefore bound by the TNC's target date of 15 February 1946.

The disagreement about the three U-boats that had been captured by US forces in Japan began in early December 1945 and resulted in two messages from the USN:

> 21 Dec 45: It has been established that the former German submarine *U-511*, at the time of its capture at the end of the Pacific war, was Japanese and therefore is not subject to allocation by the Tripartite Naval Commission.

> 14 Mar 46: Former submarines *U-IT-24* and *U-IT-25* seized by Japanese Government 6 May 1945 and commissioned in Japanese Navy 15 July 45 as *I-503* and *I-504* respectively. Nationality at time of capture Japanese therefore not subject to the decisions of Tripartite Naval Commission.[7]

This protracted debate ended with a joint decision by the Senior National Delegates to the TNC that the three IJN U-boats which had surrendered in Japanese waters in August 1945 should be sunk under arrangements to be made by the USN in accordance with the agreements about the disposal of the whole Japanese fleet. The USN had successfully argued that these three U-boats were IJN submarines when they surrendered and that the TNC had no jurisdiction over them. They were not therefore sunk until April 1946.

The RN could have taken the same approach as the USN with regard to the timing of the disposal of the four IJN U-boats under British control in the Far East but as they were in any case to be destroyed by sinking it accepted that they should be sunk no later than 15 February 1946 in accordance with the recommendation in the TNC's Final Report.

The fates of the four U-boats in British custody were:

U-181, which had been taken over by the IJN in the Seletar Naval Base, Singapore and commissioned as *I-501*. It was captured there by the RN in September 1945 and on 15 February 1946 it was towed by HM Tug *Assiduous* to the Straits of Malacca, off Singapore where it was scuttled by the frigate HMS *Loch Glendhu*.

U-195, which had been taken over by the IJN in Surabaya, Java and commissioned as *I-506*. It surrendered there on 15 August 1945 and for a time its diesel engines were used to provide electricity for the city. It was scuttled by the RN in the Bali Sea, east of Kangean Island on 15 February 1946 possibly by the cruiser HMS *Sussex*.

U-219, which had been taken over by the IJN in Batavia, Java and then moved to Surabaya, Java for servicing and commissioning as *I-505* on 15 July 1945. It then returned to Batavia where it surrendered on 15 August. It was sunk by gunfire by the Royal Netherlands Navy destroyer HNMS *Kortenaer* (ex-HMS *Scorpion*) south of the Sunda Strait, between Java and Sumatra on 3 February 1946.

U-862, which had been taken over by the IJN at Seletar Naval Base, Singapore and commissioned as *I-502* on 15 July 1945. It was captured there by the RN in September 1945 and on 15 February 1946 it was towed into the Straits of Malacca, off Singapore by HM Tug *Growler* and scuttled there by the frigate HMS *Loch Lomond.*

Finally, the USN complied with the agreed disposal arrangements set out in the Japanese surrender documents and details of the sinking of the three former U-boats in American custody in April 1946 were:

U-511 was commissioned into the IJN as *RO-500* on 16 September 1943. On 15 August 1945, rather than surrendering immediately, *RO-500*'s crew decided to join the fight against the USSR and it departed from the IJN's Maizuru naval base on 18 August 1945. However, the C-in-C of the IJN submarine force learned about this and instructed *RO-500* to return to Maizuru on the same day. It therefore surrendered at Maizuru on 18 August where it was eventually captured by US forces in September. *RO-500* was scuttled with demolition charges by the USN in Wakasa Bay near Maizuru in the Sea of Japan on 30 April 1946.

U-IT-24, which had started life as the Italian submarine *Commandante Cappellini*, had been captured by the IJN in Singapore on 10 September 1943 and handed over to the Kriegsmarine on 22 October 1943. It was recaptured by the Japanese after the German surrender whilst in dock in Kobe and was taken over by the IJN. Though commissioned into the IJN as *I-503* on 15 July 1945, it took no part in operations. After the Japanese surrender on 15 August, it was captured in the Mitsubishi Shipyard in Kobe by US forces on 2 September 1945 and sunk by the USN on 16 April 1946 in the Kii Suido between the Japanese islands of Honshu and Shikoku.

U-IT-25, which had started life as the Italian submarine *Luigi Torelli*, had been captured by the IJN in Singapore on 10 September 1943 and then handed over to the Kriegsmarine on 22 October 1943. It was recaptured by the Japanese after the German surrender whilst in dock at Kobe and was taken over by the IJN. Though commissioned into the IJN as *I-504* on 15 July 1945, it took no part in operations. After the Japanese surrender on 15 August, it was captured at the Kawasaki Shipyard in Kobe by US forces on 2 September and subsequently sunk on 16 April 1946 by the USN in the Kii Suido.

East Germany

The then East Germany raised two U-boats but it did not commission either into service. The Type VIIC *U-1308*, which was scuttled on 1 May 1945, was raised off Warnemunde in February 1953. In November 1953 it was taken to Stralsund in the Baltic but it was found to be beyond repair and was broken up in early 1955. The other was the Type XXIII *U-2344* which had been sunk in the Baltic on 18 February 1945 after a collision with *U-2336*. It was raised on 22 January 1955 for intended use for anti-submarine warfare training but although it was taken to Rostock for refit it was found to be beyond repair and was broken up in 1958.

West Germany (inc. The US Bremen Enclave)

The then West Germany raised and put into service three U-boats which had been scuttled at the end of the war. The Type XXIII *U-2365* was scuttled in the Baltic north-west of Anholt Island on 8 May 1945 and was raised in June 1956. It was commissioned into the West German Navy on 15 August 1957 as *Hai* (*S-170*) and used for training until 14 September 1966 when it was lost in the North Sea near the Dogger Bank. It was raised on 19 September but was decommissioned on 24 September and finally scrapped at Emden in 1968.

The Type XXIII *U-2367* was scuttled in the Baltic south-east of Schleimunde on 9 May 1945 and was raised in August 1956. It was commissioned into the West German Navy on 1 October 1957 as *Hecht* (*S-171*). It was decommissioned on 30 September 1968 at Kiel and scrapped there in 1969.

The Type XXI *U-2540* was scuttled near Flensburg on 4 May 1945 and was raised in June 1957. It was rebuilt at Kiel and commissioned into the West German Navy as a research vessel on 1 September 1960. It was decommissioned on 28 August 1968 for engineering work but re-commissioned in May 1970 as *Wilhelm Bauer* and then used for experimental purposes. It was damaged in an under-water collision with a destroyer on 6 May 1980 and was taken out of use on 18 November 1980 before being finally retired on 15 March 1982. It was then acquired by the German Maritime Museum at Bremerhaven and has been on display there since 27 April 1984.

Two U-boats had been captured afloat but out-of-commission in May 1945 in the US Bremen enclave in the British Zone in north-west Germany. These were *U-1197* and *U-1232*, both of which were scheduled for demolition. Repair work on these U-boats had been suspended in early 1945 and except for small demolition teams the crews had been disembarked and allocated to other duties.

U-1197 had arrived in Bremen on 21 March 1945 for repair and maintenance at the Deschimag-Weser AG shipyard. It was severely damaged during a USAAF air raid on Bremen on 30 March and could not be repaired. When the Allies advanced into Bremen in late April *U-1197* was moved down the Weser River to provide power to the Bremer-Vulkan shipyard at Vegesack. It was then moved further down the river to the dockyard at Wesermunde where it was decommissioned on 25 April. When the Wesermunde dockyard was evacuated on 30 April *U-1197* was moved back up the Weser River, this time to the small port of Brake on the west side of the Weser. However, when *U-1197* arrived at Brake the port was found to be under British control and so it returned to Wesermunde where it was captured by US troops. Whilst *U-1197* was not in commission in May 1945 and did not therefore surrender its final disposal needed to be formally undertaken by the USN. This was because it was defined in the TNC's Final Report as one of the unallocated U-boats which had to be sunk no later than 15 February 1946. Thus, *U-1197* was towed out into the North Sea and sunk by the USN in mid-February 1946.

U-1232 had been decommissioned in Wesermunde in April 1945 after being damaged in action earlier in the year and it was captured in early May. It too was classified by the TNC as an unallocated submarine afloat and was therefore subject to the recommendation that it should be sunk in the open sea by 15 February 1946. Unfortunately, the USN's experience with *U-1232* was not good. First, on 18 February 1946 it sank during heavy weather after which it was raised by the USN before being towed out to sea to be sunk. However, on 4 March the U-boat foundered in 21 fathoms in the mouth of the Weser Estuary whilst under tow to the sinking area and this was followed by a message from the USN on 7 March saying that it was proposed to destroy *U-1232* on the seabed with explosive charges when the weather permitted diving operations. On 9 March the USN reported the details of the saga suggesting that earlier cannibalisation by the German Navy prior to the capitulation plus subsequent deterioration and lack of maintenance had weakened the hull to such an extent that the strain of the tow and the force of the sea had caused structural failure. These facts were then passed to the TNC and the Senior UK and Soviet Representatives agreed that enough was enough and that they considered that *U-1232* had been satisfactorily sunk in accordance with the TNC's recommendation.

Yugoslavia

Yugoslavia raised, commissioned and operated *U-IT-19* (ex-Italian *Nautilo*) under the name of *Sava* (*P-802*). *U-IT-19* was one of the Italian submarines captured intact by the Germans in Pola after the Italian surrender in September 1943 but though it was given a Kriegsmarine U-boat number it was never formally commissioned into the German Navy. It was sunk in Pola during a USAAF air attack on 9 January 1944 but in 1947 it was raised and repaired by Yugoslavia and taken into service with the Yugoslav Navy until 1968 before being finally broken up in 1971. There were reports in the 1950s that *U-81*, which had been sunk in Pola on the same day as *U-IT-19*, had also been raised and put into service with the Yugoslav Navy. However, these reports were not confirmed and it is much more likely that after it was raised on 22 April 1944 it was scrapped as being beyond repair.

Spain

Two U-boats were interned in Spain during the War. The first was *U-573* which had been interned in Cartagena in south-east Spain after being badly damaged in an Allied air attack north-west of Algiers on 1 May 1942. *U-573* arrived in Cartagena on 2 May and was granted a three-month period to make any necessary repairs. However, the damage was too severe and it was decided to sell the U-boat to Spain. Thus it was decommissioned by the Germans on 2 August 1942 and became *G-7* in the Spanish Navy on the same day. After that, the slow and lengthy repairs took five years to complete and it was not until 5 November 1947 that *G-7* was re-commissioned. The U-boat, which had been re-named *S-01* in June 1961 then began a 23-year career in the Spanish Navy until it was decommissioned on 2 May 1970 before being sold for scrap and broken-up.

The other was *U-760* which had been badly damaged in an Allied air attack off Cape Finisterre on 6 September 1943. It initially entered Vigo in north-west Spain on 8 September but was then interned in El Ferrol, near Corunna, where it remained until May 1945 before being moved back to Vigo. Although *U-760* had been classified as a war loss the Spanish authorities handed it over to the RN after the German capitulation albeit that it was not part of the formal surrender process. It was then moved to Loch Ryan on 23 July arriving on 3 August under tow by the salvage tug HMS *Frisky*. On arrival it was found to be in a very bad state. Also, its twelve live torpedoes were still on board, with one jammed in No 3 tube. As a result *U-760* needed to be beached before the torpedo could be removed. Thereafter *U-760* was treated as though it was one of the 156 U-boats which had surrendered at the end of the war in Europe. It was inspected by the TNC in early September and subsequently earmarked for disposal. Finally, on 11 December 1945 it was towed out of Loch Ryan for sinking in Operation 'Deadlight'.

Additionally, *U-167* which had been scuttled in shallow water close to the south coast of Gran Canaria after being damaged in an Allied air attack on 6 April 1943 was raised by a Spanish salvage company in December 1951. After a first unsuccessful attempt on 23 December, it was fully refloated on 27 December and after the holes in the hull were plugged and the water pumped out *U-167* gave the impression of being in good condition. At the end of January 1952 it was towed north to Las Palmas in Gran Canaria where it was docked in the Spanish Naval Base to the east of the town. However, the Spanish Navy had no interest in the U-boat and at the end of 1952 it was ordered to be removed from the naval dock. Thus, it was transferred to an exposed anchorage in Shelter Bay to the west of Las Palmas. The salvage company made several unsuccessful attempts to sell *U-167* but there was no interest. So, after its engines were sold and its remaining torpedoes were removed it was broken up for scrap in 1953.

Portugal

The two U-boats which had been scuttled off the coast of Portugal, *U-963* in May 1945 and *U-1277* in June 1945, were listed in the TNC's Final Report as being submarines which had scuttled in shallow water and the report therefore recommended that they should be destroyed to preclude the possibility of salvage and possible use for naval purposes. However, the TNC possessed no powers of direction over the Portuguese Government and no further action was taken. Both U-boats therefore remain where they were scuttled. *U-1277* which was found in October 1973 lies about two miles north-west of Oporto and although it has not been pinpointed *U-963* is believed to lie off Nazare to the north of Lisbon.

Italy

Other than *U-IT-24* (ex-*Commandante Cappellini*) and *U-IT-25* (ex-*Luigi Torelli*) which surrendered under the Japanese flag, Italy was responsible for raising several of the sunken Italian *U-IT* submarines during the clearance of the Italian harbours after 1945. But only one U-boat (*U-IT-7*) was found to be of any further substantive use. *U-IT-7* (originally *Bario*) had been captured by the Germans in an unfinished state at Monfalcone on 9 September 1943. However, although it was launched on 23 January 1944 it was damaged at Monfalcone during an air raid on 16 March 1945 and scuttled on 1 May 1945. It was raised later in 1945 but it was not until 1953 that it was taken in hand for reconstruction and modernisation. It was relaunched as *Bario* on 21 June 1959, had its name changed to *Pietro Calvi* and was commissioned into the Italian Navy on 16 December 1961. It was used for training until it was laid up in 1971 being finally discarded in April 1973.

Additionally, two 92-ton midget submarines which had been allocated *U-IT* numbers but which were never used by the Kriegsmarine were in evidence post-May 1945. The first of these was *U-IT-17* (ex-*CM1*) which had been captured by the Germans in Monfalcone on 9 September 1943. It was transferred to the Italian Fascist Navy and completed on 4 January 1945. Thereafter it was taken over by a partisan crew and moved south to re-join the Italian Navy in April 1945. It was discarded on 1 February 1948 before being broken up. The second was *U-IT-18* (ex-*CM2*) which had been captured by the Germans in an unfinished state at Monfalcone on 9 September 1943. It was never completed and was damaged on its slipway in a USAAF air raid on 25 May 1944. It was scuttled on 1 May 1945 but was refloated in October 1950. In 1951 it was transferred to the Naval Museum at Trieste in 1951 where it was on display for several years.

Sweden

On 5 May 1945, whilst in transit from the Baltic to Norway, *U-3503* was damaged during an attack by RAF aircraft in the Kattegat. As a result, it took refuge in Swedish territorial waters and entered Vinga on 6 May. On the evening of 8 May the U-boat began to sink (possibly scuttled by the crew), eventually sinking in the Gothenburg Skerries in 8–9 fathoms of water. Despite this it was listed by the TNC as having sunk in shallow water in the British Zone of North Germany. In early 1946 the Swedish Government asked for permission to raise and scrap *U-3503*. This request was granted and the retrieval operation started on 3 May. The U-boat was raised on 24 August and moved to Gothenburg where it was docked on 27 August. It was then made watertight and transferred to the Swedish Navy Yard in Gothenburg for investigation and dismantling, finally being scrapped by July 1947.

The Netherlands

The ex-Dutch submarine *O-27*, which had been captured by the Germans whilst still on its building slip in May 1940 and which had been commissioned as *UD-5* on 30 January 1942, surrendered in Bergen on 9 May 1945. It was transferred to Lisahally, arriving there on 2 June and was handed back to the Royal Netherlands Navy (RNeN) on 13 July being re-commissioned as Hr.Ms. *O 27* on the same day. It sailed from Lisahally with a Dutch CO and crew on 24 July for Dundee which was where the Dutch submarine service had been based throughout the war. After the German capitulation in May 1945 the Dutch were unable to return all their ships to the Netherlands because of the damage to their home ports. So Dundee remained the base of the Dutch submarines throughout the remainder of 1945. Also, *O 27* was in a poor state, with damage to its bow, and it was therefore retained at Dundee until February 1946 whilst it was repaired and whilst its new crew were trained. It was then transferred to Rotterdam and used by the RNeN until 14 November 1959 when it was struck from the active list. Finally, it was sold for scrap on 23 December 1960 and broken up in Antwerp in 1961.

Poland

The Type II U-boats *U-4*, *U-6* and *U-10* were decommissioned in July and August 1944: *U-4* in Gotenhafen on 31 July, *U-6* in Gotenhafen on 7 August and *U-10* in Danzig on 30 July. They were then cannibalised for spares in support of other U-boats in the area and it is generally assumed that they were captured there by the Russians in March 1945 and scrapped in situ. This is, however, incorrect as these three unserviceable U-boats had been towed west to the Polish port of Stolpmunde sometime in early 1945 where their decommissioned hulks were captured by the Russian forces. The TNC's initial Agreed List dated 25 August 1945 which set out details of the U-boats that had surrendered and which had been prepared from information provided by the American, British and Russian delegations to the TNC listed these three U-boats as 'afloat, being repaired' in Stolpmunde. The TNC Baltic Inspection Team therefore visited Stolpmunde on 28 August 1945 where they viewed *U-4*, *U-6* and *U-10*. Subsequently the TNC's Final Report listed them as 'U-Boats that have been dismantled'. Thus, they were obviously afloat at the time of their capture by the Russians and at least some parts of them must have been visible above the water at the time of the TNC inspection visit.

Whilst the TNC's Final Report required no formal follow-up from the Soviet naval authorities the final disposal of these three Type II U-boats involved them being sunk in Stolpmunde harbour in late 1945. However, in the autumn of 1949 the Polish authorities in Stolpmunde were concerned that the harbour was being blocked by the three wrecks and that they were an obstacle for the fishing boats using the harbour. Thus, although the Russians were not keen to help, the wrecks were raised and refloated by the Polish harbour maintenance organisation in 1950. The first was raised on 23 March 1950, the second on 8 May 1950 and the third on 11 July 1950. There was some temporary interest in possibly preserving one of the U-boats as a museum exhibit but this came to nought and all three were scrapped in the latter half of 1951.

The Remaining Unserviceable U-Boats

As described in Chapter 10, the TNC's Final Report listed large numbers of U-boats which were defined as having been scuttled in shallow water and which were primarily located in the Baltic and other ports in northern Germany. Most of them had been discovered during the TNC inspection visits, thus accounting for the TNC's decision to extend its Terms of Reference and to include recommendations for the disposal of such U-boats.

For practical reasons, as well as the need to adhere to the TNC recommendations, there was a great deal of harbour-clearance activity in and around the German ports and shipyards in the second half of 1945 and early 1946. There was also a considerable amount of confusion as the salvage crews sunk and/or demolished all the U-boats that they found.

Many could neither be identified individually nor aligned to the U-boat numbers listed in the TNC's Final Report. These included U-boats which had been damaged, decommissioned, destroyed, scrapped and scuttled during the war, as well as the many U-boats that had been deliberately scuttled in Operation 'Regenbogen'. Others had not been completed in the German shipyards where they were being built or assembled.

Unsurprisingly, this clearance process has spawned reports about U-boats, other than those specifically mentioned in this and earlier chapters, having been raised since 1945. However, it is believed that no significant historical fact is ignored by discounting them.

CHAPTER 20

The Surrender List – When and Where

U-Boat No	When	Where (inc Arrival Dates)
143	5 May	in port – Heligoland, Germany
145	5 May	in port – Heligoland, Germany
149	5 May	in port – Heligoland, Germany
150	5 May	in port – Heligoland, Germany
155	5 May	in port – Baring Bay, nr Fredericia, Denmark
170	9 May	in port – Horten, Norway
190	11 May at sea	from sea – Bay Bulls, Canada – 14 May
218	12 May	direct from sea – Bergen, Norway
234	12 May at sea	from sea – Portsmouth, USA – 19 May
244	12 May at sea	from sea – Loch Eriboll, UK – 14 May
245	9 May	direct from sea – Bergen, Norway
249	9 May at sea	from sea – Portland, UK – 10 May
255	14 May at sea	from sea – Loch Eriboll, UK – 17 May
278	9 May	direct from sea – Narvik, Norway
281	9 May	in port – Kristiansand (S), Norway
291	5 May	in port – Cuxhaven, Germany
293	10 May at sea	from sea – Loch Eriboll, UK – 11 May
294	9 May	in port – Narvik, Norway
295	9 May	in port – Narvik, Norway
298	9 May	in port – Bergen, Norway
299	9 May	in port – Kristiansand (S), Norway
310	9 May	in port – Trondheim, Norway
312	9 May	in port – Narvik, Norway
313	9 May	in port – Narvik, Norway
315	9 May	in port – Trondheim, Norway
318	9 May	direct from sea – Narvik, Norway

U-Boat No	When	Where (inc Arrival Dates)
324	9 May	in port – Bergen, Norway
328	9 May	in port – Bergen, Norway
363	9 May	in port – Narvik, Norway
368	5 May	in port – Heligoland, Germany
369	9 May	in port – Kristiansand (S), Norway
427	9 May	in port – Narvik, Norway
481	9 May	in port – Narvik, Norway
483	9 May	in port – Trondheim, Norway
485	11 May at sea	from sea – Gibraltar – 12 May
510	9 May	in port – St Nazaire, France
516	10 May at sea	from sea – Loch Eriboll, UK – 14 May
530	10 July	direct from sea – Mar del Plata, Argentina
532	10 May at sea	from sea – Loch Eriboll, UK – 13 May
539	9 May	in port – Bergen, Norway
541	10 May at sea	from sea – Gibraltar – 12 May
637	9 May	in port – Stavanger, Norway
668	9 May	in port – Narvik, Norway
680	5 May	in port – Baring Bay, nr Fredericia, Denmark
712	9 May	in port – Kristiansand (S), Norway
716	9 May	in port – Narvik, Norway
720	5 May	in port – Heligoland, Germany
739	13 May at sea	from sea – Emden, Germany – 13 May
764	13 May at sea	from sea – Loch Eriboll, UK – 14 May
773	9 May	in port – Trondheim, Norway
775	9 May	in port – Trondheim, Norway
776	14 May at sea	from sea – Portland, UK – 16 May
778	9 May	in port – Bergen, Norway
779	5 May	in port – Cuxhaven, Germany
802	9 May at sea	from sea – Loch Eriboll, UK – 11 May
805	9 May at sea	from sea – Portsmouth, USA – 15 May
806	6 May	direct from sea – Aarhus, Denmark
825	10 May at sea	from sea – Loch Eriboll, UK – 13 May
826	9 May at sea	from sea – Loch Eriboll, UK – 11 May
858	9 May at sea	from sea – Lewes, Delaware, USA – 14 May
861	9 May	in port – Trondheim, Norway
868	9 May	in port – Bergen, Norway
873	11 May at sea	from sea – Portsmouth, USA – 16 May

U-Boat No	When	Where (inc Arrival Dates)
874	9 May	in port – Horten, Norway
875	9 May	in port – Bergen, Norway
883	5 May	in port – Cuxhaven, Germany
889	10 May at sea	from sea – Shelburne, Canada – 13 May
901	13 May at sea	from sea – Stavanger, Norway – 15 May
907	9 May	in port – Bergen, Norway
926	9 May	in port – Bergen, Norway
928	9 May	in port – Bergen, Norway
930	9 May	in port – Bergen, Norway
953	9 May	in port – Trondheim, Norway
956	11 May at sea	from sea – Loch Eriboll, UK – 13 May
968	9 May	in port – Narvik, Norway
975	9 May	in port – Horten, Norway
977	17 Aug	direct from sea – Mar del Plata, Argentina
978	9 May	in port – Trondheim, Norway
991	9 May	in port – Bergen, Norway
992	9 May	direct from sea – Narvik, Norway
994	9 May	in port – Trondheim, Norway
995	9 May	in port – Trondheim, Norway
997	9 May	in port – Narvik, Norway
1002	9 May	in port – Bergen, Norway
1004	9 May	in port – Bergen, Norway
1005	14 May	direct from sea – Bergen, Norway
1009	9 May at sea	from sea – Loch Eriboll, UK – 10 May
1010	11 May at sea	from sea – Loch Eriboll, UK – 14 May
1019	9 May	in port – Trondheim, Norway
1022	9 May	in port – Bergen, Norway
1023	10 May at sea	from sea – Portland, UK – 10 May
1052	9 May	in port – Bergen, Norway
1057	9 May	in port – Bergen, Norway
1058	9 May at sea	from sea – Loch Eriboll, UK – 10 May
1061	9 May	in port – Bergen, Norway
1064	9 May	in port – Trondheim, Norway
1102	13 May	direct from sea – Hohwacht Bay, Germany
1103	5 May	in port – Cuxhaven, Germany
1104	9 May	in port – Bergen, Norway
1105	9 May at sea	from sea – Loch Eriboll, UK – 10 May

U-Boat No	When	Where (inc Arrival Dates)
1108	9 May	in port – Horten, Norway
1109	12 May at sea	from sea – Loch Eriboll, UK – 12 May
1110	14 May at sea	from sea – List, Sylt, Germany – 14 May
1163	9 May	in port – Kristiansand (S), Norway
1165	9 May	in port – Narvik, Norway
1171	9 May	in port – Stavanger, Norway
1194	9 May	direct from sea – Cuxhaven, Germany
1198	8 May	direct from sea – Cuxhaven, Germany
1202	9 May	in port – Bergen, Norway
1203	9 May	in port – Trondheim, Norway
1228	9 May at sea	from sea – Portsmouth, USA – 17 May
1230	5 May	in port – Heligoland, Germany
1231	11 May at sea	from sea – Loch Eriboll, UK – 13 May
1233	5 May	in port – Baring Bay, nr Fredericia, Denmark
1271	9 May	in port – Bergen, Norway
1272	10 May	direct from sea – Bergen, Norway
1301	9 May	in port – Bergen, Norway
1305	10 May at sea	from sea – Loch Eriboll, UK – 10 May
1307	9 May	in port – Bergen, Norway
1406	5 May	in port – Cuxhaven, Germany
1407	5 May	in port – Cuxhaven, Germany
2321	9 May	in port – Kristiansand (S), Norway
2322	9 May	in port – Stavanger, Norway
2324	9 May	direct from sea – Stavanger, Norway
2325	9 May	in port – Kristiansand (S), Norway
2326	11 May at sea	from sea – Dundee, UK – 14 May
2328	9 May	in port – Bergen, Norway
2329	9 May	in port – Stavanger, Norway
2334	9 May	in port – Kristiansand (S), Norway
2335	9 May	in port – Kristiansand (S), Norway
2336	15 May	direct from sea – Kiel, Germany – 15 May
2337	9 May	in port – Kristiansand (S), Norway
2341	5 May	in port – Cuxhaven, Germany
2345	9 May	in port – Stavanger, Norway
2348	9 May	in port – Stavanger, Norway

U-Boat No	When	Where (inc Arrival Dates)
2350	9 May	in port – Kristiansand (S), Norway
2351	5 May	in port – Flensburg, Germany
2353	9 May	in port – Kristiansand (S), Norway
2354	9 May	in port – Kristiansand (S), Norway
2356	5 May	in port – Cuxhaven, Germany
2361	9 May	in port – Kristiansand (S), Norway
2363	9 May	in port – Kristiansand (S), Norway
2502	9 May	in port – Horten, Norway
2506	9 May	in port – Bergen, Norway
2511	9 May	in port – Bergen, Norway
2513	9 May	in port – Horten, Norway
2518	9 May	in port – Horten, Norway
2529	9 May	in port – Kristiansand (S), Norway
3008	11 May at sea	from sea – Kiel, Germany – 21 May
3017	9 May	in port – Horten, Norway
3035	9 May	in port – Stavanger, Norway
3041	9 May	in port – Horten, Norway
3514	9 May	in port – Bergen, Norway
3515	9 May	in port – Horten, Norway
4706	9 May	in port – Kristiansand (S), Norway
UD-5	9 May	in port – Bergen, Norway

CHAPTER 21

The Final Account

ONE HUNDRED AND FIFTY-SIX Kriegsmarine U-boats surrendered at the end of the war in Europe in May 1945, and seven U-boats in service with the Imperial Japanese Navy (IJN) surrendered at the end of the war in the Far East in August 1945. Today, only one of those U-boats still survives (*U-995*) and it is on display at Laboe, near Kiel in Germany. Of the other three U-boats on display in museums, one was captured during the war and two were raised after the war.

All the other U-boats which surrendered were either sunk or scrapped, the majority in Operation 'Deadlight' when, between November 1945 and February 1946, the Royal Navy sunk 116 U-boats from Loch Ryan and Lisahally in the North Atlantic to the north-west of Northern Ireland. Also, thirty U-boats were allocated equally between the UK, the USA and the USSR, where they were used for various testing and experimental purposes before being sunk or scrapped. Additionally, four of the U-boats which surrendered were taken over by the Royal Norwegian Navy and one was taken over by the French Navy.

The aim of this book has been to show that, despite the British objective of ensuring the early destruction of all the remaining U-boats just as soon as possible after the end of the war, a limited number remained operational for several years with various navies, albeit that a number of these were originally classed as war losses and then raised and/or repaired after the war. It was not until 1970 that *U-573* was retired after service with the Spanish Navy, and it was not until 1971 that the very last of them (*U-IT-7*) was retired from the Italian Navy.

The final disposal details of the 156 U-boats which surrendered at the end of the war in Europe and the seven U-boats which surrendered under the IJN flag at the end of the war in the Far East were as follows:

Note: 'Li' indicates Lisahally, 'LR' indicates Loch Ryan.

U-143   Sunk by RN in Op 'Deadlight' (LR) off N. Ireland on 22 Dec 45

U-145   Sunk by RN in Op 'Deadlight' (LR) off N. Ireland on 22 Dec 45

U-149   Sunk by RN in Op 'Deadlight' (LR) off N. Ireland on 21 Dec 45

U-150   Sunk by RN in Op 'Deadlight' (LR) off N. Ireland on 21 Dec 45

U-155   Sunk by RN in Op 'Deadlight' (LR) off N. Ireland on 21 Dec 45

U-170   Sunk by RN in Op 'Deadlight' (LR) off N. Ireland on 30 Nov 45

U-190   Allocated to UK (Canada). Sunk by RCN off Halifax on 21 Oct 47

U-218   Sunk by RN in Op 'Deadlight' (LR) off N. Ireland on 4 Dec 45

U-234   Allocated to USA. Sunk off Cape Cod on 20 Nov 47

U-244   Sunk by RN in Op 'Deadlight' (Li) off N. Ireland on 30 Dec 45

U-245   Sunk by RN in Op 'Deadlight' (LR) off N. Ireland on 7 Dec 45

U-249   Sunk by RN in Op 'Deadlight' (LR) off N. Ireland on 13 Dec 45

U-255   Sunk by RAF in Op 'Deadlight' (LR) off N. Ireland on 13 Dec 45

U-278   Sunk by RN in Op 'Deadlight' (Li) off N. Ireland on 31 Dec 45

U-281   Sunk by RN in Op 'Deadlight' (LR) off N. Ireland on 30 Nov 45

U-291   Sunk by RN in Op 'Deadlight' (LR) off N. Ireland on 21 Dec 45

U-293   Sunk by RN in Op 'Deadlight' (LR) off N. Ireland on 13 Dec 45

U-294   Sunk by RN in Op 'Deadlight' (Li) off N. Ireland on 31 Dec 45

U-295   Sunk by RN in Op 'Deadlight' (LR) off N. Ireland on 17 Dec 45

U-298   Sunk by RN in Op 'Deadlight' (LR) off N. Ireland on 29 Nov 45

U-299   Sunk by RN in Op 'Deadlight' (LR) off N. Ireland on 4 Dec 45

U-310	Remained in Norway and scrapped in Trondheim in 1947
U-312	Sunk by RN in Op 'Deadlight' (LR) off N. Ireland on 29 Nov 45
U-313	Sunk by RN in Op 'Deadlight' (LR) off N. Ireland on 21 Dec 45
U-315	Remained in Norway and scrapped in Trondheim in 1947
U-318	Sunk by RN in Op 'Deadlight' (LR) off N. Ireland on 21 Dec 45
U-324	Remained in Norway and scrapped in Trondheim in 1947
U-328	Sunk by RN in Op 'Deadlight' (LR) off N. Ireland on 30 Nov 45
U-363	Sunk by RN in Op 'Deadlight' (Li) off N. Ireland on 31 Dec 45
U-368	Sunk by RN in Op 'Deadlight' (LR) off N. Ireland on 17 Dec 45
U-369	Sunk by RN in Op 'Deadlight' (LR) off N. Ireland on 30 Nov 45
U-427	Sunk by RN in Op 'Deadlight' (LR) off N. Ireland on 21 Dec 45
U-481	Sunk by RN in Op 'Deadlight' (LR) off N. Ireland on 30 Nov 45
U-483	Sunk by Raf in Op 'Deadlight' (LR) off N. Ireland on 16 Dec 45
U-485	Sunk by RN in Op 'Deadlight' (LR) off N. Ireland on 8 Dec 45
U-510	Taken over by France in St Nazaire. Sold for scrap on 23 Nov 59
U-516	Sunk by RN in Op 'Deadlight' (Li) off N. Ireland on 3 Jan 46
U-530	Allocated to USA. Sunk off Cape Cod on 21 Nov 47
U-532	Sunk by RN in Op 'Deadlight' (LR) off N. Ireland on 9 Dec 45
U-539	Sunk by RN in Op 'Deadlight' (LR) off N. Ireland on 4 Dec 45
U-541	Sunk by RN in Op 'Deadlight' (Li) off N. Ireland on 5 Jan 46
U-637	Sunk by RN in Op 'Deadlight' (LR) off N. Ireland on 21 Dec 45
U-668	Sunk by RN in Op 'Deadlight' (Li) off N. Ireland on 1 Jan 46
U-680	Sunk by RN in Op 'Deadlight' (LR) off N. Ireland on 28 Dec 45
U-712	Allocated to UK. Scrapped at Dunston-on-Tyne, Newcastle in 1949/50

U-716	Sunk by RAF in Op 'Deadlight' (LR) off N. Ireland on 11 Dec 45
U-720	Sunk by RN in Op 'Deadlight' (LR) off N. Ireland on 21 Dec 45
U-739	Sunk by RN in Op 'Deadlight' (LR) off N. Ireland on 16 Dec 45
U-764	Sunk by RN in Op 'Deadlight' (Li) off N. Ireland on 3 Jan 46
U-773	Sunk by RN in Op 'Deadlight' (LR) off N. Ireland on 8 Dec 45
U-775	Sunk by RN in Op 'Deadlight' (LR) off N. Ireland on 8 Dec 45
U-776	Sunk by RN in Op 'Deadlight' (LR) off N. Ireland on 3 Dec 45
U-778	Sunk by RN in Op 'Deadlight' (LR) off N. Ireland on 4 Dec 45
U-779	Sunk by RN in Op 'Deadlight' (LR) off N. Ireland on 17 Dec 45
U-802	Sunk by RN in Op 'Deadlight' (Li) off N. Ireland on 31 Dec 45
U-805	Sunk by US Navy off Cape Cod on 8 Feb 46
U-806	Sunk by RN in Op 'Deadlight' (LR) off N. Ireland on 21 Dec 45
U-825	Sunk by RN in Op 'Deadlight' (Li) off N. Ireland on 3 Jan 46
U-826	Sunk by RN in Op 'Deadlight' (LR) off N. Ireland on 1 Dec 45
U-858	Allocated to USA. Sunk off Cape Cod on 21 Nov 47
U-861	Sunk by RN in Op 'Deadlight' (Li) off N. Ireland on 31 Dec 45
U-868	Sunk by RN in Op 'Deadlight' (LR) off N. Ireland on 30 Nov 45
U-873	Allocated to USA. Sold for scrap in New York in Mar 48
U-874	Sunk by RN in Op 'Deadlight' (Li) off N. Ireland on 31 Dec 45
U-875	Sunk by RN in Op 'Deadlight' (Li) off N. Ireland on 31 Dec 45
U-883	Sunk by RN in Op 'Deadlight' (Li) off N. Ireland on 31 Dec 45
U-889	Allocated to USA. Sunk off Cape Cod on 20 Nov 47
U-901	Sunk by RN in Op 'Deadlight' (Li) off N. Ireland on 6 Jan 46
U-907	Sunk by RN in Op 'Deadlight' (LR) off N. Ireland on 7 Dec 45

U-926	Taken over by Norway. Sold for scrap in May 65
U-928	Sunk by RN in Op 'Deadlight' (LR) off N. Ireland on 16 Dec 45
U-930	Sunk by RN in Op 'Deadlight' (Li) off N. Ireland on 29 Dec 45
U-953	Allocated to UK. Scrapped at Hayle, Cornwall in 1949/50
U-956	Sunk by RN in Op 'Deadlight' (LR) off N. Ireland on 17 Dec 45
U-968	Sunk by RN in Op 'Deadlight' (LR) off N. Ireland on 28 Nov 45
U-975	Sunk by RN in Op 'Deadlight' (Li) off N. Ireland on 10 Feb 46
U-977	Allocated to USA. Sunk off Cape Cod on 13 Nov 46
U-978	Sunk by RN in Op 'Deadlight' (LR) off N. Ireland on 11 Dec 45
U-991	Sunk by RN in Op 'Deadlight' (LR) off N. Ireland on 11 Dec 45
U-992	Sunk by RN in Op 'Deadlight' (LR) off N. Ireland on 16 Dec 45
U-994	Sunk by RN in Op 'Deadlight' (LR) off N. Ireland on 5 Dec 45
U-995	Taken over by Norway. Sold to the German Navy Ass'n on 14 Oct 65
U-997	Sunk by RAF in Op 'Deadlight' (LR) off N. Ireland on 11 Dec 45
U-1002	Sunk by RN in Op 'Deadlight' (LR) off N. Ireland on 13 Dec 45
U-1004	Sunk by RN in Op 'Deadlight' (LR) off N. Ireland on 1 Dec 45
U-1005	Sunk by RN in Op 'Deadlight' (LR) off N. Ireland on 5 Dec 45
U-1009	Sunk by RN in Op 'Deadlight' (LR) off N. Ireland on 16 Dec 45
U-1010	Sunk by RN in Op 'Deadlight' (Li) off N. Ireland on 7 Jan 46
U-1019	Sunk by RN in Op 'Deadlight' (LR) off N. Ireland on 7 Dec 45
U-1022	Sunk by RN in Op 'Deadlight' (Li) off N. Ireland on 29 Dec 45
U-1023	Sunk by RN in Op 'Deadlight' (Li) off N. Ireland on 9 Jan 46
U-1052	Sunk by RN in Op 'Deadlight' (LR) off N. Ireland on 9 Dec 45

U-1057 Allocated to USSR. Struck from Soviet Navy List on 16 Oct 57

U-1058 Allocated to USSR. Struck from Soviet Navy List on 25 Mar 58

U-1061 Sunk by RN in Op 'Deadlight' (LR) off N. Ireland on 1 Dec 45

U-1064 Allocated to USSR. Struck from Soviet Navy List on 12 Mar 74

U-1102 Sunk by RN in Op 'Deadlight' (LR) off N. Ireland on 21 Dec 45

U-1103 Sunk by RN in Op 'Deadlight' (LR) off N. Ireland on 30 Dec 45

U-1104 Sunk by RN in Op 'Deadlight' (LR) off N. Ireland on 15 Dec 45

U-1105 Allocated to USA. Sunk in the Potomac River on 19 Sep 49

U-1108 Allocated to UK. Scrapped at Briton Ferry, S Wales in 1949

U-1109 Sunk by RN in Op 'Deadlight' (Li) off N. Ireland on 6 Jan 46

U-1110 Sunk by RN in Op 'Deadlight' (LR) off N. Ireland on 21 Dec 45

U-1163 Sunk by RAF in Op 'Deadlight' (LR) off N. Ireland on 11 Dec 45

U-1165 Sunk by RN in Op 'Deadlight' (Li) off N. Ireland on 31 Dec 45

U-1171 Allocated to UK. Scrapped in Sunderland in 1949/50

U-1194 Sunk by RN in Op 'Deadlight' (LR) off N. Ireland on 22 Dec 45

U-1198 Sunk by RN in Op 'Deadlight' (LR) off N. Ireland on 17 Dec 45

U-1202 Taken over by Norway. Sold for scrap in 1962

U-1203 Sunk by RN in Op 'Deadlight' (LR) off N. Ireland on 8 Dec 45

U-1228 Sunk by US Navy off Cape Cod on 5 Feb 46

U-1230 Sunk by RN in Op 'Deadlight' (LR) off N. Ireland on 19 Dec 45

U-1231 Allocated to USSR. Struck from Soviet Navy List on 13 Jan 68

U-1233 Sunk by RN in Op 'Deadlight' (LR) off N. Ireland on 29 Dec 45

U-1271 Sunk by RN in Op 'Deadlight' (LR) off N. Ireland on 8 Dec 45

U-1272 Sunk by RN in Op 'Deadlight' (LR) off N. Ireland on 8 Dec 45

U-1301 Sunk by RAF in Op 'Deadlight' (LR) off N. Ireland on 16 Dec 45

U-1305 Allocated to USSR. Sunk in Barents Sea in atomic test on 10 Oct 57

U-1307 Sunk by RN in Op 'Deadlight' (LR) off N. Ireland on 9 Dec 45

U-1406 Allocated to USA. Sold for scrap in New York in May 48

U-1407 Allocated to UK. Scrapped in Barrow in 1949

U-2321 Sunk by RN in Op 'Deadlight' (LR) off N. Ireland on 27 Dec 45

U-2322 Sunk by RN in Op 'Deadlight' (LR) off N. Ireland on 27 Nov 45

U-2324 Sunk by RN in Op 'Deadlight' (LR) off N. Ireland on 27 Nov 45

U-2325 Sunk by RN in Op 'Deadlight' (LR) off N. Ireland on 28 Nov 45

U-2326 Allocated to UK (France). Lost in accident off Toulon on 5 Dec 46

U-2328 Sunk by RN in Op 'Deadlight' (LR) off N. Ireland on 27 Nov 45

U-2329 Sunk by RN in Op 'Deadlight' (LR) off N. Ireland on 28 Nov 45

U-2334 Sunk by RN in Op 'Deadlight' (LR) off N. Ireland on 28 Nov 45

U-2335 Sunk by RN in Op 'Deadlight' (LR) off N. Ireland on 28 Nov 45

U-2336 Sunk by RN in Op 'Deadlight' (Li) off N. Ireland on 3 Jan 46

U-2337 Sunk by RN in Op 'Deadlight' (LR) off N. Ireland on 28 Nov 45

U-2341 Sunk by RN in Op 'Deadlight' (Li) off N. Ireland on 31 Dec 45

U-2345 Sunk by RN in Op 'Deadlight' (LR) off N. Ireland on 27 Nov 45

U-2348 Allocated to UK. Scrapped in Belfast in 1949

U-2350 Sunk by RN in Op 'Deadlight' (LR) off N. Ireland on 28 Nov 45

U-2351 Sunk by RN in Op 'Deadlight' (Li) off N. Ireland on 3 Jan 46

U-2353 Allocated to USSR. Struck from Soviet Navy List on 17 Mar 52

U-2354 Sunk by RN in Op 'Deadlight' (LR) off N. Ireland on 22 Dec 45

U-2356 Sunk by RN in Op 'Deadlight' (Li) off N. Ireland on 6 Jan 46

U-2361 Sunk by RN in Op 'Deadlight' (LR) off N. Ireland on 27 Nov 45

U-2363   Sunk by RN in Op 'Deadlight' (LR) off N. Ireland on 28 Nov 45

U-2502   Sunk by RN in Op 'Deadlight' (Li) off N. Ireland on 3 Jan 46

U-2506   Sunk by RN in Op 'Deadlight' (Li) off N. Ireland on 5 Jan 46

U-2511   Sunk by RN in Op 'Deadlight' (Li) off N. Ireland on 7 Jan 46

U-2513   Allocated to USA. Sunk off Key West on 7 Oct 51

U-2518   Allocated to UK (France). Sold for scrap on 21 May 69

U-2529   Allocated to USSR. Struck from Soviet Navy List on 1 Sep 72

U-3008   Allocated to USA. Sold for scrap in Puerto Rico on 15 Sep 55

U-3017   Allocated to UK. Scrapped in Newport, S Wales in 1950

U-3035   Allocated to USSR. Struck from Soviet Navy List on 25 Mar 58

U-3041   Allocated to USSR. Struck from Soviet Navy List on 25 Sep 58

U-3514   Sunk by RN in Op 'Deadlight' (Li) off N. Ireland on 11 Feb 46

U-3515   Allocated to USSR. Sold for scrap on 30 Nov 59

U-4706   Taken over by Norway. Not repaired. Sold 14 Apr 50. Scrapped in 1954

UD-5   Returned to Royal Netherlands Navy at Lisahally on 13 Jul 45

U-181   Japanese *I-501*. Sunk by the Royal Navy off Singapore on 15 Feb 46

U-195   Japanese *I-506*. Sunk by the Royal Navy in the Bali Sea on 15 Feb 46

U-219   Japanese *I-505*. Sunk by the Dutch Navy in the Sunda Strait on 3 Feb 46

U-511   Japanese *RO-500*. Sunk by the USN in the Sea of Japan on 30 Apr 46

U-862   Japanese *I-502*. Sunk by the Royal Navy off Singapore on 15 Feb 46

U-IT-24 Japanese *I-503*. Sunk by the USN in the Kii Suido, Japan on 16 Apr 46

U-IT-25 Japanese *I-504*. Sunk by the USN in the Kii Suido, Japan on 16 Apr 46

Sources

Chapter 1: Allied Policy for the Surrender of the U-Boats
1 FRUS, Diplomatic Papers, 1944, Vol 1, General – On-line at the University of Wisconsin Digital Library. **2** History of COSSAC 1943-1944 – On-line at www.ibiblio.org/hyperwar. **3** TNA Kew, WO 205/5A – Operation Rankin Case 'C'. **4** TNA Kew, ADM 116/5123 – Surrender of the German Fleet **5** Records of the Joint Chiefs of Staff, 1942-1945, The European Theater, UPA Microfilm Project (1981), Reel 9. **6** NARA Washington, RG 38 – Records of the Chief of Naval Operations. **7** TNA Kew, ADM 116/5202 – German U-Boat Fleet, Preparations for Surrender. **8** NARA Washington, RG 43 – Records of International Conferences. **9** TNA Kew, ADM 1/18187 – Special Orders for German Naval Command. **10** NARA Washington, RG 313 – Records of ComNavEu – Surrender and Occupation of Germany 1944-1945. **11** TNA Kew, ADM 1/16180 – Disarmament of Enemy Naval Services. **12** NARA Washington, RG 313 – Records of ComNavEu – Germany, Naval Surrender.

Chapter 2: UK Plans for the Surrender of the U-Boats
1 TNA Kew, ADM 116/5202 – German U-Boat Fleet – Preparations for Surrender. **2** NARA Washington, RG 313 – Records of ComNavEu – Germany, Naval Surrender. **3** TNA Kew, AIR 15/449 – Surrender of U-Boat Fleet at Sea – 'Pledge One' Operation Order. **4** TNA Kew, ADM 1/16384 – Post War Experiments and Tests on Captured U-Boats. **5** TNA Kew, On-line Chiefs of Staff (COS) Papers, CAB 80/48 – COS Memoranda, April to August 1945. **6** TNA Kew, ADM 223/20 – Admiralty Operational Intelligence Centre – U-Boat Trend Reports. **7** TNA Kew, ADM 199/2317 – Admiralty War Diary, 1 to 15 May 1945.

Chapter 3: US Plans for the Surrender of the U-Boats
1 NARA Washington, RG 38 – Records of the Chief of Naval Operations. **2** TNA Kew, ADM 1/16384 – Post-War Experiments and Tests on Captured U-Boats. **3** NARA Boston, RG 181 – Records of Boston Naval District and Portsmouth Navy Yard.

Chapter 4: The Surrender of the U-Boats
1 TNA Kew, DEFE 3/744 – Intercepted German Radio Comms, 5 to 24 May 1945. **2** NARA Washington, RG 242 – Records of the German Navy, T-1022, PG-31801m. **3** TNA Kew, ADM 199/2317 – Admiralty War Diary, 1 to 15 May 1945. **4** TNA Kew, AIR 15/449 – Operation Pledge One. **5** TNA Kew, HW 18/221 – German Naval Messages, March 1942 to May 1945. **6** TNA Kew, ADM 223/21 – Admiralty Operational Intelligence Centre – U-Boat Situation Reports and Weekly Statements. **7** NARA Washington, RG 313 – Records of ComNavEu – Surrender and Occupation of Germany. **8** TNA Kew, CAB 122/824 – Policy for Surrender of German Fleet. **9** TNA Kew, ADM 116/5512 – Disposal of German Fleet. **10** TNA Kew, CAB 80/94 – Chiefs of Staff (COS) Memoranda, 23 April to 16 June 1945. **11** Records of the US Joint Chiefs of Staff, 1942-1945, The European Theater, UPA Microfilm Project (1981), Reel 9.

Chapter 5: The Kriegsmarine's Operation 'Regenbogen'
1 Admiral Karl Dönitz, *Memoirs: Ten Years and Twenty Days* (1959). **2** NARA Washington, RG 242 – Records of the German Navy, Microfilm Reel T-1022, PG 31801-K. **3** TNA Kew, DEFE 3/578

– German Naval Messages 3 to 17 May 1945. **4** TNA Kew, DEFE 3/579 – German Naval Messages 17 to 23 May 1945. **5** TNA Kew, DEFE 3/744 – Intercepted German Radio Communications 5 to 24 May 1945. **6** NARA Washington, RG 242 – Records of the German Navy, Microfilm Reel T-1022, PG 31801-M. **7** Walter Ludde-Neurath, *Regierung Dönitz: Die Letzten Tage des Dritten Reiches* (1999) German edition. **8** NARA Washington, RG 242 – Records of the German Navy, Microfilm Reel T-1022, PG 31801-L. **9** Bernhard Asmussen, 'Regenbogen uber der Geltinger Bucht' – *Chronik des Kirchspiels Steinberg* – Sonderband 4 (1995). **10** OKM War Diary 1939-1945 ('Kriegstagebuch der Seekriegsleitung'), Part A, Volume 68, 1 to 20 April 1945, with a supplementary document for 21 April to 22 May 1945 (1997) – Page 434-A. **11** TNA Kew, ADM 1/18325 – Report of Proceedings of the Royal Naval Submarine Party attached to the Command of Flag Officer, Western Germany – 30 May 1945. **12** TNA Kew, WO 235/632 – DJAG No. 131 – Defendant: Gerhard Grumpelt. **13** TNA Kew, ADM 1/18270 – Allied Occupation of Heligoland and Dune: Report of Proceedings 11 to 17 May 1945. **14** TNA Kew, AIR 15/449 – Surrender of U-Boat Fleet at Sea – Pledge. **15** TNA Kew, ADM 199/2317 – Admiralty War Diary 1 to 15 May 1945. **16** Law Reports of Trials of War Criminals, Vol I, English Edition, HMSO (1947) – The Scuttled U-Boats Case, 12/13 February 1946. **17** Walter Ludde-Neurath, *Unconditional Surrender* (2010) English edition. **18** Hessler/MOD (Navy), *The U-Boat War in the Atlantic 1939-1945* (1989). **19** Wolfgang Frank, *The Sea Wolves: The Story of the German U-Boats at War* (1955). **20** Peter (Ali) Cremer, *U-Boat Commander* (1987). **21** Dan van der Vat, *The Atlantic Campaign* (1988). **22** Clay Blair, *Hitler's U-Boat War* (1998). **23** Horst Bredow (Cuxhaven Archive) – E-mail message to the author – 18 December 2013. **24** Chris Madsen, *The Royal Navy and German Naval Disarmament 1942-1947* (1998). **25** Lieutenant. Wolfgang Heibges, 'U-999 auf Kursk Regenbogen' – *Chronik des Kirchspiels Steinberg* – Sonderband 4 (1995). **26** Michael Salewski, *Die Deutsche Seekriegsleitung 1935-1945*, Vol II (1975) (*The German Naval War Command 1935-1945*). **27** Joachim Schultz-Naumann, *The Last Thirty Days* (*Die Letzten Dreissig Tage*) (1991) – The OKW War Diary (20 April to 22 May 1945). **28** Captain S W Roskill, *The War at Sea 1939-1945*, Vol III, Part II (1961). **29** Dr Axel Niestlé, *German U-Boat Losses during World War II* (2014).

Chapter 6: The Assembly of U-Boats in the UK in May, June and July 1945 – Operation 'Pledge'

1 TNA Kew, AIR 15/449 – Surrender of U-Boat Fleet at Sea (Pledge One). **2** TNA Kew, ADM 1/18187 – Special Orders for German Naval Command. **3** Teddy Suhren, *Ace of Aces – Memoirs of a U-Boat Rebel* (2005). **4** TNA Kew, HW 18/222 – German Naval Messages, 8 to 15 May 1945. **5** TNA Kew, ADM 199/2318 – Admiralty War Diary – 16 to 31 May 1945. **6** TNA Kew, ADM 199/139 – Report of Proceedings, 9th Escort Group. **7** TNA Kew, ADM 199/2317 – Admiralty War Diary – 1 to 16 May 1945. **8** TNA Kew, ADM 199/22 – Operation Pledge – Surrender of U-Boats at Sea – 9 May to 6 June. **9** TNA Kew, ADM 217/702 – Diary and General Survey of Events in Western Approaches – 15 to 31 May 1945. **10** TNA Kew, On-line Chiefs of Staff (COS) Papers, CAB 80/94 – COS Memoranda – 23 April to 16 June 1945. **11** TNA Kew, On-line Chiefs of Staff (COS) Papers, CAB 79/33 – COS Minutes – 2 to 23 May 1945. **12** TNA Kew, ADM 205/48 – Office of the First Sea Lord – Correspondence with the US Naval Authorities. **13** TNA Kew, ADM 116/5512 – Disposal of German Fleet. **14** TNA Kew, ADM 116/5202 – Arrangements for Surrender of German Submarines. **15** TNA Kew, ADM 1/18319 – HMS *Hargood* – Report of Proceedings June 1945.

Chapter 7: The Hunt for the 'Walter' U-Boats

1 TNA Kew, ADM 199/2317 – Admiralty War Diary – 1 to 15 May 1945. **2** TNA Kew, ADM 228/2 – German U-Boats – Policy for Disposal and Requirements for Post-War Experiments and Tests. **3** TNA Kew, HW18/436 – Extracts from Reports Containing Information about the Activity of German U-Boats. **4** TNA Kew, ADM 1/17561 – Report of Captain Roberts' Visit to Germany. **5** TNA Kew, ADM 228/8 – German U-Boats – Reports. **6** TNA Kew, ADM 199/2320 – Admiralty War Diary – 13 to 20 June 1945. **7** NARA Washington, RG 313 – Records of ComSubLant. **8** TNA Kew, ADM 116/5566 – TNC Reports. **9** TNA Kew, ADM 116/5569 – TNC Reports.

Chapter 8: Potsdam – Pre-Conference Proposals

1 TNA Kew, CAB 122/824 – Policy for Surrender of German Fleet. **2** The Soviet Bureau of Information, Moscow – Press Release – 30 March 1945. **3** Hansard, House of Commons – Written Answers – 7 April 1945. **4** FRUS, Diplomatic Papers, The Potsdam Conference 1945, Vol 1. **5** Records of the Joint Chiefs of Staff, 1942-1945, The European Theater, UPA Microfilm Project (1981), Reel 9. **6** The

Admiral Leahy Papers, US Navy H & H Command, Washington DC. **7** Documents on British Policy Overseas, The Conference at Potsdam 1945. **8** TNA Kew, CAB 66/67/17 – Cabinet Paper – CP (45) 67 – 7 July 1945. **9** TNA Kew, On-line Cabinet Papers – Cabinet Conclusions 14 (45) – 12 July 1945.

Chapter 9: The Potsdam Conference and Agreement – July–August 1945

1 Foreign Relations of the United States (FRUS) – Diplomatic Papers – The Potsdam Conference 1945, Vol 2, Document No. 710 (9). **2** Foreign Relations of the United States (FRUS) – Diplomatic Papers – The Potsdam Conference 1945, Vol 2, Document No. 710 (10). **3** Documents on British Policy Overseas – Butler & Pelly (HMSO 1984) – Series 1, Volume 1 – The Conference at Potsdam 1945, Document No. 170. **4** Documents on British Policy Overseas – Butler & Pelly (HMSO 1984) – Series 1, Volume 1 – The Conference at Potsdam 1945, Document No. 178. **5** Documents on British Policy Overseas – Butler & Pelly (HMSO 1984) – Series 1, Volume 1 – The Conference at Potsdam 1945, Document No. 181. **6** Foreign Relations of the United States (FRUS) – Diplomatic Papers – The Potsdam Conference 1945, Vol 2, Document No. 1007. **7** Documents on British Policy Overseas – Butler & Pelly (HMSO 1984) – Series 1, Volume 1 – The Conference at Potsdam 1945, Document No. 194. **8** Documents on British Policy Overseas – Butler & Pelly (HMSO 1984) – Series 1, Volume 1 – The Conference at Potsdam 1945, Document No. 224. **9** Documents on British Policy Overseas – Butler & Pelly (HMSO 1984) – Series 1, Volume 1 – The Conference at Potsdam 1945, Document No. 271. **10** Foreign Relations of the United States (FRUS) – Diplomatic Papers – The Potsdam Conference 1945, Vol 2, Document No. 1011. **11** Foreign Relations of the United States (FRUS) – Diplomatic Papers – The Potsdam Conference 1945, Vol 2, Document No. 1013. **12** Documents on British Policy Overseas – Butler & Pelly (HMSO 1984) – Series 1, Volume 1 – The Conference at Potsdam 1945, Document No. 450. **13** Documents on British Policy Overseas – Butler & Pelly (HMSO 1984) – Series 1, Volume 1 – The Conference at Potsdam 1945, Document No. 466. **14** Foreign Relations of the United States (FRUS) – Diplomatic Papers – The Potsdam Conference 1945, Vol 2, Document No. 1014. **15** Documents on British Policy Overseas – Butler & Pelly (HMSO 1984) – Series 1, Volume 1 – The Conference at Potsdam 1945, Document No. 469. **16** Documents on British Policy Overseas – Butler & Pelly (HMSO 1984) – Series 1, Volume 1 – The Conference at Potsdam 1945, Document No. 495. **17** The Admiral Charles Maynard Cooke Papers, Hoover Library, Stanford University, California, USA – Collection No. 68005, Box No. 21 – Disposition of the German Navy & Merchant Marine 1945. **18** Foreign Relations of the United States (FRUS) – Diplomatic Papers – The Potsdam Conference 1945, Vol 2, Document No. 1015. **19** Documents on British Policy Overseas – Butler & Pelly (HMSO 1984) – Series 1, Volume 1 – The Conference at Potsdam 1945, Document No. 509. **20** Documents on British Policy Overseas – Butler & Pelly (HMSO 1984) – Series 1, Volume 1 – The Conference at Potsdam 1945, Document No. 522. **21** Documents on British Policy Overseas – Butler & Pelly (HMSO 1984) – Series 1, Volume 1 – The Conference at Potsdam 1945, Document No. 603.

Chapter 10: The Tripartite Naval Commission

1 NARA Washington, RG 333.4 – Records of the US Navy Element of the TNC. **2** TNA Kew, ADM 205/54 – Disposal of Captured Enemy Fleets. **3** TNA Kew, ADM 228/35 – Minutes of TNC Meetings. **4** TNA Kew, ADM 116/5571 – TNC – Disposal of German Vessels in British Hands. **5** The Times Digital Archive – 23 January 1946. **6** TNA Kew, ADM 1/18495 – Russian Complaint about UK TNC Representative. **7** TNA Kew, ADM, 116/5566 – TNC Reports. **8** Records of the Joint Chiefs of Staff, 1942-1945, The European Theater, UPA Microfilm Project (1981), Reel 9. **9** TNA Kew, ADM 116/5569 – TNC Reports. **10** House of Commons, Hansard – Written Answers – 5 November 1947. **11** The Admiral Robert L Ghormley Papers, Joiner Library, East Carolina University, Greenville, NC – Series 1, Box 10, Folder 1153. **12** TNA Kew, ADM 116/5564 – Admiral Miles' Report on TNC – 8 November 1945.

Chapter 11: U-Boats in the UK

1 TNA Kew, ADM 220/1703 – Report on the German GSR equipment ATHOS fitted on U-249. **2** TNA Kew, ADM 1/17322 – Visit of HM Submarine U-776 to British Ports. **3** TNA Kew, ADM 1/18416 – Tour of Coastal Towns by ex-German U-Boats. **4** The Times – 18 May 1945. **5** The Barrow News – 26 May 1945. **6** TNA Kew, TS13/3189 – Prize Cases for Cargo: S/M U-Boat 532. **7** The

Western Telegraph – June 1945. **8** *The Birkenhead News* – 8 September 1945. **9** *The Birkenhead News* – 29 September 1945. **10** TNA Kew, ADM 1/18557 – Trials of Captured German U-Boats. **11** TNA Kew, ADM 1/18328 – Trials of German Submarines U-2502 and U-2326. **12** TNA Kew, ADM 1/18949 – Explosion on Board ex-German Submarine U-3017. **13** TNA Kew, FO 371/57146 – German Fleet, Report of the TNC. **14** RN S/M Museum, Gosport – File No: A1994/097 – Trials with HMS *Meteorite*. **15** RN Historical Branch, Portsmouth – Admiralty 'Acquaint' 3530 – 16 July 1949. **16** RN Historical Branch, Portsmouth – Admiralty 'Acquaint' 3597 – 15 December 1949.

Chapter 12: The Sinking of U-Boats in Operation 'Deadlight'

1 TNA Kew, ADM 228/35 – Minutes of TNC Meetings. **2** World Ship Society/NHB Manuscript, January 1986 – Operation Deadlight. **3** TNA Kew, ADM 116/5569 – TNC Report, Destruction of U-Boats in British Hands. **4** TNA Kew, ADM 1/18537 – Sinking of Captured German U-Boats. **5** *The Times*, 10 October 1945. **6** NARA Washington, RG 333.4 – Records of the US Navy Element of the TNC. **7** TNA Kew, ADM 1/18689 – Disposal of German Fleet, Allied Communiqué. **8** TNA Kew, ADM 116/5513 – Disposal of the German Fleet. **9** House of Commons, Hansard, Written Answers, 21 November 1945. **10** *The Times* – 12 December 1945. **11** *The War Illustrated* – Volume 9, Number 223 – 4 January 1946. **12** Royal Navy S/M Museum Gosport, File No: A 1945/007 – Loch Ryan Monthly General Letters. **13** World Ship Society/NHB Manuscript, January 1986 – Operation Deadlight (Loch Ryan Section). **14** World Ship Society/NHB Manuscript, January 1986 – Operation Deadlight (Lisahally Section). **15** Royal Navy S/M Museum Gosport, File No: A 1945/008 – Lisahally Monthly General Letters.

Chapter 13: U-Boats in the USA

1 NARA Washington, RG 313 – Records of US Navy Commander Submarines Atlantic (ComSubLant). (NARA Entry No: E 275, 370/41/12/5-6, Boxes 11 and 14). **2** NARA Washington, RG 19 – US Navy Bureau of Ships (BuShips). (NARA Entry No: E 1266, 470/9/6/3, Boxes 424 and 425, and 470/27/2/1, Box 767). **3** NARA Washington, RG 333.4 – Records of the US Navy Element of the TNC. (NARA Entry No: E 15, 190/31/19/01-02, Boxes 1 and 5). **4** Portsmouth Navy Yard Museum and Archive, and on-line Internet website: 'uboatarchive.net' – Design Studies of Surrendered U-boats, U-2513, Portsmouth Naval Shipyard, Report No. 2G-21.

Chapter 14: The Capture and Use of *U-505* by the US Navy

1 NARA Washington, RG 38 – Navy Department and USS *Guadalcanal* papers – CNSG Library (NARA Entry No: A1030 – Box 198 -5750/351). **2** NARA Washington, RG 24, Deck Logs – USS *Guadalcanal*, USS *Abnaki*, USS *PCE(R) 851* and USS *PCE(R) 852*. **3** Museum of Science and Industry, Chicago – *U-505* Display Board. **4** 'The Battle of the Atlantic and Signals Intelligence: U-Boat Situations and Trends 1941-1945' (1998), The Navy Records Society. **5** NARA Washington, RG 38.2.4 – World War II War Diaries 1941 to 1945 – War Diary of Naval Operating Base Bermuda (RG38, Entry A1-353, 370/45/28/7, Boxes 449-450). **6** NARA Washington, RG 389 – US Army Provost Marshal General, Prisoner of War Operations Division (Entry 452, Boxes 1395, 1936 and 1397). **7** Wesley Harris, *Fish out of Water: Nazi Submariners as Prisoners in North Louisiana during World War II* (2004). **8** MOD (Navy), *The U-Boat War in the Atlantic 1939-1945* (1989). **9** Andrew Bermingham, Chairman of the Bermuda Historical Society, *Bermuda Military Rarities Revisited: German Submarine U-505* (2012), Chapter X. **10** Timothy Mulligan, 'A Community Bound by Fate: The Crew of U-505', in Theodore P Savas (ed), *Hunt and Kill: U-505 and the U-Boat War in the Atlantic* (2004). **11** NARA Washington, RG 38 – Office of Naval Intelligence, Special Activities Branch, OP-16-Z, Day Files and Administrative Files (NARA Stack 370/15/8/7). **12** C. Herbert Gilliland and Robert Shenk, *Admiral Dan Gallery* (1999). **13** *New York Times*, 30 May 1945 – 'Nazi U-Boat Lures Bond Buyers Here'. **14** 'World War II on the Savannah Waterfront – U-Boat 505 Visits Savannah', 7 November 1945 – City of Savannah, Research Library and Municipal Archives – 29 August 2008. **15** Admiral Samuel Eliot Morison, *History of United States Naval Operations in World War II: The Atlantic Battle Won May 1943 – May 1945*, Volume X (1956). **16** NARA, Boston, RG 181 – 1st Naval District, Boston. **17** NARA, Washington, RG 19 – Bureau of Ships. **18** Museum of Science and Industry, Chicago – Archives. **19** Keith Gill, 'Project 356: U-505 and the Journey to Chicago', in Theodore P Savas (ed), *Hunt and Kill: U-505 and the U-Boat War in the Atlantic* (2004). **20** *Chicago Daily Tribune* – 7 March 1953. **21** *Chicago American* – 22 April 1953.

Chapter 15: U-Boats in Russia

1 NARA Washington, RG 333.4 – Records of the US Navy Element of the TNC. **2** British Library – The Cunningham Papers. **3** TNA Kew, ADM 116/5513 – Disposal of the German Fleet. **4** U-Boat Archive Cuxhaven, Volume 8 (2005), Operation 'Cabal'. **5** TNA Kew, ADM 1/19405 – Passage of HMS *Icarus* to Libau. **6** TNA Kew, ADM 116/5566 – TNC Reports, The State of the German Fleet. **7** TNA Kew, ADM 116/5569 – TNC Report, Destruction of U-Boats in British Hands. **8** TNA Kew, FO 1030/6 – Report to the Council of Foreign Ministers from the Allied Control Authority. **9** FRUS: Foreign Relations, 1947, Vol II, Council of Ministers. **10** House of Commons, Hansard, Oral Answers, 19 March 1947. **11** House of Commons, Hansard, Written Answers, 5 November 1947. **12** NARA Washington, RG 38.4.3, ONI Files.

Chapter 16: U-Boats in France

1 TNA Kew, FO 371/50907 – Disposal of the German and Italian Fleets. **2** TNA Kew, On-Line Cabinet Papers, CP (45) 67. **3** NARA Washington, RG 333.4 – Records of the US Navy Element of the TNC. **4** FRUS, The Potsdam Conference 1945, Vol 2. **5** The Admiral Cooke Papers, Hoover Library, Stanford University, California. **6** TNA Kew, ADM 116/5500 – French Claims to a Share of the German Fleet. **7** TNA Kew, ADM 205/54 – Disposal of Captured Enemy Fleets. **8** TNA Kew, ADM 116/5564 – TNC Recommendations on the Allocation of the German Fleet. **9** The Times Digital Archive, 10 October 1945. **10** The Times Digital Archive, 26 October 1945. **11** Documents on British Foreign Policy Overseas, Series 1, Vol V, Germany and Western Europe Aug-Dec 45, HMSO 1990 and TNA Kew, ADM 116/5500. **12** TNA Kew, FO 371/57146 – TNC Report, Disposal and Destruction of Submarines and Warships. **13** TNA Kew, On-line Cabinet Papers, CP (46) 49. **14** TNA Kew, On-line Cabinet Papers, CM 15 (46). **15** TNA Kew, ADM 1/19510 – Report of Proceedings, HMS *Tremadoc Bay* – Handing Over of 2 German U-Boats to France.

Chapter 17: U-Boats in Canada

1 *Ottawa Journal* – 7 May 1945. **2** TNA Kew, ADM 199/2317 – Admiralty War Diary – May 1945. **3** *Halifax Herald* – 14 May 1945. **4** *Ottawa Journal* – 14 May 1945. **5** Library and Archive of Canada (LAC) Ottawa. RG 24, Series D-12, Vol.11935, File 8000-U-190: General Information U-190. **6** LAC Ottawa. RG 24, Series D-10, Vol.11565, File D20-35-3: HMCS U-889. **7** LAC Ottawa. RG 24, Series D-10, Vol. 11116, File 66-1-1: Canadian NRE Report PHx-59 dated 7 November 1945: 'Report on ex-German Submarine U-889, with Appendix on ex-German Submarine U-190'. **8** TNA Kew, ADM 213/308. Canadian NRE Report PHx-56 dated 28 September 1945: 'Listening Gear in U-889 and U-190'. **9** 'Knots, Volts and Decibels: An Informal History of the Naval Research Establishment, 1940-1967' – John R Longard (1993). Chapter IV: NRE's Submarines. **10** LAC Ottawa. Series D-1-c, Vol. 8043, File 1206-12: Exhibitions and Displays – Captured German Submarines. **11** Canadian Department of Heritage and History (DHH). Ship's Movements Cards, U-889, DHH File No. 2010/15, Box 7, and LAC Ottawa RG 24, Series D-2, Vol.7962: U-889 Deck Log – 28 August to 1 December 1945. **12** DHH. Ship's Movements Cards, U-190, DHH File No. 2010/15, Box 7, and LAC Ottawa, RG 24, Series D-2, Vol.7962: U-190 Deck Logs – 31 May to 27 August and 28 August to 1 December 1945 . **13** LAC Ottawa. RG 24, Series D-10, Vol. 11116, File 66-1-1: RCN Submarines – General (ex-German Submarines). **14** LAC Ottawa. RG24, Series D-10, Vol.11601, File SCH8000 – 476/2: General Information HMCS U-190. **15** LAC Ottawa. RG 24, Series D-2, Vol. 7962: U-190 Deck Log – 31 May to 27 August 1945. **16** LAC Ottawa. Series D-10, Vol. 11117, File 66-1-4: RCN Submarines (Disposition of German Submarines). **17** NARA Washington, RG 333.4 – Records of the US Navy Element of the TNC. **18** LAC Ottawa. RG 24, Series D-1-c, Vol. 6730, File NS8000 – 476/2: General Information HMCS U-190. **19** LAC Ottawa. RG24, Series D-10, Vol.11536, File AC8000 – 476/2: General Information U-190. **20** RCN Press Release No. 445 – 15 July 1947 – DHH File No. 81/520, Box 88, HMCS U-190. **21** RCN Press Release No. 562 – 18 October 1947 – DHH File No. 81/520, Box 88, HMCS U-190. **22** RCN Press Release No. 589 – 29 October 1947 – DHH File No. 81/520, Box 88, HMCS U-190.

Chapter 18: U-Boats in Norway

1 TNA Kew, DEFE 3/744 – Intercepted German Radio Communications. **2** NARA Washington, RG 457 – SRMN-037 – US Navy Intelligence Summary, 20 April 1945. **3** TNA Kew, ADM 199/2319

– Admiralty War Diary – 1 June to 12 June 1945. **4** TNA Kew, DEFE 3/743 – Intercepted German Radio Communications. **5** TNA Kew, ADM 116/5566 – TNC Reports – State of the German Fleet. **6** TNA Kew, On-Line Chiefs of Staff (COS) Papers, CAB 80/98. **7** TNA Kew, On-Line Chiefs of Staff (COS) Papers, CAB 79/40 and CAB 80/50. **8** National Archives of Norway, Box Dyi-12978 – Ministry of Foreign Affairs. **9** NARA Washington, RG 333.4 – Records of the US Navy Element of the TNC. **10** TNA Kew, ADM 116/5500 – French Claim to Share of the German Fleet. **11** National Archives of Norway, Box D-0016 – Sjoforsvarets Overkommando. **12** Royal Norwegian Navy Museum (Marinemuseet), Horten, Norway. **13** RNoN (Forsvarets Krigshistoriske Avdeling) Letter dated 27 July 1966.

Chapter 19: U-Boats in Other Nations

1 NARA Washington, RG 457 – SRGL No. 2958 – Intercepted German/Japanese Radio Communications. **2** SWNCC 150/2 dated 12 August 1945 – On-line Internet Website: 'www.ndl. go.jp'. **3** Foreign Relations of the United States (FRUS) – Diplomatic Papers 1945, The Far East, Vol VI. **4** TNA Kew, On-Line Chiefs of Staff (COS) Papers – CAB 80/50. **5** The Admiral Cooke Papers, Hoover Library, Stanford University, California. **6** NARA Washington, RG 313.5.2 – Records of US Navy Atlantic Fleet – ComSubLant. **7** NARA Washington, RG 333.4 – Records of the US Navy Element of the TNC.